feminist science studies

FEMINIST SCIENCE STUDIES

a new generation

Edited by

Maralee Mayberry
Banu Subramaniam
Lisa H. Weasel

Routledge
New York   London

Published in 2001 by

Routledge
29 West 35th Street
New York, NY 10001

Published in Great Britain by

Routledge
11 New Fetter Lane
London EC4P 4EE

Routledge is an imprint of the Taylor & Francis Group.

Library of Congress Cataloging-in-Publication Data
Mayberry, Maralee.
    Feminist science studies : a new generation / Maralee Mayberry,
    Banu Subramaniam, Lisa H. Weasel.
      p.   cm.
    Includes bibliographical references and index.
    ISBN 0-415-92695-5 —   ISBN 0-415-92696-3 (paper)
    1. Science—Social aspects.   2. Feminism.   3. Women in science.
    I. Subramaniam, Banu, 1966–   II. Weasel, Lisa, 1966–
    III. Title.
    Q175.5 .M385   2001
    500'.82—dc21   00-062726

10   9   8   7   6   5   4   3   2   1

Contents

ALTERED STATES
TRANSFORMING DISCIPLINES FROM WITHIN

STORIES FROM THE FIELD
IMPLEMENTING FEMINIST SCIENCE STUDIES IN THE ACADEMY

DESTINATION
REINTEGRATING SCIENCE, COMMUNITY, AND ACTIVISM

Adventures Across Natures and Cultures

An Introduction

───▶ Maralee Mayberry, Banu Subramaniam, and Lisa H. Weasel

Origin Stories

As always, introductions are read first but written last. As we trace the conception of this anthology, we sift through our individual and collective adventures in the worlds of natures and cultures. We have each traversed different paths — personal and professional, disciplinary and interdisciplinary, academic and geographic. *Maralee Mayberry*, trained as a sociologist, found a passion for researching and writing about the pedagogical implications of "women *in* science" and "feminism *and* science" approaches to science curriculum reform. This work has convinced her that there are important reasons for feminist educators to move toward pedagogical reforms that raise critical questions about science and the co-constituting relations between social, cultural, and scientific knowledge. She co-founded the Project for Multicultural and Interdisciplinary Studies in Education (PROMISE) to put her ideas into action.[1] *Banu Subramaniam* is a plant evolutionary biologist who turned to women's studies to explore her own dislocation as a third world woman in the sciences in the United States. This exploration has made her a committed feminist and scientist, convinced that each location enriches the other. Working in women's studies, science studies, and plant biology, she seeks to reconnect the worlds of natures and cultures in her work. By bringing together scholarship from women's studies, biological sciences, science studies, postcolonial studies, and ethnic studies, she is attempting to develop academic practices that are informed and shaped by experimental and theoretical practice in the sciences, humanities, and social sciences. *Lisa Weasel* is trained as a cell and molecular biologist in the field of *Drosophila* developmental genetics. As a graduate student she noticed the persistent infiltration of gender, class, and race into the science she was taught to practice, and no acknowledgment of these aspects within the methodological and theoretical traditions into which she was being inducted. Attempting to find ways to do this, she turned to feminist science studies in search of resources for integrating these aspects into

1

science, only to recognize the converse need for a richer incorporation of science into women's studies. She now makes her home in a biology department with an affiliation in women's studies, where her primary focus is on stimulating constructive alliances that can expand both feminism and science at all levels, from action and outreach projects to teaching and research to philosophical and theoretical perspectives.

The three of us met and this anthology began casually enough. Meeting at conferences, we often found ourselves at the same talks, and were delighted by the questions we heard each other asking. Over e-mail we articulated our isolation as scholars working on different aspects of a field increasingly being called the feminist studies of science. The field has no common conferences, no professional associations, no professional journals, no common departments or disciplines. And yet we were each involved with a growing network of scholars who did related work or at least work that interested us and informed our own work.

Our heterogeneous backgrounds reflect the backgrounds of the contributors to this anthology. They include scholars from molecular biology, cultural theory, hydrology, sociology, cell biology, history, women's studies, genetics, literary criticism, philosophy, animal behavior, evolutionary biology, rhetoric, engineering, mathematics, education, psychology, developmental biology, plant pathology, environmental science, and immunology, as well as academic and community activists and academic administrators. We have all come from different places, charted a diverse set of journeys into the worlds of natures and cultures, experienced these worlds through numerous and diverse disciplinary and methodological lenses, and negotiated varying disciplinary, interdisciplinary, and multidisciplinary terrains. Despite our differences, what brings us together is a passion for a common set of questions: How do natures and cultures interact? How do we produce knowledge about the natural and cultural landscapes we inhabit? What consequences does this knowledge have? The heterogeneous, multi- and interdisciplinary field devoted to exploring these questions has been increasingly called "feminist science studies."

Needless to say, for us, feminist science studies represents one of the most exciting areas of study in the academy today. It involves tackling the last and most difficult barrier to interdisciplinarity—between the humanities and social sciences and the natural/physical sciences. While the humanities and social sciences have produced a breadth of interdisciplinary fields such as women's studies, cultural studies, American studies, and ethnic studies, and the natural and physical sciences have created a myriad of interdisciplinary fields such as biophysics, chemical engineering, biomathematics, biochemistry, the boundaries of the study of natures and the study of cultures have remained relatively stable within institutions. Yet, as this anthology demonstrates, these boundaries repeatedly have been disrupted, transgressed, and redefined. We present scholars who work at the interstices of natures and cultures to show us how inextricably interconnected these two worlds are. Through their narratives, which map the personal, epistemological, methodological, and disciplinary heterogeneity of feminist science studies, we can imagine bold and brave new worlds.

Morphogenesis: A Methodological Tale

And so the three of us, Maralee in Las Vegas, Banu in Los Angeles and Tucson, Lisa in Irvine and Portland, began to develop this anthology. Our backgrounds, interests, and concerns became part of our "Call for Proposals," which we then sent on its way via Internet connections into feminist networks and Internet communities. When friends informed us that other people had independently sent them the call for proposals we knew it was traveling well. And when it created a heated debate on the History of Astronomy Discussion Group Listserv we knew it was traveling widely and stirring controversy. We were pleased! We assembled the proposals received, and rather than imposing any predetermined structure, we allowed the book to morph into a self-generating form, as pieces with natural affinities for one another took shape in the four sections presented here. While we cannot fully predict the future metamorphosis of feminist science studies, each section in this book portrays one of the ways in which feminist science practices are now being forged—through disciplinary border-crossing, interdisciplinary research, pedagogical interventions in the classroom and across disciplines, and community activism. While the essays composing each section all explore the interconnections between natures and cultures, some authors have mapped their journey into feminist science studies in more theoretical terms, whereas others draw more specifically from their own personal experiences and practices to illustrate interdisciplinary interventions. After much lively debate about how best to present this assortment of voices, we have chosen to arrange the essays within each section in a manner that explicates both the practice and the theory occurring in those sites where feminist science projects are situated.

We were committed to developing an anthology in which the whole would be greater than the sum of its individual parts—an approach designed to provide a picture capturing the rich topography of the field. We viewed our editorial role as one of guiding pattern formation in a morphogenetic field—the submissions provided a picture for us of what the field was about—and we wanted the final vision to reflect both synergy and heterogeneity, while simultaneously characterizing the commonalities and differences of the contributions. The heterogeneity of styles and theories as well as the discontinuities of foundational knowledge that we observed across our contributors and their contributions spurred many ideas about the myriad of ways to put together a representative yet cohesive volume of essays. We are well aware that in the history of feminist scholarship some of the most radical and pathbreaking theories have come from the margins. Therefore, as self-reflexive feminists, we have allowed this unevenness to mark the anthology. Although not uniform along any particular disciplinary axis, each piece has its individual strength—either in disciplinary depth or interdisciplinary breadth, in cultural imagery and literary richness or in methodological insight, in incisive critique or practical application—that adds to the volume as a whole. Intentionally, we have retained the anthology's strengths in its richness to map out the rugged contours of the landscape of this field.

Working on this anthology has been more fun and invigorating than we ever could have imagined. We deliberated on the audience for it, and were unanimous in wanting to reach as wide an audience as possible. This meant that the pieces had to be as accessible and as jargon free as possible. As we read the pieces and sent out our suggested revisions for the authors, we pushed many contributors to write accessibly and to reach beyond their disciplinary boxes. We quite honestly were nervous about how contributors would respond to our ambitious suggestions for revisions, only to be rewarded by their passionately crafted responses. Several of the contributors remarked that they were writing in a style they had never used before, or were excavating intellectual territories they had not known existed, and they found this at times frustrating but also energizing and refreshing. As we mapped out the new terrain that this volume collectively represents, we experienced a similar sense of energy and excitement at bringing these various voices together into a totipotent whole. Recognizing that this collection represents but one stage of development in a complex and ever changing field, we look forward to a continual generation and regeneration of feminist science studies in the future.

Etymology of Our Anthology

Coming together from three different places, histories, genealogies, and geographies—in both the social and material worlds—led us on adventures across natures and cultures. Natures and cultures represent foundational terms that are highly contested in feminisms and the sciences; each term ranges in meaning from material realities to abstract processes and forces. Feminist science studies has interrogated the nature of culture and the culture of nature to reimagine both materiality and human productions. To us this anthology is an embracement of natures and cultures in all their definitions and complexities, as well as the intersections, interstices, overlaps, unions, complications, and ambiguities involved in simultaneously inhabiting both natures and cultures. As we interrogate this constructed dichotomy, we also travel back and forth along an axis inscribed by academic and intellectual histories in the creation of the sciences and the humanities. However, as Bruno Latour (1993) points out, despite our delusion about the separation of nature and culture, hybrids of nature and culture are all about us. In using the term *natures and cultures,* we embrace Donna Haraway's (1999) notion of "naturecultures," which she describes as being "inside history as well as being inside the wonder of the natural complexity . . . implosions of the discursive realms of nature and culture" (105, 26).

In tracing the roots of the terms we use to describe this anthology, we offer the following etymology:

> GENERATION (jen'e'ra'shen) n. 1. The act or process of generating esp. procreation, origination, or production. 3. A class of objects derived from a preceding class. 4. A. a group of contemporaneous individuals. B. a group of individuals considered as sharing a common contemporaneous cultural or social attribute <the beat generation>

By using the term *a new generation* we mean to characterize the field of feminist science studies rather than its scholars. We mean to suggest that feminist science studies has developed into a mature field, rich and diverse in its goals, theories, actions, activisms, methodologies—its productions and effects. Although the field is founded on the inextricable interconnections between race, class, gender, and science and technology, these interconnections are complex and complicated. Multiple models, frameworks, analyses, and theories coexist for the natures, processes, and forms of these interconnections. In using the term *generation* we also want to delve into the creative, generative, original aspects, and organic quality of scholarship in the field. We want to highlight a diverse group of individuals collectively united, a group of scholars who share a common and overlapping set of goals, theories, and understandings of feminisms and the sciences that allows dissension, when it occurs, to fuel collective energies rather than distract from our aims. Finally, by *a new generation* we wish to acknowledge the brilliant and important legacy of feminist science scholarship over the last two decades that has shaped the contributors and contributions of this anthology.

> FEMINIST SCIENCE STUDIES (fem'anist si'ens stud'ez) 1. A field under construction. 2. A body of work that applies feminist analyses to scientific ideas and practices to explore the relationship between feminism and science and what each can learn from the other. 3. A field that explores the intersections between race, class, gender, and science and technology. 4. The effort to work out the implications of "situated knowledges" (knowledge seen as a social activity embedded in a certain culture and worldview). 5. A scholarship in which "gender politics are not simply about relationships about men and women but are focused precisely on how to understand agency, body, rationality, and the boundaries between nature

and culture" (Rouse 1996). 6. A disruption of the dichotomy between scientific inquiry and policy through examination of the connections between scientific knowledge and scientific practices.

Defining a field in motion is never easy. Feminist science studies over the last
two decades has elaborated the relationship and distinctions between "science,"
"technology," "engineering," and "health." The majority of proposals we received
in response to our call focused on the traditionally defined natural and physical
"sciences." As a result, our primary focus has remained on these "sciences," although technology, health, and engineering have shaped (and are represented in)
certain pieces. For those interested in these fields, we recommend several recent
anthologies that explore these topics in greater depth.[2] Because our focus is primarily limited to presenting work in the natural and physical sciences, we have
chosen to use the term *feminist "science" studies* rather than other commonly used
yet cumbersome terms such as SMET (science, mathematics, engineering, technology). Additionally, a related body of work on "women in science" and "minorities in science" deals with the historical and current underrepresentation and
status of these groups and examines a variety of strategies to increase the participation of these disenfranchised groups. Again, some recent anthologies have explored this body of work.[3] While we believe such strategies are necessary, we do
not believe they are sufficient. The history of the development of science within
the Western clerical tradition as "a world without women" (Noble 1992) has
shaped not only the underrepresentation of white women and people of color
but also the social relations of science, its methodologies and epistemologies.
Over the last two decades, feminists have highlighted how gender, race, and class
are implicated in the development of science. One of the insights fundamental
to feminist science studies is that in addition to increasing access to the sciences,
we must also expand the basis of what constitutes "science" and "scientific inquiry." Our volume focuses on this latter set of concerns.

Anatomies: Situating Thematic Narratives

Section I of the anthology, "(Un)Disciplined Identities: Forging Knowledge
Across Borders," provides autobiographical accounts from transdisciplinary
scholars who work across the boundaries demarcated by women's studies, and
science and engineering fields. These accounts provide an important entry point
to the volume, for they offer us the voices of those who have charted new paths
through the academy, both interrogating the rigidity of fixed disciplinary boundaries and institutionalizing new hybridizations of fields formerly thought to be
unrelated. All of the scholars writing in this section have creatively made places
for themselves and their scholarship within the academy, despite the challenges

of disciplinary and institutional boundaries that can at times lead to feelings of isolation. Indeed, a common theme that we heard resounding through these pieces was one of idiosyncrasy ("my situation as a feminist scientist is idiosyncratic or unique to me") and we found it striking that this was indeed a field replete with what we like to call "intrepid travelers." What ways have scholars developed to creatively circumvent disciplinary, intellectual, and institutional boundaries? How can we begin to respond to the challenges of occupying the liminal space of the insider-outsider and to the challenges presented by transdisciplinary work? And what are the practical effects of conducting transdisicplinary work? What feminist and scientific questions—practically and theoretically—emerge from border-crossing perspectives?

In answering these questions, our contributors explore their experiences and career trajectories as scholars working in two different cultures simultaneously. Their stories provide the current generation of feminist science scholars as well as those to come with role models and roadmaps for successfully navigating the thickets and underbrush of a well-disciplined academia. While earlier generations of feminist science scholars may have bravely crossed disciplinary boundaries without the benefit of well-laid trails in front of them, the growing proliferation of feminist science scholars within the academy is slowly creating established paths along which future generations can travel. We choose to begin the anthology in a manner that articulates the personal, practical, and theoretical pathways to and through interdisciplinary feminist work in and on the sciences.

Section II, "Altered States: Transforming Disciplines from Within," moves us from personal narratives to the fruits of feminist border-crossing. This section presents the contributions of feminist scholars *in* and *on* the sciences. While the spectrum of these scholars' work is wide—spanning philosophy, sociology, history, molecular biology, animal behavior, and rhetoric—they all have reached across traditional disciplinary boundaries to demonstrate the ways in which they use feminist frameworks and research tools to redefine and reorient their own disciplinary practices. How have feminist scientists incorporated feminist research into their everyday practices? How can we reenvision scientific theory and methodology? How have scholars from the humanities incorporated feminist science inquiry into their own work? The disciplinary diversity of these accounts shows how far-reaching the effects of feminism on science have been, particularly in terms of building beyond discursive critiques into the important realm of reconstruction. The work described in this section represents an important turning point in feminist science studies, one in which critique is matched by reconstruction, and feminist principles guide rather than follow the trail of science.

The fact that the authors in this section successfully bring feminist science studies to bear on their disciplinary frameworks is in part a result of the growing integration of feminist science studies into the background and training of those who study science. While previous generations of feminist science scholars may not have had the privilege of institutionalized frameworks such as women's studies programs or courses that integrate the study of natures and cultures, we now see a growing number of curriculum reform projects—within and outside the sciences as well as engineering and mathematics—integrating feminism and science in a variety of creative ways. The authors in Section III, "Stories from the Field: Implementing Feminist Science Studies in the Academy," address the pedagogical and curricular transformations occurring in a wide range of fields and disciplines that both investigate the interrelationships between feminism and science and interrogate their disjunctions. What strategies can we develop to translate theories from feminist science studies into innovative science and engineering programs? How can these theories be used to integrate knowledge of science into other disciplines such as women's studies? Several chapters in this section present curriculum modules that can be used as resources for educators in a range of disciplines, while others provide theoretical and foundational strategies that can serve as guides for developing interdisciplinary projects, transforming classroom practices, and opening rhetorical spaces for scholars to forge connections across disciplines. The spectrum of the approaches and courses represented in this section attest to the progress that feminist science studies has had in institutionalizing curricular and pedagogical changes across the academy. However, as the introduction to the section discusses, the ideas offered are only a partial view of what is possible and necessary to fully institutionalize feminist science curricula in all forms and structures of higher education. The full incorporation of feminist science coursework and pedagogy across the educational domain is an exciting challenge that will continue to develop and evolve in this and coming generations. The chapters in this section provide many starting points to meeting that challenge.

The first three sections of the book focus on innovations and alterations taking place with respect to feminist science studies in academia. However, both feminism and science have deep involvement with and extensive impact upon communities beyond the university. Section IV, "Destination: Reintegrating Science, Community, and Activism," presents authors who describe their attempts to cross yet another artificial boundary—that constructed between theory and the academy on the one hand and activism and the community on the other hand. Like the other border-crossers represented in the anthology, all of these scholars work to extend their field of vision and their work beyond that prescribed by narrowly defined disciplines, fields, and institutions. While the majority of contributors to this section are based in academic settings, all of them illustrate the rich potential that feminist science studies brings to questions relating to community and activism. What new ways of thinking about and doing science have been created that link scientific work with community needs? How can the theoretical and practical strategies developed by feminist science scholars working inside and outside the academy be used to rebuild the intersections of science, community, and activism that have been severed by disciplinary practices and policies? What are the intersections of science, politics, and activism, and how can science be used for liberatory purposes? Although the anthology ends with this section, it provides a promising beginning for constructing transformative links between feminist science studies as it has developed in the academy, and the pressing concerns (environmental, health, safety, and so on) facing communities to which the tools of feminist science scholarship can be effectively applied. As the field of feminist science studies continues to grow and intertwine in expansive and exciting ways, we look forward to new and fruitful alliances between the academy and the community in further articulating the goals and directions of the interdisciplinary adventures that have begun on these pages.

Evolutions: Reflections on the Scope and Future of Feminist Science Studies

Working on this anthology, we had many debates on what kind of future we imagine for feminist science studies. We wondered if it was wise to present a volume named "feminist science studies," as though such a field had been codified. Did we want to circumscribe the scope and contours of such a field? Did we want to categorize, name, and label what seems like a rich, diverse, heterogeneous, and somewhat amorphous set of visions and perspectives? In so doing, would we create margins where none existed and make invisible what we have not named? There are always dangers to "disciplining." Our intention in this volume is not to codify, name, or create centers and margins where none exist. We have tried throughout this introduction and this anthology to continually stress the fluidity, movement, and heterogeneity of feminist science studies. We hope the "field" will never lose this fluidity. Our decision to use "feminist science studies" in naming this anthology was ultimately a pragmatic decision. Over two decades ago, feminists expanded their attention to the sciences, and we are astonished and exhilarated by where this journey has led and how the theoretical, methodological, and epistemological tools have evolved and shifted. Presenting these rich and heterogeneous studies of "science" seemed to us to be an important endeavor. Second, the three of us belong to a network of scholars who have struggled to keep up with the ever growing breadth of the field. While we do not want to stunt or slow the proliferation of new configurations of natures and cultures, creating a network of scholars, disciplines, and interdisciplines, and presenting the breadth and range of the disciplines and interdisciplines seems to us to be a useful enterprise. It is for both these reasons that we have chosen "feminist science studies" to define this volume.

The term *feminist science studies* has evolved along with two other terms that are often used interchangeably—*gender and science* and *feminist critiques of science*. We, along with many scholars, have come to prefer *feminist science studies* because the field does more than critique. It allows for progressive, positive readings of science, and of reconstructions of science consistent with feminist theories, ideals, and visions. We envision a future in which feminism and science are no longer oxymoronic practices but instead partners in creating a more equitable and just world. Second, by not privileging gender, the term *feminist science studies* allows for coconstituting social variables of race, ethnicity, class, sexuality, nationality to be considered alongside gender. We feel this is important for reasons discussed below.

We are proud of the scope of this anthology, which provides a glimpse of what the future holds. The number of graduate students and junior faculty working in the field who have moved into uncharted territory and taken the risk of making their scholarship in this field visible by contributing to this anthology is noteworthy. It seems that so many of these young scholars have used feminist science studies as a bridge to traverse, connect, and link various disciplinary and interdisciplinary locations. While some of our contributors evocatively describe the institutional problems of doing interdisciplinary work within the disciplines, they also show us that such work is possible, and indeed enriching. What seems striking to us is that rather than letting academic structures define and limit what they can and cannot do, the new generation of feminist science studies scholars have found ways to do the intellectual work they love through new and interesting institutional locations and career paths. The ability of young scholars to circumvent and overcome the barriers and obstacles of the academy are encouraging and exciting. However, it is also clear that we must find ways to ease the route to such innovations.

In exploring interdisciplinary scholars' institutional locations, academic career paths, and professionalization, the boundaries and borders within the academy in disciplines and interdisciplines and between the academy and the world outside, the institutionalization of feminist science studies and its impact on courses and curriculum, we have explored a diverse array of intellectual and institutional projects. However, in working and observing this field for a number of years and more recently in working on this anthology, we are also struck by certain silences. Feminist science studies is plagued with the same problem of exclusion that has haunted feminist scholarship at large. While it is commonplace to speak of the importance of race, class, nationality, ethnicity, and sexuality, in practice these variables rarely shape the final analyses presented. As Patricia Hill Collins (1999) suggests, rather than viewing these social variables as "parallel" dimensions where we can focus on one dimension and not others, we must see the relationship as one of "intersections":

> feminist analyses of gender and scientific knowledge might benefit from closer association with emerging scholarship on intersectionality. The

construct of intersectionality references two types of relationships: the interconnectedness of ideas and the social structures in which they occur, and the intersecting hierarchies of gender, race, economic class, sexuality, and ethnicity. Viewing gender within the logic of intersectionality redefines it as a constellation of ideas and social practices that are historically situated within and that mutually construct multiple systems of oppression (263).

What is at stake, as Collins suggests, is not only a fuller account of gender but also a fuller account of science. Ignoring these intersections distorts our account of gender, science, and the knowledge we create about natures and cultures. We need to explore how fundamentally intersectionality and multiplicity can transform our knowledge of identities, gender, race, science, nationality, and scientific inquiry and practice, and its impact on the community.

We also wish to note that most of the analyses and focus in this anthology and in the field at large is on the biological and natural sciences, suggesting that the physical sciences are marked by a different climate both in the absence of women in the disciplines but also in the object of study. As a result, it would be a mistake to directly export analyses developed on and about the biological sciences into the physical sciences. The sciences represent a heterogeneous and diverse set of disciplines and our analyses must be contextual and shaped by the practices of these disciplines.

Having told you our origin stories, described the morphogenesis of this anthology, opened its guts up to explore its anatomy, speculated on what we see as emerging themes and the wonderful vistas that await our multidirectional evolutions, we leave you with the voices of a new generation of feminist science scholars.

Acknowledgment: *Feminist Science Studies: A New Generation* is a collaborative venture. Although our names are listed in alphabetical order, we do not wish this to imply a hierarchy of efforts. The preparation of this anthology was partly supported by the NSF under Grant No. HRD–9555731.

Notes

1. PROMISE aims to transform three components of earth science education at UNLV (University of Nevada, Las Vegas): the *form* of earth science teaching, by implementing feminist pedagogy; the *content* of earth science curricula, such that it is transdisciplinary and contextualized; and the *use* to which scientific knowledge is put by examining its political, social, and economic implications. For more information, see the PROMISE website (http://www.scsv.nevada.edu/~promise/index.html).

2. See, for instance, Adele Clarke and Virginia Olesen (1999), Jennifer Terry and Melodie Calvert (1997), Susan Hawthorne and Renate Klein (1999), E. Arnold and W. Faulkner (1985), D. MacKenzie and J. Wajcman (1985), and G. Kirkup et al. (1991).

3. See, for instance, Margaret A. Eisenhart and Elizabeth Finkel (1998), Sue V. Rosser (1990, 1995, 1997), Susan Ambrose et al. (1997), Cinda-Sue Davis et al. (1996), and Julia Evetts (1996).

Works Cited

Ambrose, Susan, Kristin Dunkle, Barbara Lazarus, Indira Nair, and Deborah Harkus (Eds.). *Journeys of Women in Science and Engineering: No Universal Constants.* Temple University Press, 1997.

Arnold, E., and W. Faulkner (Eds.). *Smothered by Invention: Technology in Women's Lives.* London: Pluto, 1985.

Clarke, Adele, and Virginia Olesen (Eds.). *Revisioning Women, Health, and Healing.* New York: Routledge, 1999.

Collins, Patricia Hill. "Moving beyond Gender: Intersectionality and Scientific Knowledge." In *Revisioning Gender*, ed. Myra M. Ferree and Judith B. Hess. Thousand Oaks, CA: Sage, 1999.

Davis, Cinda-Sue, Angela Ginorio, Carol Hollenshead, Paula Rayman (Eds.). *Gender and Career in Science and Engineering.* San Francisco, CA: Jossey-Bass Education Series, 1996.

Eisenhart, Margaret A., and Elizabeth Finkel. *Women's Science: Learning and Succeeding from the Margins.* Chicago: University of Chicago Press, 1998.

Evetts, Julia. *Gender and Career in Science and Engineering.* Bristol, PA: Taylor and Francis, 1996.

Haraway, Donna. *How Like a Leaf: An Interview with Thyrza Nichols Goodeve.* New York: Routledge, 1999.

Hawthorne, Susan, and Renate Klein. *CyberFeminism: Connectivity, Critique + Creativity.* North Melbourne, Australia: Spinifex Press, 1999.

Kirkup, G., and L. Smith Keller (Eds.). *Inventing Women: Science, Technology, and Gender.* Cambridge, UK: Polity, 1991.

Latour, Bruno. *We Have Never Been Modern.* Cambridge, MA: Cambridge University Press, 1993.

MacKenzie, D., and J. Wajcman (Eds.). *The Social Shaping of Technology.* Milton Keynes: Open University Press, 1985.

Noble, David. *A World without Women: The Christian Clerical Tradition of Western Science.* New York: Knopf, 1992.

Rosser, Sue V. *Re-Engineering Female-Friendly Science.* New York: Teachers College Press, 1997.

——— . (Ed.). *Teaching the Majority: Breaking the Barrier in Science, Mathematics, and Engineering.* New York: Teachers College Press, 1995.

——— . *Female-Friendly Science; Applying Women's Studies Methods and Theories to Attract Students.* Elmsford, NY: Pergamon Press, 1990.

Rouse, Joseph. *Engaging Science: How to Understand Its Practices Philosophically.* Ithaca, NY: Cornell University Press, 1996.

Terry, Jennifer, and Melodie Calvert (Eds.). *Processed Lives: Gender and Technology in Everyday Life.* New York: Routledge, 1997.

(UN)DISCIPLINED IDENTITIES

Forging Knowledge Across Borders

Section I

Proud to be an Oxymoron!

From Schizophrenic to (Un)Disciplined Practice

Angela B. Ginorio

Schizophrenic

Because of my dual interests in violence and science, for a long time I described my scholarly work as "schizophrenic"—the dissociated aspects of schizophrenia. My training in psychology gave me a vocabulary that defined my world with words such as *normal* and *schizophrenic*. *Normal* has two meanings: the clinical meaning refers to behavior that falls within the parameters of healthy responses, and the statistical meaning refers to the distribution of a population so that two-thirds of the population falls within one standard deviation of the mean of a normal distribution. *Schizophrenia* is a clinical term that describes types of psychosis characterized by the development of symptoms that signal "the intrusion of primary process material" from the unconscious into everyday behavior (Cameron 1963, 578).

When I applied clinical psychology to my own life, I wanted to be defined as "normal" in its clinical sense. But often I found myself with experiences that were best described by feelings of being split or torn, "feelings that familiar places, events, and even the self have somehow become unfamiliar" (Cameron 1963, 338), or what clinical psychologists call a "mild dissociative reaction." As a cross-cultural social psychologist, I could well explain my experiences as a Puerto Rican woman in the mainland United States by reference to processes such as acculturation and assimilation, or in-group and out-group contact. But the immediacy of my own experiences called for an internal explanation; "schizophrenic" fit the bill and had the advantage of needing no further explanations when used to communicate to others my internal state. (The fact that I could communicate effectively with others proved that I was not "truly" schizophrenic!)

And so I have continued this schizophrenic existence—personally, as a Puerto Rican woman in mainstream America, and professionally, as an interdisciplinary scholar working on the seemingly unrelated issues of violence and science. At face value, the two areas I was studying, gendered violence and women and/in

14

science, have nothing to do with each other. Of course, female and male scientists are likely to be victims of violence and/or aggressors at the same rate as other people of similar class and race. The first conceptual crossover between these two fields occurred for me while discussing the dynamics of a scientific lab with a woman scientist. During our conversation about the lab, I realized that the personal and professional dynamics of the lab she described became more predictable when I used the concept of the "abusive family" to sort the information. As I explained my interpretation and the analogy, she immediately resonated with the idea and went on to derive useful conclusions from that analysis.

Beyond such individual cases I found that the knowledge I gained in one field illuminated issues I was studying in the other. For example, concepts from social psychology such as "moral community" could be applied equally to my work on violence and to the experiences of women scientists. A moral community refers to a group that holds common values (Opotow 1990). In such a community there are mechanisms of exclusions and inclusions to determine who has access to the resources of the community. Individuals who are excluded from communities and defined as outsiders are more likely to be subjected to discrimination, whether in the form of violence (Opotow 1990) or by denial of access to resources (Rossiter 1984, 1995), as in the case of women scientists. Thus, not only can concepts from one discipline be used to facilitate the understanding of concepts in another, but there are also concepts that apply and work in both realms.

Another example is that the most typical connection between science and the study of violence has been through studies of the biological underpinnings of violence. Most claims of the "biology" of violence come from sociobiological theories that suggest that men, like many animals, are aggressive by their evolutionary nature (Barash 1979) and that violent acts such as rape and warfare are "adaptive" and provide evolutionary advantages to the men who commit them (Barash 1979; Thornhill and Thornhill 1983). The claims of sociobiology that continue to this day (Thornhill and Palmer 2000), however, have a long history of critique by feminist scholars (Bleier 1984; Fausto-Sterling 1985). Another connection between science and violence comes from postcolonial critics of science (Nandy 1988; Shiva 1988; Alvares 1994) who claim that science by its very nature is violent. Citing epistemological practices of abstraction and reductionism as well as the development of vivisection and intrusive experimentation, these scholars argue that the very philosophical and epistemological foundations of "Western" science are intrinsically violent.

My research on both violence and science has largely used methodological approaches from the social sciences, including empiricist epistemologies and quantitative analyses that are integral to and used in the natural sciences. For example, in my work on gender and violence, I use scientific methods such as control groups when doing surveys of the incidence of sexual harassment (Ginorio and

Brown 1983). However, unlike the methodological expectations in the natural sciences, I recognize the impossibility of using control groups in the study of certain kinds of violence. To me, the expectation of such controlled experiments in issues such as rape is evidence of the assumption of decontextualization and control in science. It was such a mentality that justified the Tuskegee syphilis experiments.

Being located in one of the few women studies departments with a social science orientation in the United States means that my department is methodologically attuned to my training as a social psychologist, especially since I am not a pure empiricist. Even before joining the women studies department, I was moving away from exclusive reliance on surveys and quantitative measurements, the traditional modes of study in social psychology. My work on violence has shifted from surveys of sexual harassment to analyses of the sociocultural context in which violence is examined: classrooms (Ginorio 1998), investigators' offices (Remick and Ginorio 1996), and the role of socially defined identities in violence (Ginorio, in progress). In my work on women and/in science I use both quantitative and qualitative measures with two particular populations: practicing women scientists and female students interested in science at sixteen rural high schools in the state of Washington. This work has expanded to using oral histories—narratives of girls and women—to understand whether and how their interest in science develops and is nurtured.

To give you a flavor of how I came to such research, I want to briefly describe two projects, the "Women Scientists Oral Histories Project" and the "Rural Girls in Science" project. Both began as a result of a meeting with thirty women scientists in which we presented data on the status of women scientists at our university. During the free-flowing discussion that followed the meeting, Dr. Lillian McDermott, then the only woman in the faculty of the physics department, raised the issue of why women scientists persisted in their profession in the face of the obstacles to success identified in the data. The ensuing discussion made it obvious that there were living histories among us that needed to be recorded. The thirty-two oral histories we have collected thus far have a dual focus: they record the lives of the women scientists from birth to the present, and they assess their involvement with feminism and other social justice movements.

In the same meeting, we also discussed the educational backgrounds of the women present. Consistent with extant research, most of the women had a relative who was a scientist or a teacher of mathematics or science at the precollege level, or had attended a single-sex educational institution. However, a small but significant number of the women had attended small rural schools. Thus began our efforts to assess the effect of rural upbringing on the development of interest in science and to foster that interest among rural students, with particular attention to girls of color (mostly Latinas and American Indian girls in rural Washington).

What surprised me about my work on women scientists was that it was easier to find congruence in the two dissimilar areas of my own scholarship than it was to find affinities between women scientists and women's studies scholars. Even the 25 percent of the scientists who claimed to be "feminists" did not feel "women's studies" was a place where they belonged. They saw the scholarship of women's studies faculty as too abstract and esoteric and irrelevant to women scientists. The foremost concerns for the women scientists we interviewed were related to gaining equal access to science, gaining resources once they were inside, and in proving that women could do science (Ginorio, Marshall, and Breckenridge 2000). Many had read a few works in feminist science studies—mostly Rosser (1990), Keller (1985, 1992), and Rossiter (1984, 1995)—and several had read Traweek (1988). What captured the imagination of most of these scientists were the stories of discriminatory practices against women in the past (McGrayne 1993; Rossiter 1984, 1995) or the present (Gornick 1990; Massachusetts Institute of Technology 1999). Sheila Widnall's (1988) presidential address to the American Association for the Advancement of Science (AAAS), with its focus on discrimination against women, was still prescient. The need to develop a document such as the 1992 Baltimore Charter (Urry 1999), whose first sentence reads, "We hold as fundamental that: Women and men are equally capable of doing excellent science," highlights some of the basic issues still faced by practicing women scientists.

My colleagues in women's studies, in turn, do not have much sympathy for the difficulties faced by women who are located in science departments, which have many more privileges (lower teaching loads, higher average salaries) than women's studies. Furthermore, feminist scholarship has long suggested and shown that recruiting more women into any discipline will not change the masculinist culture of academe. What is needed, they argue, is not just a documentation of discriminatory practices, but a recognition that these practices are the result of scientific history and practice. Ultimately, we need to change the culture of science, a culture into which both men and women scientists are enculturated. When feminists among these scientists began to infuse their ideas into their scientific departments, tension resulted with both feminist and nonfeminist colleagues. With their nonfeminist colleagues the argument focused on the desirability of changing science at all; and with feminists, the ways of changing science. Few among them were in positions where they could implement projects flowing from feminist science studies in their discipline. Many of them channeled their energies into issues of access and discrimination, where they could see more immediate benefits.

Oxymorons

Thirty years ago, Barnard College initiated a conference series called "The Feminist and the Scholar," to point to the existence of such creatures at a time when feminist scholarship was considered an oxymoron. Today, while feminist scholarship is no longer considered an oxymoron, feminist scholars are still largely white and upper or middle class, working in the humanities and social sciences. However, among academics, in many people's minds, the terms *feminist scientist*, *woman of color scholar*, and *woman of color scientist* are still seen as contradictory and curious. Most people who think of women of color or feminist scientists as oxymorons may not be as blatant as the professor who asked Yolanda Flores-Niemann, "What are you, a Chicana or a scholar?" (Flores-Niemann 1999).

As this anthology shows, we have much work left to do in creating opportunities and sustaining women of color in the sciences and in women's studies. Critiques of mainstream feminism and the marginalization, exclusion, and alienation that women of color described in anthologies such as *This Bridge Called My Back* (Moraga and Anzaldúa 1981) and *All the Women Are White, All the Blacks Are Men, but Some of Us Are Brave* (Hull, Bell-Scott, and Smith 1982) still resonate and reverberate with the experiences of most women of color in the academy today—twenty years later. The effects of faculty and students' inability to envision us as scholars makes it necessary for women of color in the academy, as well as feminist scientists, to spend time working on agendas often not of our own choosing. Ensuring access to science for students of color while also "trying to prove that we can do good scholarship" are two such agendas, both of which consume a great deal of time and energy. However, such work is often defined as service rather than scholarship (and is often seen as self-serving to boot). Thus, women of color and feminist scientists are often carrying on multiple agendas that may be defined as (un)disciplined. As Bartsch states in this volume, "Working in this undefined space is seen as unfocused rather than demanding, creative, and synthetic." As the narratives in this section demonstrate, it requires huge levels of discipline and a sense of balance to "fit and survive" in systems built to ensure the survival of only the fittest.

(Un)Disciplined

After years of schizophrenic existence, those of us who have survived in the academy have had to redefine our approach to our multiple allegiances. Our initial posture may have been one of extreme discomfort (schizophrenic), followed by resistance to being cast as oxymorons. But many of those who have survived thus far have moved on to a position of reclaiming and redefining the terrain—to being proud to be an oxymoron, to playing to that strength. We thus belong to no one discipline or identity group, yet belong to many or all. This embrace of the interdisciplinary and the vision of the progressive possibilities of multiple locations and identities is what I find most encouraging in the narratives that follow.

Reading these narratives, I have two positive experiences. First, I gain a sense of normalcy about my bifurcated interests and identity—like the feelings I experienced when I heard about Donna Hughes, a scholar in molecular biology and antiviolence work (Hughes 1995). It is the joy of seeing kindred spirits who have embarked on similar journeys. Second, I am buoyed by the possibilities of transdisciplinarity that includes the sciences. The diversity of terms used to describe these bifurcated interests indicates the level of ferment of the ideas at this time. Using both their own as well as borrowed terms, the authors in this section use the following metaphors to describe themselves and their actions: insider-outsider (Picart), meandering river (Whitaker), self-reflexive boundary-straddling (Clarke), dual citizen (Allen), resident alien (Bartsch), boundary-crossing (Flower), and naturecultures (Subramaniam quoting Haraway). The images evoke an array of disciplinary parameters, from the external force of the meandering river to the internal self-reflexion of the boundary-straddler; from the resident alien and boundary-crosser to the inhabitant of naturecultures. These pithy oxymorons provide empowering prisms to use in decoding the experience that my first discipline would have labeled as maladjusted at best and schizophrenic at worst.

The most encouraging sign for transdisciplinarity I find in these narratives is the diversity of locations of these scholars. Among the authors, there are scientists who are making feminist science projects the focus of their work from science departments (Allen, Whitaker) as well as from women's studies departments (Bartsch, Subramaniam) and other unique and interdisciplinary locations (Flower). There are scholars from the social sciences (Clarke) and the humanities (Picart) who are focusing on feminist science studies from within their own disciplines in sociology, philosophy, and rhetoric.

It is exciting and heartwarming to see these interdisciplinary scholars forge new ground intellectually and institutionally within disciplines and in interdisciplinary programs. It will be interesting to watch the academic future of these scholars and see where in the structure of their institutions they will be in ten years. It will be an index of limited success of these projects if the scientists currently in science departments move out of them, and those who have joint appointments end up with only one affiliation. And, while it will be an unlikely feat if any of the nonscientists move to science departments, I am also looking forward to the day when more women's studies programs will make science or technological literacy a priority for a full-time hire. The narratives that follow give me hope that existing disciplines will someday welcome interdisciplinary, transformative scholarship and develop mechanisms to facilitate areas of study in naturecultures, unmarked by quotation marks and no longer considered oxymoronic or schizophrenic.

Works Cited

Alvares, Claude. *Science, Development, and Violence: The Revolt against Modernity*. Delhi: Oxford University Press, 1994.

Barash, David. "Sociobiology of Rape in Mallards: Responses of the Mated Male," *Science* 197 (1979): 788–789.

Bleier, Ruth. *Science and Gender*. Elmsford, NY: Pergamon Press, 1984.

Cameron, Norman. *Personality Development and Psychopathology: A Dynamic Approach*. Boston, MA: Houghton Mifflin, 1963.

Fausto-Sterling, Anne. *Myths of Gender*. New York: Basic Books, 1985.

Flores-Niemann, Y. F. "The Making of a Token: A Case Study of Stereotype Threat and Racism in Academe." *Frontiers: A Journal of Women's Studies* XX (1999): 111–35.

Hughes, Donna M. "Significant Differences: The Construction of Knowledge, Objectivity, and Dominance." *Women's Studies International Forum* 18 (1995): 395–406.

Ginorio, Angela B. "The Role of Socially Defined Identities in the Experience of Violence." In progress.

———. "Contextualizing Violence in a Participatory Classroom: A Socially Defined Identities Approach." *Psychology of Women Quarterly* 22 (1998): 77–96.

Ginorio, Angela B., Terry Marshall, and Lisa Breckenridge. "The Feminist and the Scientist: One and the Same." *Women's Studies Quarterly* XXVII, nos. 1 and 2 Spring/Summer (2000): 271–295.

Ginorio, Angela B., and Marsha Brown. "Female Bonding as a Solution to Sexual Harassment among Students." Paper presented at the Association for Women in Psychology Annual Conference, Seattle, WA, 1983.

Gornick, Vivian. *Women in Science: 100 Journeys into the Territory*. New York: Touchstone Books, 1990.

Hull, Gloria, P. Bell Scott, and B. Smith, (Eds.). *All the Women are White, All the Blacks are Men, but Some of Us Are Brave*. New York: The Feminist Press, 1982.

Keller, Evelyn Fox. *Secrets of Life, Secrets of Death: Essays on Language, Gender, and Science*. New York: Routledge, 1992.

———. *Reflections on Gender and Science*. New Haven, CT: Yale University Press, 1985.

Massachusetts Institute of Technology. "A Study on the Status of Women Faculty in Science at MIT." Cambridge, MA: Author, 1999.

McGrayne, Sharon Bertsch. *Nobel Prize Women in Science: Their Lives, Struggles, and Momentous Discoveries*. New York: Birch Lane Press, 1993.

Moraga, Cherrie, and Gloria Anzaldúa (Eds.). *This Bridge Called My Back: Writings by Radical Women of Color*. New York: Kitchen Table Press, 1981.

Nandy, Ashis. *Science, Hegemony, and Violence*. Delhi: Oxford University Press, 1988.

Opotow, S. "Moral Exclusion and Injustice: An Introduction." *Journal of Social Issues* 46 (1990): 1–20.

Remick, H., and A. Ginorio. "Dealing with the 'Sexual' in Sexual Harassment." *Initiatives* 57 (1996): 27–35.

Rosser, Sue V. *Female-Friendly Science: Applying Women's Studies Methods and Theories to Attract Students*. Elmsford, NY: Pergamon Press, 1990.

Rossiter, Margaret W. *Women Scientists in America: Before Affirmative Action, 1940–1972.* Baltimore, MD: Johns Hopkins University Press, 1995.

———. *Women Scientists in American: Struggles and Strategies to 1940.* Baltimore, MD: Johns Hopkins University Press, 1984.

Shiva, Vandana. *Staying Alive: Women, Ecology, and Development in India.* London: Zed Press, 1988.

Thornhill, Randy, and Craig T. Palmer. *A Natural History of Rape: Biological Bases of Sexual Coercion.* Cambridge, MA: MIT Press, 2000.

Thornhill, Randy, and N. Thornhill. "Human Rape: An Evolutionary Analysis." *Ethology and Sociobiology* 4 (1983): 137.

Traweek, Sharon. *Beamtimes and Lifetimes: The World of High Energy Physicists.* Cambridge, MA: Harvard University Press, 1988.

Urry, Meg. "The Baltimore Charter and the Status of Women in Astronomy." *Status: A Report on Women in Astronomy* (June 1999): 6–10. Available at: www.aas.org/~cswa/bc.html

Widnall, Sheila. "AAAS Presidential Lecture: Voices from the Pipeline." *Science* 241 (1988): 1740–1743.

What Do You Do Over There, Anyway?

Tales of an Academic Dual Citizen

→ Caitilyn Allen

Since 1992, I have held a joint academic appointment in natural science and women's studies at the University of Wisconsin-Madison. More precisely, 41 percent of me belongs to the women's studies program, leaving the remaining 59 percent for the Department of Plant Pathology. I thus find myself a citizen of two very different academic cultures. This unusually interdisciplinary position divides my energies between profoundly dissimilar departments with very different ideas about what it means to be a productive and effective faculty member. Over the years, it has become clear to me that the two disciplines not only study different subjects, but they do so in fundamentally different ways. My position offers me the opportunity to gather up and unite these disparate perspectives, and to create a connection between two academic cultures. In effect, I hope to be a translator who is fluent in multiple intellectual approaches. To extend the metaphor, I hold dual citizenship in the country of natural science and the less easily defined territory of women's studies, an interdisciplinary area that spans the humanities and social sciences but is united by feminist theory. Viewed in the largest possible context, my job is to mediate a real exchange of ideas and foster mutual understanding and respect between science and feminism.

However lofty and high-minded these goals may sound, I also confront the practical challenge of earning tenure in an academic area (biology) that does not always understand or respect the methods and premises that shape my academic appointment in women's studies. It is my responsibility to ensure that the biologists who will evaluate me understand the intellectual basis of women's studies and my role in that discipline. In several undergraduate classes, I teach the value and scholarly worldview of biology to non–science majors (including women's studies students). These classes include Plant Pathology/Botany 123, "Plants, Parasites, and People," a non–science majors course enrolling several hundred students a year, which covers plant disease and its social impacts, with special emphasis on tropical agriculture and colonial cash crops as well as biotechnology and agriculture. Through women's studies, I teach "Biology and Gender," a critical analysis of

22

biological explanations for gender differences, which enrolls approximately forty women's studies majors and minors, usually upper-level nonbiologists. In addition to examining the quality and content of the science itself, we also consider how the science of gender differences is presented through the media.

In a process that is in many ways parallel to my work with students, I must also teach the scholarly worldview and value of women's studies to the biology faculty who will decide whether or not I am promoted. I approach this in various ways, including presentations of official seminars and other more informal routes. My seminars cover the assessment of the Women in Science and Engineering dorm project here, of which I am faculty director, and the content of my "Biology and Gender" course, in which I deliver the message that I am teaching rigorous and high-quality human biology, rather than what others may perceive to be politically biased ideology glommed on to science. Other tactics I use are more subversive—for example, taking the form of discussing a current paper in *Science*, an article in the newspaper, or even the behavior of my colleagues' children ("You know, you might think that she's dropping out of calculus because she's a girl, but you might like to know that a study published last year suggests that . . ."). The responses to this approach vary widely. Everyone is polite, but some are merely indulgent, while others are genuinely listening. Either way, I must perform this job as an ambassador in order to keep my job as a scientist.

Training and Background

Although my bachelor's degree was in botany, I took many history and literature classes as an undergraduate. It was with some difficulty that I eventually decided to major in natural science rather than humanities (literature is still a great source of personal pleasure for me). I earned my doctorate in plant pathology, an intensely interdisciplinary field by biological standards. A plant pathologist not only knows about basic botany, microbiology, ecology, and the specifics of dozens of plant diseases and pathogens, but also agriculture and something of its social context. My research interests incline toward the basic biology of plant-pathogen interactions rather than applied practical research. In particular, I'm interested in the genetics of plant pathogenic bacteria. How do they make plants sick? How do they control the expression of the genes they use to cause disease? How do they survive latently inside a host plant without causing disease? These and related questions motivate my research laboratory and are the focus of my scientific grant proposals, publications, and seminar presentations. In common with many other women's studies faculty, I have no formal training in women's studies, though I have read extensively in the feminist literature. In truth, I never supposed that I could find a job that would marry my interest in feminism with my passion for science.

Plant pathology hired me for my science; they were glad to have women's studies create the position and pay a portion of my salary. Later, they were puzzled when I told them I didn't want them to try to "buy out" the women's studies part of my position so I could do only lab science. Women's studies, on the other hand, hired me to teach "Biology and Gender" and to be a working bench researcher. There was no requirement that I publish in the women's studies literature (although I have) before tenure. Nevertheless, being a part of the women's studies community here and reading in the feminist science studies literature ensures that I am always both inside and outside of the scientific enterprise. I want women's studies undergraduate students to know a woman scientist who publishes in the biology primary literature and who also sees her work and that of others in a social context. I want the graduate students who work in my lab and whom I teach in classes to see a model of collaborative, interactive, community-based research, and to know that there are many different ways of successfully practicing science. I want them to see that I have a balanced life, and that you don't have to be a single-minded workaholic to succeed in science.

My job asks me to be simultaneously a working bench scientist and a feminist critic of science. In the first capacity I'm fully engaged in conducting research, training graduate students, and pursuing research funding. However, as a feminist critic of science, I'm also required to stand outside the discipline in which I was trained and analyze it from an entirely different scholarly standpoint. This can be awkward and uncomfortable. The world of the working scientist has a very immediate and driven quality; there is a strong and often unexamined sense that the work we do is both urgent and important. We work long hours to understand the workings of the natural world and often try to develop technologies to control, to exploit, or, increasingly, to protect the natural systems we study.

The training of scientists has much in common with joining a medieval guild. Aspiring members learn the trade and prove their loyalty through a long apprenticeship as a graduate student under a powerful and knowledgeable master. They then move on to become journeymen as semi-independent postdoctoral fellows and untenured faculty. This training is acknowledged to be a nearly all-consuming task, commensurate with the importance of the work. A very high level of commitment and a tight intellectual focus are absolute prerequisites for success in science. An interest in the philosophy of science or a critique of scientific approaches is widely viewed as weakness (except in emeritus faculty, where it can be a charming eccentricity). The taint of dilettantism can be fatal for a young scientist; one of the most damning things one can say about a student is that she's not serious about science. In short, the narrow focus and intense effort that is traditionally a part of scientific training actively mitigates against development of an objective, critical analysis of the scientific process.

Teaching Across the Gap

It is therefore quite unusual for active research scientists to devote professional energy to the issues that appear central to feminist science studies. These issues might include such questions as: How do gender-related expectations bias scientific research on seemingly gender-neutral subjects like biochemistry and agriculture? What difference might it make if scientists as a population were more diverse? Is any fact objectively knowable? These kinds of questions can seem respectively irrelevant, trivial, or downright heretical to many of my scientific colleagues.

One of the challenges I face in defining my women's studies position to my scientific colleagues is distinguishing the "women-in-science" problem from feminist science studies. Scientists tend to assume that feminists are primarily concerned with increasing the number of women pursuing science careers. The idea that feminists might critique the way in which science is performed and the fundamental assumptions upon which experimental science is based is so unexpected as to be shocking. The entire problem of objectivity and standpoint, which for years has been a fundamental issue in the humanities and social sciences, has simply not arisen for most working scientists. It can be daunting, to say nothing of intimidating, for an untenured professor to present the entire concept of feminist postmodern approaches to science to an incredulous senior scientific colleague. "Why, that's utter rot!" sputtered one eminent full professor. "Science is objective, and experiments uncover truths. Any fool can see that it's different from writing about history, where you can just put down whatever you want."

Clearly, this wasn't a very successful interaction. Bluntly advancing the idea that there are no objectively knowable facts undermines the whole foundation of science and can earn contemptuous dismissal. If there is no common set of assumptions about what is valuable and worth doing, a useful discussion is impossible. On the other hand, I have bridged this gap in perspective by getting down to specifics and discussing particular experiments to document my points. Science is unalterably data driven. Using the work of someone like Sandra Harding, one can argue for "strong objectivity" and suggest the argument that "feminist science is good science that eliminates bias," especially effective when supported with indisputable examples of sexism corrupting research data (Harding 1991, 136).

At the other end of campus, many of my women's studies colleagues have their own suspicions about scientists. To a scholar in a traditional humanities discipline, research science can appear narrow-minded, dully practical, and spiritually empty. I acquired a vivid sense of this perspective when a literary colleague shared with me her undergraduate memories: "In my romantic poetry class we were talking about the birth of the soul, and I felt that all the things that truly mattered were finally being put into words. Meanwhile in biology, we memorized the parts of the stomach. It was not very interesting." In company with many other biologists, I find that the natural world sings with meaning, and that the study of bacteria can be intensely and spiritually satisfying; unfortunately, few introductory biology classes effectively convey this perspective. It is no secret that scientists could be much better advocates for their profession; we have an unhappy reputation for being socially awkward loners, and often do not explain our work well to nonscientists. This failing can result from hubris, from absorption in our work (that very commitment and focus that is a celebrated part of the scientific mystique), or simply from poor communication skills.

Certainly, there are very different ideas about classroom pedagogy in the two cultures. The cooperative, student inquiry–driven approaches that are standard practice in the humanities or social science classroom qualify as wild-eyed radicalism in laboratory science (although fortunately that is changing). It is no wonder that non–science majors taking science courses to fulfill breadth requirements sometimes feel they've entered a hostile, alien world from which they can't wait to escape. But done well, teaching offers an opportunity for scientists, especially those who teach courses for non–science majors, to showcase the fascination, power, and extraordinary beauty of the natural world.

Another barrier to mutual understanding is that educated nonscientists may feel that scientists are frequently guilty of applying new, possibly dangerous technologies without rigorous examination of their long-term effects or ethical implications. A student in my first women's studies class, "Biology and Gender," told me that she was taking my course only because her major required a science class. "Science is a tool of the patriarchy," she told me sternly, "and as Audre Lorde (1984, 112) said, 'the master's tools will never dismantle the master's house.'" Now there was a teaching challenge.

A primary goal of teaching biology to women's studies students is to develop in students a well-informed skepticism about the ability of biologists to remain objective when researching provocative subjects like the biology of sex differences. At the same time, another central goal of the course is to give students an appreciation for the power of the scientific method, properly applied, to overcome bias. In practice, these goals are not contradictory. In my view (and there are many other views), effective feminist critique of science addresses the ways in which science fails to live up to its own best aspirations. Failures of objectivity result in bad science, whether those failures derive from sexist bias or some other cause. An example: Is premenstrual syndrome (PMS) a social construct or a biological reality? Every woman has an opinion on this matter, based on her own personal experience. Is this personal experience scientifically relevant? Maybe. Is it objective? No. Is it relevant to her experience? Yes. Does it allow one to distinguish between biological and social forces? Probably not. How could we design an experiment to answer this question more conclusively? Hmmm. This topic forms a sizzling teaching opportunity, and it emerges that non–biology students are entirely capable of designing a clean, well-controlled experiment concerning the biology of PMS without disavowing their own experiences. In the process, they develop an understanding of both the strengths and the limitations of science.

Practical Effects of Working Across Disciplines

Some of the cultural differences between bench science and women's studies have direct impacts on the career progress of those working across the disciplines. The most substantive issue is that of evaluating scholarly productivity. Scientists are promoted and rewarded based on their ability to obtain large outside research grants and to publish peer-reviewed articles in highly regarded journals. In general, big outside grants have less importance for most women's studies scholars (there are exceptions), and publication of books is more important than journal articles for promotion. If mishandled, these differences have the potential to create intractable dilemmas for interdisciplinary appointees, and indeed to scuttle their academic careers.

However, such problems can be avoided by open communication and respectful acknowledgment of these differing expectations. In my own case, the women's studies program has a history of working with biologists and thoroughly understood what I needed to do to earn tenure and professional credibility in my natural science department. It was additionally helpful that my tenure home was explicitly identified at the time of my hire, so there was no ambiguity about the fact that I was expected to develop an externally funded research program in bacterial genetics. Moreover, in deference to the time needed to launch a bench research program, the women's studies program protected me from heavy teaching loads as an assistant professor.

Certainly, the onus for explaining key cultural differences must be on the appointee; nonscientists need to be told that multiple authorship is the norm in many science disciplines and is not an indicator of weak scholarship. Counterintuitively, last authorship on a science paper is often more significant than first authorship, since last authorship usually designates the P.I. (primary investigator), the person who conceived, directed, and obtained funding for the research.

It is also important for cross-disciplinary scientists to help their women's studies colleagues understand that the position of women in many scientific fields remains very tenuous. As mentioned above, the sciences generally demand a fierce loyalty to the profession rather than rewarding thoughtful, constructive critique of it. This is particularly true for women, still substantially underrepresented among science faculty. If we assume that each scientist can defy convention in one area without endangering professional position, women have already used up that single exception simply by being female. As they are working to establish themselves in their careers, women often try to avoid being labeled as trouble-makers or unfocused. Marginalization can be lethal in a discipline that still runs largely on an "old-boy" network. For example, the prestigious oral presentations at the major meetings in my own field are by invitation only; as a result, we hear from the same two dozen scientists year after year. It can be very difficult to break into the inner circle, and so women are understandably reluctant to do anything that might undermine their scientific reputation.

Transcending Boundaries

None of this is to say that the boundaries between these disciplines are uncross-able. There is already a small but robust cadre of scholars who work effectively and productively in science and women's studies. Below I offer some suggestions to help ensure success for institutions considering cross-disciplinary appointments such as my own, and for the faculty who find themselves in such positions.

For Institutions

- Consider hiring senior faculty for joint science–women's studies posi-tions. Tenured professors are much less vulnerable to cultural pressures within disciplines and can more freely pursue unconventional lines of research.
- Define the job expectations as explicitly as possible. In particular, it is im-portant to unambiguously identify the candidate's tenure home and en-sure that he or she understands what the expectations are for tenure there.
- If you expect someone to build a bridge, you cannot assess his or her success solely by measuring what's at either end of the bridge. Find ways to acknowledge and value the effort required to successfully occupy an interdisciplinary position.
- Actively develop interaction between the two home departments; espe-cially in the case of junior faculty, it is essential that the respective chairs or mentoring committees are delivering a consistent message.

For Cross-Disciplinary Faculty

- Attend scholarly meetings in both disciplines to acquaint yourself with the culture of the fields.
- Communicate thoroughly with both departments so that they are aware of all your activities. I successfully used a departmental seminar as a forum to explain the feminist critiques of science to my biology department.
- Although they are not directly relevant to feminist science studies, "women-in-science" issues can form a useful common enterprise between science and women's studies. My involvement in a special program

for women science and engineering majors is valued by both my home departments.

- Identify and aggressively pursue any special resources (grants, fellowships) intended to encourage interdisciplinary scholarship.
- Use teaching in the two disciplines to develop and refine your scholarly perspectives. All teaching faculty do this to a degree, but in my experience, the classroom is a particularly valuable source of inspiration, focus, and incentive in the area of feminist science.

Combining research in natural science and women's studies is undoubtedly challenging, but it is also both important and rewarding. Although efforts in this area may be met with initial suspicion, feminist critiques can and will improve scientific theory and practice. Because they are inside the scientific enterprise, working natural scientists can offer particularly effective and credible analyses. To do so, however, they must understand these two cultures well enough to successfully develop dual professional personae as respected scientists *and* feminist critics. They must become dual citizens, fluent in at least two scholarly languages.

Works Cited

Harding, Sandra. *Whose Science? Whose Knowledge? Thinking from Women's Lives.* Ithaca, NY: Cornell University Press, 1991.
Lorde, Audre. *Sister Outsider.* New York: Crossing Press, 1984.

Resident Alien

A Scientist in Women's Studies

———————————————————————————————➤ Ingrid Bartsch

In 1996, a reporter for a local newspaper wrote an article on my new academic position entitled "She Balances Science, Feminism" (Karp 1996). From his perspective, my position was clearly unusual and one that he couldn't fully reconcile. During our four-hour interview, he often returned to the questions: "What do you do in women's studies?" and "What qualifies you to be a professor of women's studies?" To the best of his understanding I studied barriers, forms of discrimination for women scientists. He concluded that my training and faculty position were a "mismatch." Over the last five years, I have come to discover that it is not unusual for people to simplify issues of "feminism and science" to those of "women in science." It is far less difficult to understand the factors that have limited women's accomplishments in the sciences than it is to engage in the cultural deconstruction of science that feminism demands.

I want to emphasize that prior to accepting the position in women's studies, I had no formal training in women's studies. However, I did have experience with the field of geography, which was helpful in understanding the nature of interdisciplinary work. Being centered in women's studies has also allowed me to think about the lives of women scientists and the conditions for women (young and old) in the sciences, including my own. I now know of, and teach others about, the importance of mentors, family, support, special programs (preferably same-sex), and role models for recruiting and retaining girls and women in the natural sciences. I now appreciate the barriers women face and have come to the startling realization that my earning a Ph.D. in the natural sciences was remarkable. I had no mentors or role models, attended coeducational public schools my entire life, and am the only member of my family to have attended college (let alone pursue science as a career). Moreover, I began my doctoral program when my son was six months old, and completed my degree, including three summers of field research, in four years. So much for the notion that women can't have children while pursuing research and that, if they do, they need special favors (like more time) to help them get through.

Switching from the natural to the social sciences was not a trajectory I had anticipated in my training. Like other scientists, my perception of what I could and should do was very limited (and limiting). What brought me to women's studies was partly necessity and partly my willingness to change my identity. I came to the University of South Florida with my spouse but without a permanent position—not an uncommon situation for dual-career academics. I began my work here as an adjunct, first in the natural sciences (biology) and then expanding my teaching into the social sciences (geography). It became clear after a few years that there would be no opportunities for a tenure-earning position in either of those two departments. During this period, I was asked by the biology department to develop and teach a selected topics course entitled "Women and Science," which I agreed to do. As I taught this course, it occurred to me that there might be another location from which to offer this material and I approached the chair of the women's studies department. To my good fortune, women's studies had actually been considering hiring a "scientist" and when the department discovered that there was, in fact, a scientist on campus willing to combine women's studies and science they advertised the position. I now have a tenure-track position in women's studies, a rather unusual location for a natural scientist. And through women's studies I have developed and continue to teach the "Women and Science" course, although from a much different perspective. When I offered the course in the biology department, it was a "women in science" course, taught from a liberal feminist perspective and devoid of information on gender and feminism. I still begin with this perspective when I teach the course, since students from outside women's studies, and particularly those from the natural sciences, resist being expected to immediately dive into feminist critiques of science. However, I now incorporate feminist content midway through the semester, and most students, I find, develop an appreciation for the concepts and issues addressed in feminist science scholarship.

My reason for telling this story is to encourage other scientists to seek these kinds of opportunities and consider offering a "Women and Science" course in their home departments. Not only is the perspective of scientists important to women's studies and to the future development of feminist science studies—scholarship that is frequently dismissed by "hard" scientists who believe that only they understand the nature of science—but scientists must and should engage in the questioning of science in order to produce better science (see Harding 1991). In particular, I am convinced that scientists must be doing the questioning if transformations in the culture of science are to occur. Thus, I join others in recognizing the importance of locating the work of feminist science scholars within the natural sciences (that is, within the core science curricula), where, for the most part, it is unknown and even intentionally disregarded.

Working across the boundaries of the natural and social sciences makes possible rich analyses produced by multiple interests and perspectives. Allowing these boundaries to be permeable has shaped my research by allowing me to work with people from such widely (but artificially) separate disciplines as special education and economics and also has given me an opportunity to include scientific knowledge in social and cultural analyses. For example, in a recent interdisciplinary project with a rhetoritician and a political theorist, my knowledge of basic ecological processes allowed us to create a unique argument around the construction of identity. Because I had an appreciation for identity politics, I was able to provide examples from the "natural" world to support our contention that identities (race, class, gender, and so on) are relative and unsustainable, and that we—feminists and scientists—need to focus on the relationality between and among categories to reach fuller understanding of the natural world and respect for all living and nonliving things.

Combining disciplines, however, is not without disadvantages. As with any nontraditional position that does not conform to disciplinary and institutional boundaries, my role has challenged traditional categories and expectations. I am now an outsider in the scientific community, although still capable of acting as a consultant or as a (semi-)legitimate member of theses and dissertation committees. Unfortunately, a common perspective among my science peers is that I have accepted a demotion by leaving the elite ranks of science to join, of all things, women's studies. University administrators have asked me if I plan to "go back" to biology after I get tenure. Of course I have no intention of abandoning women's studies and, if I did, I would confront other obstacles—my publications, as perceived by the science community, are in the wrong journals; I have not generated enough grant money for scientific research; and I have not been a major advisor for graduate students or postdoctoral fellows in the natural sciences. These obstacles make quite clear the fact that, in academia, you are expected to be in a discipline, and crossing or fusing academic boundaries is institutionally discredited.

Working across women's studies and the natural sciences poses other questions as well, such as how interdisciplinary scholarship is "counted" toward a faculty member's research program. Often, working in this undefined space is seen as unfocused rather than demanding, creative, and synthetic. Part of the difficulty is that few colleagues understand that my research focus is on the *connections* between feminism and science, feminism and environmentalism, science and education, feminism and science education. And, as a yet untenured faculty member, I am quite sensitive to their claims that my work "lacks focus." While sometimes there is institutional support for interdisciplinary work, there are also powerful forces of resistance.

A major advantage of having a tenure home in women's studies (and I acknowledge that most science faculty, especially junior faculty, do not have this luxury) is that my position allows me to choose feminist science studies (or any other feminist scholarship) as my major research area. Rather than feeling discouraged by the fact that I don't fit neatly into a category, I find it empowering and actively resist being placed in a "box." My position allows me the freedom to be as creative and imaginative as I wish. It allows me to offer surprising alternatives and create unusual combinations where most people expect a single focus. For example, interrogating the need to put disciplines into boxes that limit people's identities is itself a subject of feminist science inquiry—categories, identities, and boxes have a long history in the sciences with practices such as craniometry and race and sex difference research.

It is difficult for women's studies, a field dominated by scholars from the social sciences and humanities, to attract natural scientists to their programs. At a practical level, given the well-established disciplinary norms in the social sciences and the humanities, women's studies programs seldom recruit faculty from the natural sciences. When they do, the advertisement is not placed in *Science*, where scientists look for jobs, thus limiting response to the advertisement. So, although there are a growing number of, primarily, women scientists with joint positions in natural science and women's studies, they are still relatively rare. Women with Ph.D.s in natural science who engage in interdisciplinary work early in their career and seek tenure in women's studies are extremely rare.

However, scientists should be aware that there is a rapidly growing body of scholarship on the intersections of feminism and science that needs greater contributions from people trained in the natural sciences. Moreover, if historians, literary critics, and sociologists are entitled to hold faculty positions in women's studies, why not biologists? It is a disservice to both the natural sciences and women's studies if this bridge does not exist. And although being in women's studies has modified my role as a scientist, I have not abandoned the body of scientific knowledge that I have acquired. I use my scientific expertise and credentials when I teach environmental science classes, when I am a member of graduate student committees in biology, and when I conduct empirically based field research (typically, small and unfunded projects).

What might happen if more scientists chose to become more fully engaged in women's studies? From my experience, I know that they would, at least, teach differently. Having a women's studies perspective has certainly changed the way I teach by giving me the necessary tools to employ feminist pedagogy in all my classes, including those based in environmental policy or the natural sciences. Even if scientists did not modify their teaching approach, they might at least take steps to introduce the names of women scientists in their science classes or offer to act as mentors for other women scientists. These are small changes, but they are important. Most scientists in my experience do not realize that there exist specific issues for women scientists and that, even today, women often still receive less support than men do. Raising a feminist awareness among scientists would make it difficult, if not impossible, to continue to ignore women and might even lead to some reorganization of research efforts. Such awareness might provoke scientists into examining the currently unexamined language and practices of science. This could generate different knowledges, allowing for new interpretations and questions. I fully recognize that dismantling the barriers between women's studies and the natural sciences would make it difficult to continue to conduct science in its current configuration; it is very hard to simultaneously practice and deconstruct science, which is perhaps why many natural scientists who engage in feminist science studies eventually leave the sciences. As feminist science studies grows, as more scientists engage with feminism and feminists within the sciences, we can imagine and create new configurations—intellectual and institutional—of what it means to do science, be a scientist, and participate in this grand enterprise we call science.

Works Cited

Karp, David. "She Balances Science, Feminism." *The St. Petersburg Times*, January 31, 1996.

Harding, Sandra. *Whose Science? Whose Knowledge? Thinking from Women's Lives*. Ithaca, NY: Cornell University Press, 1991.

From Biologist
to Sociologist

Blurred Boundaries and Shared Practices

→ Jan Clarke

Women working as scientists are often distanced from those of us who are educated in science and then cross disciplinary boundaries, choosing interdisciplinary studies or pursuing other creative outlets. In this chapter, I draw on my experiences shifting from biologist to sociologist to question what can be learned when ideas, concepts, and methods are taken from one discipline to another, and how such shifts contribute to feminist science studies.

To describe the ways my scientific training informs my feminist practice, I draw on my understanding of science as everyday knowledge and my practice of technoskepticism, using women's experiences as a starting point, with self-reflection as an essential part of this process (Reinharz 1992; Smith 1999). To provide social context, I trace my transdisciplinary transformation from biologist to sociologist, and highlight turning points in my uneven career path. At one level, my experience with blurring disciplinary boundaries taught me to value science not only as expert knowledge, but also as everyday knowledge, which can be taken into community-based contexts as a means to empower rather than limit people's actions. At another level, a background in science and technology means my analysis is informed by technoskepticism—an enthusiasm for technosciences while at the same time questioning ways in which social contexts of technosciences can enable and limit women's lives and social change.

Transdisciplinary Transformations

Becoming a sociologist has not meant I have discarded my interests in science and technology. Instead, graduate study in sociology has allowed me to interpret science and technology within a historical, social, and political context that I had previously ignored or overlooked. At the same time, my education and experiences in science and technology allow me to critique technosciences from the standpoint of feminist and social studies of science.

I use the phrase *transdisciplinary transformations* to describe a process of shifting from one discipline to another, across disciplinary boundaries that normally remain intact. This process implies a shaping of ideas linked to shifts in career, sometimes hesitant and other times bold. With my shift in career, I took ideas and insights from biology to sociology and vice versa. This shaping of my ideas is now reflected in topics that draw together my interests in technosciences and social sciences (Clarke 1998, 1999).

After an undergraduate degree in biology and microbiology, I worked for several years in different research labs, making a series of lateral moves to maintain my interests—from immunochemistry to developmental botany to neuropathology. With each lateral move to a new research lab, I studied different areas of science to become knowledgeable enough to take my position as the skilled hands and astute eyes of scientists I worked for. These lateral shifts not only exposed me to different topics, they also required learning different research techniques and procedures. For instance, in an immunochemistry research lab my work involved protein biochemistry techniques and animal testing, based on precise measurements that conformed to standard scientific research practice of an objective investigator (Benston 1982). In another position, in a developmental botany lab, my work required manual dexterity for optical microscopy and transmission electron microscopy, plus an ability to interpret black-and-white prints that captured complex graphics of highly magnified plant cells. In comparison to precise quantitative measures of immunochemistry with little margin for error, developmental botany was a qualitative form of research dependent on the art of photography.

In both jobs I learned from creative and dynamic scientists, and gained an appreciation of their commitment and enthusiasm for their research programs. In the developmental botany lab I worked for a woman scientist, so I was exposed to the systemic sexism she experienced from her colleagues and students. At that time, I was reminded of Margaret Benston's observation that men can do science "with little or no role conflict," and "no need to examine or change basic assumptions about the world" (1982, 52).

As I became more politically active—involved in union work and local women's movement activities—my paid work in biology research seemed isolated from people and issues around me. To resolve the contradiction, I found a way to shift from lab research work to government-funded research projects that required my science education to interview scientists, engineers, and tradespeople in order to develop questionnaires and write occupational research reports. To research these occupational areas, I worked with people and took advantage of my science education and training. I also became a self-employed independent social researcher, and enjoyed the freedom of extensive travel across Canada.

For this social research, my lateral moves in science gave me a far more diverse scientific knowledge than any graduate degree in science could offer. Instead of intense attention to details characteristic of graduate work, I had acquired a broad yet specialized knowledge of many areas of science. With an understanding of scientific practices, the logic of scientific information, and a general knowledge of many areas of science, I easily grasped technical and occupational jargon used by scientists and technologists. This was key to these occupational studies, because I quickly understood interviewees' detailed descriptions of everything from medical research, engineering standards, and underground mining techniques, to how to fell massive old-growth trees in British Columbia.

When I started these social research projects, I naively tried to lift my experience in science and impose similar methods onto occupational studies. I approached social research projects with what Benston (1982) describes as the assumptions of scientific practice based on objectivity and reductionism. I felt, therefore, that I could control the social context and readily measure people's skills and maintain a value-free distance. But I discovered that by no means were all the methods of lab research directly transferable to social research. There was a fundamental difference between science and social science research—people simply do not cooperate with a researcher in the same way chemicals and plant roots conform to scientific method. Participants in social research also socially interact with a researcher, whereas chemicals and plants do not. I experienced firsthand the contrast between experiments under my control versus the social world that at first seemed more likely to control me.

A goal of these projects was to understand skills from the perspectives of those in each occupation; therefore, different interpretations that interviewees had of their work had to be taken into account. The social world was complex, and identifying patterns of skills within occupations was surprisingly difficult. I had complex puzzles to solve that involved an interpretive process quite different from scientific research. Nonetheless, making sense of patterns in the social world was equally challenging in a new way. On the one hand, the complexity of the social world was obvious to me, and the interpretive process of understanding skills intrigued me. On the other hand, this same complexity challenged my sense of being an objective researcher in control of research data that often seemed unmanageable. Early on I partially resolved this dilemma by requesting feedback from interviewees on initial drafts of questionnaires. Only later, when studying social science methodologies, did I realize that this practice was often integral to action research and to feminist social research (Reinharz 1992).

My habit of asking questions had always been a source of criticism in my life. In occupational studies I found that asking people questions was not only valued, it was key to conducting social research. I realized that what I enjoyed about social research projects was learning what people did, how they made sense of their lives, and the multiple layers that informed their interpretations. Another benefit of this social research was that it took me to places women seldom entered, to learn about occupations that have traditionally excluded women. I had assumed that one effect of the second wave of the women's movement was that more women worked in male-dominated workplaces. What I found was that women had made little impact on those areas of work, which remained strong-holds for men. At the time this was a disturbing insight; subsequently I recognized it as an important part of an analysis of the sexual division of labor in women and work literature (Armstrong and Armstrong 1990).

As an independent research consultant I felt constrained, unable to answer questions that puzzled me. I could see potential for interesting social research projects all around me, but my analytical tools for social research were limited. My questioning of gendered social relations of work informed my choice to return to academia and pursue graduate studies in sociology, particularly feminist sociology, and subsequently to make serious stabs at an academic career.

During my graduate studies, straddling boundaries between academia and community-based activism was a conscious feminist strategy (Clarke 1996). Linking theory and practice as a reflexive process was a key element of feminist theory and methodology (Reinharz 1992; Smith 1999) that continues to inform my studies and teaching. It is also an invaluable methodological contribution to feminist science studies, because it offers possibilities to expand debates about technosciences as accessible and potential sites of social change.

The focus of my doctoral research drew on my work experience in occupational research and my interest in action-oriented research by and for women. My research on women and work issues centered on questions of technologies as social relations, skills as complex gendered social constructions, and action-research projects conducted by women's groups and unions around technological change issues (Clarke 1998). When studying women, work, and technologies for my doctoral research, my emphasis was on the social relations of technology, focusing on the ways women information workers understand technologies they work with and ways that technologies are gendered in women's work lives. I was not only interested in how women individually understood technologies, but also in actions taken by and for women around issues of technological change.

During my graduate program, social studies of science seemed an obvious fit with my experiences; however, my initial response to them was mixed. At first, the emphasis on science institutions and the history of machinery dulled my enthusiasm, because I was interested in a materialist analysis of gendered social relations. The continual questioning of value-free studies bored me, because I had experienced the overt subjectivity that is so much a part of the social construction of everyday practices of science. Later I was drawn to the work of feminists like Margaret Benston (1982), Hilary Rose (1983), and Judy Wajcman (1991), who offered materialist insights into the practices of technoscience and potential strategies for change that remain relevant. Reading Donna Haraway's (1991) refreshing take on technosciences and cyborgs was a source of challenge, intrigue, and frustration, but seldom boredom. Paula Treichler's (1999) and Donna Haraway's (1991, 1996) efforts to combine a poststructural perspective with social movements analysis provided an intellectual challenge that continues to spark my imagination.

Initially, I kept my academic projects in feminist sociology and social studies of science separate, unable to synthesize these interests or impose a hard-hitting materialist critique of the practices of science with which I still felt affiliated. Over time, I have managed to draw together my interests in feminist sociology and social studies of science so that my current interests benefit from my diverse background. This synthesis is reflected in my doctoral research on women, work, and technology, and more recent research on the intersection between biomedical research, clinical practice, and political activism (Clarke 1999).

As a lecturer in sociology and women's studies I often draw on earlier work experiences, and I find myself revaluing my uneven career path, realizing that my transdisciplinary transformations have blurred boundaries. Analysis and anecdotes about being the skilled hands and astute eyes for a scientist, donning a miner's outfit to join the men [*sic*] in underground mines, or participating in community-based activism provide important examples in lectures. My range of knowledge and experience means I can readily encourage students' interests in a wide variety of topics in sociology and women's studies.

Practice of Technoskepticism

A dilemma I experience in sociology and women's studies is to find a place for my enthusiasm and curiosity for science and technology, while at the same time critically analyzing the production of knowledge and practices of technosciences as both enabling and limiting, and considering access points for potential intervention. I refer to this enthusiasm and critical analysis of technosciences as technoskepticism, and feminist technoskepticism when specifically linked to feminist science studies.

My movement to technoskepticism was informed by Carol Stabile (1994), who makes a useful distinction between technophobia—"reactionary essentialist formulations"—and technomania—"fragmentary and destabilized theories of identity" (1). Stabile uses these concepts of technophobia and technomania to describe the tendency to fall on one side or the other of a determinism based on either nature or culture.

I propose that the practice of technoskepticism can be a useful addition to feminist science studies, which goes beyond the limitations of both technophobia and technomania, and yet is grounded in everyday realities. To consider the practice of technoskepticism in academic and activist projects involves a complex analysis that includes an enthusiasm for technosciences tempered by a critical analysis of ways that practices and products of technosciences are enabling and limiting, often both at the same time. One way that I include what I call a technoskeptical analysis in feminist critiques of technosciences is to investigate actions taken by social movement participants to address technoscience issues, particularly for women.

As part of my doctoral research (Clarke 1998), I employed this approach to investigate the actions taken by and for women workers around technological changes, by women's groups and unions in Canada. This made the social relations of technologies visible because it is the site where activists engaged in strategies that included a critique of the ways in which technologies are enabling and limiting, and allowed them to develop strategies based on this analysis. By practicing feminist technoskepticism in this research I was able to make gendered social relations of technologies visible, and to problematize actions taken by and for women around technological changes.

My recent research (Clarke 1999) also involves the practice of technoskepticism for analysis of social movements and biomedical technosciences. My interest here is in studying the intersection between biomedical research, clinical practices, and political activism in order to understand how and why social movements contribute to and shape the production of knowledge and the practices of science. By tracing the actions specific to clinical trials taken by women's health movements and AIDS treatment activists, the gendered shaping of knowledge production and clinical practices is evident. Clinical trials are specific sites where complex intersections exist between technoscience research, state regulation, social activism, and clinical practice, and where otherwise hidden complex gendered social relations become exposed.

My recognition of technosciences as complex gendered social relations, resembling a jumbled puzzle to be pieced together, is informed by my diverse experiences and background. My transdisciplinary transformations from biologist to sociologist allow me to include puzzle pieces from both science and the social world as integral to understanding a complete picture of technosciences in particular cultural and historical contexts.

Works Cited

Armstrong, Pat, and Hugh Armstrong. *Theorizing Women's Work.* Toronto: Garamond, 1990.

Benston, Margaret. "Feminism and the Critique of Scientific Method." In *Feminism in Canada,* ed. Angela Miles and Geraldine Finn. Montreal: Black Rose Books, 1982.

Clarke, Jan. "Intersection between Biomedical Research, Clinical Practice and Political Activism in AIDS Treatment Activism and Women's Health Movements." Paper presented at the Society for Social Studies of Science Annual Meeting, San Diego, CA, 1999.

———. *Changing Technologies and Women's Work Lives: A Multimethod Study of Information Workers, Feminist and Union Action Research in Canada*. Ph.D. thesis in sociology, York University, Ontario, 1998.

———. "Straddling Boundaries between Academia and Community-Based Activism." Paper presented at the National Women's Studies Association Conference, Saratoga Springs, NY, 1996.

Haraway, Donna. "Modest Witness: Feminist Diffractions in Science Studies." In *The Disunity of Science*, ed. Peter Galison and David J. Stump. Stanford, CA: Stanford University Press, 1996.

———. *Simians, Cyborgs, and Women*. New York: Routledge, 1991.

Reinharz, Shulamit. *Feminist Methods in Social Research*. New York: Oxford University Press, 1992.

Rose, Hilary. "Hand, Brain, and Heart: A Feminist Epistemology for the Natural Sciences." *Signs* 9 (1983): 73–90.

Smith, Dorothy. *Writing the Social*. Toronto: University of Toronto Press, 1999.

Stabile, Carol A. *Feminism and the Technological Fix*. Manchester: Manchester University Press, 1994.

Treichler, Paula A. *How to Have Theory in an Epidemic*. Durham, NC: Duke University Press, 1999.

Wajcman, Judy. *Feminism Confronts Technology*. University Park, PA: Pennsylvania State University Press, 1991.

Through the Lens of an Insider-Outsider

Gender, Race, and (Self-)Representation in Science

→ Caroline Joan ("Kay") S. Picart

The philosopher Maria Lugones's (1992) vision of the "new mestiza consciousness" is born from the complex interplay between oppression and resistance, where resistance is understood as a social and collective activity. *Mestizaje*, as she characterizes it, is marked by "the development of tolerance for contradiction and ambiguity, by the transgression of rigid conceptual boundaries, and by the creative breaking of a unitary aspect of new and old paradigms" (34). In Lugones's reading of Gloria Anzaldúa's *Borderlands/La Frontera*, which deals with the psychology of oppression, she imagines a consciousness that resists dualistic thinking, and acknowledges the need for racial, ideological, cultural, and biological "cross-pollination" in order for Chicanas and other women of color to remain self-critical and self-animated pluralities rather than "hyphenated being[s], . . . dual [personalities] enacted from the outside, without the ability to fashion [their] own responses" (35).

In "Playfulness, 'World'-Travelling, and Loving Perception," Lugones (1987) uses slightly different terms to describe this *mestiza*-ness she advocates. Playing across the various levels of (constructed) selves to which the "outsider" is subject, she glories in the ambiguous, funny, and survival-rich experiences of being a two-imaged self. Her exposition aims at a description of "a particular feature of the outsider's existence: the outsider has necessarily acquired flexibility in shifting from the mainstream construction of life where she is constructed as an outsider to other constructions of life where she is more or less 'at home'" (3).

Lugones's terminology is useful, as it gets at the politicocultural chiaroscuro of inside-outsideness I live. I occupy the liminal realm of the *mestiza* and the metaphorical "cyborg" personally; I am Filipino by birth, but my family is of mixed ancestry: my father has French-American roots, and my mother has a hint of Spanish-Chinese blood. But I also inhabit this in-between space professionally as a trained molecular embryologist and philosopher, and semiprofessional visual artist and ballroom dancer. My training in science makes me appreciative of the rigor it takes to attempt to "discipline" nature and to generate elegant generalizations from chaotic masses of data shot through with anomalies. I still have vivid memories of teeming tissue cultures lost en route to producing the ideal culture medium, perpetually refining procedures, smoothing those proverbial bumps in the road. My experiences have taught me that doing science entails as much manual skill as it does political artistry. To engage in science, I have learned, one must effectively mount a battle at both the laboratory bench (to capture a potentially recalcitrant specimen), and the scientific conference or in a research paper (to persuade a potentially disbelieving audience). Conversely, my training in philosophy predisposes me to being critical of the assumptions and values that undergird claims to scientific facticity.

Furthermore, my training as a visual artist and dancer render the notion of "knowledge" even more complex. These activities entail embodied epistemologies, overlaid in science and philosophy; these experiences also render me sensitive to how scientists often fall back upon some notion of aesthetics when they are asked to evaluate the veracity of a truth claim, such as the criterion of "elegance" or "simplicity." Ultimately, my involvement in these diverse fields leads me to view the often-commonsensical binary dichotomies of "objective-subjective," "nature-culture," and "science-art" as obscuring a more dynamic dialectic, which could yield a richer epistemology and ethic if explored.

This essay attempts to evoke the survival-rich and ambivalent experiences of perpetually negotiating fluctuating borders—neither completely inside nor completely outside of conventional mainstream categories. Donna Haraway's (1991) concept of the "cyborg"—a monstrous hybrid both artifactual and natural, a "creature of social reality as well as a creature of fiction" (149)—similarly evokes the lived experience of perpetually violating borders, of rupturing sacred boundaries, of destabilizing easy dichotomies. The resultant ricocheting motions binding the personal and the political realms, which are very much in keeping with narratological and qualitative autoethnographic studies,[1] are essential to one of my central aims: the exploration of a lacuna where not *only* the personal is necessarily political, and where the "political" does not require such a macroscopic and detached vantage point that it loses its grounding in lived experience.

I am currently an assistant professor of literature and philosophy at Florida State University. I find that my training as both a philosopher and scientist, and my experiences as a semiprofessional artist, have enabled me to circumvent various disciplinary, intellectual, and institutional boundaries, and have allowed me to incorporate pragmatic issues concerning gender and science into the work I do as a teacher and scholar. To illustrate, I will provide several examples.

Because of the inevitable "cross-pollination" that resulted from my hybrid background, much of my work as a teacher involves dealing with cognitive paradigms in science and art or the humanities. In "Introduction to Philosophy" and "Philosophy of Science" courses, I use the following material to varying extents.

In a section called "Kuhn vs. Laudan: The Darwinian Shift," based on my twin fascinations with the evolving face of Darwinism and Kuhn's fertile theoretical framework, I identify several crucial questions in contemporary philosophy of science. One of the fundamental issues I repeatedly encounter is the question of whether science can be both progressive and rational, while being historically, socially, and linguistically rooted. Eventually, this module uses a historical-philosophical genealogy of Darwin's conversion from creationist-fixism (the then scientific view that species are immutable, created to fit perfectly into an ecological niche within a larger scheme) to evolutionism (the then budding possibility that species change through time, with their ability to adapt being the decisive criterion for survival). I use this case study in order to create a rapprochement between Kuhn's historical sociology and Laudan's attack upon the "Kuhnian" notion of incommensurability, which seems to imply that because different paradigms have no common measure, objectivity (and therefore scientific "progress") is impossible. Ultimately, in resolving what seem to be mainly "scientific" and "epistemological" issues, both Kuhn and Laudan eventually fall back upon aesthetic criteria, such as "elegance" (meaning that the least complicated among the variations of solutions is probably the best) and "fertility" or "fruitfulness" (meaning that that which is able to yield not only answers but also more potential areas of inquiry or "problems" is probably the most progressive), in order to speak about how a paradigm becomes the dominant paradigm or how a paradigm can be judged as more "progressive" than its rivals. Such a rupture in the all too easy dichotomy between science and aesthetics is useful for the interdisciplinarity that compels me.

In discussing epistemology and metaphysics, I weave art and science, in a section called "Memory, Pictoriality, and Mystery: (Re)Viewing Husserl via Magritte and Escher" (Picart 1997a). This section was an outgrowth of conversations with Pierre Kerszberg of Pennsylvania State University. What drew me to this topic was a fascination with how Magritte's and Escher's art, though they are stylistically very different, visually pun upon the same issues of representation that inspire Magritte's phenomenology. Using widely divergent but parallel paths, they evoke the absurdity and sense of mystery that comes with realizing the limits and potentials of how images and words latch on to and yet fail to encompass the heart of "reality"—an issue that aligns these artistic and philosophical projects with the scientific quest for the "truth" of "things out there" as we represent them. These teaching modules revolve around a comparative analysis of philosophical, sociological, and phenomenological approaches to the question of how a scientific fact is generated, how science appeals to aesthetic criteria, and how phenomenological approaches also grapple with issues of the subject-object dichotomy, and the problem of intentionality characteristic of epistemological issues in both the philosophy of science and aesthetics. Finally, they intersect with the following key questions posed by the biological, psychological, and sociological sciences: What is the nature of mind, and how do perceptual, rational, nonrational, and symbolic processes contribute to our survival, and to the socially constructed linguistic conscious entity we call "self"? What is the relationship between individuals and social institutions in the generation of science and art?

My latest project, "Visualizing the Monstrous in Frankenstein Films" (2000),[2] spotlights the politics of gender in artistic representations and mythic popularizations of science. Exploring the intersectionalities of science and art, I trace evolving artistic representations or re-creations of scientific activity, projecting ahead to scientific dystopias, and gesturing to its genealogical roots, of which an analogue is the story of Dionysus's birth from the thigh of Zeus—a son born of a father, much like Frankenstein's unnamed creature is (re)produced by his "father"-creator, devoid of feminine participation. What drew me to this topic was the realization that these filmic reworkings of the Frankenstein myth reflect anxieties regarding technology (differentiating the "artifactual" or "cultural" from the "natural") and the politics of gender (demarcating the "masculine" from the "feminine"). I was also struck by how the films, functioning as the contemporary repositories of "myth," understood as the symbolic representation/deformation of the prevailing culture's most intense aspirations and most feared nightmares, illustrate how the visual and textual aspects of the evolving Frankenstein narrative are locked in a complex dialectic.

Ultimately, the notion of the "monstrous," which is derived from the Latin words *monere* ("to warn") and *monstrare* ("to show" or "to point to" [the fearful or horrifying]), is a fruitful concept in charting how various borders—between science and the humanities, between the "masculine" and the "feminine," between the "Same" and the "Other"—are policed and negotiated. As a woman of multiply hybrid professional and racial heritages, I am reminded of how the work I do (and at times my very physicality), violates these borders and often runs the risk of being regarded as "monstrous." As someone who lives the contradictions of looking and being Eastern and Western in language and values, I am constantly reminded of how engagement in such interdisciplinarity entails a commitment that

> a truly post-modern philosophy must abandon the notion of a universal "human nature" and instead assume a complex web of differences that binds and separates us to varying degrees. Such a philosophy must locate itself within the prevailing socio-politico-economic conditions. To me, that entails a commitment to trying to understand and participate in the broader framework of the political and ethical struggles of the marginalized—in a still primarily patriarchal, neo-colonial world (Picart 1997b, 3).

Thus, such research and teaching enable me to reenvisage how scientific and artistic activities are not isolated practices indulged in by solitary geniuses.

Rather, this scholarship-teaching provides me with a perspective that connects the two in a dynamic manner, analogous to the way in which two compass legs are separate and yet conjoined, and their area of intersection lies in the realm of the public imaginary. As Ludwik Fleck (1979) argues, a scientific fact becomes a scientific fact only when it has been successfully transplanted, through the hieratic authority of the scientific popularizer, from arcane laboratories to the invisible, "everyday" realm of the layperson. Similarly, what is enshrined as "beautiful" or "grotesque" or what is ordained as aesthetically pleasing or appropriate to a man or to a woman, has to be adjudicated within the realm of the public imaginary. At a more overt level, an examination of the popular filmic reconstructions of the Frankenstein myth (Picart 1998) leads me to reflect upon shifting, contemporary anxieties concerning the embattled demarcations traditionally separating the "masculine" from the "feminine," the "natural" from the "mechanical," the "pure" from the "impure." Ultimately, this type of work enables me to dissect the gendered presuppositions that underlie Baconian science, with its unapologetic aspirations to "penetrate into the secrets of nature"—a deliberately erotic metaphor steeped in the violent imagery of rape, ambivalently counterpoised against Bacon's idealistic dream of producing an earthly utopia through its domination of nature. Far from vilifying all scientific and philosophical activity as inescapably "malestream," inconsequential intellectual masturbation and petty politicking, this type of inquiry leads me to confront the challenge of actively revisioning the borders of power, at both the scholarly and pedagogical levels—where a genuine wrestling with the politics of representation in science and the humanities is most concrete.

By employing the tensions of being an insider-outsider to various professional, institutional, gendered, and racial borders, I am able to give personal and professional weight to my explorations of these themes in both my scholarship and teaching. If nothing else, when I have female students who are genuinely contemplating a career in science or philosophy, and who ask for an account of my experiences of being a scientist who turncoated to become a philosopher, I can speak to them with quiet conviction of the humorous, painfully ambivalent, and creatively survival-rich experiences, of being at the limen—and invite them to join in the cautious destabilization and joyous reworking of these borders.

Notes

1. See, for example, Reed-Danahay (1997), Stoller (1997), Constable (1997), and Ellis and Bochner (1996).
2. This project evolved from the tutelage of Raymond Fleming, professor of comparative literature then at Pennsylvania State University, and Thomas Benson, professor of

communication, also at Penn State, as well as professional correspondences with Janice Rushing and Thomas Frentz, both film critics and rhetors.

Works Cited

Constable, Nicole. *Maid to Order in Hong Kong: An Ethnography of Filipina Workers.* Ithaca, NY: Cornell University Press, 1997.

Ellis, Carolyn, and Arthur Bochner. *Composing Ethnography: Alternative Forms of Alternative Writing.* Ethnographic Alternatives Series, Series #1. Walnut Creek, CA: Alta Mira Press, August 1996.

Fleck, Ludwik. *The Genesis and Development of a Scientific Fact,* ed. T. Trenn and R. K. Merton. Chicago and London: University of Chicago Press, 1979.

Haraway, Donna. "A Cyborg Manifesto: Science, Technology, and Socialist-Feminism in the Late 20th Century." In *Simians, Cyborgs, and Women: The Reinvention of Nature.* New York: Routledge, 1991.

Lugones, Maria. "On *Borderlands/La Frontera:* An Interpretative Essay." *Hypatia* 7 (1992): 31–37.

———. "Playfulness, 'World'-Travelling, and Loving Perception." *Hypatia* 2 (1987): 3–19.

Picart, Caroline J. S. "Visualizing the Monstrous in Frankenstein Films." *Pacific Coast Philology* 35 (September 2000): pp. forthcoming.

———. "James Whale's (Mis)Reading of Mary Shelley's *Frankenstein*." *Critical Studies in Mass Communication 15* (1998): 382–404.

———. "Remembering within Remembering in Husserl and Magritte." *Philosophy Today* 41 (1997a): 118–126.

———. "Inside Notes from the Outside." *Research/Penn State* (January 1997b): 3–5.

Reed-Danahay, Debora. *Auto/Ethnography: Rewriting the Self and the Social.* New York: Berg, 1997.

Stoller, Paul. *Sensuous Scholarship (Contemporary Ethnography).* Philadelphia: University of Pennsylvania Press, 1997.

Oases in a Desert

*Why a Hydrologist Meanders between
Science and Women's Studies*

Martha P. L. Whitaker

> My career resembles the path of a river. While the general direction of
> flow from a river's headwaters to its outlet may remain relatively stable,
> the specific path that a river takes is typically not a straight one. Rivers
> are not static entities; they are dynamic, shifting laterally, deviating
> from straight paths, often creating sinusoidal curves called meanders.

I am a doctoral candidate in the Department of Hydrology and Water Resources
at the University of Arizona, while simultaneously pursuing a master of arts in
the Department of Women's Studies. My educational background is saturated
with science: my undergraduate degree is in geology, and I also have a master of
science in hydrology. I identify myself as a scientist, but I also consider myself to
be a feminist, which is why I began taking classes in women's studies.

Toward the end of my master's work in hydrology, when I initially enrolled in
women's studies classes, it quickly became clear to me that what I love about the
curriculum—the open engagement of feminism, politics, and social issues—is
often avoided in hydrology, and likewise, what I love about hydrology—the
quantitative, practical means by which to understand numerous natural
processes—is often absent from women's studies. For example, hydrology classes
are ideal for conveying straightforward facts like flow equations and discussions
regarding computer models of hydrologic processes. It is immensely empowering
to comprehend how a hydrologic system works and have practical, quantitative,
analytical tools with which to build such an understanding. However, the format
for many hydrology classes is such that they are bereft of other issues about
which I am also deeply passionate. Some of these issues include water politics,
environmental issues and ethics, and feminism.

My initial enrollment in women's studies courses was inspired by my need to
engage in an intellectual pursuit outside of hydrology that addressed my additional interests. I had completed some courses on environmental policy and water
law, but I was hungry for an academic environment in which I could openly and

unabashedly identify myself as a feminist. Women's studies provided such an environment, and simultaneously offered qualitative, theoretical tools with which to understand social and political processes. However, as biologist and feminist theorist Anne Fausto-Sterling observes, "women . . . have been socialized to think that [scientific ignorance] is okay. . . . This is the essential challenge facing women's studies scholars: to face and overcome our reluctance to engage with the segment of human knowledge we call science" (1992, 337, 348).

In making these observations, Fausto-Sterling proposes that women's studies scholars need basic scientific knowledge as much as scientists need to recognize that their research is a social enterprise that exists in a specific historical context. I thoroughly agree with Fausto-Sterling's assessment, as the theoretical tools I obtained from women's studies have became particularly important in helping me to understand that scientists' analyses and quantification of earth and natural processes *are* social and political processes. While initially unclear to me how women's studies and feminism might directly relate to my research in hydrology, I have begun to understand more generally that "the sciences need to legitimate *within scientific research*, as a part of scientific practice, critical examination of historical values and interests that may be so shared within the scientific community, so invested by the very constitution of this or that field of study, that they will not show up as a cultural bias between experiments or between research communities" (Harding 1991, 147).

It has taken several years for me to recognize that the tools of hydrology and women's studies need not be mutually exclusive, like opposite sides of a river that ostensibly never meet. Each discipline can benefit from the other: if one side of the river is women's studies and the other is hydrology, then we can imagine that knowledge, like sediment, can be gleaned from both river banks. It can be carried and blended in the "river of interdisciplinarity," and eventually redeposited in a different place and time as a new formation.

In some ways, this erosion and redeposition is similar to Donna Haraway's (1997) notion of diffraction as a means of stimulating social change. Haraway refers to diffraction as a tool to be used by a character she describes as a "modest witness." Haraway's "queered" modest witness is one who "works to *refigure* the subjects, objects, and communicative commerce of technoscience into different kinds of knots" (23). She borrowed the term *modest witness* from Steven Shapin and Simon Schaeffer's *Leviathan and the Air-Pump: Hobbes, Boyle, and the Experimental Life* (1989):

> In order for the modesty . . . to be visible, the man—the witness whose accounts mirror reality—must be invisible, that is, an inhabitant of the potent "unmarked category," which is constructed by extraordinary conventions of self-invisibility. . . . This self-invisibility is the specifically modern, European, masculine, scientific form of the virtue of modesty" (Haraway 1997).

The term *modest witness* still holds regard for Haraway's genealogical roots in science, yet she also mutates the concept of the modest witness to demonstrate the importance of the witnesses' historical and cultural subjectivity. Accordingly, Haraway's modest witness is also a feminist for whom invisibility is not an option. She is one who queers the distinctions between binary perceptions by diffracting the meanings and borders between the technical and the political.

Diffraction, another important concept for me, is the metaphor Haraway uses to describe the process of queering binary perceptions. She distinguishes diffraction patterns from reflections, which merely displace the same elsewhere: "diffraction can be a metaphor for another kind of critical consciousness . . . one committed to making a difference and not to repeating the Sacred Image of Same . . . diffraction is a narrative, graphic, psychological, spiritual and political technology for making consequential meanings" (1997, 273).

I view myself and other scholars who meander between disciplines as modest witnesses. I see the erosion, mixing, and redeposition of knowledge from different disciplines as a form of diffraction. The difficult task for me has been to negotiate this diffraction, because while the sediment erodes easily from both banks, it resists redeposition into a new formation. On the women's studies side of the river, science is often identified as important, but women's studies programs traditionally lack a rigorous analysis of its importance. On the hydrology side of the river, objectivity is valued, and the roles of politics and social issues are—at best—seen as important, but irrelevant to the discipline. Feminism and women's studies are usually not even acknowledged. This is particularly frustrating for me, as I recognize that neither bank of the river is completely different from the other. They are often comprised of essentially the same sediments, temporarily separated by a curvilinear body of water. To treat the banks of women's studies and hydrology as separate entities, and to focus on the overall direction of the academic river's flow with little attention given to the various sediments through which it flows, is the product of disciplinary training.

This is where disciplinary training becomes tenuous for students who are interested in meandering among disciplines. The traditional route encourages students to channel their energy into a single discipline in order to follow a direct, conventional career path. On the whole, this is a good idea and makes a great deal of sense, because students usually appreciate an academic curriculum that paves a clear path from student to professional, and academic administrators enjoy easy calculations of conventionally successful students. On the other hand, channelization of students' academic interests can limit a student's inclination to build a career utilizing the strengths of various disciplines.

According to a classic geology text (Press and Siever 1986, 195), "channelization is the artificial straightening of a sinuous river channel. It is sometimes done in an attempt to improve drainage and flood control, but in many cases, channelization projects have led to adverse environmental effects, such as deterioration of aquatic life, acceleration of erosion, and even poorer flood control." What channelization is to rivers, disciplinary training is to academia.

Disciplinary training in academia aims to straighten the meandering interests of pupils. Whereas a liberal arts undergraduate foundation may have encouraged a student to maneuver among various colleges, the intent of graduate school is to sharpen the student's focus and area of expertise—to engineer an authority in a specific discipline. Unfortunately, in many cases the channel walls become blinders for students; peripheral acuity is diminished, if not lost altogether. The path itself—the sinusoidal, meandering process—becomes less important; the focus has become instead the final destination, which is wherever the concrete-walled channel has been designed to end. But for rivers, it is important to note that meandering dissipates energy more evenly along the length of a channel; it is a more stable condition.

As Haraway's modest witness aims to produce difference of patterns in the world by diffracting the meanings of seemingly stable categories, I seek to reform the disciplines of hydrology and women's studies by meandering between them, obtaining knowledge from either bank and from other tributaries of disciplined knowledge, and finally redepositing the reworked sediments in a new formation, which is also subject to further erosion, reworking, and redeposition. As a graduate student, however, my authority and ability to modify concrete channel walls and redeposit reworked knowledge sediments successfully is somewhat limited, but the mere process of meandering between disciplines has provided me with the opportunity to redeposit small amounts of sediment from each bank onto the other; I can thus imagine a new formation comprised of both hydrology and women's studies by integrating and depositing sediments from both disciplines on either bank.

For example, although my dissertation research is a small part of a relatively large political project, my actual experiment is seemingly devoid of politics that might affect my research results: it is comprised of electronic instrumentation, data collection, and computer modeling. However, the results produced by my research will likely affect some water policy decisions.

My dissertation research was conducted along the river banks of the San Pedro River in southeastern Arizona, in the San Pedro Riparian National Conservation Area (SPRNCA). The SPRNCA was established by the United States Congress in 1988 to protect riparian (the various components of an ecosystem in the vicinity of a river) resources along 60 kilometers of the river, north of the U.S.-Mexico border. It is operated by the U.S. Bureau of Land Management (BLM), which oversees the conservation, protection, and enhancement of the riparian ecosystem. Unfortunately, several factors that are beyond the control of the BLM adversely affect the San Pedro River and its ecosystem. While several

problematic factors exist outside of the BLM's jurisdiction, in Mexico, the great-
est concern is excessive groundwater pumping within Arizona by the city of
Sierra Vista and the nearby army base, Fort Huachuca, both of which are located
outside of the SPRNCA border. The removal of groundwater from an aquifer
causes a cone of depression. The concern is that the cone produced by Sierra
Vista and Fort Huachuca has intercepted the water on its way to the San Pedro
River (USAG 1997).

If local pumping is diminishing groundwater flow to the aquifer, the resultant
drop in the water table and water flow in the river itself could kill many riparian
plants (Stromberg 1993) and destroy the protected habitat within the SPRNCA.
This possibility has catalyzed environmental activists into demanding government intervention; they have even engaged the trinational Commission on Environmental Cooperation to study the potential transborder impact of habitat loss
on migratory birds (Earthlaw 1997). In response, the army base and city and
county governments have implemented numerous water conservation projects,
but many people believe that these efforts are both inadequate and overdue. Goff
and his colleagues (1998) observe that "the overall effect has been to polarize various segments of the community, confuse others, and increase distrust in government efforts to resolve the problem."

My role in this complex political battle is to provide data on one small but
critical part of the water cycle. Specifically, I installed instruments in a portion of
the San Pedro's river banks, and these instruments provide data that will help
evaluate how, when, and how much river water flows laterally into the river
banks on daily, seasonal, and flood-event timescales. These data are important in
determining whether the floodwaters that periodically infiltrate the river banks
are of sufficient magnitude to affect the regional water balance. If the volume is
indeed significant, the data I collect will affect computer models of the hydrologic system, which, in turn, are used to determine the extent of Sierra Vista and
Fort Huachuca's cone of depression, which is suspected of drawing water away
from the SPRNCA.

It is comfortable and easy for me to distinguish the political from the scientific aspects of my research: my experiments, data, and results are scientific, and
the effects and use of my results are political. By meandering into women's studies, however, I have learned to loosen my grasp of such delineations. Feminist
theory has helped solidify my understanding that the scientific research I conduct is unavoidably interbedded with politics and other social activities that are
influenced by cultural biases. Feminist philosopher Sandra Harding clarified this
point when she quoted Stephen J. Gould as saying:

> I criticize the myth that science itself is an objective enterprise, done properly
> only when scientists shuck the constraints of their culture and view the world

as it really is. . . . Science, since people must do it, is a socially embedded activity. It progresses by hunch, vision and intuition. Much of its change through time does not record a closer approach to absolute truth, but the alteration of cultural contexts that influence it so strongly (Harding 1991, 145).

Additionally, while I understand that scientific research is interbedded with cultural biases, I have not lost confidence in the quality and usefulness of my research. Cultural biases and reliable science are not mutually exclusive. As feminist theorist Karen Barad (1996, 162) has observed, "The fact that scientific knowledge is socially constructed does not imply that science doesn't 'work,' and the fact that science 'works' does not mean that we have discovered human-independent facts about nature."

I recognize that, although I have only begun to carry sediment from one field into the other, I am only at the beginning of my meandering, interdisciplinary career. I hope to pursue a career that not only allows me to continue meandering, but also encourages the deposition and perpetual reworking of an interdisciplinary formation between hydrology and women's studies. I envision a scientific position in which I, as a member of a team of diverse colleagues, could conduct hydrology research and simultaneously engage in the political and social aspects of it. While traditional careers in hydrology are either academically disciplined, research-oriented government positions, or private consulting jobs—none of which have a clear relationship with science studies or women's studies—I remain optimistic that my meandering tendencies will weather a comfortable path among the incised sedimentary banks of various disciplines.

Works Cited

Barad, Karen. "Meeting the Universe Halfway: Realism and Social Constructivism without Contradiction." In *Feminism, Science, and the Philosophy of Science*, ed. L. H. Nelson and J. Nelson. Boston, MA: Kluwer Academic Publishers, 1996.

Earthlaw. "Earthlaw Wins First U.S. NAFTA Petition: International Commission to Investigate Harm to Southwest's Last Real River." *Newsletter* (May 26, 1997), Denver, CO. Internet document: http://www.envirolink.org/orgs/elaw/Feature/river.htm

Fausto-Sterling, Anne. "Building Two-Way Streets: The Case of Feminism and Science." *NWSA Journal* 4 (1992): 336–349.

Goff, Bruce, Dave Goodrich, and Ghani Chehbouni. *Semi-Arid Land-Surface-Atmosphere Program (Salsa) Working Science Plan* (1998). Internet document: http://www.tucson.ars.ag.gov/salsa/archive/documents/plans/science_plan_current.html

Haraway, Donna. *Modest_Witness@Second_Millennium.FemaleMan©_Meets_OncoMouse™: Feminism and Technoscience*. New York: Routledge, 1997.

Harding, Sandra. *Whose Science? Whose Knowledge? Thinking from Women's Lives.* Ithaca, NY: Cornell University Press, 1991.

Press, Frank, and Raymond Siever. *Earth.* New York: W. H. Freeman and Company, 1986.

Shapin, Steven, and Simon Schaeffer. *Leviathan and the Air-Pump: Hobbes, Boyle, and the Experimental Life.* Princeton, NJ: Princeton University Press, 1989.

Stromberg, J. C. "Fremont Cottonwood-Goodding Willow Forests: A Review of Their Ecology, Threats, and Recovery Potential." *J. Arizona-Nevada Academy of Science* 26 (1993): 97–110.

USAG. *Environmental Assessment, 1995 Base Realignment and Closure, Fort Huachuca, Arizona.* "Appendix A: Synopsis of Hydrogeological Studies." Fort Huachuca, AZ: U.S. Army Garrison, Directorate of Engineering and Housing, 1997.

And the Mirror Cracked!

Reflections of Natures and Cultures

→ Banu Subramaniam

Ever since I can remember, mirrors and their reflections have fascinated me. I remember what a source of amusement the fun-house mirrors were: they made me long and short, narrow and wide. What intrigued me was that I could never "know" what I looked like. Mirrors produce "mirror images" and my mind could not wrap itself around the idea of reversing sides. Photographs conjure up problems of scale—I sometimes seemed small and other times large depending on angles and magnification. Could I ever see the "real" me? I wondered.

While it was the biological sciences that consumed me and that I went on to study, these optical illusions kept me amused, and the optical metaphor continued to inform my philosophical musings. It seemed to me that as an experimental biologist, I was trying to produce as accurate and as "natural" a nature as possible. Experiments then were like mirrors—one tried to produce as accurate a mirror as possible, so that the reflection of nature we saw would be free of distortions. While an experiment is designed to control certain variables and observe shifts in others, field biologists (like me) try to make this albeit contrived scenario as natural as possible. Little did I realize how complicated this philosophical question was and where these musings would take me—from the natural sciences to the social sciences and the humanities, through interdisciplinary programs such as women's studies, cultural studies, postcolonial studies, and ethnic studies. Weaving across these disciplines and interdisciplines, the journey has profoundly shaped my intellectual and institutional trajectories as well as my relationship with mirrors and reflections.

I grew up in secular, postcolonial India, consumed by the wonder and power of science. The future of India, its "development" and "progress" (I implicitly believed then in the paradigms of development and progress), the eradication of poverty, the fight for the equality of women and religious minorities lay in my young mind squarely in my faith in science. Science, to me, was our savior from the darkness of religious superstition, poverty, prejudice, and blind faith. Science's commitment to rationality and objectivity, the creation of a "scientific

55

methodology" that made the identity of the scientist irrelevant, seemed extremely enticing and egalitarian. My classes, books, family, and teachers inspired this reverence for science. My dreams were shaped by the dead white men that filled my textbooks (with the exception of C. V. Raman and J. C. Bose there were no Indian men mentioned in my science textbooks and certainly no Indian women). The naturalist adventures of David Attenborough and Jacques Cousteau fed my fantasies of uncovering nature's secrets. A good dose of *Star Trek* fueled my fictionalized sciences. A poster of Charles Darwin, my idol, who inspired my passion for evolutionary biology, hung above my desk. The incongruity and irony of a first-generation postcolonial girl filled with ambitions of the great white explorers escaped me. My commitment for this naive, textbook version of science remained untouched until I entered the halls of science as a graduate student in evolutionary genetics in the United States.

Life as a graduate student was not easy. At first, I was able to dismiss my growing invisibility and uneasiness as nothing more than culture shock. My insecurities grew, and there came a point when I could no longer ignore them.[1] In an attempt to understand my dislocation as a third world woman in the halls of Western science, I began searching for answers outside my department and discipline. Thanks to some wonderful people in women's studies,[2] I started taking classes and learning fields such as women's studies, science studies (including disciplinary explorations of the history, sociology, and philosophy of science), postcolonial studies, cultural studies, and ethnic studies. In contrast to my naive visions of science, my experiences in the halls of science showed me that the social categories I thought were invisible were everywhere, shaping and structuring the world of science. The more I read, the more I realized that the production of scientific knowledge was not unaffected or removed from the social world it inhabited. Initially, these frameworks helped me understand the social world of science and situate my experiences as a third world woman in science. But the more I read, the more I realized that the social studies of science explained more than its social relations; it also explored scientific processes and knowledge production.

While I worked on my dissertation, my doctoral work in biology remained quite separate from all that I was reading in my interdisciplinary forays into the humanities and social sciences. I must at this point confess that I love experimental biology. I enjoy formulating hypotheses, designing experiments, being out in the field, planting seedlings, watching them grow, counting the seeds, entering the data, and then watching patterns emerge from the numbers I entered into the computer. There is something about the materiality of the process that I find deeply satisfying, and it was an interest I wanted to continue to nurture. But how could I bring these schizophrenic interests in feminist science studies and evolutionary biology together? What would it mean to be a researcher in science studies and evolutionary biology who used the scholarshop in both disciplines to do experiments on flower color variation in morning glory (*Ipomoea purpurea*) populations? Whether this was academically viable or not, I decided to embark on a research program that would bring these two interests together. I managed to find postdoctoral and faculty positions that allowed me to continue to work in both disciplines.

I met Mike Witmore, a contributor to Section II of this anthology, while we were both on a fellowship at UCLA.[3] The theme of the fellowship during our two years was "Science and the Humanities: The Two Cultures Debate Revisited." He was trained primarily in the humanities, and I in the sciences. As it did for Mike, I found Evelyn Fox Keller's persuasive work on language and science extremely compelling. Keller's work suggested that the transparency of language that scientific training advocated was far from true. In the sciences, the actual writing of the dissertation is perhaps the easiest part—it comes after years of experimentation, months of analyses, weeks of developing tables, figures, and charts. The actual paper is often strictly proscribed by disciplinary traditions into discrete sections—introduction, materials and methods, results, discussion, and a conclusion. Keller's work convinced me that the ease and "naturalness" with which my dissertation flowed from my fingertips were far from transparent and instead betrayed years of biological "disciplining."

Other scholars taught me and continue to teach me to examine other facets of scientific investigation. Anne Fausto-Sterling's careful work reminded me to look closely at the details of the experiments themselves, their structures and functions. Helen Longino and Sandra Harding's words nudged me to examine the claims I made and how I came to make them. During my graduate years, the richness with which feminist scholars of science such as Ruth Bleier, Sue Rosser, Margaret Rossiter, Evelynn Hammonds, Donna Haraway, Katherine Hayles, Ruth Hubbard, David Noble, Vandana Shiva, Sharon Traweek, and Nancy Tuana argued the connections between feminism and science, shaped my imagination and theories.

I began a project that seemed an obvious "enactment" of the field of feminist science studies—namely to take insights from the feminist/social/cultural studies on and about the sciences into innovative practice *in* the sciences. Most of feminist science studies seemed to me to be loosely called a project of deconstruction—that is, taking apart the visible workings of science to highlight the invisible factors that shaped the interconnections between nature and culture, science and society. The project I wished to embark on was one of reconstruction—to use these insights of deconstruction to rebuild a practice that was scientifically rigorous but also informed by the rigors of feminist politics and scholarship. At first I saw this as a project of translation—translating feminist science studies into the sciences. As a speaker of multiple languages, how hard could translation be, I wondered? While I made inroads into this work of translation, I must say that it was incredibly difficult and painful to translate between languages and worlds without dictionaries. As I got deeper into the project, I realized that what I was setting myself up to do was to use the tools and methodologies from fields of science and women's science to deconstruct knowledge I had constructed using the tools and methodologies from another field (evolutionary genetics).

What began as an easy interdisciplinary project on feminism and science grew in its complexity, and the more I deconstructed, the more it grew. I soon realized that the tools from science studies were not so easy to translate into scientific practice. If science had been constructed as "a world without women," feminism was constructed as a "world without science." I needed to work on both sides simultaneously, creating a language and a dictionary that would allow dialogue.[4] It seemed like the proverbial peeling of an onion: there was always a layer inside— and sometimes the onion split to reveal two. What lay under these layers was a constantly shifting vision of the connections between natures and cultures.

In his piece in Section II of this anthology, Mike Witmore has described the process of our collaboration and what it meant to him as a humanist. In this piece, I embrace the metaphor of the mirror Mike evokes and complement his analysis of the humanities to explain what this collaboration has meant to me in the sciences. Working with Mike has made me even more committed to collaboration as an important mechanism for interdisciplinary intellectual growth. I still remember the day Mike sent me his analysis of my paper. My reaction was wonder! Did my experiments on morning glory flower color variation really say all that? Tropes of race, machines, allegories of invisible agents, control, insulation. Ghosts of multiculturalism, economics, experience, identity began to haunt me. My earlier conception of the experiment lay more in the material process of doing science and less in the representation of it as text. Ridding my mind of the material morning glories, images of flower pigmentation, statistical tables of analyses, diagrams and graphs, and memories of many a hot North Carolina summer seemed impossible at first. At first, I was ready to dismiss it as an overinterpretation and an overreading. But one of the first lessons I learned about collaboration was never to dismiss anything but always to let it simmer. The crux of Mike's reading was not only what "I" as a scientist had intended or not intended in my writing but also what "I" as a scientist had inherited from my discipline as history, language, metaphors, and frameworks to organize and describe the natural world. As I delved into the history of my discipline, I was able to get more distance from my work, and engage with Mike's reading.

While feminist science studies had given me the abstract tools to know that culture entered into my thinking of the natural world, I had had a difficult time seeing it in my own work. Working with Mike and having him analyze my work, and engaging with his reading of it, were profoundly illustrative and enabling.

Interdisciplinary work has changed me forever. It is impossible to go back to my "naive" conceptions of scientific practice and process. The process of interdisciplinary work has made bare for me the fundamental assumptions of evolutionary biology, making visible the basic skeletal structure of my discipline. The familiar structure of epistemology, methodology, rules of evidence, and argument in the construction of scientific work became part of my "disciplining" in the academy. My disciplining in the biological sciences made visible logical argument, good experimental design, appropriate statistical analyses, and careful interpretation of results. The same disciplining, I realized, made invisible language, history, culture, and politics in my mediations with the natural world. I had learned that scientific writing was merely a vehicle that mirrored the logic of experiments. Writing seemed trivial, transparent, and even irrelevant in elucidating the evolutionary processes and nature's mysterious and perplexing organization.

The "perfect" mirror of nature I had constructed had, quite simply, cracked! It's not shattered but cracked. I still see reflections of nature and natural processes, but in fragments. Each of these fragments is important, "real," and gives us a glimpse of a cross section of natural processes across time, place, space, and context. In between these fragments of nature are the cracks of culture that weave and connect nature with culture, science with society. Scholarship in the humanities and social sciences, I would suggest, are fragments of culture held together by cracks of nature. These fragments of natures and cultures symbolize to me the life in "naturecultures" that Haraway suggests (2000, 26).[5] We are "of," "in," and "about" these naturecultures.

Central to the life in these naturecultures is the realization that nature and culture are coproducers of knowledge, or in Keller's words, how nature and culture "interact in the production of scientific knowledge" (1987, 90). One of the exciting aspects of the collaboration with Mike was understanding some of these boundaries as well as the imbrications. So, for example, while he convinced me that there were different ways in which I could have written the experiment—using different metaphors, different language, different conclusions that would have substantially shifted our meaning and presentation of evolutionary processes—I convinced him that "nature" had told us something in this experiment and the data "constrained" what stories we could tell about nature. Given the particular data set that the experiment produced, one could not make up any story one wanted. Experiments, data, and, most important, nature is the crucial part that guides our analyses and stories. Ultimately, our human-constructed experiment influenced by culture had interacted with nature to produce knowledge that told us something about natures and cultures.

As I have delved deeper into the philosophical questions of knowledge-making, the metaphor of mirrors and two-dimensional reflections seems impoverished. Optics is a rich field that offers other metaphors such as convex and

concave lenses, prisms, lasers, and fiber optics that refract, diffract, distort, am-
plify, focus, fracture, diffuse, multiply, and divide light. Indeed, at the heart of it
all is the question of the essence of light—particle or wave. The heterogeneity of
optical processes that transmutate and transform light can yield powerful
metaphors of the cultural processes that shape knowledge construction. For example, Haraway suggests that diffraction patterns record the history of interaction, interference, reinforcement, difference (1997). These myriad metaphors
allow us to incorporate the complexities of historical, sociological, psychological,
and philosophical processes and trace the ways in which natures and cultures are
connected together (Haraway 1997; Latour 1999).[6]

My project of tracing the connections of natures and cultures is like the
project of tracing the transmutations of light traveling through these optical
metaphors. My task, then, is to understand the various processes that produce
the final pattern of light, or in my case, the results of the experiment on morning
glory flower color variation. I have learned to trace these webs or interactions
that produce the results of the experiment. For example, one simple string of
connections[7] would be: me, a third world feminist from a formerly colonized
world—trained in the United States—trained in the field of evolutionary biology and population genetics—shaped by the histories of these fields—(chose to
work with morning glories, a species with its own history of migration and immigration)—designed an experiment in consultation with her graduate advisor,
dissertation committee, and fellow graduate students in her lab group and department, each with an individual history—collected experimental plants from
fields where morning glories were the nuisance weed for farmers growing tobacco—conducted experiments in fields owned by farmers—planted experiments with friends and colleagues—maintained experiments, warded off deer
and other animals—(plants grew, produced seeds, displayed a pattern of pollination and reproduction that shaped the results of the experiments)—funded by
private and federal agencies—published in scientific journals—producing
knowledge about evolution and morning glories.

The above is a very small sketch of the series of events, each with their own
histories, that shaped the results about morning glory flower color variation.
Each of these series of events have diverse histories and are layered in meaning.
However, each of these histories and processes have interacted and shaped the results of the experiment. Had the farmers in North Carolina not grown tobacco,
perhaps a different set of genotypes would have been selected. Had agencies not
funded my doctoral work, could this project have gone forward? Had friends not
helped in building an electric fence to ward off deer, the deer might have destroyed the experiment or changed the results due to their eating preferences.
Had the morning glories not had their particular selection history, perhaps their
pollination and reproductive patterns would have been different. Had I not been

trained by the particular set of scholars, perhaps my intellectual priorities might have been different. Had the history of population genetics not been so closely tied to the history of eugenics, perhaps the notion of the "maintenance" of variation would be a commonly expected outcome and not be constructed as a problem needing explanation in the world of the fittest survivors.

What I have learned through these collaborations is to pay attention to these connections and to trace their connections and convolutions through and between natures and cultures. What the results of the experiment ultimately tell us is not some static conception of a mythic nature, but rather the coproduction of natures and cultures. What I am committed to is an account of science that places the materiality of the world as a central part of that account, and to make the nonhuman actors a central part of the account (Haraway 1997; Latour 1999). We can make nature say what we want it to say, if we do experiments badly, but if we design experiments well, we can make nature say something meaningful about processes and organization that shape the natural world. But designing experiments well means that we must pay attention to the various processes that produce experimental results, that necessarily include natural and cultural productions. I am by no means suggesting that such knowledge will be objective (or "always true," in its absolute totalizing sense). Knowledge to me will always be situated (Haraway 1991), always historical and contextual within and between the worlds of natures and cultures.

On reflection, the project of "reconstruction"—using the tools and methodologies of women's studies, science studies, and evolutionary biology together to construct knowledge about the natural and cultural worlds—has been a difficult project precisely because the tools each of these disciplines have created were not for the reconstructive project at hand. Disciplinary tools are primarily designed to answer questions individual disciplines focus on. In order to do this work of naturecultures we need to craft new tools and methodologies that can integrate our investigations of natures and cultures. That is the challenge that faces us.

How do we weave our intersectional identities with the intellectual and institutional histories of our disciplines and interdisciplines, with the natural histories of the organisms and objects we study, with the political and cultural histories of our world? How do we trace these distortions, diffractions, and transmutations of situated knowledges of naturecultures? This is the exciting work ahead of us in feminist science studies—collaborations across the sciences, engineering, humanities, and social sciences. As an enjoyable and exhiliarating first step, I recommend you contact your closest rhetorician!

Notes

1. For more discussion on my experiences, see Subramaniam (1988).

2. I will always be indebted to the ideas, kindness, and generosity of Jean O'Barr, Nancy Rosebaugh, and Mary Wyer.

3. We were both fortunate to be at UCLA on a two-year Andrew W. Mellon fellowship.

4. See Anne Fausto-Sterling (1992), "Building Two-Way Streets." In this piece she argues that the difficulty of the project of feminism and science is as much a problem with women's studies as with the sciences.

5. "Living inside biology is about living inside nature-cultures. It is about being inside history as well as being inside the wonder of the natural complexity."

6. I am deeply indebted to the work of Donna Haraway and Bruno Latour in imagining the connections, as in Haraway's material-semiotic actors and Latour's actor-networks.

7. Bruno Latour's analyses in chapters 2 and 5 of *Pandora's Hope* (1999) have strongly influenced this vision of connections.

Works Cited

Fausto-Sterling, Anne. "Building Two-Way Streets: The Case of Feminism and Science." *NWSA Journal* 4 (1992): 336–349.

Haraway, Donna. *How Like a Leaf: An Interview with Thyrza Nichols Goodeve*. New York: Routledge, 2000.

———. *Modest_Witness@Second_Millenium.FemaleMan©Meets_OncoMouse™: Feminism and Technoscience*. New York: Routledge, 1997.

———. "Situated Knowledges: The Science Question in Feminism and the Privilege of Partial Perspective." In *Simians, Cyborgs, and Women: The Reinvention of Nature*. New York: Routledge, 1991.

Keller, Evelyn Fox. "Working Scientists and Feminist Critics of Science." *Daedalus* 116 (1987): 77–91.

Latour, Bruno. *Pandora's Hope: Essays on the Reality of Science Studies*. Cambridge, MA: Harvard University Press, 1999.

Subramaniam, Banu. "A Contradiction in Terms: Life as a Feminist Scientist." *The Women's Review of Books* 15 (1998): 25–26.

Technoscientific Literacy as Civic Engagement

Realizing How Being at Liberty Comes to Matter[1]

Michael J. Flower

One important line of inquiry about the genre of autobiography argues that it has its origins in the idea of conversion (Hawkins 1985). Thus I can say with some justification, "Once I was *there* and was *that*; now I am *here* and *this*." I once taught developmental biology as well as the cellular and molecular term of a year-long introductory biology course for majors at what was then Southern Oregon State College. I also established a research laboratory and published studies of cell differentiation during vertebrate limb development, a project supported by the National Institute of Child Health and Human Development (Flower 1973). I worked amid incubating eggs, chick embryos, culture media, microdissection instruments, Sephadex-filled glass columns used for preparing cell growth factors, a laminar flow hood, petri dishes, dissecting microscopes, cell culture incubator, binders filled with technical and experimental protocols, copies of the journal *Developmental Biology*, and, down the hallway, a 4°C cold room where dissociated limb bud cells were fractionated into predifferentiative subpopulations on bovine serum albumin gradients. I now have a joint appointment in the University Honors Program and Center for Science Education at Portland State University, where my scholarly work is characterized as interdisciplinary science studies. My major effort has shifted from investigating the link between mechanisms of embryonic morphogenesis and cell differentiation to the even more complex task of reconceiving the notion of science literacy and reconfiguring a university-level science curriculum.

I begin with a brief recollection of the boundary-crossing trajectory and intellectual alliances that constitute my academic career, and then turn to a precarious concatenation of molecular biology, political theory, science studies, and feminist writings within which I am carrying out pedagogical reform. Reverberating throughout this concatenation is a politico- and ethicoscientific recasting of political liberty. This understanding is for me both the lens of scrutiny I have turned back on the natural sciences and a way of situating and making plausible important questions arising in feminist science studies.

Being Reconfigured

I once was a developmental biologist; now I am engaged in an interdisciplinary mix of projects that resists easy definition. My interdisciplinary trajectory/conversion has been a matter of encountering and knotting together the ideas of several provocative theorists. Thus I constitute my day-to-day work as a specific intellectual[2] who is partially situated[3] in material-semiotic[4] practices and events. These in turn constitute in part the reasonably radical border-crossing pedagogies[5] I employ as the armature of a curricular reform of science education. In these efforts I attempt to take seriously the agential reality[6] of the products of science-in-action,[7] practices that produce strongly objective accounts[8] simultaneously reconfiguring the power-knowledge[9] frameworks of technoscientific governmentality[10] as well as the places and spaces[11] of an agonistic democracy indicative of and responsive to the problematic relation between identity and difference.[12]

This heterogeneous assemblage of colleagues, concerns, and projects is my work, my conversion; it is the framework within which the claims of feminist science studies are not only plausible but persuasive. I hope the obligation I owe to a number of my feminist science studies colleagues will be clear in what follows. It is feminist science studies writings that have most forthrightly called for an engaged, civic-minded technoscientific sensibility and commitment that most closely fits with my own. I would like to think that my science education reform focus on science in the making and open-ended inquiries that link to real, situated public questions is in line with Haraway's (1997) call to be partial:

> The point is to make a difference in the world, to cast our lot with some ways of life and not others. To do that, one must be in the action, be finite and dirty, not transcendent and clean. Knowledge-making technologies, including crafting subject positions and ways of inhabiting such positions, must be relentlessly visible and open to critical intervention (36).

Haraway says that "to study technoscience requires an immersion in worldly material-semiotic practices, where the analysts, as well as the humans and nonhumans studied, are all at risk—morally, politically, technically, and epistemologically" (190). I think I can say with assurance and integrity that such risky business has been and remains my intent as well as my link to feminist science studies.

Appreciating Technoscience Congeries

Key for me in my early thinking, moving, and teaching across disciplinary boundaries were frameworks of actor-networks (Latour 1993, 1996, 1999; Callon 1992; Law 1994) and material-semiotic apparatuses (Haraway 1988, 1997). These frameworks have opened a way for me to craft intersections that link technoscientific webworks of practice to vexing questions of political liberty. Latour (1993) writes of a single, composite story that illuminates this webwork:

> On page four of my daily newspaper, I learn that the measurements taken above the Antarctic are not good this year: the hole in the ozone layer is growing ominously larger. Reading on, I turn from upper-atmosphere chemists to Chief Executive Officers of Atochem and Monsanto, companies that are modifying their assembly lines in order to replace the innocent chlorofluorocarbons, accused of crimes against the ecosphere. A few paragraphs later, I come across heads of state of major industrialized countries who are getting involved with chemistry, refrigerators, aerosols and inert gases. But at the end of the article, I discover that the meteorologists don't agree with the chemists; they're talking about cyclical fluctuations unrelated to human activity. So now the industrialists don't know what to do. The heads of state are also holding back. Should we wait? It is already too late? Towards the bottom of the page, Third World countries and ecologists add their grain of salt and talk about international treaties, moratoriums, the rights of future generations, and the right to development.
>
> The same article mixes together chemical reactions and political reactions. A single thread links the most esoteric sciences and the most sordid politics, the most distant sky and some factory in the Lyon suburbs, dangers on a global scale and the impending local elections or the next board meeting. The horizons, the stakes, the time frames, the actors—none of these is commensurable, yet there they are, caught up in the same story (1).

This is not an example of science *and* politics or of nature *and* society. Latour calls this nature-culture assemblage a *collective*; it is a heterogeneous composite. "Is it," he asks, "our fault that networks are *simultaneously real, like nature, narrated, like discourse, and collective, like society?*" Haraway (1997) invites us to inspect the liveliness of such webworks:

> Any interesting being in technoscience, such as a textbook, molecule, equation, mouse, pipette, bomb, fungus, technician, agitator, or scientist, can—and often should—be teased open to show the sticky threads that make up its tissues. . . . Which thread is which remains permanently mutable, a question of analytical choice and foregrounding operations. The threads are alive; they transform into each other; they move away from our categorical gaze. The relations among the technical, mythic, economic, political, formal, textual, historical, and organic are not caused. But the articulations are consequential; they matter (68).

It follows from such rhizomic conceptions of scientific practice that science and technology do not simplify our understandings of such things as global warming, the link between gene expression and behavior, or the moral status of human em-bryos. As Latour (1998b) insists,

> Activists as well as scientists and politicians do not expect science to decrease the complex web of their lives. On the contrary, they expect research to multiply the number of entities with which they have to deal in their collective life. . . . That is what has changed most. Science does not enter a chaotic society to put order into it anymore, to simplify its composition, and to put an end to its con-troversies. It does enter it, but to add new, uncertain ingredients . . . to all the other ingredients that make up the collective experiments (209).

We are more and more entangled, and it is the capacity to trace and engage in the play of such politicoscientific filigrees that I take to be at the core of technoscien-tific literacy. Haraway (1997, 11) argues similarly, claiming that to read such maps differentially, attuned to asymmetries of power, opportunity, benefit, and suffer-ing, is to be technoscientifically literate. I would make the further claim that shap-ing such a literacy should be the goal of reformed science courses such that they connect to the critical practices of democracy, liberty, and moral sensibility in the face of such "entanglements." Hence my particular way of conceiving and going about course and curriculum design (Flower, Ramette, and Becker 1997).

Being at Liberty to Come to Matter

Assemblages of the sort noted above come to matter; that is, they are materialized arrangements-of-consequence arrived at through the labor of scientific practices. Haraway's (1997) "feminism and technoscience" project and Barad's (1998) sophisti-cated elaboration of the coming-to-matter of phenomena ground my explorations of the play of liberty in these practices of the natural sciences. As Barad asks, How does matter come to matter; what does it matter—and to whom—that we realize some phenomena and not others? I would also ask, How is it that we are at liberty to realize otherwise? These seem to me important political and moral questions.

Complex, category-mixing, boundary-crossing assemblages are the stuff of my concern, now understood as things that come to matter in important and entan-gled politico- and ethicoscientific ways. My conception of these entanglements as sites and practices of liberty owes much to my encounter with Foucault's render-ing of freedom as the "continuous reversibility and substitutability of things" (Scott 1990, 90). This rendering seems to me an apt definition of technoscientific liberty.[13] It recalls Haraway's (1997) insistence that "the threads [constituting the beings of technoscience] are alive; they transform into each other; they move away from our categorical gaze" (68). Indeed, I would argue that science-in-the-mak-ing, the practices/sites of articulation and assemblage of persons/texts/things of which Latour writes, is a contest of liberty.[14] To articulate a webwork of associations is to realize phenomena as points of departure for further articulations. Furthermore, if technoscientific liberty is the situated freedom of association constituted by science-in-action and a rearticulation of sociopolitical terrains—then sites of civic responsibility include such places as the laboratory, field station, and clinical facility. Our task, then, is to promote a citizenry literate in the ways of (re)making technoscience at those sites and change in ways we are bound up with one another and the things of the world.[15] As Latour (1998a) argues, we can no longer allow "Science" to claim that it does not do politics when it "takes all the important decisions" (104). After all, "All of us have become members [of] collective experiments on global warming, the influence of genetic engineering, conservations of species . . . [and we] thus all have to practice something which, until recently, was the calling of very few specialists, namely *science policy*" (105).

For Foucault, liberty is neither a metaphysical nor a transcendental concept. It is neither opposed to determinism nor does it affirm some reserve within the human subject that is capable of breaking the bondage of relations of power (May 1993, 119). As Foucault (1980) claimed, "there are no spaces of primal liberty" (142); thus liberty is not a state of being "free from" constraint nor is it, as Dumm (1996) has said, "a space unfettered or alone"; rather it is "a busy intersection" (25). We ought to conceive liberty as "coterminous with, rather than opposed to, the space of politics" (4). Dumm's "busy intersection" can easily be taken as aptly referring to one of Haraway's rhizomatically imbricating category hybrids. Liberty is not an essential state we can achieve but is the continuous activity of differently and differentially articulating—because of their possible reversibility and instability—our associations with others and the things about us. The greater the number of associations, the greater our liberty—technoscientific degrees of freedom, as it were. Actor-networks, Haraway's material-semiotic assemblages, and Barad's agential realizations that matter are practices and products of liberty. Liberty is the possible "coming undone," the possible reversibility of orders of knowledge and practice, a changing of the order of things, including the rearticulations of the social that take place within the making of science and technology.

In a technoscientific world, freedom is not liberation aided by the truths of science; it is neither an action or an end that a pure, objective science can enable nor a location outside the forces of history or desire. Paraphrasing and turning Rajchman (1985, 92–93) to the purpose at hand, I would join him in claiming that liberty is not an ideal we make practical with the help of science and technology; it is not a state grounded in a presumed transcendental Nature knowable by science. Instead, liberty has the properties of a verb rather than a noun; it has the properties of "making" rather than "the made." Scientists are "makers" of liberty as they work in their laboratories but not because they are free of relations of politics and power, or because the knowledge they produce "sets us free." Rather they effect significant reconstitution and realignment of the social and the discursive through their gradual constitution of claims, phenomena, and "things."

They are Barad's agential realists. It will matter to our practices of liberty just what sorts of heterogeneous assemblages of persons/texts/things are advanced at the constitutive, uncertain margins of science, for it is there that our being at liberty is being fundamentally reconfigured.

If, as Latour (1998a) has argued, we "nonscientists" are entitled to due process through our role as civic-minded science policy practitioners, then all that has been said above applies to us as well. We too are agential realists. This complex interplay I am calling technoscientific liberty presumes and names our real capacity to change the practices by which we and our world are constituted. It names the struggle within and about the "politics of technoscientific truth" of our world, a politics that operates to unsettle old and facilitate new politicoscientific associations; that is, a changing human/nonhuman polity. This is the imbricated politics into which my conversion has thrown me.

Notes

1. The multiple possibilities of reading the subtitle are intended. To "realize" is not simply to "get it" but also to bring to fruition by a considerable labor. Coming to matter is not only about being of significance but also about being important in material ways. Being at liberty is an ongoing process of material, embodied realization; it is the practice of realizing.

2. See Foucault (1980, 126, 132). In contrast to the universal intellectual who believed he could speak of transcendental principles, the specific intellectual operates in the localities of her expertise and is very much caught up in this world.

3. See Haraway (1988). She is arguing for "politics and epistemologies of location, positioning, and situating, where partiality and not universality is the condition of being heard to make rational knowledge claims" (589).

4. Haraway (1997) notes, for example, that realization is at once "deeply contingent, physical, semiotic, tropic, historical, international" and involves "institutions, narratives, legal structures, power-differentiated human labor, technical practice, analytic apparatus, and much more" (142).

5. Giroux (1992, 90) pushes us to recognize that institutions of higher education are places that legitimate existing views of the world; the university is a place that is deeply political and unarguably normative, authorizing and shaping particular social relations. After science studies we have no reason to believe that the natural sciences are not implicated in this authorizing function.

6. Barad (1998) argues that "reality is not composed of things-in-themselves or things-behind-phenomena, but things-in-phenomena" (104). The scientist, his or her practices, the instruments used—all are implicated in and constitutive of this entangled reality.

7. See Latour (1987).

8. See Harding (1991).

9. What recommends Foucault's (1980, 1982) treatment of power is his conception of "it" as a complex relationality, as action upon other actions. Power is not a thing; it is enacting, performing. Foucault (1982) says that "something called Power, with or without a capital letter, which is assumed to exist universally in a concentrated or diffused form, does not exist. Power exists only when it is put into action" (219).

10. Foucault (1997) says, "I intend this concept of 'governmentality' to cover the whole range of practices that constitute, define, organize, and instrumentalize the strategies that individuals in their freedom can use in dealing with each other" (300).

11. Brown (1995) has remarked that "our [political] spaces, while requiring some definition and protection, cannot be clean, sharply bounded, disembodied, or permanent: to engage postmodern modes of power and honor specifically feminist knowledges, they must be heterogeneous, roving, relatively noninstitutionalized, and democratic to the point of exhaustion" (50).

12. Connolly (1991) argues that "agonal democracy *enables* (but does not require) *anyone* to come to terms with the strife and interdependence of identity-difference. . . . When democratic politics is robust, when it operates to disturb the naturalization of settled conventions, when it exposes settled identities to some of the contestable contingencies that constitute them, then one is in a more favorable position to reconsider some of the demands built into those conventions and identities. One becomes more able to treat one's naturalized assumptions about identity and otherness as conventional categories of insistence" (192–193).

13. Perhaps the most intriguing and accessible examination of Foucault's notion of liberty as an alternative to Isaiah Berlin's well-known rendering of negative and positive liberty is that of Thomas Dumm (1996). Dumm's work is a wonderful entrée into the sense of liberty I have been discussing. What makes it even more intriguing is its treatment of the spaces of politics, especially what are termed heterotopias, which to my mind have characteristics similar to the hybrid assemblages of Haraway and Latour.

14. So long as we understand technoscientific practice in terms of heterogeneous assemblages of persons/texts/things (and we also understand "texts" in terms of discursive practices), we get some help from Scott (1990), when he notes that liberty "is found in the discontinuities and ruptures of discourses" (90).

15. Latour (forthcoming) seeks to move us away from notions of liberty as emancipation by noting that "the question to be addressed is not whether we should be free or bound but whether we are well or poorly bound." "If it is no longer a question of opposing attachment and detachment, but instead of good and poor attachments, then there is only one way of deciding the quality of these ties: to inquire of what they consist, what they do, how one is affected by them." The view of liberty I am arguing for is consistent with Latour's.

Works Cited

Barad, K. "Getting Real: Performativity, Materiality, and Technoscientific Practices." *Differences: A Journal of Feminist Cultural Studies* 10 (1998): 87–128.

Brown, W. *States of Injury: Power and Freedom in Late Modernity*. Princeton, NJ: Princeton University Press, 1995.

Callon, M. "Techno-Economic Networks and Irreversibility." In *A Sociology of Monsters: Essays on Power, Technology, and Domination*, ed. J. Law. London: Routledge Sociological Review Monograph, 1992.

Connolly, W. E. *Identity/Difference: Democratic Negotiations of Political Paradox.* Ithaca, NY: Cornell University Press, 1991.

Dumm, T. *Michel Foucault and the Politics of Freedom.* Thousand Oaks, CA.: Sage Publications, 1996.

Flower, M. "Cellular Heterogeneity in the Chick Wing Mesoblast: Analysis by Equilibrium Density Gradient Centrifugation." *Developmental Biology 28* (1973): 583–602.

Flower, M., C. Ramette, and W. Becker. "Science in the Liberal Arts at Portland State University: A Curriculum Focusing on Science-in-the-Making." In *Student-Active Science: Models of Innovation in College Science Teaching*, ed. A. P. McNeal and C. D'Avanzo. New York: Saunders College Publishing, 1997.

Foucault, M. "The Ethics of the Concern for Self as a Practice of Freedom." In *Ethics: Subjectivity and Truth*, ed. P. Rabinow. New York: New Press, 1997.

———. "Afterword: The Subject and Power." In *Michel Foucault: Beyond Structuralism and Hermeneutics*, ed. H. L. Dreyfus and P. Rabinow. Chicago: University of Chicago Press, 1982.

———. *Power/Knowledge: Selected Interviews and Other Writings, 1972–1977.* New York: Pantheon Books, 1980.

Giroux, H. *Border Crossings: Cultural Workers and the Politics of Education.* New York: Routledge, 1992.

Haraway, D. *Modest_Witness@Second_Millennium.FemaleMan©Meets_OncoMouse™: Feminism and Technoscience.* New York: Routledge, 1997.

———. "Situated Knowledges: The Science Question in Feminism as a Site of Discourse on the Privilege of Partial Perspective." *Feminist Studies 14* (1988): 575–599.

Harding, S. *Whose Science? Whose Knowledge? Thinking from Women's Lives.* Ithaca, NY: Cornell University Press, 1991.

Hawkins, A. H. *Archetypes of Conversion: The Autobiographies of Augustine, Bunyan, and Merton.* Lewisburg, PA: Bucknell University Press, 1985.

Latour, B. "Factures/Fractures: From the Concept of Network to that of Attachment." *Factura, special issue of RES*, ed. J. Loerner (forthcoming).

———. "On Recalling ANT." In *Actor Network Theory and After*, ed. J. Law and J. Hassard. Oxford: Blackwell Publishers, 1999.

———. "Ein Ding is Ein Thing: A Philosophical Platform for a Left European Party." *Concepts and Transformations 3* (1998a): 97–112.

———. "From the World of Science to the World of Research?" *Science 280* (1998b): 208–209.

———. "On Actor Network Theory. A Few Clarifications." *Soziale Welt 47* (1996): 369–381.

———. *We Have Never Been Modern.* Cambridge, MA: Harvard University Press, 1993.

———. *Science in Action.* Cambridge, MA: Harvard University Press, 1987.

Law, J. *Organizing Modernity.* Cambridge, MA: Blackwell Publishers, 1994.

May, T. *Between Genealogy and Epistemology: Psychology, Politics, and Knowledge in the Thought of Michel Foucault.* University Park: Pennsylvania State University Press, 1993.

Rajchman, J. *Michel Foucault: The Freedom of Philosophy.* New York: Columbia University Press, 1985.

Scott, C. E. *The Question of Ethics: Nietzsche, Foucault, Heidegger.* Bloomington: Indiana University Press, 1990.

ALTERED STATES

Transforming Disciplines from Within

Section II

Over the Edge

Developing Feminist Frameworks in the
Sciences and Women's Studies

———————————————————————————➤ Mary Wyer

The term *feminist science studies* captures a wide variety of approaches and per-spectives. It is a field of study that has no institutional "room of one's own," and therefore lacks the privileges and constraints a bounded room suggests. Those working in the field share the basic conviction that a focus on gender, race, class, and sexuality and their intersections enriches our understanding of the emergence and use of scientific knowledge within and through social processes. Beyond this, overarching generalizations about a "canon" or "consensus" on issues are difficult to make about any specialized area within women's studies, since they are neces-sarily disciplinarily informed and by definition multi- and interdisciplinary. Yet, unlike those working in the field of literary criticism, for example, people who work in feminist science studies seldom are located in a department that has a concentration of feminist science scholars with whom to work, nor do universities have reputations built around identities associated with one or another school of thought. As a result, the theory and research that emerges does not fit into the neat dimensions of prevailing frameworks. Indeed, such theory and research is at its best when it can catalyze work that challenges these frameworks.

Despite the isolation in which early feminist critics of science worked in the 1970s, this generation of scholars produced a major feminist challenge to the idea that science was necessarily neutral and objective by developing the key insight that the exclusion of women from scientific fields was entangled with the con-struction of gender *in* science and the question of what is considered "scientific."[1] The historical roots of this equation were most famously mapped out by Evelyn Fox Keller's reading of the metaphors used by Francis Bacon (Keller 1980). Quot-ing his vivid use of graphic and sexual imagery to capture a scientist's relationship to nature, Keller writes that Bacon represented nature as a bride to the scientist suitor, coy but conquerable. "I am come in very truth leading you to Nature with all her children to bind her to your service and make her your slave" (301).

Feminists have continued to develop, sustain, and enrich a theoretical frame-work for feminist science studies. The "early" works included Rosser's *Female-*

Friendly Science (1990), Bleier's *Science and Gender* (1984), Keller's *Reflections on Gender and Science* (1985), and Fausto-Sterling's *Myths of Gender* (1985), but there were also important edited collections such as the Genes and Gender series (now in its sixth edition), Tuana's *Feminism and Science* (1989), Bleier's *Feminist Approaches to Science* (1986), and Hubbard, Henifen, and Fried's *Women Look at Biology Looking at Women* (1979). Emerging from this early generation of work is a growing body of research and theory that has reimagined the cornerstone role of "objectivity" in the practices and purposes of creating scientific knowledge.[2]

These imaginings have some stirring implications attached to them, most notably that human knowledge (as we gather, teach, and transmit it to the next generation) is the product of human action and intention. Feminist theoretical insights about language, gender, and the social construction of knowledge have suggested, for instance, that scientific "fact" is less a product of objectivity and experimental method than of social consensus about the adequacy of experimental evidence (Longino 1990; Hawkesworth 1989). Though the framework developed by early feminists of science outlines the paradigmatic implications of feminist theory for rethinking biology (Bleier 1984; Hubbard and Lowe 1983; Spanier 1986), gender (Fausto-Sterling 1985), and the history and philosophy of science (Keller 1985), research that extends this work to specific topics and specialties within contemporary science and engineering has been all too rare.

Still, current work in this territory is under way and advancing at a rapid pace.[3] Some of the most recent scholarship under the rubric of feminist science studies addresses discipline-specific questions: for instance, research about the history of women in science that recovers lost information and perspectives in order to correct the historical record of women's participation in science (Rossiter 1982, 1995; Schiebinger 1987, 1989; Cabré, in this volume). Other work focuses on rethinking how and to what effect scientific research impacts women's lives, including research exposing the uses and abuses of reproductive technologies (Clarke and Olesen 1999; Gordon 1990; Martin 1987; Shiva 1989) that draws on gynecology, anthropology, and history. Yet others focus on the ways in which gender- (and race-) based assumptions distort knowledge of the natural world (Keller 1987; Hammonds 1997; Harding 1991; Jackson, in this volume); and the ways in which the practices, priorities, and products of science speak to/for/as artifact (Haraway 1989). Still other work focuses on the ways in which science is taught in the classroom, that is, the ways in which gender-based assumptions about teaching and learning shape both what and who is taught to think scientifically (Rosser 1990; Mayberry and Rose 1999; Davis et al. 1996; Henry, in this volume; Phillips and Hausbeck, in this volume.)

In short, most theory and research in feminist science studies raises questions about who does the science, how they do the work, why, for whose benefit, and what anticipated and unanticipated meanings and social consequences arise—

questions emerging from cornerstones of feminist theory (Jaggar 1983; Hartsock 1984; MacKinnon 1982; Hartmann 1979). The inverse—research that emerges from within science in order to raise questions about feminist theory—is uncommon, and it is this conversation that the authors in the following section intend to cultivate.

In retrospect, it could be said that feminist theory has had both deconstructive and reconstructive tasks in the humanities and social sciences. The first task was to critique the prevailing body of knowledge. We needed to understand how the absence of women, as legitimate subjects of study, distorted or directed what we knew about our social world and our representations of it. This work is by no means concluded, but the worthiness of the effort is now widely recognized where once it was dismissed. The complementary task has been to develop new theories to organize the gathering of new knowledge, with the goal of reshaping the terrain of ideas in the humanities and social sciences. As a result of such efforts, in literary theory, for instance, the life-and-death circumstances of childbirth can be understood as just as vital, just as fully human, just as resonant with morality, as the life-and-death circumstances of the battlefield, although just thirty years ago, childbirth was not deemed to be an interesting topic for intellectual discovery. However, understanding that the study of literature was constrained by gender bias has not led to the abandonment of literature as an area of study. Rather, the study of women has been enriched by the perspectives offered from a new source of information, that is, literary representations.

Similarly, feminist science theory has both deconstructive and reconstructive elements. The feminist critique of science began with a reevaluation of scientific knowledge, opening the door to questions about the degree to which objectivity within male-centered scientific institutions was achievable or even desirable. Key studies demonstrated the distortions in methods and misinterpretations of data that stemmed from gender-bounded preconceptions of the material, natural world (Bleier 1984; Haraway 1978a, 1978b, 1991; Keller and Longino 1996; Rose 1983; Zihlmann 1978). There is by now a persuasive and extensive body of knowledge that details an overinvestment in the ability of the scientific method to ensure objectivity. The reconstructive work, in contrast, requires that we explore how constructions of the material worlds of science can expand feminist perspectives, methods, theories, and disciplinary scope.

In the essays that follow, the authors have stepped beyond the safety of familiar ground in search of ways to think about the social, methodological, and gender-based processes through which knowledge is constructed in light of prevailing knowledge about the material world. Leading the way is Donna Haraway, who in an interview with Thyrza Nichols Goodeve explores new epistemological territory in recasting biological phenomena as metaphors. In doing this, she does not renounce the material world, but rather quite the opposite, embracing the pleasures of a symbiotic relationship between language and our embodiment. Language itself is "an intensely physical process," according to Haraway, one that points toward the complexities that emerge from thinking about the world without relying on the neat dualities of nature-culture, mind-body, or symbolic-material.

The next essay in this section, by Elizabeth Henry, takes up where Haraway leaves off; that is, Henry experiments (as a writer and teacher of literature) with the methods of intimacy and wholeness of perception practiced by geneticist and Nobel Laureate Barbara McClintock. Henry implicitly poses the question, Could I use such a method in teaching about language and literature? Her essay closes with her lyrical account of a moment in her class, using this method, when students began to see the complexities of life and language through the biology of an ear of corn. The story is a lovely reminder of the inseparability of the tangible and the intangible, emotion and reason, the natural world and the social world, and the templates by which we interpret all of the above.

Michael Witmore, in "When the Mirror Looks Back: Nature in the Scholarship of the Humanities," also struggles with the conceptual limitations that the nature-culture distinction imposes on inquiry. In an engaging account of his collaboration with an evolutionary biologist, Witmore explains the apparent incommensurability of perspectives from the humanities with those from the sciences. He ruminates about the epistemological gap that is much noticed and seldom challenged, speaking more to the questions that cannot be asked in these areas than to those that are.

Similarly, but from the perspective of a scientist, Michelle Elekonich takes an in-depth look at the ways in which disciplinary definitions of what is or is not an appropriate research question have distorted the study of aggression in song sparrows—a field in which a male-female binary has paradigmatic influence in understanding links between biology and behavior. She details an experiment to test the degree to which female-to-female aggression parallels male-to-male aggression in both expression and hormone levels. She found that aggressive behavior was more context specific than the "sex differences model" could capture. Her results point to the limitations of interpreting the sparrows' behaviors based on the overly simplistic duality of male-female. Elekonich thus is able, through application of work by Keller on marginalization in science, and Harding on "strong objectivity," to critique her field and at the same time suggest a challenge to feminists' overreliance on a binary division between male and female in the sex-gender distinction.

In the next essay, "Sexy Science: What's Love Got to Do with It?" C. Phoebe Lostroh examines how the binary distinction between male and female works to shape interpretations in the social as well as the biological world by celebrating masculinity. She argues that the standards by which a scientific experiment is judged to be "sexy" are aligned with the practices of masculinity. These standards rest on the unexamined assumptions of a male-centered science that appropriates definitions of what is sexy, largely driven by masculinist metaphors of mastery and dominance. Sexy science is work that conquers the Frontier, taming the Wilderness of the cell in order to find the proverbial gold mine, then shouting "Eureka!" She uses this critique to develop a new vision of science and a reconstructive intellectual project in signal transduction, by describing alternate metaphors and models that contextualize the multiple players in cell function rather than individualistic heroic deeds.

J. Kasi Jackson's essay links questions about the binary concept of sex to the binary concept of gender. In her field, the study of fish coloration, the prevailing paradigm is male-centered, so that coloration displays in females are neither understood nor valued as a research area. As a result, many traits that occur in both sexes in many species are labeled as "male traits," obscuring the degree of sexual variation that exists. Preconceptions of male as norm thus work hand in hand with ignorance of female biology to restrict rather than enlarge our appreciation for the diversity of the natural world. Like other contributors to this section, Jackson offers a case study in the reconstructive vein, to explain how the details of a debate in her field point toward theoretical challenges to assumptions about sexual dichotomization. If sexual variation is high, the natural world might be better represented by something other than a binary construct. If sex is not a clearly binary construct, then what are we to make of gender, the social version thereof?

With the contribution from Montserrat Cabré, this section extends the dialogue in feminist science theory to include the "science" of the history of science and medicine. What happens, Cabré asks, if we examine our own work, in her case the historiography of women in science, in light of the concept of social construction that we embrace in critiques of scientific knowledge? As a case study, she recounts the efforts of early-twentieth-century women in science who organized an ambitious research project to document the history of medical women in the United States. The study, undertaken by Kate Hurd-Mead, resulted in two books and more than fifteen articles, all published before 1940, focusing on the history of women in medicine. Yet these works have been ignored. Again, women have been left out of the picture, she maintains, this time written out because professional historians did not judge this work to be a relevant source of information. She reevaluates the work, understanding it in the context of an attempt to place women's experiences in medicine at the center of the history of medicine at a time when, indeed, women were widely discouraged from becoming physicians. From this perspective, she argues, one can see the early work in terms of its symbolic significance for the community of women to whom it was addressed, making room for these women in the historical record.

The concluding reading in this section is by Jaime Phillips and Kate Hausbeck, both sociologists who have examined the presence and character of images of women in geoscience textbooks. As in the case of Kate Hurd-Mead, women have been left out of the picture, but this time literally. Reporting on both qualitative and quantitative content analyses of a long list of popular textbooks, they explain that in this work, women are seldom, if ever, represented as authors or scientific innovators. Only a small fraction of the photographs they analyzed included people of color, and there was a disturbing and unexamined alignment of scientific initiatives with political and economic agendas in Western countries. The authors conclude that beneath the scientific text lie worldviews and epistemological positions that need scrutiny in efforts to transform who, how, and what we teach in the science classroom.

One of the most striking qualities of the readings in this section is that they go beyond simplistic understandings of the relationship between the absence of women from science and the uses and abuses of science. As feminist science studies has demonstrated, it is far too simplistic to suggest that all we need to do to promote change is to recruit more women into the sciences. Such arguments imply that women are somehow fundamentally different from men and that if women were scientists, science would be different along the same lines. Indeed, much of the early work, such as Keller's (1978) elaboration of object relations theory and Gilligan's (1982) theories of psychological development of boys and girls, have often been used (and misinterpreted) to support such essentialist claims. These two contributions to feminist theory—from Keller and Gilligan—thus converged to suggest to many women in science that they necessarily did a different kind of science than men via a "specifically female genius." To many women in science, such feminist theory was offensive on two counts. It suggested that (1) they weren't "real" women, since they were scientists, and (2) they weren't "real" scientists either. They could only do "women's science," which was inferior science. While the notion that bodies matter most—that bodies lead to standpoints that lead to certain kinds of knowledge—is temptingly parsimonious, it does not present a complete picture of the transformations that need to take place if feminist goals are to be implemented within the sciences. Moreover, the gains to be had by feminist theory by exploring scientific questions will not necessarily or exclusively come from scientists who happen to be women but rather from those who have honed intellectually fruitful ideas within interdisciplinary inquiry, whatever their training or sex. Bringing the strengths of interdisciplinary perspectives to the examination of disciplinary content is a touchstone for feminist scholars of all stripes.

The essays in this section collectively make a strong case for the need for continued, nuanced, substantive, and deconstructive analyses in the context of reconstructive perspectives for specific disciplines and research questions. The

authors herein offer their insights as examples of knowledge-making (and un-
making, and remaking) within a framework that fully acknowledges the importance of social content in social context. Their collective commitment to
rereading the scientific record in light of gender-based assumptions, especially in
but not limited to sex difference research, and their concurrent effort to rethink
their fields and specializations in light of their rereadings, provide compelling
testimony to the synergy generated by critical, self-reflexive, and feminist inquiry. The fact that they offer their ideas as catalysts for others, taking many of
the risks assumed by that first generation of feminist scholars, deserves our undi-
vided attention.

Notes

1. As is the case with feminist theory in general, there is a longer history of science critique from feminists than is widely recognized. In particular, two feminist psychologists
published research over a hundred years ago that directly challenged scientific work
demonstrating the biological inferiority of women relative to men. See the discussion of
Mary Putnam Jacobi and Leta Stetter Hollingworth (1993), "Historical Development of
the Psychology of Women."

2. One of the earliest efforts to map out a systematic overview of what was then called
"feminist critiques of science" was a talk given at the Massachusetts Institute of Technology in the early 1980s by Hilary Rose, later published in 1986 as "Beyond Masculinist Realities: A Feminist Epistemology for the Sciences." Rose divided feminist work on the
sciences into four distinct foci: naming the exclusionary practices, recovering lost women,
reevaluating scientific research about women, and critiquing the epistemological assumptions of Western science. Rose has since added a fifth focus to her framework, this one on
the symbolic import of feminist science fiction literature (see Rose 1988). For her review
of emphases in feminist science studies, see Londa Schiebinger (1987), "The History and
Philosophy of Women in Science."

3. For a more extensive overview of related work, see Londa Schiebinger's *Has Feminism Changed Science?* (1999).

Works Cited

Bleier, Ruth (Ed.). *Feminist Approaches to Science*. New York: Pergamon Press, 1986.
————— . *Science and Gender*. New York: Pergamon Press, 1984.
Clarke, A., and V. Olesen. *Revisioning Women, Health, and Healing: Feminist, Cultural,
    and Technoscience Perspectives*. New York: Routledge, 1999.
Davis, Cinda-Sue, et al. *The Equity Equation: Fostering the Advancement of Women in the
    Sciences, Mathematics, and Engineering*. San Francisco: Jossey-Bass Publishing, 1996.

Fausto-Sterling, Anne. *Myths of Gender: Biological Theories about Women and Men.* New York: Basic Books, 1985.

Gilligan, Carol. *In a Different Voice.* Cambridge, MA: Harvard University Press, 1982.

Gordon, Linda. *Woman's Body, Woman's Right: Birth Control in America.* New York: Pergamon Press, 1990.

Hammonds, Evelynn. "New Technologies of Race." In *Processed Lives: Gender and Technology in Everyday Life,* ed. J. Terry and M. Calvert. New York: Routledge, 1997.

Haraway, Donna. "A Cyborg Manifesto." In *Simians, Cyborgs, and Women: The Reinvention of Nature.* New York: Routledge, 1991.

————. *Primate Visions: Gender, Race, and Nature in the World of Modern Science.* New York: Routledge, 1989.

————. "Animal Sociology and a Natural Economy of the Body Politic, Part I: A Political Physiology of Dominance." *Signs: Journal of Women in Culture and Society* 4 (1978a): 21–36.

————. "Animal Sociology and a Natural Economy of the Body Politic, Part II: The Past is the Contested Zone: Human Nature and Theories of Production and Reproduction in Primate Behavior Studies." *Signs: Journal of Women in Culture and Society* 4 (1978b): 37–60.

Harding, Sandra. *Whose Science? Whose Knowledge? Thinking from Women's Lives.* Ithaca, NY.: Cornell University Press, 1991.

Hartmann, Heidi I. "Capitalism, Patriarchy, and Job Segregation by Sex." In *Capitalist Patriarchy and the Case for Socialist Feminism,* ed. Zillah Eisenstein. New York: Monthly Review Press, 1979.

Hartsock, Nancy. *Money, Sex, and Power: Toward a Feminist Historical Materialism.* Amherst: University of Massachusetts Press, 1984.

Hawkesworth, Mary E. "Knowers, Knowing, Known: Feminist Theory and Claims of Truth." *Signs: Journal of Women in Culture and Society* 14, no. 3 (1989): 533–557.

Hubbard, Ruth, Mary Sue Henifen, and Barbara Fried. *Women Look at Biology Looking at Women.* New York: Schenkmann, 1979.

Hubbard, Ruth, and Marian Lowe. *Women's Nature: Rationalization of Inequality.* New York: Pergamon Press, 1983.

Jacobi, Mary P., and Leta S. Hollingworth. "Historical Development of the Psychology of Women." In *Psychology of Women: A Handbook of Issues and Theories,* ed. F. Denmark and M. Paludi. Westport, CT: Greenwood Press, 1993.

Jaggar, Alison. *Feminist Politics and Human Nature.* Totowa, NJ: Rowman and Allanheld, 1983.

Keller, Evelyn Fox. "Women Scientists and Feminist Critiques of Science." *Daedalus* 116 (Fall 1987): 77–91.

————. *Reflections on Gender and Science.* New Haven, CT: Yale University Press, 1985.

————. "Baconian Science: A Hermaphroditic Birth." *The Philosophical Forum* 11 (Spring 1980): 299–307.

————. "Gender and Science." *Psychoanalysis and Contemporary Thought* 1 (1978): 409–433.

Keller, Evelyn Fox, and Helen E. Longino (Eds.). *Feminism and Science.* New York: Oxford University Press, 1996.

Longino, Helen E. *Science as Social Knowledge: Values and Objectivity in Scientific Inquiry.* Princeton, NJ: Princeton University Press, 1990.

MacKinnon, Catherine. "Feminism, Marxism, Method, and the State." *Signs: Journal of Women in Culture and Society* 7 (1982): 515–544.

Martin, Emily. *The Woman in the Body: A Cultural Analysis of Reproduction.* Boston: Beacon Press, 1987.

Mayberry, M., and E. Rose (Eds.). *Meeting the Challenge: Innovative Feminist Pedagogies in Action.* New York: Routledge, 1999.

Rose, Hilary. "Comments on Schiebinger's 'The History of Philosophy of Women in Science.'" *Signs: Journal of Women in Culture and Society* 13 (1988): 377–379.

——— . "Beyond Masculinist Realities: A Feminist Epistemology for the Sciences." In *Feminist Approaches to Science*, ed. Ruth Bleier. New York: Pergamon Press, 1986.

——— . "Hand, Brain, and Heart: A Feminist Epistemology for the Natural Sciences." *Signs: Journal of Women in Culture and Society* 9 (1983): 73–90.

Rosser, Sue. *Female-Friendly Science.* New York: Pergamon Press, 1990.

Rossiter, Margaret W. *Women Scientists in America: Before Affirmative Action, 1940–1972.* Baltimore: Johns Hopkins University Press, 1995.

——— . *Women Scientists in America: Struggles and Strategies to 1940.* Baltimore: Johns Hopkins University Press, 1982.

Schiebinger, Londa. *Has Feminism Changed Science?* Cambridge, MA: Harvard University Press, 1999.

——— . *The Mind Has No Sex: Women in the Origins of Modern Science.* Cambridge, MA: Harvard University Press, 1989.

——— . "The History and Philosophy of Women in Science: A Review Essay." *Signs: Journal of Women in Culture and Society* 12 (1987): 305–332.

Shiva, Vandana. *Staying Alive: Women, Ecology, and Development.* London: Zed Books, 1989.

Spanier, Bonnie B. "Women's Studies and the Natural Sciences: A Decade of Change." *Frontiers* 8 (1986): 66–72.

Tuana, Nancy (Ed.). *Feminism and Science.* Bloomington: Indiana University Press, 1989.

Zihlmann, Adrienne L. "Women and Evolution, Part II: Subsistence and Social Organization among Early Hominids." *Signs: Journal of Women in Culture and Society* 4 (1978): 4–20.

More than Metaphor

───────────────➤ Donna Haraway, with Thyrza Nichols Goodeve

TNG: I'd like to ask you to describe your methodology as a cultural critic. What I'm especially interested in is how your training as a molecular and developmental biologist has influenced not just the themes of your work, but its very methodology.

DH: Words like *methodology* are very scary, you know! Rather than "methodology" I'd prefer to say I have definite ways of working that have become more conscious over the years. And most certainly my training in biology—in molecular, cellular, and developmental biology—matters to me. Particularly the way that it allows me to be alert to, and take tremendous pleasure in, biological beings and biological webs of relatedness. I'm fascinated by the internal architecture of cells and chromosomes. And there is no doubt that I frequently think in biological metaphors.

TNG: There is a kind of biologism to how you write. You take something—an object of knowledge or culture—and you move further and further inside of it, to what its structure is. And then you move inside of whatever webs of meaning you discover from that analysis and so on and so forth. You also use optical metaphors a lot in your writing, and your method really has a kind of microscopic zooming-in effect to it, without, of course, ever leaving behind the big picture.

DH: I'm fascinated by changes of scale. I think biological worlds invite thinking *at*, and *about* different kinds of scale. At the same time, biological worlds are full of imaginations and beings developed from quite extraordinary biological architectures and mechanisms. Biology is an inexhaustible source of troping. It is certainly full of metaphor, but it is more than metaphor.

TNG: You used that phrase once before. What do you mean by "it is more than metaphor"?

DH: I mean not only the physiological and discursive metaphors that can be found in biology, but the stories. For instance, all the various ironic, almost funny, incongruities. The sheer wiliness and complexity of it all. So that biology is not

81

merely a metaphor that illuminates something else, but an inexhaustible source of getting at the nonliteralness of the world. Also, I want to call attention to the simultaneity of facts and fiction, materiality and semioticity, object and trope.

TNG: You mean the way these literal biological entities are also such powerful metaphors for understanding "life"; i.e., biological and ontological systems. I think of your discussion of the microorganism *Mixotricha paradoxa* in "Cyborgs and Symbionts: Living Together in the New World Order" from *The Cyborg Handbook* (Haraway 1995).

DH: Yes. I use *Mixotricha paradoxa* as an entity that interrogates individuality and collectivity at the same time. It is a microscopic single-celled organism that lives in the hind gut of the South Australian termite. What counts as "it" is complicated because it lives in obligatory symbiosis with five other kinds of entities. Each has a taxonomic name, and each is closely related to bacteria because they don't have a cell nucleus. They have nucleic acid, they have DNA, but it's not organized into a nucleus. Each of these five different kinds of things lives in or on a different region of the cell. For example, one lives in interdigitations on the exterior surface of the cell membrane. So you have these little things that live in these folds of the cell membrane and others that live inside the cell. But they aren't in the full sense part of the cell. On the other hand, they live in obligatory symbiosis. Nobody can live independently here. This is codependency with a vengeance! And so the question is: Is it one entity or is it six? But six isn't right either because there are about a million of the five non-nucleated entities for every one nucleated cell. There are multiple copies. So when does one decide to become two? Where does this whole assemblage divide so that you now have two? And what counts as *Mixotricha*? Is it just the nucleated cell or is it the whole assemblage? This is obviously a fabulous metaphor that is a real thing for interrogating our notions of one and many.

TNG: It also sounds like it has a kind of multidimensional temporarity to it. I mean, how does one find it in the first place and what did it look like—what form did it take—when it was discovered? At which moment of its being was it discovered? And how did the researchers find all of its complexity and still see it as a whole rather than as a series of different entities? I don't know very much about biology, but my sense is that there are all sorts of things like *M. paradoxa*.

DH: Right—there are zillions of examples. Biology is an endless resource. That's why I have always preferred biology to psychoanalysis because it throws up so many more possibilities for stories that seem to get at some of our historical, psychological, political existence. Psychoanalysis pins things down too soon—it may be part of the truth but it's not the most interesting. I also just love the name *Mixotricha paradoxa*.

TNG: What does *Mixotricha* mean?

DH: Mixed threads.

TNG: That's fabulous. And *Mixotricha* is a boundary creature like the cyborg, the primate, and OncoMouse™?

DH: Right, but with the cyborg and the genetically engineered creature you have to think of the industrial artifactual, the human-built. With *Mixotricha,* this is not true, although it does need an intimate relationship with the laboratory processes that bring it into our view. Our relationship with *M. paradoxa* is produced by technoscientific relations that include the laboratory machinery, airplane travel, the whole history of zoology and taxonomy, as well as of colonial science in Australia.

TNG: You often receive the same kinds of reductionist readings of your work that experimental narrativists and artists like Yvonne Rainer[1] do for many of the same reasons. Some people refuse to engage with the kind of complexity your use of *M. paradoxa* requires. I associate this with an almost experimental or avant-gardist (to use an old term) antilinear, antiteleological aesthetic in your theory that is like Rainer's. Like you, she is constantly constructing analyses of race, gender, sexuality, desire via a complex relational-associational aesthetic that demands one does not stop her film at any one moment and say, "This is Yvonne Rainer's statement." It's the same with your work, which read unsympathetically turns into an antimaterialist, technophilic—or technophobic—social constructionist view of science. Such readings are representative of an inability to work with subtlety.

DH: It's a kind of literal-mindedness. And that's why figures are so important to me, because figures are immediately complex and nonliteral, not to mention instances of real pleasure in language. An odd literalism comes through when critics create positions that don't really exist—like recycling urban legends of people saying, "You believe in DNA!?!" How unsophisticated! This is sad, shocking, and takes away from all the pleasure in language *and* bodies that animates so much of the serious work on the cultural studies of science (see Ehrenreich and Macintosh 1997).

TNG: Finding the figural in the literal, or concrete, is very important to you. Your recent book *Modest_Witness@Second_Millennium.FemaleMan©_Meets_ Onco-Mouse*™ spends a great deal of time discussing figuration, not just in the discourses of biotechnology but in the very "flesh" of the gene itself. I'm interested in the way "flesh" has always been important to you—not just through your training as a molecular and developmental biologist, but in your deep commitment to the "flesh" of gender, race, species. "Flesh" stands in as a synecdoche for the way material reality signifies or is physically "tropic" as you put it.

DH: The first thing I'd say is that words are intensely physical for me. I find words and language more closely related to flesh than to ideas.

TNG: Roland Barthes has this great sentence, "Language is a skin: I rub my language against the other. It is as if I had words instead of fingers, or fingers at the tip of my words" (Barthes 1978, 73). In much the same way you rely on language's fleshy metaphorical juiciness.

DH: Since I experience language as an intensely physical process, I cannot *not* think through metaphor. It isn't as though I make a choice to work with and through metaphor, it's that I experience myself inside these constantly swerving, intensely physical processes of simiosis. Biochemistry and language just don't feel that different to me. There's also a Catholic dimension to all of this. My deep formation in Catholic symbolism and sacramentalism—doctrines of incarnation and transubstantiation—were all intensely physical. The relentless symbolization of Catholic life is not just attached to the physical world, it *is* the physical world. Look at the religious art of the U.S. Southwest, the Mexican, Latino, Chicano art, and you get an intense example of that. Contrast that art to the more abstemious Protestant art and then imagine the inside of a church in Mexico City. I grew up within the art world of Mexico City, so to speak, even though I grew up in Denver, Colorado. It was an Irish Catholic scene, nowhere as rich as the Latino cultural tradition, but I grew up very much inside an elaborate symbolic figural narrative world where notions of sign and flesh were profoundly tied together. I understood the world this way by the time I was four years old.

TNG: Would you define flesh?

DH: My instincts are always to do the same thing. It's to insist on the join between materiality and semiosis. Flesh is no more a thing than a gene is. But the materialized semiosis of flesh always includes the tones of intimacy, of body, of bleeding, of suffering, of juiciness. Flesh is always somehow wet. It's clear one cannot use the word *flesh* without understanding vulnerability and pain.

TNG: There's this quote I saved from the 1985 "Manifesto for Cyborgs" where you say, "Why should our bodies end at the skin or include at best other beings encapsulated by skin."

DH: And other organisms as well as built objects. There are all kinds of nonhumans with whom we are woven together.

TNG: As well as ways that our flesh is made up of artifactual flesh. I'm thinking of the way you use syntactical marks—"@", "©," "™," in *Modest_Witness@Second_Millennium.FemaleMan©_Meets_OncoMouse™*—to locate us (Haraway 1997). It is an example of the way your title successfully creates a new kind of syntax and figuration. The title *Modest_Witness@Second_Millennium.FemaleMan©_Meets_OncoMouse™* is its own technocultural poem. You visualize and theorize through the words and syntactical marks of the title, situating us in late-twentieth-century history. That is wonderful because these marks *are* the new brands.

DH: Especially with the double meaning of brand as type and mark of ownership burned into the flesh.

TNG: And rather than use the word *postmodernism*, or any other kind of category of modernity to mark the constitutional difference between the late twentieth century and earlier moments of modernity, you say, "I give the reader an e-mail address, if not a password, to situate things in the net" (Haraway 1997, 43). E-mail is familiar to almost everyone now. It is a crucial location for us in everyday life and signifies a mode of communication particular to late-twentieth-century technoculture. The "@" instantiates all the complex webs of relation (economic, ontological, social, historical, technological) that are key to postmodernism without having to engage once again in all the gnarly academic debates around the term.

DH: And it's a joke too.

TNG: Yes, humor, as much as irony, is so crucial to your theoretical style. How can we not laugh at the description you give of the transgenic tomato-fish antifreeze combination developed in Oakland, California, in 1991?[2] Since I brought up postmodernism, I'm interested in your definition of modernity.

DH: My definition of modernity is that it is the period of the intensified transportation of seeds and genes. For instance, look at the invention of the first great industrial system—plantation agriculture (which is not my idea but one I got from others)—and follow the whole relocation of populations, plants, sugar, cassava to feed populations from which male labor has been removed for colonial agricultural purposes. You can do the history of modernity as the history of the transportation of genes as well. In fact you can take each of the technoscientific stem cells I mention in *Modest_Witness*—brain, chip, gene, fetus, bomb, race, database, and ecosystem—and do the history of modernity.

Notes

1. Yvonne Rainer is a dancer, choreographer, artist, writer, and filmmaker. *MURDER and Murder* (1997) is her most recent film. For a discussion of her work, see Rainer (1997).

2. "Herbicide-resistant crops are probably the largest area of active plant genetic engineering. I find myself especially drawn by such engaging new beings as the tomato with a gende from a cold-sea-bottom-living flounder, which codes for a protein that slows freezing, and the potato with a gene from the giant silk moth, which increases disease resistance. DNA plant technology, Oakland, California, started testing the tomato-fish antifreeze combination in 1991" (Haraway 1997, 88).

Works Cited

Barthes, Roland. *A Lover's Discourse*. New York: Hill and Wang, 1978.

Ehrenreich, Barbara, and Janet Macintosh. "Biology under Attack." *The Nation* 264 (1997): 11–16.

Haraway, Donna J. *Modest_Witness@Second_Millennium.FemaleMan©_Meets_Onco-Mouse*™. New York: Routledge, 1997.

——— . Forward to *The Cyborg Handbook*, ed. Chris Hables Grey. New York: Routledge, 1995.

——— . "Manifesto for Cyborgs: Science, Technology, and Socialist Feminism in the 1980s." *Socialist Review* 80 (1985): 65–108.

Rainer, Yvonne. "Rainer Talking Pictures." *Art in America* (July 1997).

Toward a Feeling
for the Organism

Elizabeth Henry

It was Evelyn Fox Keller, in the 1985 work *Reflections on Gender and Science*, who most specifically introduced us to the concept of a gendered science. Although dismantling science's claims to objectivity was a philosophical move long ago introduced, Keller's unique slant on the scientific endeavor was to critique the discipline's alleged objectivity on feminist grounds. Keller's previous work on the biography of one of the world's foremost scientists, Barbara McClintock, undoubtedly offered her sustenance for her new vision of scientific inquiry. In 1983, just a few months after Keller's book on her was published, Barbara McClintock was awarded the Nobel Prize. The award was largely in response to be her paradigm-shifting work in the field of developmental biology, work that had for most of her life been ignored and avoided by the scientific community. McClintock's discovery of "transposition" as a means of genetic communication and development reconfigured geneticists' previous "central dogma" concerning the structure and function of genes. It took more than thirty years for McClintock's discoveries to be accepted, but once recognized and applied to species other than her own favored maize, McClintock's vision uprooted and replaced many of the previously ruling metaphors.

McClintock's is a vision of cells that reflects a less hierarchically ordered microuniverse that liberates DNA from its authoritarian past and puts it in a more responsive, more cooperative relationship with its cytoplasmic neighbors. In McClintock's work, DNA becomes a cell that interacts with other cells, an organism that does not stand apart from and is not indifferent to its environment, one whose very genetic development is influenced by the factors surrounding it.

The metaphysical shift in scientific paradigms that McClintock's assertion required was initially resisted by the scientific community at large. But the implications of its acceptance, as evidenced by her Nobel Prize as well as by the recent outpouring of scientific articles concerning McClintock's work, provide an impetus for a revision of our accepted modes of explanation not only in the sciences but perhaps in the humanities as well. McClintock reminds us that even at the

level of the smallest units of life, communication is two-way: the sender also re-
ceives, the observer affects the observed, the observed alters the observer, and
now, the outside environment may actually affect the previously autarkic individual. McClintock's work suggests a new, more ecological paradigm that includes, even emphasizes, the importance of relationship.

McClintock's singular scientific method also reveals conceptual differences
from that of her predecessors. Her very approach to the species focuses on interrelationship, system, and process rather than on more mechanism or dogmatism.
Where predecessors "employed the tools of biochemical assay to determine the
effects of critical genetic crosses, McClintock used the techniques more familiar
to the naturalist. . . . Where they sought a molecular mechanism, she sought a
conceptual structure, supported and made real by the coherence of its inferences
and its correlation with function" (Keller 1983, 8). McClintock introduced a new
metaphor to biology by way of her uniquely intimate method of scientific discovery. Her work embraces both the twentieth-century focus on experiment and
the earlier methods of the naturalist. The naturalist's approach "does not press
nature with leading questions, but dwells patiently in the variety and complexity
of organisms" (Keller 1983, 207). As Keller explains, "what for others is interpretation, or speculation, for [McClintock] is a matter of trained and direct perception" (xxi). McClintock's discoveries and methods might also be considered those
of an ecofeminist; the discovery of molecular relationships, the models of behavior, and especially McClintock's "feeling for the organism" that guides her own
methods of observation and exploration, offer a deeper, fuller, more ecological
view that science can take of nature.

As a writer and teacher of literature I can't help but wonder what such a trans-
ference might look like if applied to the act or theories of writing itself. Might
the parameters of what is acceptable under the term *academic* be expanded in the
humanities as they already have been in the sciences? McClintock's methodology
was rooted in a desire to understand the organism, in toto. How would such a
method, rooted in an intimacy with the natural environment, affect our perceptions of language, reality, the relationships between mind and nature? The word
understanding, says Keller, "and the particular meaning she attributed to it, is the
cornerstone of Barbara McClintock's entire approach to science. For her, the
smallest details provided the keys to the larger whole" (101). "Understanding,"
for McClintock, comes from combining the naturalist's skill with the theoreti-
cian's. McClintock's own words reveal the intensity of her relationship with the
tiny organism she studied under a microscope. "I was down there. I was part of
the system. I was right down there with [the cells of the species maize] and everything got big. I even was able to see the internal parts of the chromosomes — actually everything was there. It surprised me because I actually felt as if I were
right down there and these were my friends" (Keller 1983, 117).

Might not we all be able to suffuse our study with such intimacy and whole-ness of perception? This is not another argument for relativism of position, nor an argument for an all-encompassing ideology cum fascism, which many critics of the deep ecological or ecofeminist stance accuse ecotheorists of promoting. What if we ourselves were to assume a position more "naturalist" while consider-ing McClintock's microbiological discoveries; and what if we were embedding her metaphors into a worldview that would now include watching and listening instead of thrusting our own self-induced worldview upon others? As McClin-tock suggests, "the main thing is that you forget yourself" (Keller 1983, 117). That is, McClintock's powerful insights are the result of

> the knowing that comes from loss of self—from the state of subjective fusion with the object of knowledge. Einstein once wrote, "The state of feeling which makes one capable of such achievements is akin to that of the religious wor-shipper or of one who is in love." Scientists often pride themselves on their ca-pacities to distance subject from object, but much of their richest lore comes from the joining of one to the other, from a turning of object into subject (Keller 1983, 118).

It's a project that would enrich our academic studies in many fields, including my own.

Patricia Passes the Corn

It was several years ago when I first encountered Keller's (1983) book *A Feeling for the Organism* during a graduate nonfiction writing seminar at the University of Iowa. The university is surrounded by thousands of acres of pristine Iowa farm-land, rolling moraines and hills, low-lying marshlands, and lakes. We were sev-eral weeks into the fall quarter, most of us writers or students of literature who were somewhat aghast and befuddled by this tale of McClintock's discoveries. Few of us had encountered terms such as *anaphase* or *zygote* before, and we be-came as concerned with holding on to newly formed concepts of the "meiotic phase" as we were with learning about Keller's particular take on subjectivity, bi-ography, representation, and so on. These class sessions were not particularly pleasant, though the weather outside was dry and clear. Our frustration with the density of the biological material before us created more classroom tension than usual; egotistically fearing that we individual students might not be smart enough to comprehend the material, we began to compete with one another, and with Keller. The literature students positioned themselves as theoretically supe-rior to the naive MFAs; the writers scoffed at the lack of creativity evidenced by literature students' embracing of suffocating literary theory; the biologists felt more at ease, more grounded than the students of the arts, who saw the biologists as small-minded, myopic, and much too reserved. Meanwhile, we all kept struggling with passages concerning genetic transposition and began to resent Keller's authorial assumption that we even cared about it. Not surprisingly, we began to resent the professor of the course as well for selecting such a dry book for our hungry minds to waste time over.

In early October, a student named Patricia brought a corncob to class so that we might see an example of McClintock's species of study. When we entered the classroom that morning, a variegated rust and tawny and brown and pine-green cob of corn, wrapped in some spiny, cream-colored leaves that rustled autumn-dry at the slightest touch or breath sat consciously on the seminar table. As we took our seats around the table, Patricia passed the corn around, advising us to take a look at a sample of species McClintock spent her life with, each bead of color the doorway to microscopic agility, submolecular communication, and endeavor. The great variety and apparently random placement of colors on this single stalk were a shimmering monument, a vegetal testimony to millions of genetic transactions, transpositions, currents and crosscurrents, divisions, anaphases, meiotic activities—a semiotics of the energy and mystery of life. But the cob was also an individual—a creature with its own history, decisions, responses, its own specific lineage and unique combination of soils, its own particular angle on the sun. The corn seemed to be laughing, like a young child just pulled from a warm, cleansing bath—stimulated, slightly chilled, giggling all the while over its joie de vivre. As the cob was passed from hand to hand, the tension in that classroom lightened while all of us fell silent, relaxed and humbled by our new, intelligent visitor who—in its crackling, brilliant choreography of form—seemed to know more about living than we gripping, grasping, and desperate students of writing.

The complexity of the biological world, which we had stumbled over when it had been presented to us in clumsy human language, was illuminated again by patterns of color and shape, texture and sound that made up this unique organism we could see, touch, and listen to. Our perspectives on the textual material and ourselves were necessarily changed by the physical presence of this cob of corn. I like to think that Barbara McClintock's field of vision had become our own. A more intimate method of discovery, a naturalist's approach to the study of organisms or of ideas, had presented itself to us. We seemed not to press the subject with leading questions, but dwelt patiently with the questions so that it might have a voice and a resonance of its own. Class went very well that day. We were more comfortable together. We were more honest, "humble"—not self-effacing, but as the latter term's etymology suggests, simply "of the earth." One could label this experience of ours in a variety of ways—mystical, spiritual, emotional, romantic—all of them perhaps, postlapsarian fallacies. But before the label, there was this fact: not the representation of the corn, nor the theories of the corn, but the cob of corn itself.

Scientists now tell us that the outside environment may actually affect the not-so-autarkic individual. McClintock's science calls for relationship as not only an accepted practice but a required principle. McClintock reminds us of the necessity of bilateral communication and warns that our theories need always take the material itself into account. How might this scientific pedagogy be extended to study in the humanities? Might the organism's transpositional processes offer us a model for theorizing about nature that includes nature as well as theory? The good scientist will daily approach her material with new eyes, will work to develop "a feeling for the organism." Might we at least keep the organism in mind, if not a feeling for it? What our class learned the day Patricia passed the corn was to take the book back to the field, the concept to the physical being, to remember that the organism is predecessor to our theories about it, and that from nature there might still be more to learn.

Works Cited

Keller, Evelyn Fox. *Reflections on Gender and Science*. New Haven, CT: Yale University Press, 1985.

————. *A Feeling for the Organism: The Life and Work of Barbara McClintock*. New York: Freeman, 1983.

When the Mirror Looks Back

Nature in the Scholarship of the Humanities

→ Michael Witmore

Several years ago I began collaborating with an evolutionary biologist on a "rhetorical experiment." I did an analysis of the language used in an experiment in order to test some of the ways in which language and culture shape interpretations of empirical data. The evolutionary biologist, Banu Subramaniam (whose companion chapter appears in Section I), and I had both been exposed to cultural studies of science in graduate school, and both of us had independently developed an interest in feminist epistemologies of scientific inquiry. Those epistemologies and the political critiques that animate them were attractive to us for a variety of reasons. My interest has been in the potential these methods hold for cross-disciplinary work, in particular work that links political concerns with a fine-grained analysis of language and a respect for the material power of a practice like science.[1] The experiment, then, was a way of putting into practice something I somehow already believed. It also represented an attempt to intervene in the process of doing science rather than an attempt to produce a critique of science as a whole. While the latter seemed like an admirable undertaking to both of us, we decided to do something more "practical" because it had so rarely been done before.

The experiment itself was rather simple. We began with a scientific experiment from Banu's dissertation, one that described how evolution acts to preserve variation for flower color in morning glory populations (*Ipomoea purpurea*). I provided a textual analysis of the paper, elaborating how I thought the argument worked and detailing the implicit burdens of proof that the experimental report tried to satisfy. Here I tried to describe a group of "rhetorics" in action—linguistic choices (conscious or not) that could be linked to particular conceptual, ideological, and empirical consequences. Banu then revised the original paper to offer new interpretations, adopting a different set of "rhetorics" for the same set of data. Together we analyzed the empirical consequences of using these new versions. At the conclusion of the project, we felt we had isolated two significant rhetorical junctures in the experiment, the first an organizing metaphor of "bal-

ancing selection" around which observations and measurements had been ar-
rayed, and the other an allegory of race and multiculturalism attached to flower
color—the variable that underwent significant variation in the experiment.

We have described the consequences of these rhetorical junctures in detail
elsewhere (see Subramaniam and Witmore, forthcoming); here I want to reflect
on the experience of collaborating across the science-humanities divide, an experience that made me rethink some of the issues surrounding the "two cultures"
debate. What was most significant for me in this process of collaboration was a
certain persistent confusion I felt, and still feel, about what I was doing. What *we*
were doing was clear enough: we were trying to join the intellectual resources of
two disciplines, and would probably learn something whether or not the experiment was a "success." But what I was doing—a scholar of early modern literature and culture trained in rhetoric—was poaching in fields where I didn't
belong. Perhaps this was one of the enticements of the project. But I think this
feeling of discomfort may tell us something about the nature of the disciplinary
divisions we were trying to "cross."

Because of the way in which we had structured the collaboration, my role in
the project was very much that of an "intervener" rather than a knowledge producer. This is familiar territory to me, since as a professional critic of texts I am
used to isolating rhetorical structures and relating them to a variety of interpretive structures. So I began with the usual questions. In what way does this piece
offer evidence for its claims? How does the text's form embody broader assumptions about where knowledge comes from and how that knowledge ought to be
secured? What are the structuring metaphors of the text? Does the text offer itself
as a picture of nature as it naturally is, and if so, what are the political consequences of that vision? When scholars from the humanities ask these kinds of
questions about texts, they introduce a critical gap—that between the reader and
the writer—in order to produce their own interpretations. As long as I was reading across this gap, I felt untroubled about what I was doing.

But as the collaboration continued, I began to see how my own critical comments were snowballing into questions about how evolution works and how its
activities might be tested. This empirical transition—where evidence in the
world, not just in the text of the experimental report, was becoming necessary to
test a given interpretation—is one that I simply do not make in my own work.
Granted, historians and cultural critics will often ask how real people felt or
acted in a particular historical situation. But we do not arrange those people in a
situation we have contrived and then watch to see what happens. This crucial
difference, the way in which a scientist creates a situation by altering certain circumstances (or arranges to be present in a situation where those conditions already pertain), and then *waits for something to happen*, is something that
distinguishes scientific research from the interpretive work we do in the humani-

ties.[2] This difference is itself cause for division between the "disciplines." Those who are skeptical of the humanities, for example, usually cite this lack of active experimentation as the reason for dismissing all knowledge claims in the humanities as speculative or "unfalsifiable" in any meaningful sense.[3] We in the humanities usually reply that all human practices, including science, are structured by speculative intuitions, cultural traditions, and ideological pressures whose shaping power cannot be identified in the same ways one might search for, say, the presence of a gene for a certain flower color. The disciplinary impasse here is so well developed—by now it is a principled one—that one rarely gets to encounter it without already being on one side or another.

So when our interpretation began to slide toward the empirical in some of the ways I have just described, I began to get nervous. The scope of the collaboration was widening; nature was, at some point, going to be asked to "make something happen." Once I began thinking about how all of this worked, I realized that I was a latecomer in what was already a collaboration with *nature* in the production of knowledge claims. In her doctoral research, Banu had created a situation in which something "knowable" would follow from whatever nature (or as the rhetoric goes, "natural selection") did. What did this mean for the products of our collaboration? Some epistemological presuppositions of my own were now coming up for scrutiny.

As a scholar in the humanities, I am inclined to treat "knowledge" and the texts that transmit it as cultural artifacts, the end result of an interested producer or creator. I do not make such artifacts; instead, I try to account for how they are made, the experiences they enable, and the cultural interests they serve. But working on this project made it very difficult for me to maintain this position. It seemed to me, as we tried to understand how certain concepts and metaphorical terms were attached to the observations made in the field, that the natural world was not simply an empty reservoir of possibility that could be shaped for human ends. Granted, there were certainly human interests being expressed in the experiment itself, in its design, conclusions, and in what it took to be a reasonable piece of evidence. But there were also events that had to take place: populations had to change, variables had to deviate in statistically significant ways . . . one situation had to become another. Looking into the mirror of nature, as the phrase goes, I had expected that we would find another human face. Instead, the mirror looked back.

This is a dramatic way of describing what it was like to collaborate with a scientist, but I hope it captures what a striking experience it is to see the nature-culture divide start to dissolve when certain kinds of questions are asked. The nature-culture distinction seems to me more fundamental than the science-humanities split, and perhaps we can see the persistence of the latter as an attempt to fend off some truly bewildering questions about our own agency (or lack thereof) in the production of knowledge, whether we are scientists or scholars trained in the traditions of the humanities. I want to conclude with a series of questions that I have begun to ask myself about the differences between work in these two different "cultures," questions that relate to this fundamental problem of whether and how nature is involved in the production of knowledge. Some of these questions will seem out of place for those working in the humanities, but perhaps they will seem less so the more we begin to think of science and the humanities as working side by side instead of one before the other.

First, what would be the consequence of allowing nature a role in the production of knowledge within the humanities? Let me explain that this is a question of processes, not of objects. At one point it seemed desirable, indeed urgent, for scholars in the humanities to take nature as an object of critical analysis, a move that nature be turned into an artifact. Within the humanities, "nature" and the outcomes of "natural processes" are much more likely to be viewed as artifactual today (because to some extent they are rhetorical), although there is significant disagreement over the degree to which this is the case.[4] (One could, for instance, see the role of rhetoric in shaping knowledge claims as superficial or fundamental). But what if we begin to ask the question differently, thinking not so much about objects of knowledge as about the agents who produce it? This question will lead us to quite contentious areas of research within the sciences and humanities; for example, toward growing fields like cognitive psychology, which is seen by some as appropriating distinctive psychic territory from the humanities and making it the property of the natural sciences.[5] Similarly, in literary studies we see work being done on the cognitive limits of poetic imagery, an approach that places nature once again into the equation.[6] Do we even know how to evaluate this kind of research given how fundamentally it disturbs our disciplinary (and maybe even ontological) organizing categories?

Building on this first question, to what degree do we want to exclude, in advance, any appeals to nature in shaping either the artifacts we study in the humanities or the process by which we come to understand those artifacts? I am not talking here about admitting that the weather may have influenced an important battle or whether the childlessness of a particular monarch changed the course of history. Rather, I wonder if we in the humanities have fully articulated what counts as a legitimate object of humanistic research. Is collaborative work with the natural sciences appropriate in some instances, or are the approaches so at odds politically, culturally, and epistemologically as to be practically impossible? These are difficult questions to pose productively in the midst of our current millennial giddiness about the convergence of all forms of knowledge and experience.[7] Clearly we do not want to subsume the sciences into the humanities or the humanities into the sciences, and we may find that the most interesting work across the disciplines is that which helps us understand more precisely why and when the disciplines are incompatible. As we consider these questions, at least within the humanities, I think we will be returned to this scene in which the mirror of nature looks back. That is not to say we need to be afraid to look in the mirror; only that we should not be entirely sure that the mirror reflects only ourselves.

Notes

1. Particularly important in my case was the work of Evelyn Fox Keller, N. Katherine Hayles, and to some extent Donna Haraway.

2. I develop this conception of experimentation, albeit in a very different historical context, in *Culture of Accidents: Unexpected Knowledges in Early Modern England*, forthcoming.

3. The term *falsification* is from the work of Karl Popper (1959).

4. Recent debates in science studies, particularly those following the Sokal affair, have foregrounded the range of positions that cultural constructivists are able to occupy. A tiny sampling of these views can be found in *Lingua Franca*, July/August 1986; the debate expanded considerably in the pages of *Tikkun, Dissent, Libération,* and *Le Monde*.

5. As cognitive psychology and psychopharmacology expand, other models of psychic processes like psychoanalysis become increasingly the province of English departments.

6. Here I am thinking of the recent work on the poetic imagination by Elaine Scarry (1999).

7. E. O. Wilson's latest book, *Consilience* (1999), seems, despite its ironic-sounding title, like a symptom of this trend; in it he argues that we should finally embrace the Enlightenment project of creating one science for all experience.

Works Cited

Popper, Karl. *The Logic of Scientific Discovery*. New York: Basic Books, 1959.
Scarry, Elaine. *Dreaming by the Book*. New York: Farrar Strauss and Giroux, 1999.
Subramaniam, B., and M. Witmore. "Cross-Pollinations: Tropes and Consequences in Scientific Writing." In *(Re)Visions: Feminist and Gender Theory at the Turn of the Century*, ed. Gail Currie and Celia Rothenberg, forthcoming.
Wilson, E. O. *Consilience: The Unity of Kowledge*. New York: Random House, 1999.
Witmore, Michael. *Culture of Accidents: Unexpected Knowledges in Early Modern England*. Stanford, CA: Stanford University Press, forthcoming.

Contesting Territories

Female-Female Aggression and the Song Sparrow

⟶ Michelle Elekonich

One contribution of the feminist critiques of science is to require scientists to examine the assumptions that underlie their hypotheses, especially those assumptions that are based on gender ideology and culturally mediated sex roles. Scientists attribute experimenter bias to the collection and interpretation of data determined by the lens of a predetermined hypothesis. However, scientists seldom think of experimenter bias as also resulting from underlying assumptions related to a scientist's personal identity or viewpoint (Sheldrake 1998).

Science is assessed both in terms of its long-term contribution to knowledge, as well as its concordance with current viewpoints about what constitutes "good" and "interesting" science; that is, according to the "current model of reality" (Fausto-Sterling 1992). Steeped in the socially sanctioned viewpoint/model of reality, it is often difficult in practice to clearly see one's biases, let alone assumptions arising out of personal identity and viewpoints. Some feminist scholars would argue that only when one can access viewpoints outside the dominant "model of reality" can one hope to see the role of one's biases with foresight when planning and interpreting experiments (see Harding 1986, 1991). Part of a scientist's current model of reality stems from the viewpoint of previous scientists in his or her field of study. Examining the assumptions underlying previous researchers' hypotheses may expose the biases inherent in their current model of reality, often left unquestioned, thus inherited by current researchers. My own research concerns female-female aggression in song sparrows.

The hormonal control of male song sparrow territorial aggression was already well studied by the time I began to consider females' aggressive behavior (see Wingfield 1984a, 1984b, 1985). Subsequent work with resident populations in Washington State found that males are aggressive throughout the year, but that testosterone levels and aggression are correlated only during the prebreeding and breeding seasons—spring and summer (Wingfield and Hahn 1994). In fall and winter, males can be aggressive with low basal levels of testosterone, and aggressive interactions do not increase circulating levels of androgens.

The common view in the literature was that the hormonal control of the females' behavior ought to be like the males. As Arcese and his colleagues (1988,

96) state, "Androgen levels may increase in females involved in prolonged conflicts as has been demonstrated in wild male song sparrows." This expectation was due in part to the similarity of the vocalizations and postures male and female song sparrows use during aggressive interactions, but also possibly due to an unconscious bias toward defining the male birds' conditions as "normal" (Lawton et al. 1997; Riger 1992). For example, in many north temperate species of songbirds, females seldom sing, yet song is considered a primary measure of aggression, along with other male-typical behaviors like long flights over the intruder (see Wingfield 1985). Although many scientists thought that the question had been answered for all song sparrows with the data on males, the seasonality and hormonal control of female-female aggression had been unstudied. Furthermore, Wingfield's (1984a, 1984b) data on the seasonal changes in testosterone suggested that females never had the high levels of testosterone exhibited by males.

In spite of the literature and discussions with Arcese and Wingfield suggesting that females should be like males, several biological factors led me to expect the female song sparrows to be different. First, females do all of the nest-building and incubation, leaving less time in the breeding season to be territorial. Second, high levels of testosterone inhibit parental behavior (Hegner and Wingfield 1987; Searcy 1988). Therefore, high testosterone levels to support aggression might interfere with female reproduction. Third, song sparrows are sometimes polygynous, so females might have an interest in keeping other females out. Finally, although Margaret Morse Nice (1937, 1943) suggested that males define the territory boundaries that females follow, other researchers including myself (Arcese 1989a, 1989b; Elekonich 1997, 2000) believe that females pursue their own interests and territory boundaries.

But, as I later realized, I also expected them to be different simply because they were *females*. As I began contemplating the politics of male-female models, I was reminded of my own experiences as a woman from my Swiss-German, Ukrainian-Czechoslovakian immigrant working-class family. At family gatherings there were different rules for men and women that often revolved around food, children, and entertaining. If as a biologist I believe that all phenotypes, including behavior, are the outcome of genetic and environmental influences, should that not hold true for both myself and the song sparrows? However, as a feminist, I would assert that the sociocultural environment influences more of my behavior than the female song sparrows'.

Considering these different viewpoints/models of reality led to two alternate hypotheses about female song sparrow territorial aggression. The first—from the research history in biology and animal behavior—led to the hypothesis that female-female aggression is similar to male-male territorial aggression in seasonal and social context and hormonal control. The second—from the interaction between my scientific identity and encultured gender identity—led to the hypothesis that female-female aggression will be different from male-male aggression in its seasonal expression, social context, or hormonal control, or some combination of these. My focus on sex differences limited the hypotheses to two, but one could suggest others. For example, a female's response to intrusion might be due to prior experience with intrusions (a possibility I controlled for but did not test).

Methods

In order to test these hypotheses, I carefully set up the experiment to be similar to experiments on males, including using similar dependent variables (see Wingfield 1985) to give the hypothesis that females are like males every opportunity to be tested. However, I measured all female behaviors, not just aggression, and looked at female responses to a nonsparrow intruder to investigate the factors in the context of an intrusion that was important to females; that is, to try to identify a female song sparrow "standpoint" (Harding 1991). Because I expected that females could be different from males I not only measured the androgens (testosterone and dihydrotestosterone) known to be involved in male-male aggression, but also measured estradiol, progesterone, and corticosterone.

In the experiment, female song sparrows experienced one of three stimuli, either a simulated female song sparrow intrusion and blood sampling for hormone analysis, or a simulated spotted towhee intrusion (behavioral control), or blood sampling alone (hormone control). Presentations and netting occurred in the mornings during three parts of the song sparrows' reproductive cycle: prebreeding (early spring), breeding (late spring–summer), postmolt (fall). During a simulated intrusion I placed a small Sony speaker emitting a full range of taped female song sparrow vocalizations and a live caged decoy next to a mist net. For the towhee controls, I presented only a stuffed towhee and speaker broadcasting towhee songs and calls. During the prebreeding and postmolt period the speaker/decoy stimuli were placed in the center of the territory as previous researchers testing males had done (see Wingfield 1985). But during the breeding season, the stimulus was placed 10 to 15 meters from the nest toward the center of the territory, because the nest is the center of female activity at that time. I chose not to put the stimulus at the nest to ensure that the female was responding to the presence of a female on the territory rather than the presence of an intruder at her nest. Simulated female song sparrow intrusions and towhee presentations occurred for 30 minutes, or until the female was netted. This was substantially longer than typical 5- to 10-minute stimulus presentations to males (see Wingfield 1985), but I wanted to look at typical female response, and females were slower to respond during pilot tests (see Elekonich 2000 for a more detailed discussion of the study's methodology).

Results and Discussion

Principal components analysis of the behavioral data suggested that female song sparrows responded to conspecific intruders in one of three ways. Females either responded aggressively, signaled their mates, or did not respond to the intruder and instead turned to foraging or caring for the young. Female song sparrows showed more behaviors directed toward the intruder, including aggressive growls and wing wave threat displays in the prebreeding season than in the breeding season or fall. Females were also significantly more aggressive toward simulated female song sparrow intrusion than simulated towhee intrusion (see figure 1). The

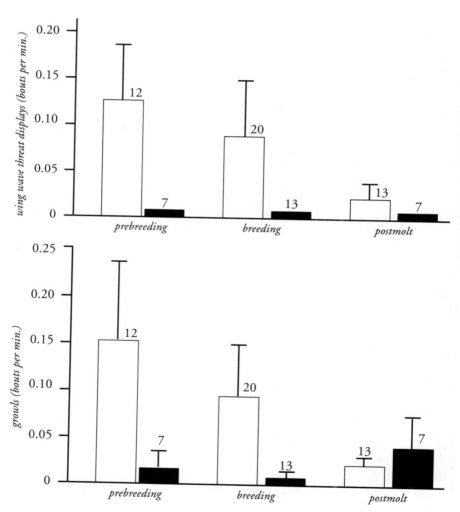

Figure 1:   Wing wave threat displays and growls by female song sparrows in response to simulated female song sparrow and spotted towhee intrusions. Light bars are simulated song sparrow intrusions, dark bars are towhee intrusions. Data are means and standard errors, numbers on top of bars indicate sample size.

chance of a female choosing to not respond, or to signal her mate, did not differ between the two types of intrusion or across the seasons.

Circulating levels of androgens (testosterone and dihydrotestosterone) were significantly lower in individuals experiencing a simulated song sparrow intrusion than in passively netted controls (see figure 2). This is exactly opposite to the data on males (see Wingfield 1985) and came as quite a surprise. Estradiol,

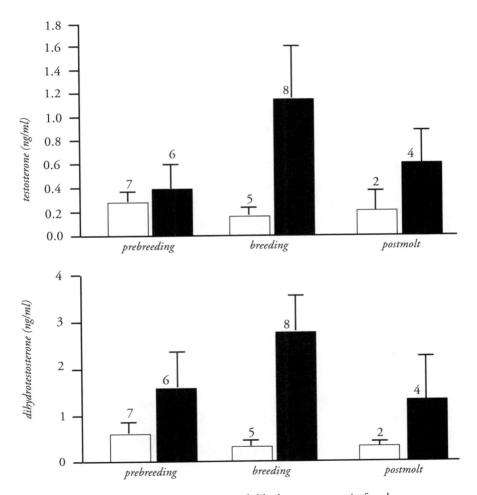

Figure 2: Circulating levels of testosterone and dihydrotestosterone in female song sparrows following simulated female song sparrow intrusion and in passively netted controls. Light bars are simulated intrusions, dark bars are controls. Data are means and standard errors, numbers on top of bars indicate sample size.

progesterone, and corticosterone levels did not differ significantly between the females experiencing intrusions and those that were passively netted. Corticosterone
levels were significantly higher in the fall than in the breeding or prebreeding
seasons.

Like males, females respond aggressively in this context throughout the year,
but unlike males their response peaks in the spring. Like males there is a role for
androgens (testosterone and dihydrotestosterone) in aggressive behavior, but androgens do not facilitate aggression. Although female song sparrows will still respond to simulated intrusion throughout the year, females appear to be more
focused on feeding and reproduction after the prebreeding season. If I had measured only typical aggressive behaviors like the studies of males, I would not have
seen the relative importance of nonaggressive and courtship behaviors indicated
by the principal components analysis. Many of the vocalizations have context-
dependent uses and measuring only aggressive behaviors would have obscured
that level of information, providing an incomplete picture of female response
(see Elekonich 2000, and Elekonich and Wingfield, forthcoming, for a more detailed discussion of the study's findings).

Conclusion

Historically there has been a large gender bias in constructing scientific discourse
about avian behavior (Lawton et al. 1997). Discussing Charles Darwin's expectations of males and females, Meredith Small (1992) points out that during his
time there was little scientific data on female behavior, and it was likely that Darwin's expectations were drawn from his observations of the upper-class Victorian
ladies around him. With the advent of the sociobiological synthesis in the 1970s,
animal behaviorists started to look at life history strategies, kin selection, and recip-
rocal altruism, all of which required carefully following marked individuals—including females. Trivers's (1972) paper on parental investment suggested that
females chose mates based on their own reproductive interests to most effectively
produce the best-quality offspring with as little cost as possible. Thus, in one
sense sociobiology "liberated" female animals. This change, at least in part, was
culturally mediated. As Small (1992) writes, "The passive role for females is replaced by a new sexual assertiveness. And females gained a further dimension
from Trivers: females are selected to address their own reproductive requirements
. . . this change in perspective . . . was socially timely and it would be naive to ignore the influence of social trends on acceptance of the theory" (148). However,
many studies of female aggression during mate choice simply used females as a
biological assay to study male traits or considered females only as resources for
males (Hrdy 1986), reproducing the conflicting messages about female sexuality
so prevalent at the time.

Added to this scientific background was a rich cultural legacy from feminist biologists who were already doing science from a female standpoint. For example, Martha McClintock's work on rat sexual behavior suggested that female proceptivity and pacing of the interaction were important to its outcome (see McClintock and Adler 1978). Sarah Hrdy (1981, 1986) explicitly pointed out the gender biases inherent in primatology and demonstrated the value of considering the world from "a female's point of view." Patricia Gowaty, working on extra pair copulations and intraspecific egg dumping (where one female lays her egg in another female's nest), revolutionized our thinking about female birds and avian monogamy by focusing on the female's interests rather than the male's "cuckholdry" (see Gowaty and Wagner 1988; Gowaty 1994). These scientists gave me concrete examples of feminists doing science and of the actualization of Small's "active female" (1992, 148).

As these studies suggest, the inclusion of "female perspectives" may provide a more complete view of the biological world. In this case, the idea that a female sparrow has her own definition of the territory's boundaries and her own priorities relative to her reproductive interests led to a more complex picture of the behavioral biology and physiology of these birds. My experiment shows how expanding our hypotheses can expand our knowledge about the natural world. This experiment expanded my hypotheses by "one," by adding one more treatment. It also added information about songbirds that the field did not know before. However, I have considered only one other option—many more are possible. The standpoints in the world are numerous and are limited only by our imagination in creating alternative hypotheses. Historically, animal behaviorists have described their findings on animal behavior as "objective." Feminist scholars have identified some of these studies as "male-centered" descriptions of the world, and feminist scientists have started to make visible female animals and to illuminate how their addition to scientific studies shifts how we understand animal behaviors and populations.

Acknowledgment: I would like to thank Angela Ginorio for comments on an early version of the manuscript and for instigating this essay when she asked me what it meant for me to be a scientist and a feminist.

Works Cited

Arcese, P. "Intrasexual Competition and the Mating System in Primarily Monogamous Birds: The Case of the Song Sparrow."*Animal Behavior* 38 (1989a): 96–111.

———. "Intrasexual Competition, Mating System, and Natal Dispersal in Song Sparrows." *Animal Behavior* 38 (1989b): 958–979.

Arcese, P., P. K. Stoddard, and S. M. Hiebert. "The Form and Function of Song in Female Song Sparrows." *Condor* 90 (1988): 44–50.

Elekonich, M. M. "Female Song Sparrow (*Melospiza melodia*) Response to Simulated Conspecific and Heterospecific Intrusion across Three Seasons." *Animal Behaviour* 59 (2000): 551–557.

———. "Female-Female Territorial Aggression and Its Hormonal Control in the Song Sparrow." *Dissertation Abstracts International* (1997): 58–08B, 4512.

Elekonich, M., and J. C. Wingfield. "Seasonality and Hormonal Control of Territorial Aggression in Female Song Sparrows." *Ethology*, forthcoming.

Fausto-Sterling, A. *Myths of Gender.* New York: Basic Books, 1992.

Gowaty, P. A. "Architects of Sperm Competition." *Trends in Ecological Evolution* 9 (1994): 160–161.

Gowaty, P. A., and S. J. Wagner. "Breeding Season Aggression of Female and Male Eastern Bluebirds (*Sialia Sialis*) to Models of Potential Conspecific and Interspecific Egg Dumpers." *Ethology* 78 (1988): 238–250.

Harding, S. *Whose Science? Whose Knowledge?* Ithaca, NY: Cornell University Press, 1991.

———. *The Science Question in Feminism.* Ithaca, NY: Cornell University Press, 1986.

Hegner, R. E., and J. C. Wingfield. "Effects of Experimental Manipulation of Testosterone Levels on Parental Investment and Breeding Success in Male House Sparrows." *Auk* 104 (1987): 462–469.

Hrdy, S. B. "Empathy, Polyandry, and the Myth of the Coy Female." In *Feminist Approaches to Science*, ed. Ruth Bleir. New York: Pergamon Press, 1986.

———. *The Woman that Never Evolved.* Cambridge, MA: Harvard University Press, 1981.

Hrdy, S. B., and G. C. Williams. "Behavioral Biology and the Double Standard." In *Social Behavior of Female Vertebrates*, ed. S. K. Wasser. New York: Academic Press, 1983.

Lawton M. F., W. R. Garstka, and J. C. Hanks. "The Mask of Theory and the Face of Nature." In *Feminism and Evolutionary Biology: Boundaries, Intersections, and Frontiers*, ed. P. A. Gowaty. New York: Chapman and Hall, 1997.

McClintock, M. K., and N. T. Adler. "The Role of the Female during Copulation in Wild and Domestic Norway Rats (*Rattus norvegicus*)." *Behaviour* 67 (1978): 67–96.

Nice, M. M. *Studies in the Life History of the Song Sparrow, II. The Behavior of the Song Sparrow and Other Passerines.* New York: Dover, 1943.

———. *Studies in the Life History of the Song Sparrow, I: A Population Study of the Song Sparrow and Other Passerines.* New York: Dover, 1937.

Riger, S. "Epistemological Debates, Feminist Voices." *American Psychology* 47 (1992): 730–740.

Searcy, W. A. "Do Female Red-Winged Blackbirds Limit Their Own Breeding Densities?" *Ecology* 69 (1988): 85–95.

Sheldrake, R. "Could Experimenter Effects Occur in the Physical and Biological Sciences?" *Skeptical Inquirer* 22 (1998): 57–58.

Small, M. F. "Female Choice in Mating." *American Scientist* 80 (1992): 142–151.

Trivers, R. L. "Parental Investment and Sexual Selection." In *Sexual Selection and the Descent of Man*, ed. B. Campbell. Chicago: Aldine, 1972.

Wingfield, J. C. "Short-Term Changes in Plasma Levels of Hormones during Establishment and Defense of a Breeding Territory in Male Song Sparrows, *Melospiza melodia.*" *Hormones and Behavior* 19 (1985): 174–187.

———— . "Environmental and Endocrine Control of Reproduction in the Song Sparrow, *Melospiza melodia,* I: Temporal Organization of the Breeding Cycle." *General Comparative Endocrinology* 56 (1984a): 406–416.

———— . "Environmental and Endocrine Control of Reproduction in the Song Sparrow, *Melospiza melodia,* II. Agonistic Interactions as Environmental Information Stimulating Secretion of Testosterone." *General and Comparative Endocrinology* 56 (1984b): 417–424.

Wingfield, J. C., and T. P. Hahn. "Testosterone and Territorial Behaviour in Sedentary and Migratory Sparrows. *Animal Behavior* 47 (1994): 77–89.

Sexy Science

What's Love Got to Do with It?

C. Phoebe Lostroh

As topics rise to ascendancy in molecular biology, scientists call them "sexy." We use this adjective to describe investigations that are particularly popular and confer status, power, and pleasure upon the researchers with special access to that research. Some nonscientists are shocked to hear that scientists think anything is sexy at all, but feminists are not surprised by sexy science because they are acutely aware of the power in designating any entity "sexy." My purpose here is to reveal the context in which sexy science is practiced, and to provide examples taken from one contemporary sexy science (signal transduction) to talk about "master molecules" as primary hallmarks of sexy science. I then give some reasons why molecular biologists and feminists should each have concerns about sexy science, and close by drawing on my personal experience as a scientist and a feminist to provide examples of ways sexy science might be resisted.

I became interested in sexy science as a graduate student at Harvard Medical School. My classmates and I learned that it was crucial that we discover what science is sexy because our careers depend on publications in the sexiest journals (for example, *Cell*, *Science*, and *Nature*). The message was clear: find an "old boy" with space in his lab, find out what sexy science turns him on, and then devote every frenzied hour possible to penetrating its mysteries. (I use "old boys" in this chapter to designate people—male or female, old or young—who hold the majority of power in molecular biology. "Old boys" of any gender and age do not challenge the status quo but instead promote its "natural" meritocracy.) The subtext of this message is that we must adopt the values of sexy science or forfeit world-class research careers (and the potential to become "old boys" ourselves). Most of us have no reason to question these values: over 80 percent of the graduate students in my program are American-born, 73 percent are white, and most of the minorities are Asians from the United States or China. Although half (thirty-seven) of us are women, only two identify as feminists and only one is not heterosexual. Just like our professors, we reflect the United States power elite—

106

rather than its general population—and we are used to having our desires (sexual and otherwise) universalized.

In this atmosphere, challenging the notion of sexy science (either socially or scientifically) is unthinkable.[1] To critique sexy science puts scientists' personal livelihoods at stake; such criticism threatens the peculiar notion that scientific truths are the most factual truths that humans can divine. Moreover, scientists are heavily invested in the production and reproduction of sexy science; maintaining their status requires not only the mystique of sexy science but also that Harvard remain among its major producers. Molecular biology at HMS, like the science published in *Cell*, is sexy science.

One common sexy science at HMS is signal transduction. Signal transduction is "a large body of knowledge about the biochemical mechanisms that regulate cellular physiology" (Ray 1999). Signal transduction biologists use genetic and biochemical methods to study changes in how proteins interact with each other. The field's basic premise is that a change in a single protein results in a change in several others, which then modify even more proteins, thus snowballing (transducing) the effect of the original single change (the "signal").[2] Signal transduction biologists then correlate these changes with macrobiological phenomena.

A recent issue of *Science* (1999) dedicated to reviews in signal transduction highlights the sexiness of the field. This issue includes signal transduction reviews in four very sexy systems: hormones, sensory detection, morphogenesis, and directional growth. While the phallic subtext of these four topics (testosterone coursing through veins, arousal in response to sight or touch) is possible to overlook, it is impossible to ignore the sexy cover art (see figure 1). The cover portrays the athletic physique of a nude dancing woman (ever-so-tastefully depicted from the rear, of course). She is superimposed on a biological clock and accompanied by an oversized fly, a mouse, and a patch of grassy plants. Although the fly, mouse, and woman are mutually oblivious, one single tall plant yearns for the dancer so much that it stretches toward her, apparently surpassing the love of (mice and) men. This cover suggests that when some scientists say that a field is sexy, they mean erotically sexy—not "interesting" or "fascinating" or even "of fundamental importance"—but literally sexy. Furthermore, the object of our desires is a "sexy" woman.

Unlike the casual slang scientists use to talk to each other, written scientific language is notoriously passive and disembodied. Discerning the actual sexiness of the written reviews is more challenging. Through extensive required reading in signal transduction during my graduate training, I learned that master molecules were sexy. Master molecules dominate other molecules, usually in heroic pursuit of a laudable biological goal. Thus, when molecular biologists' written results state that the master molecule is controlling, directing, or otherwise determining the activity of other molecules, our supposedly detached language is actually

Figure 1

sexually coded. Scientists thus endow molecules with anthropomorphized masculine traits.

The morphogenesis review paper (in the issue of *Science* with the sexy cover) on
the signal protein Notch is a good example of such professional writing in this sexy
field (see Artavanis-Tsakonas et al. 1999). Throughout, the authors use the textual
conventions described above to interpret data in ways that establish Notch as a
master molecule. For example, they describe how Notch "controls an extraordinarily broad spectrum of cell fates and developmental processes," such as fruit fly wing
and eye formation (773). They observe that it is critical in embryonic development
not merely in fruit flies, but also in such evolutionarily divergent organisms as sea
urchins and humans. Notch controls these diverse situations, the authors explain,
by determining the molecular activities of scores of other proteins. The fact that

Notch is dominant at a molecular level (and thus particularly fundamental) further enhances its status. To paraphrase the authors in less coded language, Notch is a master molecule because it promiscuously dominates numerous other molecules in myriad exotic locales. Notch biology is thus indisputably sexy.

The authors' case for Notch being a master molecule is not entirely airtight, as the authors acknowledge when they bring up several troublesome points that could threaten its status. For example, they are unsettled that "it may, perhaps, be more useful to view Notch signaling from the perspective of a 'network' rather than a linear 'pathway'" (771).[3] Similarly, they grudgingly confess that some of Notch's activities are context-dependent, thus hinting that the master may respond as well as demand. They also lament that "how Notch signaling modulates nuclear processes has been one of the most challenging problems of Notch biology" (774). An inability to connect Notch to gene expression (and thus to the patriarch of all master molecules, DNA) is worrisome, not because the problem has not been adequately researched by many fine laboratories (as they fully admit it has), but because the lack of such a connection is unthinkable (772). Control of differential gene expression is the sine qua non of central developmental molecules, so Notch simply must influence gene expression by directly contacting DNA or it is not *by definition* a developmental master.

Of course, the authors must counter any claims that might threaten Notch's status as a master molecule. For example, although they discuss numerous molecules that modulate Notch's activity, the central portrayal of heroic Notch itself relegates these molecules to the role of support staff. This textual convention further implies that Notch doesn't just respond to its modulators, it integrates the information they provide and then acts decisively. Additionally, throughout the review the authors universalize Notch's molecular activities, by uniformly describing both the mechanism and the extent to which Notch influences other proteins, as though Notch's effects were independent of the specific interacting protein(s). To more directly refute claims that Notch's activity is context-dependent, the authors even go so far as to dismiss one model for how another molecule might lessen Notch's activity as "a simplification," a deadly insult in science because it dismisses a competitor's work as not only wrong, but beneath notice (774).

The structure of the review itself also emphasizes Notch's master status by discussing its individual interactions in a linear narrative progression, passively implying that each interaction happens progressively, and in isolation. The authors also emphasize unidirectional chains of command in their figures, thus distracting the reader from data that detract from such simplistic models. The very fact that the review was written about Notch itself (as opposed to the development of any structures affected by Notch) places this single molecule at a position of greater importance than the macrobiological events it is purported to control. Collectively, all of these implicit and explicit techniques vanquish any facts that could neutralize Notch's master status; the authors have thus ensured not only the status of their molecule, but their own master status.

Although a few of my scientific peers are willing to concede that sexy science is possibly a sign of sexism in society at large, most of them don't care unless I answer the following questions: What does it have to do with biology itself? Master molecules *are* the important ones to know about, so how can calling a molecule "master" impede progress? Does sexy science hurt biology?

To explain how I believe sexy science hurts biology, I must begin with a confession: I do not believe that sexy science retards scientific progress. In fact, the elite scientists who produce sexy science push molecular biology to perform at its very limits. Rather, what bothers me is the very trope of the "master molecule." We look for master molecules, and then we universalize the molecules we find. We do not examine our intellectual investment in finding such molecules but instead naturalize our findings with the "fact" that biology is fundamentally about master molecules. Sexy science isn't bad molecular biology; it is instead hypermolecular molecular biology, master molecule masturbation carried to the extreme.

I do not object to molecular biologists' doing their job thoroughly. Rather, I object to the way the rewards and assumptions of sexy science encourage scientists to conflate understanding a molecular interaction with understanding a biological phenomenon. The most reasonable logical extension of sexy science is believing that although understanding a single molecular interaction may not be coterminus with understanding a biological phenomenon, understanding every single molecular reaction that could occur would indeed explain macro-phenomena. Sexy science thus defines molecular frontiers as the Frontier and then conveniently provides the methods by which such frontiers can be civilized. Every known molecular interaction then tames the cellular wilderness one step further.

Such intellectual expansion is deeply satisfying to those of us trained to pursue progress; the intensity of feeling (Eureka!) cannot be overstated to nonscientists. Eureka! is the scientific equivalent of an orgasm. Our big "Oh!" after a sexy science score brings not only this psychological positive feedback but also numerous professional rewards that are required for success. Sexy science is difficult to resist on many levels.

Resisting Master Molecules

Once a field is deemed sexy, it attracts connections from other fields. Such is certainly true of my own field, bacterial pathogenesis. Although in days of biological yore microbiology was at the forefront of sexy science, when I entered graduate school, bacterial genetics had an air of fustiness akin to that of ancient library stacks. We microbial geneticists are proud of just how much information can be learned with little more than a Bunsen burner and sterile toothpicks.[4]

My coworkers and I study how *Salmonella enterica* senses its environment and then, once in a mouse's intestines, breaches the intestinal epithelium and causes systemic disease. We call breaching the intestinal epithelium "invasion." We are *molecular* microbiologists, and we mostly study the genes (and gene products: proteins) that are involved in invasion. My work is focused on understanding how one single protein, HilA, turns on many of the genes *Salmonella* needs for invasion. A central hypothesis in the lab is that HilA somehow integrates all of the cues from the environment and that the production and/or activation of HilA irreversibly commits the bacterium to expressing invasion genes (see Lucas et al. 2000; see also Lostroh et al., forthcoming).

Unfortunately, this hypothesis makes HilA sound a lot like a master molecule. Even the word for the process HilA is purported to control, "invasion," suggests a military hierarchical mode of operation.[5] I could easily use typical master molecule models to report my work on HilA. Instead, I try to be true to the data and represent the complexity of HilA by choosing proactive resistance to master molecule thinking.

For example, when I present my work, I emphasize the complexity of the system and the unknowns in my work right from the start. Figure 2 is an example of a cartoon I use to introduce my work. Unlike a figure characterizing HilA as a master molecule (figure 3), this cartoon suggests that HilA's role is central but not masterful. Figure 2 uses symbols to show that other molecules have influence over its activity at many levels. Placing question marks on the picture gives me an opportunity to mention the aspects of invasion gene regulation that we still don't understand, as well as a chance to talk about what other people in my lab research, thus placing HilA (and myself) in a relational context. Figure 3, in contrast, emphasizes HilA's centrality to the exclusion of other molecules. It is the only possible focal point in the figure, reinforcing its master status.

Even though I try to give myself visual tools that place HilA in a relational context, I am often tempted to universalize HilA's activity in the name of simplicity. As I have already mentioned in discussing the Notch review, I know that universalization is more about enhancing a master molecule's power than about communicating its properties clearly and concisely. It seems so easy to simply say, "HilA activates gene expression when it binds to an HilA Box," instead of saying, "HilA activates the *invF* and *prgH* promoters when it binds to the HilA Box, a symmetrical sequence centered around -47 relative to the start of transcription in both cases." Although the distinction between these two statements may seem trivial in isolation, the accrual of statements like the first one inevitably enhances master molecule status. Another way I try to avoid universalization is to use the actual numbers that quantify HilA's effects. This strategy allows me to generalize because I can talk about the fact that the magnitude of the response is similar in both cases, but it keeps me from universalizing because, in fact, the particulars of each circumstance are not identical.

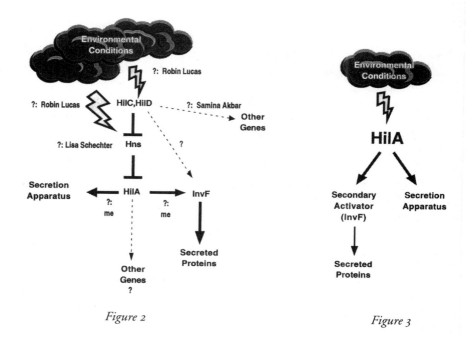

Figure 2   Figure 3

These are just a few examples of how I try to make my work participate less in sexy science. I am fortunate that my laboratory in general, although it participates in bacterial signal transduction, questions the scientific prowess of master molecules and questions many of the premises of sexy science. For example, recent experiments have shown that at least two of the genes listed in my cartoon, *hilC* and *hilD*, are also important molecules in the invasion gene cascade that apparently influence the transcription of many genes even in the absence of *hilA*. Just as the Notch review authors' status is connected to the status of Notch itself, our status is connected to that of HilA. It is the molecule that brought us into the upper tier of pathogenesis research. The idea that there are not one, but two proteins that can affect invasion gene expression in the absence of HilA could, therefore, be profoundly threatening.

Many sexy science–driven researchers in this circumstance would do everything in their power to discredit any work that removes the master from his position of supremacy, typically by discrediting "anti-master" work as either poorly done and therefore uninterpretable or as biologically irrelevant and therefore a waste of scientific energy. I am proud that my lab head's reaction to competitor labs' work (as well as our own) showing that *hilC* and *hilD* can do important things in the absence of *hilA* has not been dismissive. Instead of directing us away from experiments that dislodge *hilA*, she has directed us to wrestle with what such data mean. She has encouraged us to undertake experiments that confirm and then expand on our competitors' data and thus allow us to tell a more complete story about invasion gene expression than we could tell with a temptingly elegant unidirectional *hilA*-centric chain of command.

My lab head has a longstanding commitment to traditional bacterial genetics and to lifelong learning from collaborators and competitors alike, so our lab is predisposed toward seeing *hilA* as a molecule that functions in context and in cooperation. However, it is tempting to play our molecules up as masters in order to try to get publication in hot journals; to argue that our interpretations are likely to lead to better understandings of invasion biology than other interpretations. As a visiting speaker (and scientific "hero") once regaled the graduate students over a department-sponsored lunch, the key to a successful career is to find a sexy project early on and pursue it relentlessly until tenure and respectability are achieved. Then (and only then) can a scientist take the luxury of studying less sexy stuff or of pursuing any science using fewer of the sexy science conventions. Clearly there is a lot at stake with sexiness.

Sexy science is also steeped in the market because it requires new technologies, like gene chips, that can be mass-produced and then advertised (in the sexiest journals, of course) so that even the scientists who will never be among the pioneers in sexy science will nevertheless produce and reproduce it. In order to sell sexy science, the "old boys' network" and, by extension, their graduate students, are profoundly entwined in the network of biotech businesses that create and market new products (as well as the behemoth pharmaceutical companies that could not develop their products without the benefit of university-associated, publicly funded "basic research"). For example, "old boy" labs train the people most likely to develop patentable materials and methods. "Old boys" commonly found biotech companies that serve the basic research and biopharmaceuticals markets, and they are consultants who suggest where science will go next. Moreover, they are the people who allocate funds to buy millions of dollars' worth of product from one company instead of another, and they are leaders among the peer-review boards that decide which scientists get public money to spend in the first place. It is thus completely ridiculous to believe, as many scientists want to, that sexy science is the result of pure intellectual meritocracy. It is very much the brainchild of a narrow set of people and it is at least as much industry as scholarship.

Molecular biology's connection to hierarchical oppression at so many levels is profoundly discouraging, but I can't withdraw from a field for which I have talent, skill, and a love that predates adulthood. I believe that if more feminists practiced molecular biology and applied feminist values to the science itself as well as to the ways that we conduct the interpersonal business that goes along with being a scientist, science itself would be better. Unfortunately, we cannot know what would have happened if any twentieth-century science had been led by feminists, but if there are a few cracks in radical arguments that equate science with patriarchy, more feminist participation in twenty-first-century science could change the equation. That's a chance I have to take.

Acknowledgments: Thanks to Jen Christensen for alerting me to this writing opportunity and to Amanda Udis-Kessler for her steadfast encouragement.

Notes

1. I believe that the molecular biologists most likely to recognize sexy science as problematic are, first, marginalized for one reason or another, and second, do not wish to become fully integrated into the upper-middle-class straight white masculinist culture of science.

2. The changes are usually the addition or removal of phosphoryl groups from a protein. This chemical modification allows the protein to associate with and modify other proteins (usually by changing their phosphorylation states in turn).

3. The authors are aware that linearity and direct submission to the master make the master sexy; as the World Wide Web's popularity rises and is subsequently masculinized, I predict that signal transduction will turn to weblike models to maintain its sexy status.

4. Microbiologists interested in sexy science, of which there are many, are of course working hard to rescue microbiology from the backwaters, for example through pioneering technologies in genomics and, unsurprisingly, through finding pathogenic microorganisms that interact with animal or plant signal transduction molecules.

5. I have tried to think of *Salmonella* pathogenesis as a failed relationship optimal for neither the host nor the bacterium instead of the outcome of microbial aggression, but thus far I have been successful only at reducing the number of times I use words like "pathogenesis" or "invasion" to describe a particular phenomenon.

Works Cited

Artavanies-Tsakonas, Spyros, et al. "Notch Signaling: Cell Fate Control and Signal Integration in Development." *Science* 284 (1999): 770–776.

Lostroh, C. P., V. Bajaj, and C. A. Lee. "The Cis Requirements for Transcriptional Activation by *hilA*, a Virulence Determinant Encoded on SPI-1." *Molecular Microbiology,* forthcoming.

Lucas, R. L., C. P. Lostroh, C. C. DiRusso, M. P. Spector, B. L. Wanner, and C. A. Lee. "Multiple Factors Independently Regulate *hilA* and Invasion Gene Expression in *Salmonella enterica serovar* Typhimurium." *Journal of Bacteriology* 182 (April 2000).

Ray, L. B. "The Science of Signal Transduction." *Science* 284 (1999): 775.

Science 284 (1999): 701–864. Issue on Signal Transduction.

Unequal Partners

Rethinking Gender Roles in Animal Behavior

$\longrightarrow$ J. Kasi Jackson

> The classical story of stickleback courtship, brightly colored males vying for the attention of cryptic but choosy females, has strong parallels with heraldic competitions in medieval England. During these competitions, burnished knights arrayed in their lady's preferred colors would joust for the love of said lady, while the modestly clad object of the ritualized contest remained in the background.
>
> —*Deborah A. McLennan*

> It is theory which decides what we can observe.
>
> —*Albert Einstein to Werner Karl Heisenberg, 1926*

McLennan's critique of "the classical story of stickleback courtship" illustrates how gender role expectations have shaped animal behavior research. Feminist animal behaviorists are now developing analyses of how theories of animal behavior have been shaped and constructed by cultural assumptions about sex and gender. I am currently finishing a Ph.D. dissertation on coloration in fish and a graduate certificate in women's studies. My attempts to bring together my feminism and academic research has been difficult, and I find that my graduate work often recreates the very gender-based dichotomies that I want to resist. In this chapter, however, I want to use my graduate research experiences to explore the "gendered" conceptions that infuse my scientific work and consider how feminist approaches to scientific research can be used to challenge these conceptions.

Early in my graduate school years, I began to see how the field of animal behavior (historically dominated by male researchers) had produced male-centered theories of animal behavior and failed to consider female evolution. For instance, studies of sexual selection—which examine the evolution of traits used to acquire mates—have focused primarily on male traits and predicted that male reproduction is limited by mate number, whereas female reproduction is limited by fecundity. Therefore, it is predicted that males will display ornaments, sometimes bright and elaborate, to attract more mates, whereas females will not (Andersson 1994). It is interesting to note that theories of sexual selection originated in Victorian England, where the dominant sexual ideology was one of eager males and sexually disinterested, passive females (Russett 1989).

In hopes of challenging these culturally based gender dichotomies in animal behavior studies, I began to read feminist scientific accounts that theorized active and sexual females (Gowaty 1997; Hrdy 1981, 1986; Zuk 1993). I was particularly interested in the work of Deborah A. McLennan (1996) who emphasized signaling in both male and female stickleback fish, and in the work of Gowaty (1997) and Smuts (1995), who explored female bird and primate resistance to male domination. Soon, I began to realize that this changing representation of female animals was not due simply to the growing participation of women in science. I found male scientists who were instrumental in challenging biased conceptions of female behavior as well as female scientists who produced androcentric work. I noticed that these shifts in theories of animal behavior represented larger shifts in our cultures' changing gender roles and found it interesting that as women's workplace and political influence grew, animal behavior researchers began to reevaluate the traits observed in female animals.

The history of animal behavior illustrates how human social relations—with binary conceptions of sex and gender—have created an animal (and plant) world reflecting similar binaries. Cultural influences, as feminist science studies scholars have noted, are intrinsic to the scientific process. Our models from fish morphology to rock formation are replete with imageries of human social relations. However, as Stamps (1997) suggests, acknowledging those influences in the scientific process can be a positive attribute: it can be a source of new hypotheses, models, metaphors, and imagery that can subsequently be tested.

Using this insight, I began analyzing the social context of my own background and found that gender expectations had restricted my childhood aspirations. Activities acceptable to boys were forbidden to girls; when I got muddy playing in the creek, my mother chided that I was acting like a boy. I was also told to pity my father because there were no male grandchildren to continue the family name. Masculinelike activities, such as wearing pants, were forbidden. My religion taught me that women, as the source of original sin, were placed under men's control and moral guidance. During college, women were encouraged to seek escorts when walking at night; experiencing no such limitations, my male peers discouraged my rebellious solo forays. When I wanted to be a scientist, my family recommended that I get a teaching certificate in order to hold a job convenient to my husband's career. At my first conference, a senior scientist told me that he would never take a woman to his field sites because the country was too dangerous for women. Since maleness was desirable and femaleness undesirable, I accentuated "male" qualities such as competitiveness, aggressiveness, and strength in myself. As a scientist, I searched for desirable "male" traits in female animals. However, during my graduate school years, I began to reverse these trends. Since sexual selection research focused on ornaments, I chose to study an organism in which females were brighter than males, yet their color patterns had not been researched.

Convict cichlid female fish have gold abdominal flecks. During fieldwork, I observed female courtship toward males and aggression between breeding females. Convict cichlids presented an opportunity to show that female animals could be just as aggressive, flashy, and competitive as males. I reversed the traditional categories and hypothesized female signalers and male assessors. However, I soon realized that the fish did not fit these roles; some males displayed abdominal gold. But the standard theory of animal behavior was not correct either. In a concurrent literature review, I discovered that in many species, sexual roles, in particular the production of ornaments, are less clear-cut than current theory predicts. Females in many bird and insect species exhibit coloration labeled male (Amundsen et al. 1997; Andersson 1994; Bleiweiss 1992; Hilton 1987; Muma and Weatherhead 1989; Potti and Merino 1996; Stutchbury 1994; Tella et al. 1997). These females are described as male mimics or as showing male traits. In actuality, the coloration occurs in both sexes. What I realized was that our focus on "male" as the "norm" meant that these traits were labeled as male, obscuring the true sexual variation that exists.

In other species, females display colorations not usually seen in males. In scientific publications, I found forty-three such fish species and an additional thirty-one cichlid species in aquarium hobby manuals (Jackson, unpublished review). However, only twenty-two species have been studied experimentally, and few research papers describing the results of these experiments have been published. The most well researched species, the brook stickleback (*Culaea inconstans*), is the topic of only four publications. In contrast, there are hundreds of research publications on male sticklebacks. Why are signaling females not studied? Sexual selection's emphasis on female assessment of male signals left no theoretical space for the study of signaling females. In my work, I reversed the above roles—to study male assessment of signaling females—but did not question one basic assumption: Why do we divide the animal world into gender roles? Questioning this assumption raises other issues that I believe are central to a reconception of animal behavior. Why and how do human gender roles constrain our conception of male and female animals? Additionally, what happens to individuals who occupy the space between conceived gender roles? In my case, they were ignored. I had established two potential categories (female signalers and male assessors) into which I tried to fit all fish. If a fish did not fit into one of the categories, in a sense, I couldn't see it. Such factors operate in the work of many scientists. However, we expect the scientific method to eliminate cultural or personal influence. We don't explore how our experience shapes our science.

Unless we challenge science's culturally determined categories, gender-based representations will forever constrain our understanding of nature. An expanded definition of sexual selection or a reversal of male-female roles is not enough. Such an approach will simply re-create the dichotomous portrayal of male and female animals that has prevailed thus far. Due to feminism's impact on culture, we see greater diversity in female behavior than we did previously, yet we are still unable to account for nature's true continuity and variation.

Feminist theory, because of its multidisciplinary approach to gender and emphasis on variation, can improve the study of animal behavior. Whereas I had constructed the woman scientist as a monolithic category, women of color, lesbians, and third world women have challenged mainstream feminism's category of the universal "woman" (Hurtado 1996), suggesting that there is no monolithic "woman's experience." Gender as a social category is mediated and shaped by other categories such as ethnicity, sexuality, and class. Although categories are present, current feminist theory recognizes their fluidity. Humans move in and out of different categories in various situations. Such a perspective emphasizes the flexibility of human nature. When applied to science, these insights and methodologies encourage a flexible view of animal nature. Feminist animal behaviorists (especially primatologists) have already begun such analyses and have produced new theories and models of animal behavior. What new models, theories, and self-reflexivity my training in women's studies and animal behavior will bring remains to be seen.

Works Cited

Amundsen, T., E. Forsgren, and T. T. Hansen. "On the Function of Female Ornaments: Male Bluethroats Prefer Colorful Females." *Proceedings of the Royal Society of London B* (1997): 1579–1586.

Andersson, M. *Sexual Selection.* Princeton, NJ: Princeton University Press, 1994.

Bleiweiss, R. "Widespread Polychromatism in Female Sunangel Hummingbirds (*Heliangelus trochilidae*)." *Biological Journal of the Linnean Society* 45 (1992): 291–314.

Gowaty, P. A. "Sexual Dialectics, Sexual Selection, and Variation in Reproductive Behavior." In *Feminism and Evolutionary Biology*, ed. P. A. Gowaty. New York: Chapman and Hall, 1997.

Hilton, D. F. G. "A Terminology for Females with Color Patterns that Mimic Males." *Entomological News* 98 (1987): 221–223.

Hrdy, S. B. "Empathy, Polyandry, and the Myth of the Coy Female." In *Feminist Approaches to Science*, ed. Ruth Bleier. New York: Pergamon Press, 1986.

———— . *The Woman that Never Evolved.* Cambridge MA: Harvard University Press, 1981.

Hurtado, Aida. *The Color of Privilege: Three Blasphemies on Race and Feminism.* Ann Arbor: University of Michigan Press, 1996.

McLennan, D. "Integrating Phylogenetic and Experimental Analyses: The Evolution of Male and Female Nuptial Coloration in the Stickleback Fishes (*Gasterosteidae*)." *Systematic Biology* 45 (1996): 261–177.

Muma, C. E., and Weatherhead, P. J. "Male Traits Expressed in Females: Direct or Indirect Selection?" *Behavioral Ecology and Sociobiology* 24 (1989): 25–31.

Potti, J., and Merino, S. "Decreased Levels of Blood Trypanosome Infection Correlate with Female Expression of a Male Secondary Sexual Trait: Implications for Sexual Selection." *Proceedings of the Royal Society of London B* (1996): 1199–1204.

Russett, C. E. *Sexual Science: The Victorian Construction of Womanhood.* Cambridge, MA: Harvard University Press, 1989.

Smuts, B. "The Evolutionary Origins of Patriarchy." *Human Nature* 6 (1995): 1–32.

Stamps, J. "The Role of Females in Extra Pair Copulations in Socially Monogamous Territorial Animals." In *Feminism and Evolutionary Biology*, ed. P. A. Gowaty. New York: Chapman and Hall, 1997.

Stutchbury, B. J. "Competition for Winter Territories in a Neotropical Migrant: The Role of Age, Sex, and Color." *The Auk* III (1994): 63–69.

Tella, J. L., M. G. Forero, J. A. Donazar, and F. Hiraldo. "Is the Expression of Male Traits in Female Lesser Kestrels Related to Sexual Selection?" *Ethology* 103 (1997): 72–81.

Zuk, M. "Feminism and the Study of Animal Behavior." *Bioscience* 43 (1993): 774–778.

Toward a History of Us All

Women Physicians and Historians of Medicine

————————————————————————————————→ Montserrat Cabré

Historical Genealogies

As a feminist historian of medicine who is concerned with the creation of a space for creative dialogue between women scientists and feminist science scholars, I believe history could help to establish a common ground where conversation becomes possible, a history that could be shared by women physicians and scientists as well as women historians of medicine and science. It is now common in feminist historiography to acknowledge the past efforts to open the field of the history of science and medicine to women. In review essays and methodological overviews, we read sophisticated historical analyses about the contributions that women and men have made, sometimes from a distant past, to the writing of a history of women in science and medicine. However, I would argue that as feminist historians of science and medicine, we have left our own disciplinary origins largely undiscussed. As feminist historians of science and medicine, where do we come from? Do we have a disciplinary history beyond George Sarton and Henry Sigerist, beyond Margaret Rossiter and Londa Schiebinger? Does it matter if we do?

In what follows, I will outline answers to these questions and explain why I think they are historically and politically relevant for feminist historians of medicine and science to address. Overall, I would like to suggest that feminist historians of medicine and science have failed to acknowledge the experiences of women scientists and physicians in the writing of history, and that by doing so we have helped to enhance the gap between women scientists and physicians and feminist science scholars. It is my suspicion that during the last decades, while feminist historians of science and medicine have created a field shaped by professional standards relying on recent developments in feminist theory, women's history and the history of medicine and science have overlooked the meanings given by women scientists and physicians to history, as well as their investments in its writing. Hence, we have written a genealogy of the historiographical practice that denies agency to the very women whose history we are attempting to uncover.

120

Feminist historiography today does not acknowledge much significant early historical work on women and medicine beyond an influential nine-page article on women in American medicine by Richard Shyrock, a professional historian not trained as a physician (1950). The early historiography by women physicians on women in medicine, when occasionally acknowledged today, is often portrayed as historiographically insignificant, and is sometimes accompanied by a global dismissal of its value as uncritical historiography of "women's worthies," which does not satisfy our current professional standards. However, I would argue that the desert is less barren than we might at first think, and that these evaluations fail to acknowledge what the women scientists and physicians who pioneered some of these historiographies were looking for in history and its writing.

Not noticing or undervaluing women scientists' and physicians' investments in historiography has important political consequences in the way that feminist historians define ourselves and our field. It contributes to the definition of our field within the boundaries of the discipline (the history of medicine and science) as it was institutionalized in the academy. By engaging in such approaches, we may well be contributing to a fundamental process in which patriarchal cultures have sustained themselves: the theft of feminine genealogies (Irigaray 1993).

It is with the aim of shaping a feminine genealogy of the practice of history that I present an unacknowledged episode in the history of feminist historiography of medicine. This episode involves the foundation in 1925 of the Committee of the History of Medicine by the American Medical Women's National Association, with the explicit goal of promoting the writing of the history of women in medicine (BMWNA 1925, 27–28, 33).

The Committee of the History of Medicine was very active between 1925 and early 1941, under the direction of Kate Hurd-Mead, the physician who proposed its foundation and who led the committee until her death. Hurd-Mead decided to abandon her clinical practice in 1925 to devote herself exclusively to historical research. Her interest in the history of medicine had been cultivated initially in Baltimore, where she lived between 1890 and 1893, and where she participated in the Historical Club, which later gave rise to the Johns Hopkins Institute for the History of Medicine. When she decided to devote herself fully to historiographical activity, she injected an openly political dimension into her project (Cabré 1993). Founding the Committee of the History of Medicine, Hurd-Mead was transforming her interest in history into a collective enterprise; she, together with the politically active women physicians of her age, engaged in the writing of history as part of their political agenda.

Not long after the foundational meeting in Atlantic City, Hurd-Mead traveled around the world with her husband and for four years her contact with the committee members remained epistolary. During that period, she conducted research in European libraries and collected materials for a project on writing a history of women's medicine from antiquity to her present day. However, her life during this period was neither that of a researcher isolated from her political commitment nor that of a solitary foreign scholar devoted exclusively to the study of historical sources and bibliography. Hurd-Mead contacted the more visibly active medical women in the countries where she traveled; some she already knew through their participation in the Medical Women's International Federation, and others (who were from countries having no representatives in this association) she encouraged to join.

In spite of her long absence, her support for the American Women's National Association was not diminished, nor was her commitment to the History of Medicine Committee. During this period she wrote several articles for the association's newsletter—the *Bulletin of the Medical Women's National Association*—explaining her activities and her perceptions of the situation of medical women in the countries she visited (Hurd-Mead 1926a, 1926c, 1927a, 1927b, 1928a, 1928b, 1929a, 1930a). In addition, she gathered information about women physicians, past and present, from the medical women she was meeting and urged them to write histories of women in medicine as well as their own autobiographies. She used the materials collected during this period to write a seven-hundred-page volume entitled *Medical Women of the Eastern Hemisphere* (1943).

Hurd-Mead's contacts with the other members of the Committee for the History of Medicine allowed an ambitious research project on the history of medical women in the United States to flourish. Women from different states gathered data on early women physicians—who they called pioneers—in a literal attempt to turn feminine experience into a historical source. Through the association's bulletin, autobiographies and information on the history of women in medicine were solicited, and in its pages Hurd-Mead reported on the materials received (Hurd-Mead 1926b, 1928a, 1929b, 1930b, 1931b, 1931c, 1935, 1936, 1938b, 1940). A redefinition of the concept of historical relevance was at stake here, as well as an attempt to create new historical periodizations based on women's experiences in medicine (Hurd-Mead 1931a).

In 1929, Hurd-Mead settled back in Haddam, Connecticut, devoting herself exclusively to producing women's historical knowledge. From then until her death, she wrote two books and more than fifteen articles on the history of women in medicine. In *Medical Women of America* (1933), she drew upon the materials the committee had received. In *A History of Women in Medicine* (1938a) she presented a historical narrative appraising the medical work done by women from the origins of humanity through the nineteenth century. These works fundamentally displaced the definition of the (male) historical subject in medicine.

The Symbolic and Political Potential of History

I think that it is important for feminist historians today to rethink the roles that history has played in women's actions to attain feminine authority in medicine and science—roles that are of a symbolic and political nature. History has been invested by women scientists and physicians with the capacity to signify feminine authority in medicine and science in the present (Sartori 1994). I would argue that for feminist historians today to reevaluate the importance of physicians' experiences in the writing of history is not only a question of historical accuracy but an important political and symbolic move—a decision that concerns how we define ourselves. Historians of science and medicine are well aware that history, like science or medicine, is about privileged or forgotten traditions: we should acknowledge and challenge those we are privileging. We have a disciplinary history beyond Sarton and Sigerist, a history whose insignificance within the academy is not due to its intrinsic historiographical irrelevance but rather to the ways the history of science and medicine as a discipline has been shaped.

Given the rich historiographical project implemented by Hurd-Mead and other women physicians, I believe that it is time to reexamine why an interesting nine-page article by a William H. Welch Professor of the History of Medicine at Johns Hopkins is considered to be the turning point in the historiography of women and medicine in America (Shryock 1950). We should ask ourselves if with this disciplinary priviliging we are denying to women physicians relevant originality in the writing of women's history in medicine. Because we might be missing what women physicians are telling us about the importance of signifying and inscribing—through history—women's authority in the present, it does matter that we recognize a history for our field beyond our distant founding fathers and beyond our more recent intellectual and professional referents in the historiography of medicine and science. It does matter, because it is a political and symbolic option that allows the creation of a space that women physicians and feminist science scholars may share: an space where the authority of feminine experience is acknowledged.

Acknowledgments: I am indebted to the Archives and Special Collections on Women in Medicine, the Medical College of Pennsylvania, for a Louise Gloeckner Summer Fellowship in 1991, which allowed me to start research leading to this article; in 1998–99, I was the recipient of a postdoctoral fellowship from the Generalitat de Catalunya–Massachusetts Institute of Technology at the Program in Science, Technology, and Society, MIT, which enabled me to keep working on this project. A Spanish version of this paper was presented at the VII Coloquio Internacional of the Asociación Española de Investigación Histórica de las Mujeres "Las mujeres y el poder: Representaciones y prácticas de vida," celebrated in the Universidad Complutense, Madrid, May 27–29, 1999.

Works Cited

BMWNA. *Bulletin of the Medical Women's National Association* 9 (July 1925).

Cabré, Montserrat. "Kate Campbell Hurd-Mead (1867–1941) and the Medical Women's Struggle for History." *Collections: The Newsletter of the Archives and Special Collections on Women in Medicine* 26 (1993): 1–4, 8.

Hurd-Mead, Kate Campbell. Medical Women of the Eastern Hemisphere. Vol. 2 of *History of Women in Medicine*, ed. Eveline W. Brainerd and Dr. Esther P. Lovejoy. Haddam, CT. Kate Campbell Hurd-Mead Papers. Schlesinger Library, Radcliffe College, Cambridge, MA, 1943.

———. "Library Committee Report." *Women in Medicine* 68 (April 1940): 18–19.

———. *A History of Women in Medicine: From the Earliest Times to the Beginning of the Nineteenth Century.* Haddam, CT: Haddam Press, 1938a.

———. "History of Medical Women." *Women in Medicine* 62 (October 1938b): 17–18.

———. "Committee on History and Library." *Women in Medicine* 52 (April 1936): 14.

———. "Report the Committe on History of Women in Medicine." *Women in Medicine* 50 (October 1935): 21.

———. *Medical Women of America: A Short History of the Pioneer Medical Women of America and of a Few of Their Collegues in England.* New York: Froben Press, 1933.

———. "Report of the Committee on the History of Medicine." *Bulletin of the Medical Women's National Association* 31 (January 1931a): 11.

———. "Seven Important Periods in the Evolution of Women in Medicine." *Bulletin of Women's Medical College of Pennsylvania* LXXI-3 (January 1931b): 6–15.

———. "Medical History Committee." *Bulletin of the Medical Women's National Association* 32 (April 1931c): 9.

———. "Dr. Anna N. Shabanoff, Pioneer Woman Physician of Russia." *Bulletin of the Medical Women's National Association* 28 (April 1930a):11–12.

———. "History of Medical Women." *Bulletin of the Medical Women's National Association* 30 (October 1930b): 9.

———. "Doctoresse Legey of Maternité Indigène." *Bulletin of the Medical Women's National Association* 24 (April 1929a): 10.

———. "Report of the Committee on the History of Women in Medicine." *Bulletin of the Medical Women's National Association* 25 (July 1929b):16–17.

———. "Report of the History of Women in Medicine." *Bulletin of the History of Women in Medicine* 22 (October 1928a): 14–15.

———. "Letter from Dr. Kate Mead." *Bulletin of the Medical Women's National Association* 22 (October 1928b): 19–20.

———. "Letter from Dr. Kate Mead." *Bulletin of the Medical Women's National Association* 16 (April 1927a): 14.

———. "Medical Women in Spain." *Bulletin of the Medical Women's National Association* 16 (April 1927b): 19–20.

———. "Extract from a Letter from Dr. Kate Campbell Mead." *Bulletin of the Medical Women's National Association* 12 (April 1926a): 17-18.

———. "Report of the History of Medicine Committee at Dallas, Texas." *Bulletin of the Medical Women's National Association* 14 (October 1926b): 20.

———. "Medical London in Dress Clothes." *Bulletin of the Medical Women's National Association* 14 (October 1926c): 24–25.

Irigaray, Luce. *Sexes and Genealogies.* Translated by Gillian C. Gill. New York: Columbia University Press, 1993.

Sartori, Diana. "Women's Authority in Science." *Knowing the Difference: Feminist Perspectives in Epistemology,* ed. Kathleen Lennon and Margaret Whitford. New York: Routledge, 1994, 110–121.

Shryock, Richard H. "Women in American Medicine." *Journal of the American Medical Women's Association* 5 (1950): 371–379.

Just Beneath the Surface

Rereading Geology, Rescripting the Knowledge/Power Nexus

⟶ Jaime Phillips and Kate Hausbeck

> The history of science traces the progress of discovery, the formulation of problems, and the clash of controversy; it also analyzes theories in their internal economy; in short, it describes the processes and products of the scientific consciousness. But, on the other hand, it tries to restore what eluded that consciousness, the influences that affected it, the implicit philosophies that were subjacent to it; the unformulated thematics; the unseen obstacles; it describes the unconscious of science. This unconscious is always the negative side of science—that which resists it, deflects it, or disturbs it.
>
> —*Michel Foucault, 1970*

Scholars working in the area of feminist science studies have charged that modern Western science is a hegemonically biased discourse that can discourage or deter the participation of certain groups of people, particularly women. While the superficial layers of the language of science may be smooth, apparently value-neutral, and "objective," just beneath the surface of language lies the truth of power.

Research in feminist science studies has used various methods to bring to light the ways in which social power relations are present as a subtext in the discourse of science, including the application of poststructuralist methods to scientific texts. It is now commonplace in poststructuralist literatures to state that words are the building blocks of truth, that discourses construct reality, and that language is therefore an assertion of power. To read against dominant discourses or languages is to resist, deflect, and disturb the often invisible power structures that they construct and reinforce. This process is a necessary step toward transforming the culture of science so it may be more inclusive and contextualized in the social relations of knowledge production, exchange, and application.

This is particularly relevant to the field of geoscience, since research has shown that the numbers of women and minorities enrolled in physical science majors drop during college at a greater pace than the numbers of their white male counterparts (see NCES 1997; NSF 1999). The result is the continually disproportionate rate of participation for whites and males in science compared to other groups. In this chapter we examine educational materials, specifically textbooks used in college classes, as an important method by which to study the "unconscious of science." To do so is to learn more about the discourses of science and the knowledge/power nexus; it is also to engage in feminist praxis, as identifying bias in science texts is an important step in changing the process and practice of science itself. Here, the "unconscious of science" refers to the subtextual messages, the implicit assumptions, the unspoken but defining worldview that is infused into course materials, specifically textbooks. Content, layout, diagrams, photographs, examples, and thought questions all necessarily embody and reflect certain ideas and presumptions, and these are in turn a part of the pedagogical experience. In this essay we intend to uncover both manifest and latent discourses in geology texts in order to make explicit the messages that are imparted to students.

Results: Texts' Conscious and Unconscious Voices

Four major themes arose from and guided the geology textbook content analysis.[1] They are: (1) femininity, masculinity, and sexuality; (2) race, ethnicity, and multiculturalism; (3) the military-industrial complex; and (4) social and scientific integration. The first three themes provide important insights into the unconscious of the text, as it is almost certain that none of the authors set out to incorporate such issues in a manifest way. The fourth represents to some degree a measure of the authors' (intended or unintended) placement of the science within a social context. It is our contention that rereading introductory geology texts with an eye for these four themes helps reveal the messages existing in the textual substrata.

Femininity, Masculinity, and Sexuality

Gender is arguably the most fundamental social identity; it is a master status. It exists almost everywhere in our culture. It is not terribly surprising, then, to discover gender messages in introductory geology textbooks. We should note here that we are not essentializing gender into a binary or naturalistic distinction between men and women or masculine and feminine. Instead, we assume that gender is socially constructed and that we live in a patriarchal culture in which patterns and expectations regarding appropriate gender roles and identity are political and have ramifications for the lives, experiences, and expectations of both women and men. As such, we are looking for ways in which dominant notions of masculinity and men and femininity and women are represented in geology texts in order to find patterns of gender role socialization and gender-based discouragement within the discipline that may influence the demographics of who does science and why.

First, we performed quantitative counts of gender equity similar to those done in other fields (see Rosser 1990) to analyze the more overt gender content of the geology texts. While writers and editors of science texts have made a conscious effort to reduce or eliminate overt sexism, we found an underrepresentation of women in several important ways. The authors of the texts included in our sample were overwhelmingly male (for a discussion of the study's methodology— choice of textbooks and analysis—see Phillips and Hausbeck 2000). Out of seventeen total authors for the twelve textbooks, only one was a woman. Also, we looked to the geology texts in our study for mention of women scientists, particularly in the position of being founders or innovators (presented as contributing to major discoveries or innovations). Not surprisingly, we found women scientists to be mentioned rarely if at all in our sample of introductory geology textbooks. Whereas we counted twenty-one references to male founders or innovators for the discipline of geology, women were clearly absent from such positions in the texts. Additionally, while the usage of the "generic" *he* has seemingly been eliminated from textbooks, masculine pronouns still far outnumber feminine ones (see table 1). A world where the *he*'s are so much more common than the *she*'s can hardly be seen as a welcoming place for women. Although some improvements have been made, more needs to be done to demonstrate a commitment to representing science as a place for women as well as men.

Table 1: Men and women authors, founders/innovators, and pronouns.

	Authors	*Founders/Innovators*	*Gendered Pronouns*
Women	5.88%	0.0%	5.43%
Men	94.12%	100.0%	94.57%

Photos and diagrams/drawings of people in the textbooks are also disproportionately male (see table 2). While the quantitative data are informative in themselves, the visual representations (or lack of them) are even more interesting when analyzed qualitatively. A qualitative analysis of the selection of visual depictions of women reveals that when pictured, women are more often than men used for illustrating scale (placed next to an object to give an estimate of its size), and less often than men pictured as scientists or in a working capacity.

Table 2: Men and women depicted in photos and diagrams/drawings.

	Photos	*Diagrams/Drawings*
Women	27.91%	5.26%
Men	72.09%	94.74%

A related issue analyzed in the geology texts is the use of imagery of women, sexuality, and female bodies as representations of ideas and scientific principles. The presence of such constructed images of femininity and their use as scientific metaphor in science education is a subtle but powerful signifier of gender, sexuality, and power. These cultural representations carry meaningful messages about objectification of women's bodies and (hetero)sexualization of natural objects and processes. In one introductory geology text, for example, the "principle of isostasy," which describes the mantle's compensation for the weight of the crust above it, is visually represented through a drawing of a blond woman clad in a pink nightgown (complete with a peek hole at the top) lying on a bed. The curve of her hips is used to demonstrate the weight on the "crust" (the mattress). This is an example of literally using (hetero)sexual desire and women's bodies to construct a discourse of science. Other texts avoided sexualizing the science by demonstrating the principle of isostasy without using a woman's form. Remembering Bacon's description of science as a woman to be conquered helps us understand why the correlation of women and nature is so problematic from a feminist perspective.

Relatedly, sometimes sexual metaphors or double entendres are used to educate students in a "fun" or "playful" manner about scientific concepts. When sex is used to sell ideas and teach students, it teaches more than just the science. It teaches heterosexuality, objectification, and powerful lessons about gender, especially when taken as part of a larger system of meanings generated in and by the text. For example, one text uses the heading "When the Earth Was Young and Hot" to introduce a side section on hypotheses regarding the formation of the earth. In a literal sense, there is nothing untrue in the statement (the earth is hypothesized to have been much hotter in its geologic past). However, the phrase clearly is used as a double entendre to capitalize on its latent sexualized meaning. Similarly, a diagram is provided in the same text that shows that on the seafloor, "young, hot rock" is found near a "spreading center" while "older, cool rock" is far away from it. Again, there is nothing incorrect in this description and terms such as *spreading center* are accepted terminology in geology. The labeling of this particular diagram presents latent sexual metaphors that are avoided in some other presentations of the same concepts. Constructing a scientific discourse that rests on gendered metaphors of sexuality to represent science helps reproduce systems of power that put women at a disadvantage.

Race, Ethnicity, and Multiculturalism

The attrition of people of color from the natural sciences suggests the need to evaluate what the unconscious of science texts is saying that is different from the overt messages. We should note here that we are not supporting an essentialist perspective on racial and ethnic distinctions as natural or simplistically determinable by external, visible characteristics. However, having a skin color that has been socially defined as nonwhite has ramifications for the people so defined. Thus we cannot ignore the ways in which "nonwhite" and "white" people are presented, even in geology textbooks, and the latent messages sent by these depictions. Our data on photographs used in the geology texts showed eighty-two persons whose race could be placed in a (tentative) category of black, white, or "other." Of the eighty-two, twelve were black and seven appeared to be of a race or ethnicity other than Anglo or black (see table 3). In diagrams and drawings, there were five persons of discernable race in our sample. All were white. Out of 528 photos included in the sample, only 45 (8.52 percent) depicted non-Western images.

Table 3: Race/ethnicity in photos and diagrams/drawings.

	Photos	*Diagrams/Drawings*
Black	14.63%	0.0%
White	76.83%	100.0%
Other	8.54%	0.0%

Similar to the discussion of visual representations of women and men, the depictions of people of color and non-Western societies are even more interesting from a qualitative standpoint. Ten of the twelve black persons were in a single photograph used to represent the problem of overpopulation. The photo's caption read in part, "Until the world's growing population is brought under control, scenes like this one will become more common." While the integration of social concerns into a geology textbook is laudable, the latent racist message is not. Another qualitatively induced pattern we uncovered is the visual representation of nonwhite, non-Western people as disproportionately helplessly victimized by nature. This is compounded by the depiction of scientists in photographs as being almost always white (and male), thus indicating that the people of color are in need of assistance from what one might think of as the great white, Western hope of science. This is not apparent by viewing a single photograph or image in a text but rather is a pattern of representations and subtle messages about power. The scientists are often depicted as studying and actively working over nature with different Western technologies, while third world people of color are depicted as the ones being devastated by nature, presumably because of their lack of science and industry. With almost no other depictions of persons of color, and with geologists presented as all being white, a black student may feel that her or his presence is a "problem" to be fixed by science rather than a welcomed contribution to it.

The Military-Industrial Complex

The messages about gender, sexuality, race, and ethnicity are supplemented in this system of meaning by messages about power, specifically the apparently "natural" and "good" role of the military and the state (both overwhelmingly American and

nationalistic) in the scientific endeavor. These flows of power in the text establish
an institutional and structural context for the production of science that is apparently neutral and objective. Harding (1993) states that science in the United
States—at least for the last three decades—has primarily been continuing more
effectively than ever its long-standing service to militarism and the long history
of Eurocentric economic greed that has succeeded in continuously moving
global resources from the have-nots to the haves (53).

The relationship between science and the state, including U.S. governmental
policies and interventions, has the capacity to further relations of exploitation
worldwide. Scientific discoveries are often made possible by copious financial resources provided by the state or private industry. The failure to make these relations explicit can give the false impression of a neutral scientific research policy
that leads to "pure" knowledge accumulation. Acknowledgment of the sources of
research funding can help make the purposes for certain projects more explicit.
Additionally, the constructed nature of scientific knowledge is exposed by a consideration of what research questions are not funded, as well as what questions
are not even being asked. A critical examination of the political and/or economic
agenda being served by the support of certain scientific research projects over
others is essential to understanding modern science as socially contextualized.

In addition to the production of scientific knowledge being impacted by the
influence of the state, the presentation of the science is also shaped by this interaction. We would argue that the placement of science in a social context is a positive step toward transforming science, so it is more socially responsible and
inclusive. However, in textbooks, references to the state and the military provide
a political context to what is put forth as for the most part objective science. It is
the lack of acknowledgment of this context that presents a problem. The implicit
and explicit presentation of only one type of message—that is, an unproblematically nationalistic one—denies many other realities of the political context that
also need to be heard.

Our quantitative content analysis revealed both explicit and implicit references to the state and the military. Comparatively, implicit state and military references occurred with about the same frequency. Explicit state references,
however, occurred about seven times as often as explicit military references.
While explicit references accounted for only 43.10 percent of the total mentions
of the military, they accounted for 83.18 percent of the total references to the
state. The high occurrence of explicit references to the state was primarily related
to the chapters on geologic resources. When the data for the resource chapters
were excluded from the analysis, the number of explicit state references became
more comparable to the others. The references to the state with regard to geologic resources were interesting in that they made explicit the relationships of
various national governments to resource holdings. For the most part, however,

the politics involved in these relationships were not discussed. The involvement of our military in obtaining and maintaining access to resources was also not typically mentioned, explaining the lesser frequency of such references.

The use of qualitative examples and other imagery of the state, military, or industry in science texts cannot be seen as innocent. When used, these representations serve to construct science as exclusive rather than inclusive with regard to traditional patterns of hegemony in the institution of science. The state is embedded in one geology text with an introductory quote taken from Marcus Aurelius, emperor of Rome from C.E. 61 to 180, suffusing the content with the specter of Western historical bias and militarism.

Militarism pervades the geologic unconscious with forms named for their perceived resemblance to instruments of war—ejected volcanic lava that hardens into a lemonlike shape is referred to as a "volcanic bomb," which then becomes associated with man-made bombs and intentional destruction as if the two are synonymous; "shield volcanoes" named for their apparent resemblance to a warrior's shield. In one case, a military map from the Civil War was used to illustrate geologic formations by their importance to the Union army for planning a strategic attack position. Clearly these examples of military imagery resonate with some students differently than with others, and given the association of militarism with masculinity it is not hard to see that women might be less drawn into the science by the military metaphors. The use of these images also means that others are being excluded, constructing an educational experience that cannot but have the unintended consequence of creating its own audience. The science student's experience of this knowledge does not have to be refracted through this lens; it can be changed, in part by the recognition of the lens itself.

Social and Scientific Integration

The experience of scientific knowledge is also affected by whether science is presented as pure and uncontaminated by social processes or whether the interaction of science and society is acknowledged and critically examined. The Enlightenment-borne fantasy of science as both producible and presentable in a neutral fashion, not to mention the implicit desirability of such a neutrality, could be thought of as an andro- and Eurocentric "dreamworld"[2] that excludes others at best—and constructs them as problems to be solved at worst. Reconstructing science to work for everyone means doing away with this fantasy and making explicit the social context of science.

The degree of integration of social and scientific process was evaluated in several ways. One measure concerned references to people in the geology textbooks. Such references were coded into three distinct categories, nonspecific mentions of humans, people, society, and the like; references to specific individuals; and mention of natural scientists as an occupational group. The nonspecific references to people were generally considered a positive step toward a greater degree of social and scientific integration. There were many such references—924 in our sample (see table 4). The naming of specific people was also counted, and was notable in its almost exclusive white maleness. Mention of nonspecific scientists (geologists, geoscientists, seismologists, and so on) represented a separate category in that the intention behind these references likely differs from either of the other two groupings. Depending on the context, these references can be seen in several different ways. Sometimes they appear to be a hierarchical (and patriarchal) invocation of scientific authority; other times, a positive attempt to reveal the people and process behind the science; still other times, a depiction of an occupation for potential future practitioners. Clearly there have been improvements in the effort to humanize science by including people in the text; however, in that process we must exercise caution to ensure that more than one set of voices is heard.

Table 4: References to people.

	Frequency	Percentage of Total
Nonspecific	924	51.74%
Specific	113	6.33%
Scientists	749	41.93%

The "study" or "thought" questions and recommended readings usually located at the end of each chapter were also used to measure the integration of social and scientific process. The lists of questions and readings were coded for whether they included human and/or social dimensions or whether they dealt strictly with the science alone (no overt reference to humans, society, or culture). Of the recommended readings, strictly scientific readings accounted for 55.75 percent of the sample, while more integrated readings represented 44.25 percent. The study questions revealed a large disparity, with 84.22 percent dealing with science alone, and 15.78 percent dealing with human/social dimensions (see table 5). Thus while study questions tended to present the scientific material in a way that was, for the most part, abstracted from a social context, the recommended readings were much less so. This suggests an improved awareness on the part of textbook authors with regard to the importance of providing students with further resources to study science and society in a more integrated way.

Table 5: Social/scientific integration in recommended readings and study questions.

	Recommended Readings	Study Questions
Human/Social	44.25%	15.78%
Scientific	55.75%	84.22%

Another measure of the degree of social and scientific integration was the notation of any commentary that situated geology and/or geologists in political or legal context. These were coded as policy references and their placement in the textbook—within the main text of a chapter as opposed to set aside at the end of a chapter—was noted. There were a total of fifty-seven policy references in the entire sample, forty-eight of which were located in the main portion of the chapters, with the remaining nine at the end of the chapter. The inclusion of references to policy is a positive note with regard to recognizing the social context in which the science of geology, like all sciences, operates. It is notable that such a high percentage (84.21 percent) of the references occurred within the main body of the text, in that this would suggest a higher degree of social and scientific integration than the separated placement at the end of chapters. We would argue that this contextualization is an important step toward empowering students to become agents of social and environmental change. Additionally, the transformation of science into an enterprise that is beneficial and inviting to all requires making explicit the connections between science and society, because in "othering" either, we allow to exist a context of domination of the less powerful.

Discussion: Rescripting the Dreamworld of Science

Based on our findings, it appears that geology texts continue to reflect a modern, Western, androcentric, and Eurocentric perspective of geology and the larger relationship between people, our social environment, and our natural environment. Geology education, like the discipline itself, is still reflecting a scientific field of inquiry and profession that is predominantly masculine, Caucasian, and closely (as well as apparently unproblematically) connected to the military-industrial complex. This knowledge is embedded in a particular set of power relations in which modernization and industrialization are unquestionably superior to other forms of socionatural interaction; in which scientists are predominantly male and Caucasian; in which gender and sexuality operate primarily as metaphors used to construct particular versions of truth and relationships to the process of doing science; and in which the unarticulated assumption is that geology is a discipline devoted to the analysis of earth systems and their relationship to industrial applications, significantly more than the analysis of the dynamics between physical and social environments.

Just beneath the surface of a scientific text are a myriad of alternative perspectives and interpretations. It is these currents of different worldviews and epistemological positions that we argue need to be identified, uncovered, and rewritten. In geology, as in other scientific disciplines, this requires an analytical rereading of the languages of power using both manifest content analysis and latent discourse analysis. We argue that doing so rescripts the knowledge/power nexus that opens more than the text of science to prospective readers and authors—it offers the possibility of opening up and transforming science itself. Rescripting the language of science encourages and reflects a fundamental reshaping of the way in which science is accomplished, as well as who partakes in the process.

Such a rereading of the unconscious of science and rescripting of the language of truth in science simultaneously means a broadening of the scientific method to include and make use of alternate perspectives, thereby altering existing arrangements of power and strengthening the claims of science. It offers perhaps the best hope for a science that is powerful within its boundaries and limitations and that embraces principles of inclusion as the means to securing a more fully realized version of objectivity. As Haraway (1988, 190) points out, "not so perversely, objectivity turns out to be about particular and specific embodiment, and definitely not about the false vision promising transcendence of all limits and responsibility. The moral is simple, only partial perspective promises objective vision." Looking forward to the twenty-first century, we assert the need to apply the important insights of feminist science scholars into the more praxis-oriented task of analyzing and rewriting texts of science. This is only possible when we collectively interrogate the nexus of knowledge and power as it is configured in our classrooms and embedded in our textbooks and course materials. Making the subtext visible and the unconscious of the text audible is the first step in rescripting science and the next step in transformative feminist pedagogy.

Acknowledgment: This material is based upon work supported by the National Science Foundation under Grant No. HRD-7555721.

Notes

1. The results were generated from the twelve textbooks that constituted our sample, which was chosen from among the most widely used textbooks, in order to generate a valid but manageable selection. From this final group of twelve textbooks, the sample was further refined to a portion of each textbook. From each one, three chapters were chosen and analyzed, each of these falling into one of three categories: an introductory chapter; a chapter on weathering and soils whose content is similar across all the textbooks; and a chapter concerning geologic resources, often the final chapter in introductory-level texts. For more detailed information regarding the methodological approaches used in this study—quantitative and qualitative content analysis—see the entire version of this chapter, which is published in *Women's Studies Quarterly* (Fall/Winter 2000): "Women and Science," special issue, edited by Sue V. Rosser.

2. *Dreamworlds 2* is a 1995 film by Sut Jhally that describes music videos as representing an adolescent, white, heterosexual, male fantasy of objectified sexuality.

Works Cited

Foucault, Michel. *The Order of Things: An Archaeology of the Human Sciences.* New York: Pantheon, 1970.

Haraway, Donna. "Situated Knowledges: The Science Question in Feminism and the Privilege of Partial Perspective." *Feminist Studies* 14 (1988): 575–599.

Harding, Sandra. "Forum: Feminism and Science." *National Women's Studies Association Journal* 5 (1993):49–55.

National Center for Education Statistics (NCES). *Findings from the Condition of Education, 1997: Women in Mathematics and Science.* Washington, D.C., 1997.

National Science Foundation (NSF). *Women, Minorities, and Persons with Disabilities in Science and Engineering: 1998.* Arlington, VA: National Science Foundation, 1999.

Phillips, Jaime, and Kate Hausbeck. "Just beneath the Surface: Rereading Geology, Rescripting the Knowledge/Power Nexus." *Women's Studies Quarterly* (Fall/Winter 2000).

Rosser, Sue V. *Female-Friendly Science: Applying Women's Studies Methods and Theories to Attract Students.* New York: Pergamon Press, 1990.

STORIES FROM THE FIELD

*Implementing Feminist Science Studies
in the Academy*

Section III

Feminist Leadership in the Academy

Innovations in Science Education

————————————————➤ Leslie S. Jones and Kathryn Scantlebury

The sciences have traditionally been seen as a systematic process devoted to ob-taining objective and value-free knowledge about the natural world. In contrast, feminists have consistently pointed to the significant role science plays in the val-idation of cultural constructions of gender. Feminist critics from both inside (Bleier 1984; Fausto-Sterling 1985; Hubbard 1990; Keller 1992) and outside the sciences (Code 1991; Harding 1986; Longino 1990; Schiebinger 1999) have ex-plored how scientific authority has consistently been used to justify and reinforce inequitable gender power structures. There seem to be two fundamental mecha-nisms by which this takes place: first, a blanket acceptance that scientific knowl-edge claims are devoid of cultural influences; second, that women are virtually excluded from participating in the production of science itself. Education, both inside and outside the sciences, plays a key role in both of these practices. The chapters in this section disrupt these mechanisms by presenting pedagogical and curricular ideas and innovations that are designed specifically to translate theo-ries from feminist science studies into new and different educational approaches that interrogate the cultural underpinnings of scientific knowledge through an examination of the intersections of natures and cultures.

As secondary and postsecondary science educators with academic appoint-ments in natural science departments (biology and chemistry), we occupy un-usual and relatively rare positions since most science educators are housed within colleges of education and have little contact with science faculties. However, we find our unique positions to be particularly effective sites from which to operate as activist feminists and enact a transformative educational agenda. We can use our credentials as "scientists" for entry to otherwise inaccessible science domains, allowing us proximity to those who shape academic science disciplines. Yet, we remain insulated from some of the pressures to conform to the masculine nature of science culture by virtue of our designation as "education lines." We fall into a relatively new category of interdisciplinary scholars, border-crossers, who negoti-ate these terrains daily, and find a subversive satisfaction in the idea that neither the educational or scientific community can pin us down. The journey has many challenges and obstacles. However, the very nature of border-crossing provides the freedom to engage in the transformative feminist leadership of science education to which we are profoundly committed.

This section of the anthology provides a myriad of examples of the ways in which the field of feminist science studies has begun a constructive discourse between feminism and education. As border-crossers, Pamela Baker, Bonnie Shulman, and Elizabeth Tobin tell an intriguing story regarding the trials and tribulations they faced in their effort to carve out such a discourse on their university campus. Their struggles illuminate the challenges inherent in making connections between incongruent places and their successes illustrate what the view from the academic bridges could look like. As subsequent chapters demonstrate, by forging such connections with other academic domains, feminist educators have developed an effective critique of science and feminism, and constructed ways to integrate this critique into education in the sciences and women's studies.

Toward Feminist Science Education Reform

There is currently a widespread movement devoted to reforming K–16 science education. These efforts center on changing science curricula, teaching, and assessment practices. The various calls for reform have focused on what and how science is taught, and the best strategies for assessing students' understanding of science concepts and processes. Specifically, the emphasis has changed from placing importance on students' ability to memorize science content to students' development of an understanding and appreciation of science as a "way of knowing" and "a process for producing knowledge" (Project Kaleidoscope 1991; NRC 1996a, 1996b; NSF 1996; Rutherford and Ahlgren 1990).

As Maralee Mayberry points out in her chapter, to address this issue science educators have used constructivism as a theory of knowledge to help us understand how students learn and, in particular, how this theory may improve teaching. Social constructivism attends to the influence and impact of the social milieu of knowledge making, curriculum making, and the teaching and learning of science. Although current reform initiatives do not typically deploy the concept of gender, our work as feminist science educators illuminates the insidious ways that science education uses the construction of knowledge as a means of perpetuating the masculinity of science. For example, the credibility of the knower is important when discussing knowledge production. However, philosophers typically have treated those who construct knowledge as "featureless abstractions" and have defined knowledge as an objective and transcending experience (Code 1991). This position poses several dilemmas in discussing the culture of science teaching. If we adhere to the constructivist ideals that students create knowledge and meaning from their social interactions with their peers and teachers and also adhere to feminist perspectives that all view social relations as gendered, classed, and racial, then the knower cannot be a featureless abstraction. When knowledge is viewed as abstract, the importance and value of experience is negated. Such ideas prevent people who value experience from engaging in knowledge production. Mayberry explores these dilemmas in her discussion of the theoretical underpinnings of two pedagogical approaches to reforming science education—collaborative learning and feminist pedagogy. Her analysis illustrates how on the one hand collaborative approaches maintain existing power structures in the sciences, whereas on the other hand feminist pedagogy subverts existing structures of power to create sciences that speak from the lives of women and other marginalized groups.

To work toward a bridge between science and feminist education and enact feminist reforms in science education, it is crucial to document our experiences within the sciences so schooling can be a key part of transforming science's culture. As science educators, our daily existence makes us acutely aware of the inextricable connection between scientific pedagogy and the masculine nature of the natural sciences. As feminists, our political perspective is the infrastructure for using a transformative educational process to change the culture of science. As researchers and activists we are compelled to show the way and document this journey. It is heartening to see how closely our work parallels that of the other authors in this section of this anthology. All of us describe feminist efforts to enact transformative strategies for education at the college level and all of these efforts build a feminist analytical perspective into the goals for education.

Transforming College Science Teaching

In our case, our unique positions allow us to teach both science content and pedagogy courses to students from a variety of academic programs. Additionally, we work with graduate students and K–12 teachers. Like the authors in this section, our formal and informal teaching is interwoven in our political stance and commitment to improve the gender and racial/ethnic climate of science. While the courses described in this section have been implemented in primarily liberal arts institutions where class sizes are small, allowing for greater interaction between instructor and students, our experience suggests that the recent call for reforms to improve science pedagogy can be implemented in large classrooms in large public universities as well. Professors in these settings have incorporated hands-on activities, small-group discussions, e-mail chat rooms, and problem-based learning into their teaching to enhance students' learning (Jones, Anderson, and Dhanwada 1999).

The "typical" formal curriculum for a science major is approximately fifty credit hours of college-level science and mathematics courses. Students learn mostly through coursework taught by professors who often cover material at a fast pace and make little or no attempt to relate the material to the everyday world. In the other usual setting for learning science—teaching laboratories—experiments are often cookbook and bear little relationship or relevance to the lectures or the actual scientific process. By the end of their science experiences, students often have not posed a hypothesis, designed scientific experiments, or completed original research. Their science coursework provides very little exposure to anything other than a rigid, cold, fact-dominated memorization process (Seymour 1992). In our science courses, the goal is to challenge and transform this "typical" experience and to practice something akin to what Karen Barad terms "agential literacy." Barad challenges the current bandwagon slogan "scientific literacy" by arguing that our pedagogical work needs to move beyond facilitating common understandings of scientific literacy—which focus on a science that is not in intra-action with other practices—to teaching our students "agential literacy" or "learning how to intra-act responsibly within the world." The courses described by Barad and other authors in this section provide pilot sites for enacting these strategies.

For example, a fundamental premise we work from is that a successful general education course will provide a re-presentation of science. We strive to help our students think critically about the myth of a universal "Western" scientific thinking and the handicaps imposed by its exclusionary image. One effective way to achieve this is by passing out issues of *National Geographic* magazine and asking students to find examples of someone doing something scientific. Every issue contains multiple examples, and sharing these pictures sets the groundwork for discussions of the ubiquitous nature of scientific activity. The cultural diversity of the features disrupts the notion that science happens only in the West and also serves to frame the lesson that the standardized script of the hypothetico-deductive model presents such a limited notion that it is actually a misrepresentation of science. Students enter our classes expecting professors to be aloof and distant, and care little about them as individuals. By actively questioning and initiating discussions, the flow of the discourse becomes at least two-way, if not multidirectional. Writing assignments dramatically enhance student learning by allowing individuals to pursue personal interests in the application of the course material. Balancing the assessment of students' performance by weighing outside writing assignments on topics of their personal interest at least as heavily as test scores in the determination of their final grade changes students' class experience and improves their chances for success.

We are also interested in emphasizing the social and personal relevance of learning scientific subject matter. For example, we have found that a human biology course that integrates aspects of life such as reproduction, heredity, cancer, AIDS, and immunity readily captures the attention of the undergraduates. A unit on reproduction is an effective site to interrogate concepts such as sex/gender and male-female, and present the range of sexes and sexualities that abound in humans and animals. The chapters by Sharon Kinsman and Rebecca Herzig provide detailed course descriptions that illustrate how units similar to ours can be designed. During another unit on heredity, it is possible to take an antiracist stance and use sound biological presentations of population genetics and molecular biology to deconstruct the notion that race is a valid biological category. Tracing the origins of human evolution, it is delightful to remind the class that all Americans are of African descent, it is just that some of us—as Beverly Tatum (1997) suggests—have a more recent connection to that continent. The implicit message of social justice is made by raising students' consciousness of the inextricable nature-nurture connections by teaching sound scientific content.

Similarly, context and social issues can be incorporated into more scientific courses. For example, in chemistry, the production and use of the drug thalidomide provides an excellent explanation and rationale for naming chemical compounds and illustrates the important role of the Food and Drug Administration in drug regulation. In the 1950s and early 1960s, doctors prescribed thalidomide to pregnant women for morning sickness. The drug caused deformities in unborn babies that resulted in children with no arms and/or legs. Although many factors contributed to the continued worldwide use of thalidomide after the link had been made between the drug and the birth defects, one problem was the "naming system" used to identify the compound. The drug was banned as thalidomide in the United States, but was still being prescribed in other countries under different names. European doctors did not realize that the same drug was being repackaged by the drug company under another name. In the United States, the thalidomide case precipitated increased regulation of drug companies with regard to extensive testing of new drugs before giving approval for public use (Selinger 1989). Further classroom discussions on the role of the FDA could involve how these laws affect scientific funding for the development of drugs for patients with HIV. This example also illustrates the masculine hierachy of science, because female nurses identified the problem with thalidomide but were ignored by male doctors for several years.

The chapters by Kay Picart, Lisa Weasel and her colleagues, and Haydee Salmun provide other examples of curriculum reform models that can be applied in the humanities, physical sciences, and engineering. These interdisciplinary approaches reveal the variety of intersections linking scientific and feminist activities. All three essays deal with areas where few feminist courses have been developed or taught—art, the physical sciences, and engineering.

Educating Teachers

One aspect of our work as science educators not explored in this section concerns the need to produce subsequent generations of teachers who challenge the current version of scientific culture. Preservice teachers learn about teaching through what is taught, how it is taught, and the hidden curriculum. One approach to helping students learn about the hidden curriculum as it relates to science's culture is to raise their consciousness regarding their assumptions, associations, and educational experiences. Teacher preparation is a particular challenge but an excellent site for transformative education. We deliberately model alternative pedagogical approaches and discuss how important it is to cover nontraditional science topics. Two dominant aspects of our mission are to challenge the idea that science is neutral and value-free and that teaching is gender-neutral and without cultural bias. By examining the scientific culture and the concepts of femininity and masculinity we can help preservice teachers appreciate and understand the subtleties of the hidden curriculum. In teacher education courses, we help prospective teachers recognize the assumptions about and the associations made between gender and science, so they may begin to provide a different science education for their students.

While changing the way that science is taught at the university level can impact teacher education, new teachers have other influences on their teaching. Preservice teachers report that student teaching is the most useful and relevant requirement in their teacher education programs because schools are conservative entities replicating and reinforcing traditional racial and gender role stereotypes; preservice teachers' stereotypic attitudes can be reinforced by their field experiences (Scantlebury et al. 1996). Neophyte teachers need specific training in equitable teaching strategies and supervision by cooperating teachers who are sensitive to those issues. Because of their role in K–12 science education and influence on the development of preservice teachers, we devote considerable efforts to reaching the population of practicing schoolteachers through inservice or professional development experiences in which we discuss science's "objectivity," issues of multicultural education, antiracist pedagogy, and science content.

The current climate of reform in science education provides an unprecedented opportunity to promote equity in science education. "Science for All" serves as the centerpiece for K–12 science education reform, and this idealized goal helps us promote change in university science. The authors of this section demonstrate that this is a laudable and achievable goal. By employing a feminist perspective in research, scholarship, and service these scholars are reenvisioning their disciplines. This section illuminates the innovative course and curriculum transformations that are taking place in a variety of disciplines, but much work remains. There are few feminist revisions of the physical sciences and engineering. Likewise, the humanities and social sciences need to work harder to incorporate scientific content and practice. We are witnessing the emergence of a more positive and less masculinist/antagonistic culture of teaching in scientific disciplines, from which we can begin to undo science's masculine image, and revision the interwoven nature of gender, science, and culture.

Works Cited

Bleier, R. *Science and Gender: A Critique of Biology and Its Theories on Women.* New York: Pergamon Press, 1984.

Code, L. *What Can She Know? Feminist Theory and the Construction of Knowledge.* Ithaca, NY: Cornell University Press, 1991.

Fausto-Sterling, A. *Myths of Gender: Biological Theories about Women and Men.* New York: Basic Books, 1985.

Harding, S. *The Science Question in Feminism.* Ithaca, NY: Cornell University Press, 1986.

Hubbard, R. *The Politics of Women's Biology.* New Brunswick, NJ: Rutgers University Press, 1990.

Jones, L. S., P. L. Anderson, and K. R. Dhanwada. "Science Education for All: Effective Undergraduate General Education Classes that Turn the Rhetoric into a Reality." Sigma Xi Forum "Reshaping Undergraduate Science and Engineering Education: Tools for Better Learning." Sigma Xi Annual Meeting, Minneapolis, MN, November 4–5, 1999.

Keller, E. F. "How Gender Matters: Or Why It's so Hard for Us to Count Past Two." In *Inventing Women: Science, Technology, and Gender,* ed. G. Kirkup and L. Smith Keller. Cambridge: Polity Press, 1992

Longino, H. *Science as Social Knowledge: Values and Objectivity in Scientific Inquiry.* Princeton, NJ: Princeton University Press, 1990.

National Research Council (NRC). *From Analysis to Action: Undergraduate Education in Science, Mathematics, Engineering, and Technology.* Washington, D.C.: National Academy Press, 1996a.

————. *National Science Education Standards.* Washington, D.C.: National Academy Press, 1996b.

National Science Foundation (NSF). *Shaping the Future: New Expectations for Undergraduate Education in Science, Mathematics, Engineering, and Technology.* NSF 96–139. Washington, D.C.: Author, 1996.

Project Kaleidoscope. *What Works: Building Natural Science Communities.* Project Kaleidoscope. Washington, D.C., 1991.

Rutherford, J., and Ahlgren, A. *Science for All Americans.* New York: Oxford University Press, 1990.

Scantlebury, K., E. Johnson, S. Lykens, R. Clements, S. Gleason, and R. Lewis. "Beginning the Cycle of Equitable Teaching: The Pivotal Role of Cooperating Teachers." *Research in Science Education* 26 (1996): 271–282.

Schiebinger, L. *Has Feminism Changed Science?* Cambridge, MA: Harvard University Press, 1999.

Selinger, B. *Chemistry in the Marketplace.* Orlando, FL: Harcourt Brace Jovanovich, 1989.

Seymour, E. "The 'Problem Iceberg' in Science, Mathematics, and Engineering Education: Student Explanations for High Attrition Rates." *Journal of College Science Teaching* (February 1992): 230–238.

Tatum, B. D. *"Why Are All the Black Kids Sitting Together in the Cafeteria?" and Other Conversations about Race.* New York: Basic Books, 1997.

Reproductive and Resistant Pedagogies

The Comparative Roles of Collaborative Learning and Feminist Pedagogy in Science Education

→ Maralee Mayberry

> Why aren't women and minorities rushing into the science vacuum? I con-
> tend that an important reason is that the science curriculum itself and the
> dominant views of science as an a-historical and hyper-rational system of
> thought makes the science classroom an alien and hostile place for women
> and people of color. Students often decide whether to pursue a particular
> line of study based on a combination of intrinsic interest in the subject and
> something I might call the "comfort zone." Baldly stated, the science class-
> room is usually an uncomfortable place for women and people of color. If
> we are to address the crisis in science personnel we must ask not only about
> how we teach science but also about the subject matter itself.
>
> —*Anne Fausto-Sterling, 1991*

This chapter addresses the implications and consequences of reproductive versus
resistant or transformative pedagogies. It provides a critical comparison of two
pedagogical approaches to reforming the science classroom—collaborative learning and feminist pedagogy. The first section very briefly traces the theoretical and
epistemological development of these two pedagogies. It illustrates that collaborative learning is rooted in an interpretive epistemology that circumvents any
meaningful conversation about the gender, race, or class nature of knowledge
production, dissemination, and utilization. In contrast, feminist pedagogy is
linked to the theoretical and practical concerns of feminist theory and works to
uncover, understand, and transform gender, race, and class oppression and domination. The second section discusses the social and political consequences of implementing either collaborative learning or feminist pedagogy in science
classrooms. Educators' full awareness of these consequences is critical, because
collaborative learning is a socially reproductive pedagogy that encourages students to gain proficiency in the dominant discourse of existing science systems,
whereas feminist pedagogy is a socially transformative pedagogy that invites students to critically analyze existing science systems and their relationship to social

oppression and domination. Thus, choosing a pedagogy is not an apolitical act. The final section of the chapter concludes with some thoughts about the practical barriers science educators may face as they begin to construct feminist science classrooms. The vision of feminist educators, regardless of their discipline, is to implement a classroom pedagogy that challenges the dominant masculinist assumptions about knowledge and education, and ultimately challenges the oppressive power relations embedded in the wider society. To be successful, the movement for developing a more democratic science education for all and for building a more diverse science community will require a similar feminist vision and a more widespread awareness and implementation of feminist pedagogy.

Similar Techniques, Different Visions: A Brief Overview of Collaborative Learning and Feminist Pedagogy

Collaborative Learning: A "Conversation of Mankind"[1]

The call to restructure science education dates back to the late 1960s, when the academic preparation of U.S. students came under fire from business and scientific elites. During this period, a plethora of national "state of education" studies were sponsored to pinpoint why U.S. students appeared to be academically less prepared than their international counterparts (Coleman 1973). The common recommendation made was to replace the traditional, formal classroom environment with a new classroom culture that would involve students in a network of informal social relations and encourage them to engage in the construction of collaborative, or communal, knowledge. The reasoning behind this advice came from the era's new corporate management models that had been designed to increase worker productivity and, in turn, to ensure American business success. Across industries, top-down management styles were rapidly replaced by small problem-solving units composed of both workers and managers. American educators were slow to recognize how similar organizational arrangements, when introduced in school environments, could bolster students' math and science performance. Becker (1983) and Wells (1989) pointed out that the call to create collaborative classroom environments fell on deaf ears throughout the 1970s. Not until the mid-1980s, after years of relying on traditional approaches to educational reform (teaching basic skills and more standardized testing), did educators begin to acknowledge the research showing that students learn more when they actively participate in a network of informal social relations and work in collaborative learning settings (Astin 1985). Today, the business community (and funding sources such as the National Science Foundation) recognizes the need for a larger and more literate scientific workforce, which as a result of demographics will have to be drawn from groups who traditionally have not pursued science education or science careers.

Collaborative learning approaches restructure the educational environment within which students learn. In collaborative settings, student learning is not designed to be an individual activity; rather, learning takes place as students work in small groups and collectively pose questions, define problems, gather data, interpret findings, and share their conclusions with other class members. Collaborative settings also encourage student groups to probe deeply into course assignments and to actively search for a breadth of information regarding the topic under study. However, collaborative environments do not necessarily provide students with an adequate model of critical thinking. That is, collaborative techniques restructure the environment within which students learn, but do not question what students learn or why they should learn it. The reproductive epistemological and theoretical underpinnings of collaborative learning underscore this point.

Brown (1995) and Webb and Palincsar (1996) suggested that collaboration helps students understand the vocabularies, methodologies, and grammatical and rhetorical structures, as well as the goals of knowledge, in any particular discipline. Collaboration engages students in an ongoing conversation about these aspects of disciplinary knowledge, and in turn trains students who are capable of adapting to the "conventions of conversation" in educated communities. According to Bruffee (1994), the goal of collaborative learning is to "provide a social context in which students can experience and practice the kinds of conversation valued by college teachers . . . the normal discourse of most academia, professional, and business communities" (642–43).

Although the work on collaborative educational methods does contain some hints about the potential of collaborative learning strategies to open knowledge communities to change, the explicit model assumes that knowledge production entails the learning, practicing, and mastering of the discursive conventions embedded in existing knowledge communities—business, academic, government, and the professions. Furthermore, the model implicitly assumes that members within and between knowledge communities share similar knowledge interests. The race, class, and gender aspects of how knowledge is produced and used are not addressed. As a result, collaborative learning settings create a social context in which students (apparently disembodied from their race, class, and gender) are to learn, practice, master, and ultimately sustain the discursive conventions of professional communities (apparently devoid of race, class, and gender biases)— and in the case of science education, a science that is disembodied from the doer of science. In this sense, collaborative techniques reproduce existing forms of knowledge and provide students with the skills and tools necessary to join established knowledge communities, rather than to transform them.

Feminist Pedagogy: In Pursuit of Praxis

> Feminist theory . . . validates difference, challenges universal claims to truth
> and seeks to create social transformation in a world of shifting and uncertain
> meanings. In education, these profound shifts are evident on two levels:
> first, at the level of practice, as excluded and formerly silenced groups chal-
> lenge dominant approaches to learning and to definitions of knowledge; and
> second, at the level of theory, as modernist claims to universal truth are
> called into question.
>
> —*Kathleen Weiler, 1991*

Feminist education, Nancy Schniedewind (1993) reminded us, is "concerned
with the content of what we teach—feminist scholarship—and the ways in
which we teach—feminist pedagogy" (17). The form and content of educational
practices are inextricably linked in the feminist classroom. Feminist pedagogy
therefore embodies a concern for both what we teach and how we teach it.

The intellectual roots of feminist pedagogy lie in the lifelong work of Brazil-
ian educator Paulo Freire. Freire's (1972) vision of education subverts public
schooling's historical function of reproducing a class system in which resources
are shared unequally (Bowles and Gintis 1976). In Freire's model of education,
students and teachers work collectively to interrogate traditional forms of knowledge and social ideologies, as well as their own accepted beliefs and identities.
The classroom serves as a center of participatory democracy where teachers and
students alike engage in this dialogical experience, the aim of which is to challenge the structures of oppression, repression, and inequality.

The principles of feminist education and pedagogy are based on a Freirean
pedagogy of liberation, although they expand and enrich Freire's model. Feminist pedagogy developed in the context of a growing number of women's studies
programs nationwide, and it reflects the feminist political commitment to
women's liberation (Weiler 1991). It embraces the critical, oppositional, and activist stance of the Freirean model of education, yet expands Freire's pedagogical
vision. In particular, the absence of the analytical concept of gender in Freire's
pedagogy presents difficulties to feminists who are struggling to put their liberatory ideals into practice.

Feminist pedagogy rectifies this oversight by considering not only the class
and race aspects of knowledge production and dissemination, but also the gender
aspects. It invites students to critique the unequal social relations embedded in
contemporary society and to ask why these circumstances exist and what one can
do about them. To achieve these liberatory goals, feminist educators develop and
use classroom process skills, many of which are used in collaborative learning environments. Informal relations among class members are built by initiating stu-

dent-centered experiences such as group activities and group reports. Great care and skill go into developing a learning environment in which students work together to design group activities that demonstrate an awareness of the race, class, and gender dynamics that permeate the larger society. Through dialogue and conversation, students and teachers negotiate a curriculum that articulates their needs and concerns. These classroom strategies are designed explicitly to empower students to apply their learning to social action and transformation, recognize their ability to act to create a more humane social order, and become effective voices of change within the broader social world.

In some ways, collaborative and feminist approaches to education share similar interests. Both are concerned with the social context of learning, both apply similar pedagogical techniques to enhance informal classroom relationships in which students construct knowledge interdependently through conversational process, and both construct a classroom culture in which students feel safe participating in the learning process. However, contrary to the assumption that collaborative learning should train students to master knowledgeable discourses, the feminist classroom conversation and process of knowledge production are overtly political and aimed toward social and educational change (Kenway and Modra 1992; Maher and Tetreault 1994). In essence, feminist pedagogy is based on the desire for social transformation. It explicitly seeks to dismantle the systems of oppression that collaborative learning leaves unquestioned.

Collaborative Learning and Feminist Pedagogy in Science Education: Women in Science or Feminist Science?

The discussion of gender issues in science has evolved in two directions. One line of thinking argues that science courses need to be designed to attract and retain women. This approach, women in science, encourages educators to redesign their courses to be more female-friendly. Another line of thinking advocates the building of two-way streets between feminism and science. This approach argues that women's disinterest in modern Western sciences reflects sciences' disinterest in women and in their own social and historical context, as well as in the political and policy implications of scientific inquiry (Harding 1993, 50). I suggest that these views are not necessarily incompatible and that each makes an important contribution to feminist projects within the sciences. There are important reasons to educate more women in sciences, and there are important reasons for feminists to take on a critical examination of the sciences and to train students in the study of science. Each view, however, has different pedagogical implications. To clarify some of these differences, I will sketch their central features and concerns.

Making Science Friendly to Women

Much literature documents the barriers to success that women traditionally confront in science courses. The earliest studies concentrated on ways to enable women to fit into the way science traditionally is taught (Kahle 1985; Matyas and Malcolm 1991). The recommendations that were made centered on strengthening girls' cognitive skills (for example, spatial visualization, numerical problem-solving, logical reasoning) and affective skills (assertiveness, competitiveness, and goal-orientedness).

More recent scholarship suggests that only by changing the features of schools—the science curriculum and how science is taught—will significant changes in the participation of women in science occur (Tobias 1989, 1992). Spear (1987) described the underrepresentation of women in science as a reflection of low teacher expectations about females' ability to do science. In schools where low teacher expectations persist, female students develop the feeling that they do not belong in science courses. Consequently, they are more likely to avoid additional science coursework and less likely to pursue science degrees and careers. Rosser (1990), and Hollenshead and her colleagues (1994) examined the culture of competition that characterizes many science, math, and engineering classrooms. Their findings indicate that competitive classroom environments deter women from majoring in these disciplines. A competitive classroom culture appears to facilitate individual achievement for white men, but acts as a significant deterrent to women's achievement. Other studies suggest that the lack of curriculum images relevant to the daily lives of women (Kelly 1985; Rosser 1990) and the androcentric bias of scientific knowledge and practice (Harding 1991; Keller 1992) are additional factors involved in women's attrition from science.

In light of these findings, the current reform efforts directed at developing a science curriculum and pedagogy that is capable of attracting women to science courses and careers—a female-friendly approach—share a common set of objectives: recognize successful female scientists, teach problem-solving skills from perspectives such as home economics and nursing, incorporate and validate women's experience in the curriculum and pedagogy, use less-competitive classroom models, provide cooperative and supportive learning environments, and rely more on interdisciplinary methods of teaching science. To achieve these objectives, science education reformers call on science educators to implement an assortment of collaborative learning techniques in their classrooms: student-to-student exchange and collaboration, nonhierarchical teaching approaches, hands-on experiential learning, small-group learning and conversation, group reports, and student journaling.

Thus, within the context of programs whose goal is to add women to science, implementing these collaborative learning techniques reproduces, rather than transforms, the existing system of science. It is likely that the current science education reform movement may succeed in involving more women in some areas of scientific study. It is also likely that the popular pedagogical reforms will fail to articulate and analyze the role Western science plays in sustaining systems of inequality, and thereby will serve to continue legitimating and perpetuating the existing social and scientific systems.

Remaking Science, Remaking Society

The recent feminist thinking about science and science education provides insight into how the existing system of science sustains social inequalities and, to a lesser extent, how classroom learning might be organized to be more inviting to women *and* to achieve transformative, rather than reproductive, goals. The question "How can we make science more appealing to women?" is replaced with the question "What is it about existing science cultures and methods of inquiry that excludes women?"

Given the reframing of this question, understanding the historical and social context of science (knowledge *about* science) is high on the feminist scholarly agenda. Feminist philosopher Helen Longino (1995) reminded us that critical questions about science are raised when one considers how the sciences are inextricably related to the structures of power in modern and postmodern societies. Accordingly, feminist critics of science have examined the epistemology of Western science, the relation between social change and scientific change, the scientist's relationship to phenomena, and the effect of existing social distributions of power on scientific inquiry and implementation (Harding 1986, 1991; Longino 1995). Feminist scholars have also critically examined traditional scientific inquiry on other grounds, including its tendency to privilege the masculine, reinforce existing power structures, and promote so-called objectivity while obscuring the interactional and interdependent relations among natural and social phenomena (Bleier 1986; Harding 1986, 1991; Keller 1985, 1988). Underlying these issues is an educational concern: How can feminist scientists and educators incorporate a critical examination of science into courses in the natural sciences?

Those involved in developing a feminist science education are beginning to unravel the two seemingly conflicting pedagogical approaches to science education reform outlined above. Evelynn Hammonds (1995), for instance, suggests that women scientists whose interests lie in creating programs to increase the participation of women in science seem to have little understanding of the questions that feminist critics of science have attempted to address. The point of contention, Hammonds argues, is located in the meaning of *gender*. Hammond's research indicates that women science educators misread feminist critics' "ideas about how gender is constructed within scientific discourses as statements about women scientists" (86). For these women scientists, taking gender out of science means creating scientific learning environments that bring more women into scientific practice.

Without a clear understanding of the difference between the barriers to *women's* participation in the sciences and the feminist critique of the *gendered* characteristics of scientific culture and scientific knowledge, the pedagogical practices advocated by science educators will fail to have a truly transformative effect on science education or the uses to which science is put. Without an emphasis on illuminating the race, class, and gender dimensions of scientific inquiry and science's relationship to political processes and policy making, pedagogical techniques such as small-group learning activities, making content relevant to diverse learning styles, and legitimating experience as a valid form of knowledge may serve to entice more women to study science but will not transform scientific inquiry. Rather, these pedagogical techniques will serve the epistemological ends of collaborative learning: to reproduce existing knowledge that is in harmony with the ways of doing that the general public are "already familiar with, find useful and depend upon" (Bruffee 1993, 9–10). Without a feminist approach to scientific inquiry, it is likely that women scientists will be socialized into the masculinist view of science, and will remain unlikely to engage in transformative activities.

In contrast, when the issues raised by feminist critics of science are addressed in classroom content and process, these pedagogical techniques serve a different goal. They can help *all* students and teachers to develop a critical analysis of the epistemology of Western science, its privileging of the masculine, and its inability to reorient the relation of scientific inquiry to social policy and social development (Clover: 1995). In short, transformative potentials emerge in classrooms where the work of feminist critics of science is taken seriously and where establishing a set of values upon which the transformation of science can be grounded is the goal.

Feminist approaches to science education can serve dual, although related and complementary, purposes. As feminist scientists begin to raise important questions about Western science (for example: Who benefits and who does not from the uses to which science is put? What role does the historically specific context within which conventional science has developed and flourished play in constituting content, practice, and use in the natural sciences? What are the specific ideologies and values that are carried into scientific research? How has modern science sustained hegemonic structures and distributed benefits to some groups and cultures while ignoring or exploiting others?) and begin to create sciences that speak from the lives of women and other marginalized groups, not only will existing systems of science be challenged, but women's interest (as well as other marginalized groups' interests) in the sciences will rise (Harding 1993). Consequently, not only will the face of the scientific community become more multicultural and gender, race, and class inclusive, but members of the community will be part of an enterprise that now encourages (rather than discourages) its members to become actively involved in asking new questions from fresh standpoints. New theories, methods of investigation, and practices will be created that fundamentally alter descriptions and explanations of the natural world and question who benefits from the uses to which science is put.

The poignant examples presented in this section of the anthology (see Kinsman, Herzig, Picart, Weasel et al., and Salmun) illustrate how feminists and scientists are beginning to breach their traditional knowledge boundaries to develop an integrated feminist science education with the explicit goals of (1) constructing a science education that explores the interrelationships between natures and cultures, and (2) developing a critical consciousness empowered to apply scientific knowledge to social action and social transformation. These projects move us closer to creating sciences that respond to the needs of women and other marginalized groups—sciences in which these groups will have a vested interest.

Some Practical Concerns

Challenging the sanctity of science will not be an easy task. In the current educational climate, in which schools face increasingly conservative politics, it is unlikely that truly transformative models of science education will quickly appear. Many questions about the feasibility of implementing feminist pedagogies in schools and universities remain to be examined: How can feminist pedagogies best respond to fiscal constraints, increasingly diverse student populations, new technologies, and the conservative political climate? How can progressive academics adapt our classroom practice and course content to accommodate these challenges without sacrificing feminist learning goals? What kind of innovative courses can feminist teachers design and have administratively approved? In what ways can feminist teachers creatively circumvent disciplinary and institutional barriers as they implement courses that reflect feminist concerns? Feminist science educators will need to grapple with and write about these questions as they begin to construct feminist science classrooms. Further, as teachers develop their ability to integrate theory and practice, they will inevitably need to transform the curricular goals, course content, and daily teaching routines with which they are familiar. In so doing, feminist teachers may find themselves distanced from the traditional models of science teaching in which teachers rely on standardized approaches and course content. Tensions and conflicts over what constitutes scientific literacy and how national science standards will be met will inevitably emerge between feminist educators and the institutional settings within which they work.

Pragmatically, feminist science educators may stand a better chance of gaining credibility and support if they appeal to the current emphasis on meeting the needs of an increasingly diverse student population through curricular and pedagogical reform. Peggy McIntosh's (1983) five-phase vision for curriculum transformation provides a door through which we can move science curriculum and pedagogy from female-friendly sciences (Phase III) to "sciences reconstructed to include us all" (Phase IV). (See Fausto-Sterling 1991 for a detailed description of how McIntosh's model can be applied to science education reform.) In this case, collaborative learning traditions may be used to help feminist science educators become institutionally positioned in a place where they will be more capable of moving toward more transformative and radical reforms.

The issues and concerns raised in this essay are significant to the ongoing development of feminist educators in all disciplines. Collaborative learning techniques may provide science educators with one avenue on which to move toward building a feminist science. However, the critical examination of science as a social institution, which is a hallmark of feminist pedagogy's role in science education, cannot be ignored if we intend to transform science into a resource that is used to improve the welfare of all people around the globe. Without an appreciation of the reproductive impulse of collaborative learning and the resistant nature of feminist pedagogy, I worry that science educators who are aligned with feminist concerns will find a safe and congenial home in the collaborative learning household. As we work to apply feminist theories, practices, and values in our classrooms, we should remember the words of Audre Lorde (1984, 112): "You can't dismantle the master's house by using the master's tools."

Note

1. This section heading is taken from Bruffee's (1994) influential article "Collaborative Learning and the 'Conversation of Mankind,'" which is commonly regarded as the classic statement on the epistemological foundations of collaborative learning.

Works Cited

Astin, A. W. *Achieving Educational Excellence.* San Francisco: Jossey-Bass, 1985.
Becker, H. S. "Studying Urban Schools." *Anthropology and Education Quarterly* 14 (1983): 99–108.
Bleier, R. (Ed.). *Feminist Approaches to Science.* New York: Pergamon, 1986.
Bowles, S., and Gintis, H. *Schooling in Capitalist America.* New York: Basic Books, 1976.
Brown, L. "The Advancement of Learning." *Educational Researcher* 23 (1995): 4–12.
Bruffee, K. "Collaborative Learning and the 'Conversation of Mankind.'" *College English* 46 (1994): 635–652.

———— . *Collaborative Learning.* Baltimore: Johns Hopkins University Press, 1993.

Clover, D. "Gender Transformative Learning and Environmental Action." *Gender and Education* 7 (1995): 243–258.

Coleman, J. S. *Youth: Transition to Adulthood.* Report of the Panel on Youth of the President's Science Advisory Committee. Washington, D.C.: Office of Science and Technology, 1973.

Fausto-Sterling, A. "Race, Gender, and Science. *Transformations* 2 (1991): 4–12.

Freire, P. *Pedagogy of the Oppressed.* New York: Herder, 1972.

Hammonds, E. "The Matter of Women in Science." In *Debates and Issues in Feminist Research and Pedagogy*, ed. J. Holland and M. Blair. Philadelphia: Open University, 1995.

Harding, S. "Forum: Feminism and Science." *National Women's Studies Association Journal* 5 (1993): 56–64.

———— . *Whose Science? Whose Knowledge? Thinking from Women's Lives.* Ithaca, NY: Cornell University Press, 1991.

———— . *The Science Question in Feminism.* Ithaca, NY: Cornell University Press, 1986.

Hollenshead, C., P. Soellner-Younce, and S. Wenzel. "Women Graduate Students in Mathematics and Physics: Reflections on Success." *Journal of Women and Minorities in Science and Engineering* 1 (1994): 63–88.

Kahle, J. *Women in Science.* Philadelphia: Falmer Press, 1985.

Keller, E. F. "How Gender Matters, or, Why It's so Hard for Us to Count Past Two." In *Inventing Women: Science, Technology, and Gender*, ed. G. Kirkup and L. Keller. Cambridge, MA: Polity Press, 1992.

———— . *Reflections on Gender and Science.* New Haven, CT: Yale University Press, 1988.

———— . *A Feeling for the Organism: The Life and Work of Barbara McClintock.* San Francisco: W. H. Freeman, 1985.

Kelly, A. "The Construction of Masculine Science." *British Journal of Sociology of Education* 6 (1985): 133–154.

Kenway, J., and H. Modra. "Feminist Pedagogy and Emancipatory Possibilities." In *Feminisms and Critical Pedagogy*, ed., C. Luke and J. Gore. New York: Routledge, 1992.

Longino, H. "Conflicts and Tensions in the Feminist Study of Gender and Science." *Debates and Issues in Feminist Research and Pedagogy*, ed. J. Holland and M. Blair. Philadelphia: Open University, 1995.

Lorde, A. *Sister Outsider.* New York: Crossing Press, 1984.

McIntosh, P. *Interactive Phases of Curricular Re-Vision: A Feminist Perspective.* Wellesley, MA: Wellesley College Center for Research on Women, 1983.

Maher, F. A., and M. T. Tetreault. *The Feminist Classroom.* New York: Basic Books, 1994.

Matyas, M., and S. Malcolm. *Investing in Human Potential: Science and Engineering at the Crossroads.* Washington, D.C.: American Association for the Advancement of Science, 1991.

Rosser, S. *Female-Friendly Science.* New York: Pergamon, 1990.

Schniedewind, N. "Teaching Feminist Process in the 1990s." *Women's Studies Quarterly* 21 (1993): 17–30.

Spear, M. G. "Teachers' Views about the Importance of Science to Boys and Girls." In *Science for Girls*, ed. A. Kelly. Philadelphia: Open University Press, 1987.

Tobias, Shiela. *Revitalizing Undergraduate Science: Why Some Things Work and Some Things Don't.* Tucson: Tucson, Arizona Research Corporation.

———— . *They're Not Dumb, They're Different.* Tucson: Tucson, Arizona Research Corporation, 1989.

Webb, N. M., and A. S. Palincsar. "Group Processes in the Classroom." In *Handbook of Educational Psychology*, ed. D. C. Berliner and R. Calfee. New York: Macmillan, 1996.

Weiler, K. "Freire and a Feminist Pedagogy of Difference." *Harvard Educational Review* 61 (1991): 449–474.

Wells, A. S. "Backers of School Change Turn Sociologists." *New York Times*, January 4, 1989, 17.

Difficult Crossings

Stories from Building Two-Way Streets

———➤ Pamela Baker, Bonnie Shulman, and Elizabeth H. Tobin

In 1997, thirty-four (or nearly 20 percent) of the Bates College faculty began conversations about scientific literacy for women. The organizers of this project[1] hoped that these conversations would encourage the inclusion of scientific material in women's studies courses and the consideration of the perspectives of feminist science studies in science courses. Our work was part of a larger project funded by the Association of American Colleges and Universities, with help from National Science Foundation, entitled "Women and Scientific Literacy: Building Two-Way Streets."[2] We used our grant from AAC&U to hold two-year-long seminars, each of which met monthly, aimed at faculty teaching introductory courses. Each seminar represented one lane of a two-way street for women's studies and science faculty. The first, in 1997–98, entitled "Scientists Encounter the Feminist Challenge," included the six members of the organizing team (four scientists and two social science faculty) and sixteen other scientists (eight women and eight men), all of whom taught introductory courses in physics, chemistry, biology, geology, or math. The second, "Women's Studies Encounters Scientific Content," held in 1998–99, included five team members, four scientists from the first year (one woman and three men) and twelve faculty from humanities or social science disciplines (all women). These twelve faculty members in the second seminar all taught courses cross-listed with women's studies; two-thirds had taught or would in the future teach core courses in the women's studies program. The reading lists for the two seminars differed, as we tailored them to the participants.[3]

Our goals for this new project included the specific one of introducing new materials into courses taught at Bates, especially introductory courses. We started this project based on the premise that a more self-conscious science, alive to its social context, historical background, and the assumptions of its practitioners, can produce better and more useful results. We also believe that colleges and universities are crucial locations for taking the first steps toward a more self-conscious science: including the perspectives of people of color and women. Thus, we hoped participants in the project from the natural sciences would add material to their courses about the historical development and current uses of science, with special emphasis on gendered contexts, and that they would think about the method and presentation of their subjects, finding techniques friendly to people of color and women. The readings included some of the standard works in feminist science studies, among them essays and books by Evelyn Fox Keller (1983, 1985, 1987), Ruth Hubbard and Elijah Wald (1993), Donna Haraway (1991), Sandra Harding (1995), and Bonnie Spanier (1995), as well as writings by Angela Ginorio (1995) and Evelynn Hammonds (1986) on the experiences of people of color in science courses.

Another basic assumption was that women's studies is enriched whenever its analyses can incorporate the uses and distribution of scientific knowledge and technological products, and also whenever it can make compelling the relationship of gender analysis to the production of scientific knowledge itself. We hoped that women's studies faculty would introduce material with scientific content into their courses, encouraging students to consider scientific materials as subjects for interrogation, critique, and understanding. We used several texts with materials potentially suitable for use in women's studies courses, such as Ruth Hubbard and Elijah Wald, *Exploding the Gene Myth* (1993), Eli Minkoff and Pamela Baker, "Variation among Human Populations" (1996), and Londa Schiebinger, *Nature's Body* (1993).

Along with introducing new course materials, we had a second, equally important goal for these two seminars: that faculty in a variety of disciplines would talk with each other. In this case, we were less set on what should be discussed than on how we could begin to get over lack of knowledge and distrust of each other's disciplines. Such distrust and lack of communication has the potential to impede all interdisciplinary work. However, our earlier experience with a faculty development seminar[4] led us to believe that getting these conversations started could have long-term positive consequences for our campus. We wanted to create space for further cross-disciplinary conversations and learning.

Our goal of two-way conversation was influenced, however, by our decision to build the two-way street one lane at a time, first for scientists and then for women's studies faculty. We chose this method because our earlier faculty development seminar, and subsequent conversations with faculty, had alerted us to the fears each group had about the other, as they set out on this journey. Many scientists were curious about feminist critiques and worried that they might unintentionally be driving women and students of color away from their fields. But they also feared being labeled "politically incorrect" or being ridiculed for their lack of sophistication in nonscientific forms of analysis. Many faculty in women's studies likewise showed interest in including material about science in their courses, but appeared hesitant about their ability to present that knowledge themselves.

We realized that all participants needed to establish a common groundwork of knowledge about science and feminist science studies, and about disciplinary differences and similarities. We decided they were most likely to speak openly and freely about new and controversial subjects in groups of those with similar disciplinary backgrounds. We reasoned that each lane of this street needed to carry traffic smoothly before two-way traffic would become possible. Although we continue to believe this decision was correct, as with any construction project, the kind of foundation we built influenced our later work.

Year One: Scientists Encounter the Feminist Challenge

Perhaps the most significant barrier to open discussion in the first year was the language we used. For example, in contrast to the second year, when women's studies faculty were asked to encounter scientific content, science faculty were asked to encounter the feminist *challenge*. From the start, the scientists' worldview was being critiqued, which put them immediately on the defensive. One scientist commented,

> Most readings have a very strong slant towards a radical reconstruction of science, implying that much, if not all of what we do is not done "correctly," sensitively or in a manner beneficial to our students. I find this demoralizing in light of the hard work we all do and the great successes we all have had at Bates. This makes keeping an open mind about the seminar and the reading materials a difficult task.[5]

Team members expected to act as facilitators of conversations about the feminist critique of science. But we neglected to plan a clear response to the understandable defensiveness of those whose worldview was being challenged. As a result, instead of seeing us as resources to help explicate difficult new material, participants identified the team leaders as representing the challenge. Looking back, it seems clear that some of these difficulties were the result of our membership in different discourse communities: scientists and feminists. We had inadvertently set up a dynamic in which it was primarily the team leaders who spoke for and with an understanding of feminist theory, while the participants were not only unfamiliar with the categories of analysis taken for granted by feminists, but often antagonistic toward the very label.

People who are members of the same or similar discourse communities share common understandings and mutual frames of reference. Our language use both reflects and constitutes our different worldviews. Even though seminar leaders and participants used many of the same words, it often felt like we were speaking different languages. Within particular discourse communities, words have meanings

that cannot be easily disentangled from the contexts of those communities. Indeed, the very notion of discourse communities, so important in making sense of
our conversations, is alien to most scientists, for whom scientific language is
more transparent. Conversely, the scientists often found the language used by
feminist theorists impenetrable, and their arguments opaque. Feminists, one scientist commented, "are very verbose, quite clever, and manipulative in their language, and often repetitive."

In retrospect, we believe that much of the frustration we experienced, especially in the first half of the seminar, when we talked past rather than with each
other, can be understood by attending to the different meanings and significance
feminists and scientists attach to two words: *gender* and *objectivity*. In fact, if we
had it to do over, we would start with readings to stimulate discussion of the
terms *gender* and *objectivity*. We learned that it is important to introduce scientists early on to the feminist theory surrounding and complicating these terms.
Embedded in these categories are many of the "self-evident" assumptions taken
for granted by one group, and not shared by the others. Making these assumptions explicit early on, and returning to them throughout the seminar, is necessary "road work" to pave the way for genuine two-way traffic and productive talk
among the participants.

Feminists, of course, take for granted that one of their primary contributions
to any analytical framework is to add the lens of gender to the theorist's toolkit.
For the nonfeminist participants, however, this category was not easily assimi-
lated as a useful or even viable tool for analysis.

> I HATE these categories [male and female]!! In fact, the whole activity of insist-
> ing on dividing up the world into "feminine" and "masculine" and then analyz-
> ing the world by these two categories seems to me an astoundingly reductionist
> thing to do.

For scientists, on the other hand, discussions of objectivity seemed unneces-
sary; most seemed to believe that it simply characterized their practice as scientists. After reading Lorraine Daston (1992), who documented the historical
evolution of various connotations and meanings subsumed by this word, chemist
Thomas Wenzel remarked,

> I am not convinced that objectivity is a recent concept in science. It does seem
> to me that scientists always tried to be objective, even if they did not use that
> term to describe it.

Some examples from our earliest discussions further indicate the difficulties
we encountered in trying to talk about gender and objectivity. We began our

seminar with an exercise adopted from Catherine Middlecamp (1995) that helped us focus on how we construct and use categories. We asked participants what they would like to know about each other. They had to frame their inquiries as questions that could be answered yes or no. In other words, we made a list of categories, by which people would classify themselves as in or out: male/female, scientist/nonscientist, over-forty/under-forty, humanist/nonhumanist, and so on.

This process can be very illuminating, as it brings into question the "naturalness" of our categories, and hints that categories we have taken for granted as natural may in fact be constructed. We hoped that thinking about the significance of the categories we choose to describe and order the world, and seeing how different disciplines focus on different categories, would set the stage for our group to examine how concepts of gender may have influenced the basic categories used in science. This proved to be a far more difficult project than we had originally anticipated. In discussing this exercise, the participants saw how categories contributed to producing identity. But they were not persuaded to expand this insight to the production of knowledge more generally.

Through carefully written overviews and "maps" to each set of readings, we attempted to bridge cultural differences and introduce scientists to the language of feminist scholarship. Our first reading was *A Feeling for the Organism*, Evelyn Fox Keller's biography of Barbara McClintock (1983). Paraphrasing Keller, we began our overview with what was for us an obvious and noncontroversial observation: "A familiar metaphor in our culture is the identifying (naming) of nature as female, and mind as male." We continued, "Here is an example of how gender may influence the basic categories of science. This is one place we will begin to look for the role of gender in the construction of science." As it turned out, our first statement was not obvious and in fact highly contentious for most participants. Participants saw feminists as imposing these categories on science rather than uncovering their effects.

We needed to allow time for this metaphor/concept to sink in before we would be able to focus the group's attention on the role of gender in the construction of scientific knowledge. We have all spent years being socialized in our disciplines, being trained to ask certain questions, and to use particular methodologies. It should not be surprising that it also takes time to reorient in order to learn to communicate across these disciplinary boundaries—in effect, to learn a new language.

Using Keller's analysis of McClintock's story, we asked questions designed to expose and challenge the dualistic worldview that values and rewards objective rational thought over subjective emotional feelings. We were trying to encourage gender analysis for both the fate of the work of one female scientist and for scientific methods in general. For instance, we asked participants to "Examine the cultural assumptions embedded in our individual and/or collective (un)conscious

that imply contradictions between our cultural ideals of 'woman' and 'science.'"
But these categories were not yet familiar or relevant for most of the participants.
One woman professed ignorance of any conflict or dualistic split between the so-
cietal values associated with the two categories:

> I am unaware of any cultural assumptions that imply any contradiction be-
> tween our cultural ideals of woman and science. Maybe it is tough to look sexy
> in goggles.

Without the idea that rationality has been culturally associated with maleness,
we also had difficulty critiquing the concept of objectivity that this same rationality can theoretically create. The same woman who saw no contradiction between the ideals of woman and science wrote later in another context, "I do not
think that I was attracted to science because it was an arena free from emotions."
   This picture of science as being impersonal and free of human values is one
shared by many scientists and has often been cited as support for the claim that
science is objective (see, for example, Noble 1992, 281–82). Our participants
agreed that the notion of *the* scientific method as a unique method followed by
all scientists was a myth introduced in elementary science texts and perpetrated
by the popular media. But most still believed that a variety of scientific methods,
or habits of mind, are designed precisely to prevent error that might arise from
more subjective factors. Resistance to claims that *all* knowledge is socially constructed often manifested itself in a vigorous defense of the objectivity of scientific knowledge. Sometimes evidence of social factors (including gender)
influencing scientific theories was dismissed as a failure of objectivity, simply
"bad science." Our suggestions that gender analysis is a legitimate category in
science critique were often perceived as introducing bias into an otherwise "objective" science. This worldview is so much a part of scientific training that it was
difficult for most of the scientists in the seminar to recognize it as a construction,
to realize that "the anonymity of the picture they produce is . . . itself a kind of
signature" (Keller 1985, 10).
   Aside from differences in discourse communities, perhaps the largest obstacle
we faced was a difference in goals set by the organizers and the participants' expectations. We began with the assumption that in order to facilitate conversations and interactions between people in women's studies and the sciences, we
needed some common language, and thus our readings for the first year concentrated on bringing the scientists "up to speed" in the feminist science studies literature. However, while most scientists who enrolled in the seminar expressed
curiosity and a willingness to become familiar with feminist critiques of science,
they were not signing up for a course in feminist theory. They wanted practical
suggestions for increasing the recruitment and retention of women in their

classes. The organizers, however, felt that it was impossible to address climate and participation issues without a firm grounding in feminist critiques of science. Participants perceived the leaders as "pushing an agenda" on them.

At first, we thought we were simply encountering the resistance to new ideas that we had expected. However, on further reflection, at least one team member (Shulman) realized that she did have an agenda and had to admit that it was, indeed, different from that of the participants. Feminist critiques go beyond creating "female-friendly" classrooms, and raise questions about how scientific knowledge is constructed, and by whom. They claim that in order to make science truly more inclusive, we must make connections between the lived experiences of students marginalized in traditional science classrooms and "real" science. Feminists (and others) claim that no knowledge is value-free. Indeed, they claim that privileging aperspectival knowledge as an ideal to be achieved itself reflects a value system. Rather than letting social motives and purposes that are hidden or denied control the "progress" of science, it is better to make these assumptions explicit, and consciously direct the production of knowledge. It is denying one's biases and interests that is harmful. When we are driven by hidden agendas, we end up in places—sometimes unpleasant or even dangerous places—without understanding how we got there.

In writing this paper, we have realized the importance of this insight in understanding the difficulties we encountered in our seminar. In order for genuine communication to take place, we too had to be willing to confront and acknowledge our own deeply cherished assumptions and beliefs. We did not explicitly examine our own acceptance of the feminist critique of science, and avoided responding directly to the differences in goals, even after some participants complained. In hindsight, we see that many of our difficulties stemmed from our failure to deal openly with the fact that feminist science studies do indeed challenge the scientific worldview and our own resistance to clearly stating our feelings about the validity of these critiques. When we hide how we feel, especially from ourselves, our feelings "leak out" nonetheless, and may contribute to the perception that we are trying to impose our agenda on others.

Given the difficulties we experienced, is there any hope for a meeting of minds, a sharing of worldviews, between feminists and scientists? The short answer is yes, but it takes time. As feminist sociologist of science Sherry Turkle has astutely remarked, "Resistance to a theory is part of its cultural impact" (1997, 145). Disavowal and appropriation of ideas go hand in hand. New ideas can be accepted by people without their realizing it. They can begin speaking a language that was once foreign to them, without noticing a transition, nor recalling that words and concepts that are now self-evident and obvious were once incomprehensible and alien. Indeed, this happened in the second half of the seminar. Perhaps unconsciously, the feminist conceptual framework began to seep into the participants' thinking, and appeared in their comments and discussions.

We learned that it is very difficult to avoid the trap of equating "feminist science" with a project to merely substitute one set of metaphors and values for another. From the start, with feminists challenging scientists, we all (team leaders and participants) tended to reinscribe familiar categories of opposites. In order to walk a truly different path, we must step outside the dualistic construction that places subjective *and* objective knowledge in opposition. The more subtle and difficult task before us is to sort out how both subjective and objective factors *interact* in the production of knowledge; to try to understand how who we are, or who we believe ourselves to be—in other words, our identity—interacts with efforts to "be objective."

Year Two: Women's Studies Encounters Scientific Content

In the second year, we laid down the second lane of the two-way street. Our explicit goal was to encourage women's studies faculty to introduce scientific content into their women's studies courses. We reasoned that women's studies courses had the responsibility to discuss the role of science in women's lives (from the technology of the spinning jenny to the vacuum cleaner), the role of science in seeking to explain questions involving gender and race (from a nineteenth-century science that purported to measure the "inferiority" of African women to the creation of a contraceptive pill supposedly equally effective for all women), and the role of scientists in determining the questions appropriate for research (from the human genome project to the causes of breast cancer). Women's studies courses, at Bates and elsewhere, have often focused much more on evidence and methods from the humanitites and social sciences than those from the natural sciences and mathematics. We hoped our seminar would encourage women's studies faculty to challenge their students to try to understand the relationship of gender analysis to the construction of scientific knowledge. We believed that both faculty and their students needed to learn that they often must investigate scientific content in order to be able to evaluate the questions and products of science. We intended to give seminar participants appropriate examples of such scientific content, as well as to convince them of the importance of thinking about science, in order to stimulate further investigations about the role of science in their own research and teaching.

In order to persuade women's studies participants of the significance of this goal, we planned to engage them in considering the role of material culture in human constructions of reality. We were trying to take up the challenge to critics of science described by Keller as early as 1987.

> Although we may now see that science does not simply "mirror" nature, to say
> instead that it mirrors culture (or "interests") is to make a mockery of the com-
> mitment to the pursuit of the reliable knowledge that lies at the core of scien-
> tists' work. . . . Until we can articulate an adequate response to the question of
> how nature interacts with culture in the production of scientific knowledge,
> working scientists will continue to find their more traditional mind-sets more
> comfortable, more adequate (Keller 1987, 90).

While this topic was extremely important to those of us planning the seminar, in
part because the natural scientists in the first seminar had brought it up often in
opposition to readings that stressed the social construction of reality, we did not
talk about this goal explicitly to our participants. Frankly, we were afraid that
tackling the subject head-on would provoke hostility from faculty skeptical of
any methods that did not privilege social construction. We hoped instead to encourage the discussion through the readings. We can see now that this was a mistake, because we had difficulty in persuading our participants to consider at any
length the role of the material world until the seminar was well advanced.

We knew from our reading and from our experience in the first year that the
roles of the "material world" versus that of "social construction" in creating understandings of human experiences were likely to be represented differently by
our women's studies and natural science participants. We planned to begin by
creating knowledge about and appreciation for both the habits of mind and the
work of the natural scientists. Although the women's studies faculty who participated in our seminar almost all said they wanted to, as one said, "participate in
an exchange of ideas with colleagues," we found little interest or sympathy with
scientific habits of mind at first. One of the habits of mind of many natural scientists is a strong focus on the material world, asking questions designed to eluci-
date its constitution, nature, and modes of change. The women's studies faculty
had less interest in these questions than we had anticipated.

We started our second-year seminar with the question "What is science?" and
asked everyone to write an answer based on readings by three different scientists
(Deutsch 1958; Pert 1997; Wilson 1998). In their responses, most women's studies
faculty demonstrated their facility with analyses of cultural markers and the deconstruction of texts. They focused hardly at all on the scientific work Pert describes at length in her autobiography, *Molecules of Emotion,* and instead stressed
that the science she described was competitive and shot through with gamesman-
ship. They pointed out what was omitted, scrutinized the authors' assumptions
about truth, and analyzed sexist language. Even four months later, when we read
Nelly Oudshoorn's *Beyond the Natural Body: An Archeology of Sex Hormones*
(1994), about early research on what became known as "sex hormones," several
readers criticized her use of the terms *discourse* and *social construction,* but com-

mented little about her discussion of the physical construction of the hormones. Several ignored or said they did not understand a question about the role of scientific research in creating social constructions of the female body.

Why hadn't we been able to encourage more focus on the science in the texts, in Pert's analysis of receptors in the brain, or Oudshoorn's evidence that the practicality of certain kinds of testing influenced scientific decisions about the definition of sexual hormones? First, the discourse communities that created problems in the seminar in year one presented an obstacle in year two as well. Graduate training and association with other members of a discipline divide almost all disciplines from others through the use of terminology, the type of questions asked, and the evidence considered appropriate to answer those questions. The divide between faculty schooled in the natural sciences and those schooled in other disciplines, however, seems a more formidable chasm than that between, say, English and sociology (Burnett 1999; Traweek 1988). Second, our questions did not focus enough attention on the issue of how the material world helps determine our understanding of reality. Because we had failed to make that a central question, the seminar participants didn't think to look at the scientific evidence. Third, many of our participants practiced what we have come to call "science avoidance." Only a few women's studies participants had strong science backgrounds. Fourth, unsurprisingly, women's studies faculty concentrated on what they could do best: they tried to make our readings fit the norms of women's studies discourse. Future project leaders might consider the sheer difficulty for all academics, even those in women's studies who are committed to interdisciplinarity, in developing the ability and desire to see the benefits of the language, concepts, and norms of a seemingly distant discipline.

Even as many women's studies faculty showed reluctance to engage with the scientific content in the texts we assigned, some complained that they were not learning what they had hoped—namely "science," and, in particular, science they could use in their courses. Four of twelve of the faculty outside the natural sciences specifically expressed this criticism on their midcourse evaluations. Faculty wanted practical results; they wanted to learn "science"; they wanted "teaching modules," readings and knowledge they could use in their own courses. Our goal, however, had been to teach them the importance of engagement with the ideas, structure, and production of science. Despite the sophistication with which many of our participants could analyze the social context of the production of knowledge, they still appeared to conceive of science as something existing outside of their own work; science would have to be imported into their courses from somewhere else. At midyear, neither they nor we had realized that the science they would successfully teach in their own courses would not be copied whole from designs of ours, but would develop from the science that was already a part of their own teaching and research subjects.

What is the benefit of encouraging women's studies faculty to try to see the world from the eyes of scientists, to consider the role of the material world in the social construction of knowledge, and to take seriously the science in their own work? We were most successful in eliciting interest and understanding in matters of science and in satisfying our women's studies participants when we asked them to think concretely about a task involving scientific work. Following are three examples, for those who might be trying such ideas.

At the meeting in which we discussed Oudshoorn, we divided the participants into groups of about four people and asked them to work on very specific questions, for which they needed to understand some of the scientific work discussed in the book. For example, one question was "What exactly is a hormone?" Our women's studies faculty genuinely liked this exercise; they set to it with their texts open, waved down passing team members with questions, and resisted our attempts to bring them back together as a whole group. When they really had no choice, because we asked questions directly about the scientific evidence in our texts, women's studies faculty ceased resorting to discourse analysis to avoid it, and approached the science eagerly. Understanding the definition of the scientists "discovering" sex hormones increased the participants' ability to explain (potentially to students) how a hormonal explanation of human bodies relies both on evidence from the material world and social assumptions built into the experiments they performed.

Another successful exercise came in connection with our reading of Claudia Zaslavsky's *Fear of Math: How to Get over It and Get on with Your Life* (1994). As part of the premeeting assignment, we asked participants to work several math word problems, some of which came from Zaslavsky and some of which we wrote ourselves. Specifically, we tried to make the word problems relevant to women's studies by asking questions about statistics regarding the incidence of AIDS and about the effects of alcohol consumption. This exercise produced several wonderful "Aha!" moments, when faculty members got the right answer or figured out how to work the problem—and when they saw the high number of false positives in initial AIDS testing, and considered the possible usefulness of an understanding of statistics. A silence followed our communal conclusion that a large percentage of the alcohol ingested by humans ends up not in the bloodstream, but in the brain. We think that this thoughtful pause reflected an acknowledgment that empirical evidence, based on measurements taken of the material world, contributes to our social construction of the effects and benefits of alcohol consumption.

Finally, we ended the seminar with a half day of ten-minute presentations by seminar participants. They each spoke about how they might incorporate what they had learned into their teaching. Most women's studies faculty demonstrated that they had absorbed the readings and creatively developed ways to integrate them into the teaching of women's studies courses. For example, Cristina Malcolmson, a scholar of British literature and the chair of the women's studies program at Bates, did a close reading of a seventeenth-century British text that included ruminations about what we today might call "molecules." Cristina explained that she had previously simply ignored these references, but that now, by comprehending their role in the text, she could better understand the text as a whole.

Professor Malcolmson's presentation was one of the most striking. It also illustrates one of our most important achievements. Many participants, when they turned back to their own areas of knowledge to create this presentation, could see that aspects of science were already imbedded in their work. Like the team member Elizabeth Tobin, who had never included a word about science in the readings for her courses on modern European history before Bates's 1992–93 seminar on gender and science, faculty began to notice connections they had previously missed. Were we beginning this seminar again, we would try to design exercises earlier in the seminar that directed women's studies faculty to look for the ways in which science in all its forms might be imbedded or inscribed in their own areas of study.

The year two seminar did accomplish its goals of encouraging women's studies faculty to consider the importance of recognizing and including scientific content in their courses, as well as material on the role of science in society in general and the discipline of women's studies in particular. We did not come close, as a group, to answering the question of what role the material world plays in our social construction of reality. We hope that we did achieve some legitimacy for the question among women's studies faculty at Bates, and that this recognition of the question will promote better and more frequent communication along the two-way street.

Negotiating Content and Critique

> Whenever I read this stuff, I am reminded of an old, now-defunct television advertising campaign for Reese's peanut butter cups, where two people (one holding a jar of chocolate and one holding a jar of peanut butter) would accidentally bump into one another, and declare in shocked tones: "Hey! You got chocolate in my peanut butter!" and "You got peanut butter in my chocolate!" I always find myself thinking how appropriate it would be to make a spoof commercial for science studies, where the shocked exclamations are instead: "Hey! You got culture in my nature!" and "You got nature in my culture!"
> —*Rebecca Herzig, women's studies, specializing in gender and science*

Communication can develop despite the difficulties in speaking from different discourse communities. Shared meaning develops over time through a process of negotiation and a willingness to step outside one's own framework and look at the world through a different lens. We found in the first seminar that even groups of scientists often don't share meaning with other scientists who use different research techniques or start with different sets of assumptions. In our second seminar the more heterogeneous community of scientists and women's studies scholars began to communicate and share meaning (or at least hear each other's meanings) when they were ready and able to state explicitly and compare the definitions and usages of terms. As discussed above, in the first year the crucial terms that brought to the surface unstated differences in usage between feminists and scientists were *gender* and *objectivity*. In the second year, we stumbled over the terms *content* and *critique* and realized they also needed attention.

Scientific critique occurs in many forms: in peer review of manuscripts, in the design of new studies that fill in the blanks of previous studies, or in asking the same question in a different way, to see if the "answer" holds up. For scientists, critique is such an integral part of their process that it had not occurred to them that this fact needed to be made explicit, nor that they needed to define what they meant by "critique." Pam Baker, a scientist and team leader, was surprised at how easily women's studies faculty were able to identify and critique both overt and covert political agendas in the readings, and yet at the same time appeared willing to accept scientific data at face value. An "Aha!" moment occurred in a conversation between Pam and Cristina Malcolmson, chair of women's studies, in which Pam suddenly understood that Cristina didn't think scientists were skeptical or that they ever critiqued science.

The feminist critique and the scientific critique differ in their focus and in their purpose. We might have progressed more rapidly in our two seminars had we made the distinction between the critiques early on, and suggested the importance of urging scientists and women's studies faculty to utilize both kinds of critique. It is our belief that when applied in tandem, they will lead to a more comprehensive and self-conscious science, aware of its strengths and weaknesses and better able meet the goals of understanding the world and improving the lives of those who inhabit it.

One of the readings in the second seminar, *Exploding the Gene Myth* (Hubbard and Wald 1993), was chosen because it contains both scientific and feminist critiques of molecular biology. We made some progress toward shared meaning and communication in discussions of this book. Hubbard and Wald (using feminist critique) point out how the use of certain language—for example, "the gene for X"—leads to a feeling of the inevitability of some outcome, and discourages questions about alternatives. The book also includes rigorous scientific critique of the research; that is, a critique based on the data. In our discussions of the book, there were several moments when it was clear that participants were "hearing" (maybe for the first time) the concerns and interests of their colleagues in different disciplines. In retrospect, we could have taken better advantage of these moments by drawing attention to them, and directing the conversation toward an examination of what enables us to communicate across boundaries.

However, toward the end of the second year, we did have an interesting exchange about communication on our listserv. The postings showed that by the end of the seminar we were doing a better job of talking *to* rather than past each other. As a group, we had become more self-conscious about our own definitions of critique and content, and more willing to consider those from other disciplines.

Conclusion

The reigning metaphor of this project has been the two-way street, with traffic in both directions. We found that the two-way street wasn't an easily navigated and well-paved route; it was more like a multilane road in various states of repair. Our method of building the street, one lane at a time, was necessary, in our opinion, but that method made it more difficult for some faculty to cross over to the other side of the street. Even when both lanes were operable, some cars whizzed along so fast on familiar surfaces that they never stopped to look at the traffic going the other way. Some cars pulled into the breakdown lane early in the journey and never moved. Sometimes our own vehicle broke an axle in the potholes and we had to stop for repairs. Regardless, we think that the journey itself was worth taking.

In thinking about how to improve communication on this two-way street, we noticed that our own conversations improved in quality and understanding the more women's studies faculty knew about the habits of mind and questions of scientists, and vice versa. A few members of our group stated that their own learning took place more quickly when they were part of a group composed primarily of faculty from the "other side of the street." One scientist who participated in both seminars said that he had learned more in the second seminar, when he was one of only a few scientists in a group with many women's studies faculty. He sometimes felt amazement when listening to his women's studies colleagues; it hadn't occurred to him, for example, to think of these texts about science as narratives whose literary construction was as important as their handling of data. Likewise, a social scientist team member learned to recognize that her scientific colleagues' habit of mind of asking empirical questions did not preclude their consideration of questions regarding the social construction of knowledge.

We still find the metaphor of the two-way street very useful, especially because it draws the attention of women's studies faculty toward what they can learn from scientists. But we have also begun to think in terms of the vehicles implied in the metaphor of the two-way street. We need to conceptualize ways in which we can see, at least temporarily, from the perspective of other disciplines.

We need to cross the street and carpool, ride together until we know more about the new driver's destination, roadmap, and driving style. The two-way street won't go away; separate disciplines will continue to have different questions and destinations. Nonetheless, by driving for a time with another group, we can learn about methods and perspectives that will help us, when we get back into our familiar car, to modify our own vehicles and perhaps travel to new destinations.

Notes

1. Bonnie Shulman, trained as a mathematician and currently writing on science studies, was a facilitator of both seminars. Sharon Kinsman, an evolutionary ecologist who has taught an introductory biology course that is also a core course in women's studies, was a cofacilitator of the first year's seminar. Elizabeth Tobin, a historian who has been chair of Bates' women's studies program, helped develop the readings for the second year. Pamela Baker, a biologist, also developed the readings for and cofacilitated the second seminar. Mark Semon, a physicist, contributed suggestions for readings for year two, but dropped out as a team member.

2. The AAC&U project was funded by the NSF Experimental Projects for Women and Girls, Grant HRD95-55808. According to the AAC&U website, accessed November 22, 1999 (http://www.aacu-edu.org/Initiatives/scilit.html), "The primary goal of the Women and Scientific Literacy Project is to bridge the gulf between science and women's studies by incorporating the new scholarship in these areas into undergraduate science, engineering, and mathematics courses and also by making science a more central part of women's studies courses."

3. The syllabi and reading lists for the seminars described in this paper can be found at the AAC&U website (see note 2).

4. An active group of faculty in both the sciences and women's studies at Bates have been trying to establish personal and intellectual connections across these disciplinary lines for some years. Our most concerted previous action had been a faculty development seminar in 1992–93, called "Gender and Science," in which faculty from many disciplines considered how issues of gender impact the composition of science faculties, the kinds of questions asked by scientists, and the nature of scientific evidence. Some of the most significant moments in this seminar occurred during sessions in which seminar members tried to explain and understand the nature of each other's disciplines. Seeing the strengths and weaknesses of other methods helped us all see the strengths and weaknesses of our own.

5. Quotations from faculty members in our seminars come from three sources: (1) evaluation forms filled out at several different times during the course of each seminar, asking about goals and their achievement, (2) written responses to questions about each month's reading, and (3) e-mail comments that furthered discussion begun at meetings, or that brought up related topics. Quotations and paraphrases remain anonymous, unless the faculty member explicitly requested attribution.

Works Cited

Burnett, D. Graham. "A View from the Bridge: The Two Cultures Debate, Its Legacy, and the History of Science." *Daedalus 128* (1999): 193–218.

Dastin, Lorraine. "Objectivity and the Escape from Perspective." *Social Studies of Science* 22 (1992): 597–618.

Deutsch, Martin. "Evidence and Inference in Nuclear Research." *Daedalus* 87 (1958): 88–98.

Ginorio, Angela. *Warming the Climate for Women in Academic Science.* Washington, D.C.: Association of American Colleges and Universities, 1995.

Hammonds, Evelynn. "Never Meant to Survive: A Black Woman's Journey." *Radical Teacher 30* (1986): 8–15.

Haraway, Donna J. "A Cyborg Manifesto." In *Simians, Cyborgs, and Women: The Reinvention of Nature.* New York: Routledge, 1991.

Harding, Sandra. "Can Feminist Thought Make Economics More Objective?" *Feminist Economics 1* (1995): 7–32.

Hubbard, Ruth, and Elijah Wald. *Exploding the Gene Myth: How Genetic Information Is Produced and Manipulated by Scientists, Physicians, Employers, Insurance Companies, Educators, and Law Enforcers.* Boston: Beacon Press, 1993.

Keller, Evelyn Fox. "Women Scientists and Feminist Critics of Science." *Daedalus* 116 (1987): 77–90.

———. *Reflections on Gender and Science.* New Haven, CT: Yale University Press, 1985.

———. *A Feeling for the Organism.* San Francisco: W. H. Freeman, 1983.

Middlecamp, Catherine. "Culturally Inclusive Chemistry." In *Teaching the Majority*, ed. Sue Rosser. New York: Teachers College Press, 1995.

Minkoff, Eli, and Pamela Baker. "Variation among Human Populations." *Biology Today: An Issues Approach.* New York: McGraw-Hill, 1996.

Noble, David F. *A World without Women: The Christian-Clerical Culture of Western Science.* New York: Knopf, 1992.

Oudshoorn, Nelly. *Beyond the Natural Body: An Archeology of Sex Hormones.* London and New York: Routledge, 1994.

Pert, Candace. *Molecules of Emotion: Why You Feel the Way You Feel.* New York: Scribner, 1997.

Schiebinger, Londa. *Nature's Body: Gender in the Making of Modern Science.* Boston: Beacon Press, 1993.

Spanier, Bonnie. "Biological Determinism and Homosexuality." *NWSA Journal 7* (1995): 54–71.

Traweek, Sharon. *Beamtimes and Lifetimes: The World of High Energy Physics.* Cambridge, MA: Harvard University Press, 1988.

Turkle, Sherry. *Life on the Screen: Identity in the Age of the Internet.* New York: Simon and Schuster, 1997.

Wilson, E. O. "Scientists, Scholars, Knaves, and Fools." *American Scientist* 86 (1998): 6–7.

Zaslavsky, Claudia. *Fear of Math: How to Get over It and Get on with Your Life.* New Brunswick, NJ: Rutgers University Press, 1994.

The Forgotten Few

Developing Curricula on Women in the Physical Sciences and Engineering

→ Lisa H. Weasel, Melissa Honrado, and Debbie P. Bautista

While feminists have made bold and enduring strides into science in the recent past, the focus of a large majority of feminist projects in the sciences have tended to be on the life and social sciences, rather than the physical sciences or engineering. As feminist scholars and educators, we must ask ourselves how the relative neglect within women's studies of the situation for women in the physical sciences and engineering makes us complicit in the continuing gender imbalance between these fields. Furthermore, if women's studies is to be understood and constructed as an interdisciplinary undertaking, we must also ask ourselves why so few scientists, particularly physical scientists and engineers, teach and conduct research as part of our programs, and why our curricular offerings tend to focus on the humanities and social sciences rather than the natural sciences and engineering. To arrive at a solution, we must seek ways in which we can address and redress these imbalances through our teaching and scholarship. Here, we want to offer an agenda for developing curricula linking women's studies and the physical sciences and engineering. These suggestions aim to foster constructive bridges that will bring together students, faculty, and subject matter from women's studies and the physical sciences and engineering. These suggested interdisciplinary curriculum development efforts therefore have a dual goal: on the one hand they aim to improve the situation for women and underrepresented people of color in the physical sciences and engineering, and on the other hand they provide an important contribution to the construction and creation of new, inter- and transdisciplinary knowledges that are so important in the development of women's studies. While offering concrete suggestions, examples, and resources, our agenda is intended to present a flexible model for curriculum development, which can be adapted and fine-tuned to fit a variety of diverse institutional and educational scenarios.

Our Approach: Traversing Institutional and Disciplinary Boundaries

This project arose out of a collaborative action project developed in an undergraduate women's studies class titled "Science Studies in Feminism." After reading and discussing a broad range of feminist literature on science, several students in the class decided to address the lack of courses on campus combining the sciences and the humanities more generally, and women's studies and the physical sciences and engineering in this specific case. Curriculum development and course design is usually a matter presided over and determined by faculty and administrators; in this project, however, we aimed to develop a more collaborative, interactive model that would give students a voice in the subject and content of courses. Through the creation of an environment in which students worked together with faculty to evaluate, revise, and design course content and materials, this project provided an opportunity for increased dialogue across traditional institutional boundaries, for mentoring and role modeling to take place, and for the exchange of otherwise disparate perspectives and ideas pertaining both to subject matter and teaching styles.

Our approach to the challenge of developing courses that link women's studies and the physical sciences and engineering began with an analysis of the current curricular offerings at our university in both women's studies and the schools of physical sciences and engineering. Within our women's studies program, courses addressing science in general ("Race, Gender, and Science"; "Science Studies in Feminism") and the life sciences more specifically ("Genes and Society") have recently been implemented with great success. In analyzing these pilot courses, we determined that a critical factor in their success was their interdisciplinary nature. While these courses demonstrated the potential for collaborative coursework linking women's studies and the sciences, they were also notably focused on the life sciences rather than the physical sciences or engineering.

When we turned our attention to the courses offered in the schools of physical sciences and engineering at our university, we found few if any courses addressing or incorporating issues of gender, race, or class, or that were taught within a feminist framework. Several courses in the physical sciences and engineering included topics pertaining to social issues or applications; however, these courses were almost always designed for nonmajors, and were rarely available for credit within the major. Notable exceptions were several courses in the School of Engineering, including "Energy and Society," "Communications in the Professional World," and "Ethical Issues in Engineering," which conversely were open *only* to students in the School of Engineering. Thus, we concluded that there were few if any courses that examined the social aspects or implications of the physical sciences or engineering within an interdisciplinary, feminist context.

Based on our analysis of the current course offerings and inspired by the relative and recent success of courses linking women's studies and biology on our campus, we decided to approach the challenge of developing feminist curricula that would serve to bridge women's studies and the physical sciences and engineering. Our goal was to bring topics and subject matter from the physical sciences and engineering into the women's studies curriculum, while at the same time developing courses that would offer feminist analyses and approaches to issues of gender, race, class, and other social variables within the fields encompassed by the physical sciences and engineering. We wanted to create an interdisciplinary learning environment that would bring together not only subject matter, but also students and ideally faculty from these fields.

Course Development: Two Models

We devised two models that could be applied to the development of cross-disciplinary and interdisciplinary curricula. The first model involves the transformation and reformatting of already existing courses to include social issues directly addressing issues of gender, race, and class within a feminist framework. We chose to begin with a course offered to majors in the School of Engineering at our university, "Communications in the Professional World." Because this course is currently offered for credit to engineering majors, it is already accepted as a part of the engineering curriculum. Its emphasis on written and interpersonal communication provides opportunities for feminist intervention and the addition of subject matter concerning gender, race, class, and other social stratifications that may play an important role in communication styles within the engineering workplace. While maintaining the general structure and subject matter of the course as offered, our intervention involved the following substantial changes:

- the incorporation of subject matter pertaining to gender dynamics and communication styles in general, and the role that such dynamics play in engineering in particular;
- consideration of the concept of power differentials related to dominant and oppressed groups in the workplace, including issues of gender, race, and class;
- discussion of sexual harassment laws, cases, and policies in the workplace, with specific reference to situations in which significant gender differentials in employee composition exist; and
- expansion of the course to include non–engineering majors, and the cross-listing and credit of the course within the women's studies curriculum.

Such changes are incorporated into the course through the addition of readings, writing exercises, guest lecturers and student interaction, and role playing. Readings from the text *Women in Engineering: Gender, Power, and Workplace Culture*, by Judith McIlwee and J. Gregg Robinson (1992), provide a backbone for content and discussion, which is supplemented by written journal response assignments. Guest lectures by women engineers and engineers of color working in the community provide role models as well as insight into the dynamics of engineering workplace culture. Visits from human resource or sexual harassment officers at the university and local engineering firms also provide first-hand information regarding sexual harassment and equal opportunity issues in engineering. Actively engaging the students in role-playing and interactive group assignments around communication issues serves to demonstrate relevant points regarding gender dynamics, as well as to generate awareness and promote change.

Although this structure retains the basic outline of the original course, it incorporates new approaches and subject matter that make it appropriate for inclusion in both the engineering and women's studies curricula. The advantage of such an approach is that it requires only the revision of an existing course rather than the development and introduction of a new course. This may be particularly useful in situations where a science department as a whole shows little support for the inclusion of feminist curriculum and where the introduction of a new course would be difficult. In such cases it may be easier to identify and work with individual supportive faculty with the power to revise courses that they already teach, providing a more gradual introduction to curricular transformation. This approach also lends itself readily to team teaching, in which an engineering faculty member works together with a women's studies faculty member, who may or may not be from engineering or the sciences. This is advantageous in creating interdisciplinary alliances, and can help to alleviate situations in which qualified women's studies faculty are not able to commit to teaching an entire course. Although we have demonstrated this model with a course from engineering, this revision-intervention model can of course be extended and applied to courses from the physical sciences as well.

Our second model for curricular transformation involves the design of a new course bridging women's studies and the physical sciences, to be offered for credit to students majoring in both women's studies and physical science fields. This approach allows for a thorough and intentional structuring of the class around feminist principles and subject matter addressing and integrating subjects from the physical sciences, and works best when there is commitment on the part of and alliance between women's studies and physical science faculty and administration regarding the incorporation of such an interdisciplinary course into the curriculum. A general description and outline of the course follows below.

Gender and Belief Systems in Physical Science

Course Outline in Module Format

Course Description. How are the directions and goals of the physical sciences determined? Who gets to do science? Does their gender, race, class, sexuality, or religion affect the results they come up with? Who decides how to apply what we learn in the physical sciences? Is it possible to come up with a Theory of Every-thing, commonly referred to by physicists as "TOE"? Who decides what we study in the physical sciences and how it relates to us? Through careful study of the history, sociology, and ethics of the physical sciences within a feminist con-text combined with an open atmosphere for critical self-reflection, this class will act as a springboard for the engagement of active discourse and contemplations of these questions.

Course Texts. Sandra Harding (1991), *Whose Science? Whose Knowledge?*; Evelyn Fox Keller (1985), *Reflections on Gender and Science*; Sharon Traweek (1988), *Beamtimes and Lifetimes*; Margaret Wertheim (1995), *Pythagoras' Trousers*; David F. Noble (1992), *A World without Women*; Claudia Henrion (1997), *Women in Mathematics*; Ken Wilber (1984), *Quantum Questions*; Susan Ambrose (1997), *Journeys of Women in Science and Engineering*; Dana Zohar (1990), *The Quantum Self*; and additional selected articles listed below.

Basic Course Structure. The course is divided into several modules, which can be tailored to available numbers and structures of class segments. We present it below as we constructed it to fit our once-a-week seminar format within a ten-week quarter system; however, the flexibility of content and assignments can eas-ily be tailored to fit other types of instructional formats and schedules by adding or reducing readings, discussion, and assignments, as well as incorporating guest lecturers or field trips.

Module 1: Introduction to the Course
This module introduces students to the concepts and applications of feminism in science. Because many science majors may not have had prior background or experience in women's studies courses, establish-ing a firm foundation in this initial module is essential.

Readings
Harding, "Feminism Confronts the Sciences: Reform and Transfor-mation" (chapter 2), and "How the Women's Movement Benefits Sci-ence: Two Views" (chapter 3), in *Whose Science? Whose Knowledge?*
Wertheim, *Pythagoras' Trousers* (Introduction).

Module 2: History of Physical Science from a Feminist Perspective
This module provides historical insight into the origin of contempo-rary ideas, theories, and practice in the physical sciences and dis-cusses the role of gender, race, and class in this development.

Readings: History 1
Noble, "Mothers, Daughters, Sisters, Wives" (chapter 1), and "Revivals" (chapter 2), in *A World without Women*.
   Keller, "Baconian Science: The Arts of Mastery and Obedience" (chapter 2), in *Reflections on Gender and Science*.

Readings: History 2
Noble, "Revelation in Nature" (chapter 8), "The Scientific Restoration" (chapter 9), and "Women in a World without Women" (chapter 10), in *A World without Women*.
   Keller, "Spirit and Reason at the Birth of Modern Science" (chapter 3), in *Reflections on Gender and Science*.
   Wertheim, "The Triumph of Mechanism" (chapter 4), in *Pythagoras' Trousers*.

Module 3: Gender, Belief Systems, and Physics
This module approaches the physical sciences as a belief system and looks at intersections between gender, religion, and physics in historical and contemporary contexts.

Readings: Physics and Religion 1
Noble, "Saints: The Ascent of Clerical Asceticism" (chapter 3), "Fathers: Patristic Anxiety to Papal Agenda" (chapter 4), "Brothers: The Militarization of Monasticism" (chapter 5), and "Bachelors: The Scholastic Cloister" (chapter 7), in *A World without Women*.
   Wertheim, "All Is Number" (chapter 1), "God as Mathematician" (chapter 2), "Harmony of the Spheres" (chapter 3), in *Pythagoras' Trousers*.

Readings: Physics and Religion 2
Zohar, "Consciousness and the Brain: Two Classical Models" (chapter 5), "A Quantum Mechanical Model of Consciousness" (chapter 6), "Mind and Body" (chapter 7), and "The Quantum Vacuum and the God Within" (chapter 15), in *The Quantum Self*.
   Wilber, ed., Werner Heisenberg, "Scientific and Religious Truths"; Erwin Schoedinger, "The Eye That Is God" and "The Mystic Vision"; and Albert Einstein, "Cosmic Religious Feeling" and "Science and Religion," in *Quantum Questions*.

Module 4: Gender and the Practice of Physical Science
This module addresses the way in which the physical sciences are practiced and carried out. In the discussion and reading selections in this module, close attention should be paid to the diversity of women's experiences in the physical sciences with respect to categories of race, class, ethnicity, sexuality, and religious affiliation. This module also provides an excellent opportunity to invite a guest speaker or assemble a panel of women physical scientists to speak to the class.

Readings
Ambrose et al., eds., *Journeys of Women in Science and Engineering.*
   Henrion, "Rugged Individualism and the Mathematical Marlboro Man" (chapter 1), "What's a Nice Girl like You Doing in a Place like This?" (chapter 2), and "Double Jeopardy: Gender and Race" (chapter 5), in *Women in Mathematics.*
   Traweek, *Beamtimes and Lifetimes.*

Module 5: Gender and the Theories of Physical Science
In this module, students have the opportunity to uncover and address the ways in which beliefs about gender, race, class, and other socially constructed categories find their way into theoretical work in the physical sciences. As a way to preface this module, it may be helpful to review earlier considerations of the concept of objectivity introduced in Harding (1991) in module 1.

Readings: Gender and Theory 1, Content
N. Katherine Hayles (1992), "Gender Encoding in Fluid Mechanics."
   Carol Cohn (1987), "Nuclear Language and How We Learned to Pat the Bomb."
   Wertheim, "The Ascent of Mathematical Woman" (chapter 10), in *Pythagoras' Trousers.*
   Keller, "Cognitive Repression in Contemporary Physics" (chapter 7), in *Reflections on Gender and Science.*

Readings: Gender and Theory 2, Epistemology
Harding, "Why Physics Is a Bad Model for Physics" (chapter 4), in *Whose Science? Whose Knowledge?*
   Henrion, "The Quest for Certain and Eternal Knowledge" (chapter 6), in *Women in Mathematics.*

Wertheim, "Quantum Mechanics and a 'Theory of Everything'" (chapter 9), in *Pythagoras' Trousers*.

Karen Barad (1998), "Getting Real: Technoscientific Practices and the Materialization of Reality."

Class Assignments and Grading

Journals
Essential to developing students' ability to comprehend, analyze, and respond to the material are journal responses designed to both summarize and reflect upon the assigned readings. These three to five-page journals help students to prepare for discussion, which is an integral component of the class, as well as to keep the instructor informed of how and in which ways the students are responding to the material beyond what is brought up in class.

Research project
Students are asked to critically analyze an experiment they have performed in the past or are currently working on. If they have never participated in an experiment, they are asked to pick one of interest from the literature. The experiment should be related in some way to the physical sciences (suggestions here include light, time, space, lasers, lenses, mathematics, radioactivity, and so on). In their research paper, students are asked to document the language used throughout the experiment, and to discuss the social implications of the experiment. Who came up with the idea to study this? Why? How was the information gathered and how will it be used? Do the results and their presentation include or exclude the public? Findings will be presented in an in-class feminist science research forum.

Science fair
Students are asked to envision what a feminist science would look like, and to design a physical science experiment of their own specifically incorporating a feminist approach to interpreting or practicing science. What are the benefits of this approach? What assumptions are made? Why was this approach chosen? How could this experiment be performed differently?

Discussion/class participation
The nature of this class necessarily requires an active approach to the material on the part of both students and faculty. While some of the

material may initially seem unfamiliar to students of the sciences accustomed to memorizing facts in lecture classes, or appear intimidating to women's studies students without strong science interests or backgrounds, early establishment of active discussion and processing of the course readings should aim to encourage student participation and engagement with the materials.

Faculty and Student Support: Suggested Strategies

Obviously, successful implementation of either or both of these curriculum transformation models requires some degree of support from both faculty and students. Thus, when considering the development of such curricula, it is wise to facilitate a network of supportive faculty and students who can both champion the change and provide creative input. Our collaborative model, which involves both students and faculty working together, has been very successful in generating supportive and enthusiastic alliances at multiple levels. Through networking attempts, we have been able to identify individuals and groups on our own campus as well as at other related or nearby institutions who can be consulted as resources and for support. These include faculty, administrators, and student groups. Often the implementation of a pilot course or seminar on the topic can mobilize student interest and generate faculty curiosity. Guest appearances at student science groups, particularly those involving students underrepresented in science, and student-advising opportunities can help to both gauge and stimulate interest in such curricula. Drawing attention to statistical figures relating to the participation of generally low numbers of men of color and women in the physical sciences and engineering can often help to persuade reluctant departments and administrations. Seeking and obtaining grant or other funding or award support for such curriculum development is another way to help build enthusiasm for such projects. Often, initial small refinements in curricula can pave the way for broader changes later on, and particularly in the early stages of such a project it is important to keep in mind the direction that one is moving the curriculum toward as well as the ultimate goal.

The suggestions that we provide here have been derived from our experience as students and faculty working together at a large, public research institution, and thus our recommendations have been tempered by our specific context. However, we have tried to present our models in as broad and flexible a manner as possible, to allow for their adaptation to a variety of instructional and institutional formats. Our two models for curriculum development, one relying predominantly upon revision and transformation of already existing courses and the other building a new course from the ground up, are meant to demonstrate the diversity of approaches that can be taken in developing interdisciplinary curricula bringing together women's studies and the physical sciences and engineering. We present them not as alternatives to one another, but as representatives of just two of the many ways in which curriculum development might ideally and simultaneously proceed. In offering these suggestions for curriculum transformation, we hope to demonstrate one way in which women's studies curricula can address and collaboratively work toward changing the situation for women in the physical sciences and engineering.

Works Cited

Ambrose, Susan, et al. (Eds.). *Journeys of Women in Science and Engineering: No Universal Constants*. Philadelphia: Temple University Press, 1997.

Barad, Karen. "Getting Real: Technoscientific Practices and the Materialization of Reality." *Differences* 10 (1998): 87–120.

Cohn, Carol. "Nuclear Language and How We Learned to Pat the Bomb." *Bulletin of the Atomic Scientists* (June 1987).

Harding, Sandra. *Whose Science? Whose Knowledge? Thinking from Women's Lives*. Ithaca, NY: Cornell University Press, 1991.

Hayles, N. Katherine. "Gender Encoding in Fluid Mechanics: Masculine Channels and Feminine Flows." *Differences* 4 (1992): 16–42.

Henrion, Claudia. *Women in Mathematics: The Addition of Difference*. Bloomington: Indiana University Press, 1997.

Keller, Evelyn Fox. *Reflections on Gender and Science*. New Haven, CT: Yale University Press, 1985.

McIlwee, Judith, and J. Gregg Robinson. *Women in Engineering: Gender, Power, and Workplace Culture*. Albany: SUNY Press, 1992.

Noble, David F. *A World without Women: The Christian Clerical Culture of Western Science*. New York: Knopf, 1992.

Traweek, Sharon. *Beamtimes and Lifetimes: The World of High Energy Physics*. Cambridge, MA: Harvard University Press, 1988.

Wertheim, Margaret. *Pythagoras' Trousers: God, Physics, and the Gender Wars*. New York: Times Books/Random House, 1995.

Wilber, Ken (Ed.). *Quantum Questions: Mystical Writings of the World's Great Physicists*. Boston: Shambhala, 1984.

Zohar, Dana. *The Quantum Self: Human Nature and Consciousness Defined by the New Physics*. New York: William Morrow, 1990.

"What about Biology?"

Building Sciences into Introductory
Women's Studies Curricula

⟶ Rebecca M. Herzig

Teaching "Introduction to Women's Studies" (WS 100) last winter at Bates College (a private liberal arts college in New England), I opened the course by asking students to present their definitions of *woman*. After a few grumbles and rolled eyes about fulfilling such an elementary request, the students set about jotting down ideas. What characterizes *woman* or *women*, the alleged subject(s) of this elective course?

The difficulty of the question presented itself immediately. The term exploded. Some students characterized *woman* as a sense of being, a kind of knowledge based on shared experience. In the words of one sophomore, woman is "more of a mentality than a physical state."[1] Others rejected the significance of shared social existence in favor of individual determinations. As one junior put it, "a woman is one who chooses to identify as woman. Simple as that—self-identification." As the fissures in the category became more evident, some participants in the class steered their definitions to the seemingly safe ground of biology. One student argued, "*woman* is a person with a female body." Concurring, other members of the class listed attributes that characterize "the female body": breasts, a uterus, lactation, ovaries, eggs, a clitoris, vagina, two X chromosomes, specific hormones, hips, curves, and/or menstrual fluid. As the list grew longer and longer, one student tentatively questioned the seeming clarity of such anatomical distinctions. "What about those people with more than two chromosomes? You know—XXY and YYX or whatever it is?" Another chimed in, "What about women who don't menstruate?" Even on the terra firma of "the female," *woman* again began to waver.

At this point in the history of feminist organizing, it is hardly more than a cliché to note that "woman" does not name a neutral or universal identity. Where once the foundational subject of women's studies was generally taken for granted by those teaching and learning in the field, a generation of research and activism has successfully challenged the transparency and fixity of the category (for example, Joseph and Lewis 1981; Herdt 1994; Hull et al. 1982; Wittig 1992). Twenty-first-century feminisms must now tackle the concept of *woman* as a problem in itself (Alcoff 1989; Brown 1997). Rather than simply describing "things that have happened to women and men," contemporary women's studies typically examines "how the subjective and collective meanings of women and men as categories of identity have been constructed" (Scott 1988, 6). Accordingly, introductory courses in the field often seek to demonstrate the profound differences masked by the term *women*. At Bates, "Introduction to Women's Studies" typically explores the subjective and collective meanings of womanhood as constituted by nationality, race, religion, class, sexuality, ethnicity, language, and physical ability.[2]

Yet for many introductory-level students, sooner or later this critical approach smacks into the wall of physical embodiedness. *Ideas* about "women" may be divided and marked by the effects of history and culture, they insist, but not underlying bodies. Ironically, even as we study productions of womanhood in law, art, popular culture, wage labor, or family life, students often grow *more* confident in the immutability of fundamental, physiological "femaleness." They happily consider myriad permutations of "gender" by assuring themselves of the constancy, neutrality, and universality of "sex." Students' conceptual retreat to the neutral ground of sex occurs even despite evident variation in perceptions of "the" female body (a body that students alternately distinguish by breast milk, chromosomes, or beardlessness). In short, for all its manifest inconsistency "the female body" tends to remain protected from students' critical scrutiny.

This persistent retreat from gender to sex became starkly apparent during one recent class when we discussed a short article by Gloria Steinem titled "If Men Could Menstruate" (1988). In this playful spoof, Steinem ponders on how differently menstruation might be approached if the process were identified with men instead of women: rather than skulking to the bathroom to change tampons, men would boast about the length and amount of their bleeding, would declare themselves specially fit for military service due to their affiliation with blood, and so on. Introductory students, following Steinem's lead, often view the possibility of alternate interpretations of menstruation as testimony to the pervasive sexism in contemporary U.S. society. If men could menstruate, blood would be cause for bravado and celebration rather than shame or annoyance. To students discussing the essay in class, the essay makes systemic social discrimination perfectly clear: women have been routinely encouraged to view their bodies with distaste or abhorrence.

What also appears clear to the students is the fundamental, immutable fact of sexual difference: women cyclically expel menstrual fluid; men do not. This fact exists outside the effects of culture and history, outside the reach of what one student termed "sexist ideology." While interpretations on menstruation may be subject to analysis and change, the shape and function of "the female body" is not. Students comfortably critiqued "gender" by stabilizing definitions of "sex."

Further conversation, however, reopens the presumed fixity and universality of sexed identity in this instance. As we discussed the article and the presumption that "women" menstruate, one student quietly pointed out that women with eating disorders often stop menstruating, and yet "they're still women." Someone followed that comment by noting that some long-distance runners often do not menstruate. Others noted that women taking oral contraceptives could skip the monthly "blank" pills, postponing menstration indefinitely. With another nudge, the room of teenage students also slowly began to consider the matter of menopause. "*All kinds of women don't menstruate,*" one summarized. Quickly, strict distinctions between ideas and bodies, between gender and sex, broke down. We were revisiting questions of norms, definitions, categories, and identities—precisely the mutable, troubling issues we thought we'd corralled and left behind. "The female body" turned out to be equally subject to historical and cultural context.

Thus, to encourage a more thorough consideration of the constitution of "women" and "men" in introductory women's studies courses, I find I must begin by focusing attention on "the female body." Among students at Bates, questions regarding the irreducible *matter* of bodies persist throughout our discussions of symbolic, juridical, or literary embodiments of gender. "That's all well and good," someone invariably points out during our class discussions, "But what about biology?"

From Bodies to Science

Buried in this straightforward question is a complex set of assumptions: To what do we refer when we discuss "biology"? Chromosomes? Hormones? Neurotransmitters? Curve of hips? Coarseness of facial hair? (And how did biology, knowledge about the body, come to stand for somatic attributes—the body's very physicality?) Students' recurrent biology question reveals, however, that attention to the realm of physical bodies inevitably leads to the realm of "science." The task, then, is to formulate questions about scientific knowledge and scientific authority in such a way as to make them relevant and interesting to introductory students, to raise questions about the sciences that help them make sense of concrete, bodily examples like menstruation. What characterizes difference with respect to such biological attributes? How are standards of difference determined, and by whom? What constitutes evidence of such differences, once we identify common standards of measurement?

Such questions have been the object of discussion for a generation of feminist studies of science, medicine, and technology. Several innovative graduate and undergraduate courses have reaped the benefit of this scholarship, integrating women, gender, and feminism into basic and advanced coursework in mathematics, engineering, and the natural sciences.[3] Yet even as feminist science studies gains influence in the teaching of natural sciences, we have had less effect on the content of courses in women's studies. As Lynda Birke and Marsha Henry (1997) recently noted, aside from some material on health and reproduction, women's studies classes rarely incorporate the numerous insights of feminist science and technology studies. At times, the gap between feminist science studies and women's studies appears as pronounced as that between feminist science studies and practicing scientists and engineers. Although this chasm might be addressed through a range of topics in feminist science studies, I want to focus here on the role feminist science studies might play in illuminating the complex, contested issue of sexual difference.

Feminist theory, of course, has devoted significant attention to questions of sexual difference in recent years (Lundgren 1995; Butler 1990, 1993; Riley 1988). Yet unlike much contemporary feminist criticism, feminist science studies compel us to consider both symbolic and somatic formations of "women" (Barad 1998). The best work in feminist science studies moves beyond stale discussions of social construction, urging us to specify both the locus of agency implied in the social and the particular mechanisms veiled in the term *construction*. In its interdisciplinarity, this work subverts students' rather curious assumption that science (or rather, biology) is the realm of the material (the concrete, the fixed, the real), while feminism is the realm of the conceptual (the abstract, the mutable, the ideal). By focusing on particular examples, students toss out these presuppositions and examine the mundane, concrete formations of "women" ongoing around them.

The three modules below thus offer ways to incorporate some of the insights of recent feminist science studies into introductory women's studies syllabi.[4] Each short description includes sample readings, videos, and/or class assignments, all designed to query received knowledge about "the female body." Each module also attempts to bolster understandings of the sciences (promoting arithmetic skill or knowledge of human reproduction), while encouraging a critical examination of the methods, contents, and aims of science. The modules seek to integrate issues of regional location, race, economics, and ideology, while remaining firmly attentive to the shape, substance, and mortality of fleshy bodies—to the questions of materiality that inevitably arise in women's studies courses. All units described here have been used in actual introductory courses. I offer them not with the intention of bracketing discussion of "science" from other course content, nor with concentrating critical scrutiny of "woman" in just a few lectures. The few examples provided will I hope provoke new combinations of source materials, and new ideas for introducing sciences into women's studies curricula.

Module 1: Sexual Dimorphism
Lurking in most contemporary discussions about gender and sexuality in the United States is a presumption of the universal, timeless di-

morphism between human males and females. How empirically sound are these dualistic categories? What evidence has been presented for and against universal human sexual dimorphism? How might cross-cultural ethnographic evidence challenge biomedical assumptions of a strict two-sex model? How does the presumption of sexual dimorphism inform our understandings of human sexuality?

Readings
Anne Fausto-Sterling (1992), "The Five Sexes: Why Male and Female Are Not Enough."
  Suzanne Kessler (1990), "The Medical Construction of Gender: Case Management of Intersexed Infants."
  Anne Fausto-Sterling (1997), "How to Build a Man."
  Will Roscoe (1994), "How to Become a Berdache: Toward a Unified Analysis of Gender Diversity."
  Serena Nanda (1993), "Hijras as Neither Man nor Woman."

Videos[5]
Sex Games, Sarah Marris, producer (1993), 30 min.
  Juggling Gender, Tami Gold, director (1992), 27 min.

Assignment
Consider how you would determine which box [M or F] you should mark on a U.S. passport application. On the basis of what criteria would you make this determination? Would your criteria change if you were applying for a passport in a different national context? Why? In a short paper, explain how you came to consider these to be reliable criteria for determining your sexual identity.

Module 2: Human Conception

A number of feminist scientists and historians have described instances of "sexist science"—moments when researchers have produced deliberately skewed or constructed data in order to advance dubious claims about "women's" abilities or inabilities. While most of us could identify and critique such overt cases of bias, it is somewhat more difficult, however, to identify gender at work in *normal* science, in the production of knowledge we trust to be authoritative and legitimate. Can we identify gender in the sciences while maintaining a commitment to reliable knowledge? If so, how might we compose more accurate, more reliable knowledge of human bodies?

Readings
Emily Martin (1991), "The Egg and the Sperm: How Science Has Constructed a Romance Based on Stereotypical Male-Female Roles."
Cynthia Daniels (1997), "Between Fathers and Fetuses: The Social Construction of Male Reproduction and the Politics of Fetal Harm."

Assignment
Photocopy the description of human conception contained in your high school or college biology textbook and bring it to class. In a small group, compare the various scientific narratives you have collected, considered in light of Martin's gender analysis. Then, working together, create your own, innovative narrative of human conception to present in class. This narrative might be in the form of a skit, a dance, a song, a video, a textbook chapter, a comic strip, and so on. Think carefully about how your social locations shape the collective narrative you produce. The narrative must reveal your group's understanding of both Martin's essay and the biology texts.

Module 3: HIV/AIDS
We frequently encounter statistics regarding women and AIDS; e.g., between 1985 and 1997 the proportion of women with AIDS increased from 7 percent to 22 percent of all cases reported to the U.S. Centers for Disease Control; women make up only 16 percent of participants in clinical trials of new AIDS therapies; initial HIV diagnoses among women increased 3 percent in 1995–96, while men experienced a 3 percent decline. Yet what do such numbers tell us? Which women are represented in these numbers, and in larger public discussions of AIDS and HIV? Which women are systematically ignored?

Readings
Paul Farmer (1996), "Women, Poverty, and AIDS."
Evelynn Hammonds (1995), "Missing Persons: African American Women, AIDS, and the History of Disease."

Videos
DiAna's Hair Ego: AIDS Info up Front, Ellen Spiro, director (1990), 29 min.
Fighting for Our Lives: Women Confronting AIDS, Center for Women Policy Studies (1990), 29 min.

Assignment
Working in a small group, complete the following math problem, developed by Professor Pamela Baker for use in a faculty development seminar at Bates College:

> A false positive rate of 4 percent ("96 percent accurate") means that on average, for every 100 people tested, 4 who are actually negative will yield a positive test result. In the United States in general in 1998, the incidence of HIV infection (that is, the percentage of the population that is infected) was estimated to be 0.07 percent. Is author Margaret Cozzens correct when she claims that "only about one out of ten people who tested positive actually had the AIDS virus"?

After working through the problem, discuss the relevance of mathematical literacy as it informs HIV awareness and prevention. How necessary is it to be able to read these figures? Does numerical sophistication address the kinds of issues described by Evelynn Hammonds? Why or why not?

Playing the Wild Cards

As research in women's studies provides new methods and materials to bring to the teaching of mathematics, engineering, and natural sciences, so too can feminists from diverse backgrounds incorporate insights of recent science studies more fully into women's studies courses. Doing so, I have suggested, helps us shed new light on the problem of materiality, on the role of sexual identity and difference in contemporary gender studies. Thinking critically about science, technology, and medicine in their social contexts allows students to translate abstract philosophical considerations of "woman" to practical, specific productions of "femaleness." Students thus grow more prepared to identify, analyze, and subvert the constraints of "woman" and "man." Troubling these constraints necessarily changes our conceptual and political landscapes. As Donna Haraway notes, challenging the innocence of sex "changes the geography of all previous categories; it denatures them as heat denatures a fragile protein" (1991, 157).

While incorporating feminist studies of science in women's studies curricula can bring additional heat to the important task of "denaturing" woman, there are drawbacks to this approach. As U.S. popular culture becomes increasingly absorbed in scientific definitions of behavior, agency, and responsibility, refuting the neutrality and universality of female biology may not sit easily with many students (Hubbard and Wald 1997). I learned this the hard way when blithely lecturing on the BRCA1, the so-called breast cancer gene. After a lecture on the dangerous presumptions about race, sex, and genes embedded in two recent scientific publications on BRCA1, a student approached me to say that her mother had died of breast cancer two years earlier. Recently, the student's primary care physician encouraged her to be screened for BRCA1, raising the prospect of prophylactic mastectomy. As the student pointed out, her ability to analyze scientific productions of "woman" ran aground on her grief for her mother, her concern for her breasts, and her fear for her life.

Thinking about our conversation now, I hear in the student's comment a critical suggestion for future teaching. For better or worse, students and teachers alike embody the very sciences we scrutinize; our own flesh is understood and re-shaped with the tools of science. Feminist teachers, then, must be careful not to simply suggest the abolition of scientific definitions of *woman* or *women*. Such a task would be as unwise as it would be impossible. Nor should we simply throw out the generative, useful categories of "sex" and "gender," ignoring the important analytical work they have done for the field of women's studies. Rather, we must learn to be mindful of their deployment, to articulate how sexed identities take their shape and meaning from particular historical and cultural situations. This point was captured in one student's final paper: "I no longer see women and men as entirely separate circles. . . . Now I think of all people as playing cards, their value dependent on their number and suit, but also upon the context in which they are played; there are always wild cards."

Notes

1. All quotations in this paragraph are from students enrolled in Women's Studies 100 during the winter of 1999, Bates College, Lewiston, Maine.
2. Here it is worth noting Judith Butler's cogent remark that the presence of "those proverbial commas (gender, sexuality, race, class) suggest that feminists have not yet learned to conceptualize the relationships they mark" (Butler 1993, 168).
3. Along with other contributions to this volume, readers might consult Rosser (1995) and Eisenhart and Finkel (1998) for examples of this integration.
4. These modules were developed in conversation with Dr. Kiran Asher.
5. Videos are available through Women Make Movies, Inc., Order Department, 462 Broadway, Suite 500K, New York, NY 10013, or www.wmm.com.

Works Cited

Alcoff, Linda. "Cultural Feminism versus Post-Structuralism: The Identity Crisis in Feminist Theory." In *Feminist Theory in Practice and Process*, ed. Micheline R. Malson, Jean

F. O'Barr, Sarah Westphal-Wihl, and Mary Wyer. Chicago: University of Chicago Press, 1989.

Barad, Karen. "Getting Real: Technoscientific Practices and the Materialization of Reality." *Differences* 10 (1998): 87–127.

Birke, Lynda, and Marsha Henry. "The Black Hole: Women's Studies, Science, and Technology." In *Introducing Women's Studies*, ed. Victoria Robinson and Diane Richardson. New York: New York University Press, 1997.

Brown, Wendy. "The Impossibility of Women's Studies." *Differences* 9 (1997): 79–101.

Butler, Judith. *Bodies That Matter: On the Discursive Limits of "Sex."* New York: Routledge, 1993.

———. *Gender Trouble: Feminism and the Subversion of Identity*. New York: Routledge, 1990.

Daniels, Cynthia. "Between Fathers and Fetuses: The Social Construction of Male Reproduction and the Politics of Fetal Harm." *Signs* 22 (1997).

Eisenhart, Margaret A., and Elizabeth Finkel. *Women's Science: Learning and Succeeding from the Margins*. Chicago: University of Chicago Press, 1998.

Farmer, Paul. "Women, Poverty, and AIDS." In *Women, Poverty, and AIDS: Sex, Drugs, and Structural Violence*, ed. Paul Farmer, Margaret Connors, and Janie Simmons. Monroe, ME: Common Courage Press, 1996.

Fausto-Sterling, Anne. "How to Build a Man." In *Science and Homosexualities*, ed. Vernon A. Rosario. New York: Routledge, 1997.

———. "The Five Sexes: Why Male and Female Are Not Enough." *The Sciences* 33 (1992): 20–25.

Haraway, Donna J. "A Manifesto for Cyborgs." In *Simians, Cyborgs, and Women*. New York: Routledge, 1991.

Hammonds, Evelynn. "Missing Persons: African-American Women, AIDS, and the History of Disease." In *Worlds of Fire: An Anthology of African-American Feminist Thought*, ed. Beverly Guy-Sheftall. New York: The New Press, 1995.

Herdt, Gilbert (Ed.). *Third Sex, Third Gender: Beyond Sexual Dimorphism in Culture and History*. New York: Zone Books, 1994.

Hubbard, Ruth, and Elijah Wald. *Exploding the Gene Myth*. Boston: Beacon Press, 1997.

Hull, Gloria T., Patricia Bell Scott, and Barbara Smith. *All the Women Are White, All the Blacks Are Men, But Some of Us Are Brave: Black Women's Studies*. Old Westbury, NY: Feminist Press, 1982.

Joseph, Gloria I., and Jill Lewis. *Common Differences: Conflicts in Black and White Feminist Perspectives*. Garden City, NY: Anchor Books, 1981.

Kessler, Suzanne. "The Medical Construction of Gender: Case Management of Intersexed Infants." *Signs* 16 (1990): 3–26.

Lundgren, Eva. "Creating Bodily Gender in the Fields of Symbol and Power." *NORA— Nordic Journal of Women's Studies 3* (1995): 101–112.

Martin, Emily. "The Egg and Sperm: How Science Has Constructed a Romance Based on Stereotypical Male-Female Roles." *Signs* 16 (1991): 485–501.

Nanda, Serena. "Hijras as Neither Man Nor Woman." In *The Lesbian and Gay Studies Reader*, ed. Henry Abelove, Michele Aina Barale, and David M. Halperin. New York: Routledge, 1993.

Riley, Denise. *"Am I That Name?" Feminism and the Category of "Women" in History*. Minneapolis: University of Minnesota Press, 1988.

Roscoe, Will. "How to Become a Berdache: Toward a Unified Analysis of Gender Diversity." In *Third Sex, Third Gender: Beyond Sexual Dimorphism in Culture and History*. New York: Zone Books, 1994.

Rosser, Sue V. (Ed.). *Teaching the Majority: Breaking the Gender Barrier in Science, Mathematics, and Engineering*. New York: Teachers College Press, 1995.

Scott, Joan Wallach. *Gender and the Politics of History*. New York: Columbia, 1988.

Steinem, Gloria. "If Men Could Menstruate." In *Feminist Frontiers*, ed. Laurel Richardson and Verta Taylor. Reading, MA: Addison-Wesley Publishing, 1988.

Wittig, Monique. "One Is Not Born a Woman." In *The Straight Mind and Other Essays*. Boston: Beacon Press, 1992.

Life, Sex,
and Cells

Sharon Kinsman

For a decade, I taught undergraduate courses in biology and evolutionary ecology in conventional ways. But recently, I developed a rather unconventional course about current understandings of the evolution and consequences of sex. The biological content, feminist critiques, and teaching methods I employed were outside of my traditional training, and represented dramatic changes in my teaching. I designed "Life, Sex, and Cells"—simultaneously a core course in women's studies and an introductory course in biology—to encourage students to be curious about detailed scientific content and feminist science studies, and to use content and analysis together to investigate certain questions about sex and reproduction. I deliberately chose these questions not just because they are likely to interest young adults, but because they can lead to interesting, instructive queries about how science is done, how popular culture uses science, and how we can fruitfully investigate the influence of cultural ideas on scientists' questions, assumptions, methods, and conclusions. The venture for me was exhilarating and nerve-wracking; the pay-offs for students included some I had not anticipated. For instance, one student noted:[1]

> This class has made me see the world and myself differently. I am not afraid of science anymore. I feel like I can have a conversation with someone about biology and not run away in fear. I realize that things I learned growing up about science can be argued as not necessarily "true" as I once thought it to be. You have opened my mind to a subject I have neglected for too long.

Feminist approaches to science that I had come to embrace for my own research motivated me to design this course. This personal and professional journey had begun for me years earlier, in the course of my research in plant reproductive ecology. In closely examining research literature on questions about pollination and fertilization of flowering plants, I discovered certain unexamined problems with the field's paradigms, practices, and presentations. Feminist scholars helped me see that it is not unusual to examine science as a cultural endeavor that is not as objective as I had been trained to believe. Using feminist scholarship, I began to reexamine my field and, as a result, my approach to science changed: I now recognize how crucial it is to use and assess content (or what we call the "facts" of science) along with both "feminist" and "scientific" critiques of science. Putting into practice a feminist approach to science in my research has strongly motivated me to change what and how I teach.

In this chapter, I focus on the framework and methods of "Life, Sex, and Cells," using selected examples of course content as illustrations. I hope to characterize a potential example of how scientific content and feminist approaches can be woven together to make sense for us and our students.

Why Sex? Content and Critique

Sex—the mixing of DNA of two distinct individuals—is the unifying theme of "Life, Sex, and Cells." (In teaching, and in this chapter, I use *sex* to mean "DNA mixing." Otherwise, I use "*sex*," referring to one of the more common uses of the word, such as shorthand for "sexual reproduction," or for acts such as copulation that bring gametes close together. On occasion, I use the term *DNA mixing* in place of the word *sex*, as a reminder of the most basic definition.) Understanding sex—whether its biological role or its cultural representations or misrepresentations—compels learning both content and critique. Thus we examine not just the biology of sex, but *how* biologists approach and write about its origins, patterns, and consequences. Sex is an exceptionally good topic for students beginning to learn biological concepts and detail ("content") because investigating its biological role requires knowledge of cell structure and function, cell evolution, genetics, evolutionary biology, development of multicellular organisms, biological diversity, and behavior. But understanding sex also demands critical analysis—especially cultural and feminist critiques—not only because "sex" has multiple and confusing definitions and representations, but because its biological meaning and role often are misrepresented, or explored only for a limited set of the species, even in biological literature.

The two central questions of the course—How did sex originate and evolve? What are, and what explains, the characteristics of sex and reproduction in the many species?—provide many opportunities to identify the limitations of their popular explanations, and to explore why popular explanations reflect only a few selected species and only some of the many patterns of sex and reproduction. Our work in "Life, Sex, and Cells" suggests that these popular explanations and the narrow scientific approaches they reflect significantly limit our knowledge and understanding of the diverse patterns of sex and reproduction, and their early cellular origins.

Our journey in "Life, Sex, and Cells" is toward more broadly informed views of sex, of reproduction, of the species, and especially of science itself. Implicitly and explicitly, I ask the students to use the two central topics — the origin of sex and the patterns and consequences of sex — to consider the following questions: What constitutes knowledge, and who creates it? What are the mainstream ideas and why have they come to be favored? What shapes and what constitutes an explanatory paradigm, and what kinds of evidence are put forth to support it? Why is this particular evidence emphasized? How are the "knowledge," the "evidence," and the "explanation" presented to us? How does this presentation affect our learning, our reasoning, our questions, and our conclusions? Can we improve the presentation, the paradigm, and the evidence? Can we find or create different points of view?

These questions, first implicit, then explicit, underlie a good deal of our daily work. They lead students to identify and to question various popular characterizations of sex (for example, the idea that sex evolved *because* variation in offspring is good) and of the reproductive practices often linked to sex (for example, the idea that males "naturally" should be promiscuous). Our work requires linking content with critique, and students' accomplishments demonstrate that science can be improved by critique, and that critique based in scientific literacy can be particularly strong and insightful. By learning substantial content in order to understand and create critique, students become able to discover what the paradigms are missing, and to evaluate the paradigms' evidence and consequences. I want students to understand that all of us can contribute to (or at least assess) what constitutes the questions, kinds of evidence, and breadth of approaches for any particular "scientific" question. I insist on the difficult work that this eventually requires. We begin with more accessible tasks: defining sex, and discovering its diverse, intriguing forms.

Beginning with Basics: Definitions and Diversity

To begin the course, students must recognize multiple meanings for *sex, reproduction,* and *gender,* and become familiar with the variety of characteristics of sex and reproduction to be found among the species. They must use this information in considering the natural world and the ways humans try to make sense of the natural world. In sorting out the many ways that the words *sex* and *reproduction* are used and linked, we begin to learn about biology and representations of sex. For example, we learn that sex is most fundamentally defined as DNA mixing between individuals (Margulis and Sagan 1986). Bacteria mix DNA in conjugation, and gametes such as pollen and ovules mix DNA when fertilization occurs. We find that reproduction is not sex (and that sex is not reproduction). Reproduction is making additional independent organisms called offspring.

While many species make these offspring sexually, not all reproduction requires sex. Species that clone reproduce without DNA mixing. Many plants make offspring from fragments that take root, and certain species of lizards and insects that have no males reproduce parthenogenetically: the females make daughters from unfertilized eggs. Similarly, sex does not require reproduction. That is, DNA mixing between individuals (such as conjugation in bacteria) can occur with no subsequent production of offspring.

Sex occurs, we find, at least intermittently or for some individuals, in a majority of the 30 million or so unicellular (for example, bacteria, protozoa, and diatoms) and multicellular (for example, plants, fungi, and animals) species. This DNA mixing began with early cells. Some biologists who study cell evolution suggest that sex then became (perhaps by accident) inextricably associated with many features of organisms, including DNA repair (Michod 1995), cell structure, the multicellular condition, and the ways that multicellular individuals develop through cell differentiation (Margulis and Sagan 1986). These links may have forced certain reproductive mechanisms also to become associated with sex, particularly in multicellular organisms (Margulis and Sagan 1986). In brief, DNA mixing may not be for reproduction, even though it is now linked to reproduction (and to many other conditions) in many species.

Students see that these fundamental views of the definition and origin of *sex* are not mainstream in biology—many biologists who have studied and written about "sex" actually address not sex per se but reproduction that is sexual. Indeed, *sex* has come (erroneously) to mean "reproduction" in popular views and to many biologists, and often implicitly refers only to animals with backbones. Furthermore, ideas of gender are conjoined with ideas about sex and reproduction. Thus we find that our popular vocabulary, even our scientific vocabulary, is imprecise. To know what we are talking about in class, we must define terms that usually are used imprecisely, and we must restate our meanings repeatedly. In class we address the confusing terms and their fundamental definitions, coming to see that their conceptual linkages are not surprising: in the species we are most familiar with, reproduction usually *is* associated with DNA mixing and with structures or individuals labeled "female" (having large nutritious gametes such as plants' ovules or animals' eggs) and "male" (having small gametes such as plants' pollen or animals' sperm). Indeed, in our recent mammalian lineage, sex is inflexibly linked with reproduction and with distinct female and male conditions. No wonder we are not inclined to think about what sex really means, how it got started, and the implications of its original distinction from reproduction.

Thus our struggle to understand "sex" and "reproduction" also demands familiarity with biological diversity—particularly of the diversity and flexibility of sexual and reproductive patterns among the millions of other species. Mammals' rigid—perhaps originally accidental—coincidence of DNA mixing and reproduction (along with distinct individual female and male conditions) is far from the only pattern to be found in the array of all species. Let flowering plants frame the way you make sense of the natural world (as I do), and the picture broadens. Flowering plants are incomparably varied in mechanisms that bring about DNA mixing, in the distribution of male and female reproductive structures within and among individual organisms of a species (for example, functional hermaphroditism is very common), and in breeding systems (for example, many are self-fertile). Many can clone (make offspring nonsexually), switch back and forth between biological male and female reproductive conditions, abort selectively, mate simultaneously with multiple partners, and employ other species (the birds and the bees, the bats and the beetles) to bring their gametes close together prior to sex. Considering the flowering plants alone, it's not a dull world!

Toss in the bacteria, the obscure but diverse protista (for example, diatoms, amoebas, algae), insects, marine invertebrates, and certain fishes: now the patterns of sex and reproduction burgeon to a truly riveting array. Just a sample might include hermaphroditic slugs and roundworms, fish that change from male to female, aphids and other invertebrate animals that rampantly clone, sister societies of yellow jackets and bees, intermittent DNA mixing triggered by shrinking body size in diatoms, pregnant male pipefish, female-only species of insects and fish, and female insects that make egg yolk from fatty sperm packets collected from males. These intriguing phenomena—often treated by popular literature as anomalies or "just so" stories—are strands of a colorful tapestry of a variety of norms.

Because most of us are not familiar with the species, and with the diverse patterns of DNA mixing and reproduction they embody, our struggles to understand humans (and especially human dilemmas about "sex," "gender," and "sexual orientation") are impoverished. Our students, I think, need to know about the flowering plants, the fishes, the aphids, and the gulls. Shouldn't a fish whose gonads can be first male, then female, help us determine what constitutes "male" and "female"? Shouldn't an aphid fundatrix ("stem mother") inform our ideas of "mother"? There on the rose bush, she neatly copies herself, depositing minuscule, sap-siphoning, genetically identical daughters. Aphids might lead us to ask not "Why do they clone?" but "Why don't we?" Shouldn't the long-term female homosexual pair bonding in certain species of gulls (Bagemihl 1999) help define our views of successful parenting, and help students reflect on the intersection of social norms and biology? I want students to adopt a broad view of sex and reproduction based on biological diversity. I ask them to peer into aphid colonies with interest. I insist that they inform their investigation of sex, reproduction, and gender, and of the ways that biologists approach and present these topics, with knowledge of the diversity of sexual and reproductive ways among the multiplicity of species of all lineages.

Learning Methods: Expectations and Environment

While the first topics—definitions and diversity—provide a framework for investigating sex, the first class meetings set expectations for very active learning. Students can best practice the kind of learning and application I expect via the wide variety of pedagogical techniques often called "feminist." Learning from my women's studies colleagues, I (nervously but successfully) dispense with exams and frequent lectures, and use teaching methods that emphasize participation, reflection, and explanation in lively interactions that involve everyone.

I emphasize participation because I want students to be comfortable thinking about, evaluating, and applying content. With twenty to forty students per section, who represent many majors and all four college years, participation works well. Our work with basic definitions and with biological diversity provides good examples. In the first class meeting, good-willed laughter ensues when we share some of our written definitions of *sex, reproduction,* and *gender.* I give students tacit permission to express a variety of responses by asking them to identify the most surprising, or unbelievable, or unattractive method of intimacy their reading presents. Our class review of the varied ways animals bring eggs and sperm close together prior to DNA mixing (Kevles 1986) models matter-of-fact discussion of potentially embarrassing topics and terms. In identifying themes revealed by these examples of animals' intimacies, we also review animal diversity, concluding that a wide variety of reproductive practices are, simply, "normal."

Participatory learning works very well. One student commented: "There was no way to hide in the corner because a great deal of participation was necessary and encouraged." The pay-off in their confidence is especially obvious later, when small groups must design an efficient design for meiosis (the type of cell division that reduces the number of chromosomes per cell). Their insights and responses are impressive. The students' ownership and participation are so effective that they complain outright that books have never taught them to think about the fact that mechanisms of cell division are constrained because they evolved from earlier conditions. This kind of confident questioning soon embraces critique. We often ask "why": Why are there two states—female and male—and not three? Why do we have the ideas we do of "female" and "male" animals? Why has the astonishing variety of "sexual" and reproductive patterns deviating from the heterosexual "norm" been described forthrightly only recently (Bagemihl 1999)? Why do aphids clone, while humans do not? Why is functional hermaphroditism absent in most vertebrates, and how does this affect our representations and views of hermaphroditism?

Just as participation encourages critical thinking, so do close reading and responsible writing. For nearly every reading, students must answer questions that demand that they learn the scientific content, consider carefully the material and

the author's intent, and use information from earlier classes. Culminating writing assignments similarly emphasize detailed learning and responsibility. Students write short passages designed for college biology textbooks and chapters for popular books, as well as analytical reviews that demand substantial knowledge and well-supported argument. Ideally, writing to educate others helps students understand that this field, and "science" as a whole, is an accessible human endeavor strongly influenced by culture and by individuals.

Introducing Critique: Conceptions of Conception[2]

In order to introduce analyses of content and critique, we turn to internal fertilization in animals. Students are familiar with popular concepts of fertilization, but are unfamiliar with the idea that presentations of science can be misleading. We begin by reading commentary by primary researchers Heide Schatten and Gerald Schatten (1983) in their article "The Energetic Egg," and evaluating it using Ruth Bleier's (1986) suggestions for standards for "good science."

Next, we turn to learning more about the biology of fertilization (or "content"). We work hard to thoroughly understand current knowledge of the steps in fertilization, reviewing cell types (prokaryotic and eukaryotic) and learning about the structures and functions of the components of eukaryotic cells (such as nuclear envelope, cytoskeleton, membrane, and the processes by which cell parts move and change). In small groups students consult several references, discovering that "scientific" sources can disagree and/or use different emphases, images, and methods. In listing the steps in fertilization, we try to use neutral language and imagery. Vowing to eschew metaphors and stereotypes in their own recounting of fertilization, students come to see that metaphors often are helpful, and also see that their choices of metaphors are consequential.

Now, well informed about the biological details, including recent discoveries such as how components of the cytoskeleton are built and disassembled, we return to critique. We read Emily Martin's (1991) or the Biology and Gender Study Group's (1988) accessible, thought-provoking feminist critique of some traditional presentations of egg as passive bride and sperm as competitive, conquering hero. These analyses of classical (often hilarious) depictions of egg and sperm in mammalian fertilization provide concrete examples of the value of a feminist critical approach. The students' detailed knowledge of fertilization means that the critiques are easy to understand—and, in fact, to critique. Most students are very pleased with the power of their scientific literacy. One student commented: "I finally felt like I was learning for the sake of understanding, applying, and building on previous knowledge."

Now the students are well positioned to apply their learning. Specifically, for a college-level biology textbook ("known for accuracy, clarity, and interesting tone"), they write a section that presents an updated, accurate, detailed account of cellular events in mammalian fertilization. The assignment requires explicit revision of outdated, stereotyped depictions of conception. Many of these student papers are outstanding. Even self-confessed "science-phobes" produce excellent work. They learn and use scientific content, act as scientists informed about biases via feminist critiques, and improve science presentation. Their work reflects both the critiques they explore and their sense of having been sold short when they themselves were first taught about fertilization.

Next, we more formally identify our critical approach as feminist, using Ruth Bleier's (1988) "A Decade of Feminist Critique in the Natural Sciences." Bleier sets forth examples of feminist critiques in the form of questions that the students now recognize as tools of analysis. These themes repeat throughout the course as we investigate two larger paradigms, and use critiques overt and obscure, feminist and scientific.

Practiced in active learning and in ways to link scientific literacy with critique to improve science, we turn to the course's two central questions. For the question "How did sex originate and evolve?" we focus on cell biology. In exploring "What are the consequences of sex for the patterns of sex and reproduction?" we focus on the behavior of vertebrate animals.

Origins and Consequences of Sex

The origin question most often is linked to what can be called the "why sex?" paradigm. This popular approach implies that sex occurs as a result of the benefit it confers on parents who reproduce sexually: the benefit of genetically varied offspring (quantitatively a fascinating dilemma of genetic costs and benefits). In its simplest form, the argument implies that sex is good, so species have it. (Note that "sex" by this reasoning is equated or strongly linked with "sexual reproduction.") While this paradigm does suggest how natural selection might *maintain* sex in multicellular lineages with complex bodies, such as the plants and animals, it does not address the *origin* of DNA mixing. To broaden students' understanding, I rely especially on the revolutionary work of Lynn Margulis and Dorion Sagan (1986). Clues about the origin of sex lie in little-known organisms dating from a distant time: especially the bacteria and protista, and their ancestors and early multicellular descendants. Sex probably began as a consequence of peculiarities of the evolution of cells, or DNA, or both, and then seems to have become linked to the demands of multicellularity. We may have sex because we're stuck with it, not because it's good for us. (The genetically varied offspring many species enjoy may be just a serendipitous, albeit sometimes beneficial, side effect of sex having become linked with reproduction.) I aim for students to learn and enjoy the challenging logic of the Margulis and Sagan reasoning, and to use this reasoning in concert with literacy about cell biology to critique the "why sex?" paradigm.

Next, we examine the consequences of sex, choosing for particular focus animal behavior and the "parental investment" paradigm. This is an area that has a rich and recent history of feminist approaches and critiques in fields such as primatology and anthropology. We examine the theories of the parental investment (or "Trivers/Bateman") paradigm, which contends that differences in parental investment between females and males both characterize and explain animals' reproductive behavior. As we have done for fertilization, we "decompose" the parental investment model to be sure to understand it and we evaluate the types of evidence offered to support the model. One student remarked, "it made me rethink my ideas about sex and gender, even in terms of humans." Sarah Blaffer Hrdy's (1986) classic essay "Empathy, Polyandry, and the Myth of the Coy Female" is key in modeling how to identify problems with the assumptions, reasoning, and predictions of a theory (in particular, the parental investment model). Having teased apart and understood the components of the parental investment paradigm, students can appreciate and respond to Hrdy's implicit demonstration of how feminist critiques can be built and supported. Students must use their knowledge of the model to identify the assumptions, reasoning, and predictions that Hrdy explicitly challenges. Then, they must explain and judge how she challenges each component, and how she supports each challenge. We discuss who "consumes" science, how this paradigm is used by the popular press, why the popular press is more likely to emphasize the paradigm than to highlight Hrdy's critique, and how work like Hrdy's can empower us to evaluate troubling or limited models.

The students now must synthesize their knowledge of biology and their skills of learning and critique in a difficult assignment. To prepare to write a chapter that could be included in a book on the evolution and consequences of sex, they must "translate" two original research papers that report experimental research on specific questions about mate choice by vertebrate animals. Reading and summarizing primary biological research is entirely new to most. Senior biology majors join us to assist in small learning groups, translating statistics and helping the students understand every detail of the experiments. We review, more than once, each paper's difficult introduction, referring to our schemes of the components of the parental investment paradigm. Students not only must identify each author's central question, they must then explain the question's purported importance, identify the hypothesis and its predictions, and determine the kinds of data that would support the distinct predictions. They must evaluate how well the experiments address the question, and how appropriately the authors use the data.

All of this is quite daunting. I hear a good deal of complaining about the turkeys, guppies, parasites, and pigments we encounter in the mate choice research articles. But then come breakthroughs: students finally can outline the experiments, and are shocked and pleased when I agree with their suggestions that there are certain faults with the experiments, or with the presentation and use of data. They also must come to see the limitations imposed on researchers (in how many replicates can you use a certain guppy?) and to judge whether or not the resulting research is "robust."

Again, hard work to "own" scientific literacy pays off. I am struck by how involved some of the students become. I believe that this is the result of the responsibility they are given: to understand primary research, to judge primary research, and to translate it accurately and competently, without bias, in a theoretical context, for a more general audience.

Coda

For most students, this course and the accomplishments and understanding it demands strongly countered their ideas of science and their ideas of their own competence. The few biology majors who took this course had particularly complex reactions. As had been true for me, critiquing their own profession was first scary, then revealing, and finally empowering. One confessed to feeling betrayed by all her earlier biological education, and struggled as she continued to be silenced in other science classrooms. Needless to say, I have never had a better classroom teaching experience. I have not yet dramatically changed my other courses, which predate this experiment. But I have colleagues en route who "think that the journey itself [is] worth taking,"[3] and students who remind me that curriculum that integrates science content with feminist analysis is needed throughout science courses: "I was afraid of science because it seemed too much like a truth and a final answer . . . facts that could never be disputed . . . I have become aware of so many different components."

Acknowledgments: I am grateful to many individuals for assisting, encouraging, and teaching me: Jean Potuchek, Bonnie Spanier, Scott Gilbert, Lucinda McDade, the editors of this volume, Alice Elliott, pollination biology coresearchers, Suzie and Jane Kinsman, and not least: members of the Bates College Women and Scientific Literacy project team—Bonnie Shulman, Elizabeth Tobin, Pam Baker, and Georgia Nigro. Funds for developing "Life, Sex, and Cells" were provided by a grant from the Hughes Council of Bates College.

Notes

1. All student quotes used in this article are from anonymous evaluations by students enrolled in "Life, Sex, and Cells."

2. Scott Gilbert used this title ("Conceptions of Conceptions") for a talk presented at Bates College.

3. Pamela Baker, Bonnie Shulman, and Elizabeth Tobin. See their chapter, Difficul-Crossings: Stories from Building Two-Way Streets," in this anthology.

Works Cited

Bagemihl, Bruce. *Biological Exuberance: Animal Homosexuality and Natural Diversity.* New York: St. Martin's Press, 1999.

Biology and Gender Study Group (Sarah Bailey, Athena Beldecos, Scott Gilbert, Karen Hicks, Lori Kenschaft, Nancy Niemczyk, Rebecca Rosenberg, Stephanie Schaertel, and Andrew Wedel). "The Importance of Feminist Critique for Contemporary Cell Biology." *Hypatia* 3 (1988): 61–76.

Bleier, Ruth. "A Decade of Feminist Critique in the Natural Sciences." *Signs* 14 (1988): 186–195.

——— (Ed.). *Feminist Approaches to Science.* New York: Pergamon Press, 1986.

Hrdy, Sarah Blaffer. "Empathy, Polyandry, and the Myth of the Coy Female." In *Feminist Approaches to Science*, ed. Ruth Bleier. New York: Pergamon Press, 1986.

Kevles, Bettyann. *Females of the Species: Sex and Survival in the Animal Kingdom.* Cambridge, MA: Harvard University Press, 1986.

Margulis, Lynn, and Dorion Sagan. *Origins of Sex: Three Billion Years of Genetic Recombination.* New Haven, CT: Yale University Press, 1986.

Martin, Emily. "The Egg and the Sperm: How Science Has Constructed a Romance Based on Stereotypical Male-Female Roles." *Signs* 16 (1991): 485–501.

Michod, Richard E. *Eros and Evolution: A Natural Philosophy of Sex.* New York: Addison-Wesley Publishing, 1995.

Schatten, Gerald, and Heide Schatten. "The Energetic Egg." *The Sciences* 23 (1983): 28–34.

Working at the Limen

Repositioning Authority in Science and Art

$\longrightarrow$ Caroline Joan ("Kay") S. Picart

Conventionally, issues of feminism and science, and gender and art, have been pursued as separate areas of inquiry. What such an approach obscures, however, are the natural intersections and common themes that bind the epistemologies, politics, and ethics of scientific and artistic activities. The honor's colloquium I designed, "Gender, Authority, and the Politics of Representation in Science and Art," seeks to disrupt the pervasive science-art and nature-culture dichotomies.[1]

Among the questions this course challenges students to grapple with, which are crucial to excavating and revisioning invisible mechanisms directing the production and consumption of scientific and artistic activities, are: How is authority established in science and art? How has nature been gendered in both science and art? How do the artistic conventions and popular views of science continually come together, for example, to regenerate the Frankenstein myth—a myth of male self-birthing, steeped in anxieties concerning the control of nature, technology, and the "feminine other"? How does one decenter the subject of Enlightenment science and Romantic or colonial art? In what ways has the historical exclusion of women from the spheres of science and "high" art contributed to the rise of patriarchy? How does one move from a politics of exclusion in science and art to one of integration? What historical cases illustrate the correlation between scientific and artistic representations and the resultant political and economic hierarchies, differentiated along gendered, racial, and class lines? Is there such a thing as an essentially "feminine" type of science or art? Can one make an argument for a distinctively "feminist" epistemology based on biological or sociological grounds, rooted in representations in/of science and art? What would be the conditions of possibility within which one could speak of a "feminist" ethics that addresses concrete issues aligned with scientific or artistic activity? What feminist strategies can be employed to move toward a more just and humane world, particularly as rooted within scientific and artistic modes of production, representation, and consumption?

Traditional political theory links the issue of *author*-ity with the entitlement to speak, and conventional modes of representation in both science and art have implicitly set up standards of who is speaking versus who listens; who dissects and who is dissected; who gazes and who is gazed upon. In contrast, feminist and postcolonial critiques have focused on destabilizing and unmasking the complex genealogies that underlie traditional assumptions and historical configurations of power rooted in specific cultural and economic contexts. These conversations constitute an especially fertile ground for examining and reenvisaging the nature of authority, and of recognizing and redirecting the political nature of representation in science and art, and its numerous ramifications in ethics and social and political theory.

Part of my self-perceived role as educator is maximizing multidisciplinary inquiry, particularly with respect to the reconfiguration of the science-art and nature-culture divides as veiling complex, weblike interconnections. Hence, precisely in order to disrupt these pervasive and commonsensical dichotomies, during the first two sessions, I juxtapose Mary Shelley's novel *Frankenstein* (reprint 1991) with slides of Henri Fuseli's *Nightmare* and video excerpts from classic filmic iterations of the Frankenstein narrative (for example, James Whale's *Frankenstein* and *Bride of Frankenstein*) and more contemporary versions (for example, Kenneth Branagh's *Mary Shelley's Frankenstein*) in order to trace the changing face of the "monstrous" in relation to gender and technology. The modern tradition, beginning with Francis Bacon, likes to paint the portrait of the scientist as a Promethean figure who tames the terrifying wildness of nature (configured as a woman) to become a beautiful and domesticated slave-spouse. In other words, within the modern paradigm, the realm of the scientific saves humanity from the realm of the "monstrous"; yet as I show in many twentieth-century film interpretations of *Frankenstein*, particularly the Hammer series (which ran from the 1940s until the 1970s), the scientist is the real monster, who manipulates and outlives his mindless and ubiquitous creations. The term *monstrous* is etymologically traceable to *monstrare* (to point; to demonstrate); and *monere* (to warn), and I find it instructive to pose the questions: Against what are we being warned? How do figures of the "feminine" and the "masculine" fit within this embedded narrative that juxtaposes categories of power and impotence with demarcations of beauty, health, and the "natural" as contrasted with those of the grotesque, the sickly, and the "unnatural"? And even more significantly, whose voice/authorship are we implicitly urged to believe in these accounts? Is this voice or locus of authorship gendered or raced in any way?

In addition, I integrate several texts as supplementary critical frames. Anne Mellor's (1988) work on the politics of gender in Romantic art illustrates the close interconnection between the spheres of the erotic and the violent, and lays bare the nature of the masculine gaze onlookers are encouraged to peer through, in such pieces as Fuseli's *Nightmare*—a gaze whose coercive/voyeuristic power parallels the clinical "scientific" gaze in the Frankenstein narrative. Similarly, Janice

Hocker Rushing and Thomas Frentz's (1995) work underlines how popular films serve as contemporary repositories of myth, and how such narratives reveal and reconstruct anxieties concerning demarcations of the "masculine" from the "feminine," and of the "human" from the "artificial." I also bring in my own work on the myth of parthenogenesis (that is, the story of a father who gives birth to his son devoid of female participation) alongside the repression of the scandalous body of the female-as-monstrous as constituting the core of the evolving Frankenstein narrative.

All three approaches illustrate how the masculine-feminine and subject-object positions are precariously constructed in parallel positions in both science and art. The conjunction of these various texts not only enables a dynamic continuum across the spheres of scholarship and teaching, but also drives home the point that the academic and the popular are not simplistically opposed: namely, Romantic literature, contemporary film, and the rise of modern science overlay each other to form a complex portrait of power in relation to gender in science, as artistically and popularly depicted.

From there, I usually find it instructive to revisit Kuhn's (1996) evolving notion of "paradigms" and "disciplinary matrices" to illustrate how the subject position created by the modern conception of science is historically and socially generated, rather than by a natural a priori stance. The notion of paradigms—"concrete scientific achievements" that provide, for a time, model problems and their solutions for a particular, historically grounded community of scientific practitioners—is often a watershed for many students. The idea that the logical positivist model of science—that science is a value-neutral, unambiguously progressive cumulative stockpiling of facts, involving the unprejudiced exorcism of superstition, insulated from the contingencies of history, culture, and politics (and naturally, socially constructed narratives of gender and sex)—is simply one among competing theoretical frames on how science works often leads to vociferous debates concerning "truth" and "reason." Ultimately, the insertion of issues of race, gender, and sexuality into the debate, which was framed by sociologists and feminists rather than Kuhn, challenges students to examine deeply held assumptions concerning the construction of knowledge.

The class composition when I taught the honor's colloquium was evenly split among scientists and artists. Somewhat predictably, science majors hung on, with some tenacity, to the positivistic view of science, and art majors clung just as stubbornly to the view that art, unlike science, is devoid of any constraints of "objective" reference because art is necessarily private and subjective. It is only after we had gone into several sessions dealing with the intertwined issues of critical judgement and representation in activities like constructing a scientific model or creating a piece that does more than mimetically reproduce an object that the two groups began to forge a new vocabulary that transcended these dichotomies. With some reluctance, science majors conceded that scientific equations and models fall back upon some types of aesthetic criteria such as simplicity or "fruitfulness" (maximal predictive power with the least convoluted explanation), and art majors in turn reluctantly conceded that insofar as art objects are produced within a social and historical matrix, much like scientific paradigms, their status as "art" falls back in some way upon standards of "intersubjective" or communal judgment.

Another crucial concept derived from Kuhn's fertile framework is "incommensurability," broadly construed from the fact that if different paradigms have their own metaphysical, epistemological, and linguistic foundations, then there is no value-neutral vantage point from which to compare paradigms (Kuhn 1996). Thus, paradigms have "no common measure," and hence are "incommensurable." The term *paradigm* acquires an even more concrete dimension when these budding artists and scientists find out that they play different language games even when they use the same terms, such as *modernism* or *realism*. In the creative tension, the students found themselves problematizing the twin notions that science is universally objective with no subjective dimension, and that art is its mirror image: necessarily solitary and subjective, and impervious to any level of critical inquiry by virtue of the ever present appeal to the standards of "taste."

From these foundations, the course radiates outward to focus on selected nodes. Sandra Harding's "Why Physics Is a Bad Model for Physics" (1988) and "'Strong Objectivity' and Socially Situated Knowledge" (1988) are juxtaposed alongside Trinh Minh-ha's "Questions of Images and Politics" (1991) and selected clips from her film *Naked Spaces—Living Is Round*. The juxtaposition underlines a fundamental similarity-difference. Both argue passionately for the incorporation of types of standpoint theories—that is, they both argue for debunking the positivistic view of science as value-neutral and ahistorical, and aim to substitute a framework that is conscious and critical of its historical and political roots. For Harding, the incorporation of standpoint theory must pragmatically reset the direction of scientific research priorities, such that marginalized voices may disrupt the coercive conjunction of economic, racial, and gendered hegemonies masked as universal scientific values. Similarly, for Minh-ha, the incorporation of the "view from below" should create a disturbing rupture in the seamless visual consumption of documentary images concerning ethnic women, which is characteristic of the "natural" (an aesthetic criterion), "authentic" (a scientific criterion), and "realistic" (a criterion that straddles both scientific and aesthetic domains) "look" of commercial or conventional film. Nevertheless, Harding and Minh-ha employ very different rhetorical and political tactics to practice their brands of feminist activism. Harding writes clearly and incisively within the tradition of a Western philosophy of science, steeped in the traditions of Hegel and Marx; Minh-ha, in contrast, employs what Heléne Cixous calls a "feminine" form of writing (fluctuating across words and images) that relies upon gaps, silences, and fissures that jar the narcotizing seamlessness and omniscient perspective assumed by the conventional documentary film. Yet both focus upon the political differences separating the first world from the third world as crucial to the practice and consumption of science and art. Both Harding and Minh-ha offer frameworks through which a genealogy of parallel paths, which Enlightenment science and colonial art have taken, may be gleaned. These different but converging paths have led to the relegation of women, "the feminine," and the racial "other" to the object position. Similarly, their projects enable a revisioning of the conditions of possibility within which power, gender, and race in science and art may be configured, leading to a more dialectical and less tyrannical schema that destabilizes the parallel and intersecting dichotomies of masculine-feminine, subject-object, and culture-nature.

Finally, I integrate a spectrum of texts by Donna Haraway (1989), Moira Gatens (1996), and Londa Schiebinger (1993) to form a crucial counterpoint to articles by Mary Garrard (1995), Alice Adams (1997), and Christine Moneera Laennec (1997). Their parallel dissections of the scientific and artistic (re)constructions of the porous boundaries separating and linking nature and culture provide compelling cases that illustrate the correlation between scientific and artistic representations, and political and economic hierarchies, differentiated along gendered, racial, and class lines, which these representations engender and maintain, while masking them as "natural" or "inevitable." Haraway's detailed genealogies of the gendered and political dimensions of anthropological and psychological experiments simultaneously demarcating and building an affinity among monkeys, apes, and humans, alongside Gatens's compelling account of the "imaginary" body as being between the lived experience of the "phantom limb" and the phenotypically male or female body, form a challenging tandem to Schiebinger's humorous and ironic accounts of how patriarchal/religious/ideological dimensions concerning sexuality actively shaped Carolus Linnaeus's botanical system of binomial nomenclature. Along a parallel track, Garrard argues that a critical analysis of Da Vinci's paintings reveals him, compared to his contemporaries, to display protofeminist sympathies because of the way he depicts female portraits as resisting/transcending the male gaze, and of celebrating nature's power, which he depicts as an immense female body. Alice Adams dissects the scientized aesthetic of women's sexual and reproductive bodies operative in Dr. James Burt's notorious "love surgery"—a procedure that, in line with the myth of exterminating women's sin of original ugliness, sought invasively to realign the vagina and remove the covering of the clitoris, which ironically left women sexually crippled. Finally, Christine Moneera-Laennec argues that early-twentieth-century fashion photography captures the shift from the romantization of the natural female body as soft and domesticated to the idealization of the engineered, hard "techno-body." All these accounts draw their persuasive force from the active and critical engagement in what Minh-ha calls the battle-ground of "warring fictions"—writ large against interweaving backdrops of science and art in the gendered characterization of what constitutes the "natural." Taken together, these texts problematize any "essentialist" view of science and art as "male" or "female"; they destabilize the constructed opposition between what exists "in nature" and what is "mechanical" or "artificial."

In keeping with the questions it poses at the beginning, the course closes with a brief look at ethical questions, particularly in relation to biomedical dilemmas. Tom Beauchamp and James Childress's (1989) analytic, principle-driven approach to dilemmas concerning women's reproductive rights form an instructive contrast to Helen Bequert Holmes and Laura Purdy's (1992) continental and case-driven approach. Beauchamp and Childress argue that four clusters of principles—namely (1) respect for autonomy, (2) nonmaleficence (not causing harm), (3) beneficence (providing benefits and balancing benefits against risks and costs), and (4) justice (distributing benefits, risks, and costs fairly)—form a necessary framework for beginning to wrestle with claims of competing moral obligations in professional-patient relationships. In contrast, Holmes and Purdy examine the inadequacies of "malestream" medical ethics, and using specific medical cases as starting points, broadly sketch the outlines of an ethics of care as an important dimension of a "feminist prescription for the healing of medicine." Juxtaposing the two approaches enables the students to pursue practical strategies and to tease out ramifications that flow from such strategies. While Beauchamp and Childress's approach uses a deductively driven trajectory, and benefits from a formal simplicity and coherence, at least at the outset, Holmes and Purdy's principally casuistic anthology of approaches uses a predominantly inductive approach, and in turn benefits from its specificity and rootedness in experiences, though it seems weaker in forming a basis for generalizable normative guidelines. In the course of comparing the strengths and weaknesses of both theoretical perspectives, I pay particular attention to how the framing of the ethical problem and its resolution relies heavily upon more invisible epistemological and aesthetic considerations, which are often gendered in terms of who occupies the subject and object positions.

With its broad interdisciplinarity and heavy emphasis on honing critical skills of reading, interpreting, speaking, and writing, it is an ideal humanities elective; yet in addition to that, based on an individual student's request, the course was eventually accepted as a substitute for a required natural science elective. The request was accepted principally because the colloquium not only employed concrete historical and medical cases to illustrate theoretical as well as practical issues in fields such as physics, chemistry, biology, and medicine, but also rooted these dilemmas within the contemporary international context, which entails the "first world–third world divide." The course illustrated the impact of science (and art) in action within the larger matrix of politics, history, and culture. That is, the course built upon the student's rudimentary knowledge of such scientific terms as *species* or *molecule* to produce a more sophisticated appreciation for the constellation of epistemological and metaphysical postulates that undergird these terms. It also enabled a more nuanced understanding of scientific language as a system of representation that is not insulated from hierarchies of power and implicit value judgments. Ultimately, it enhanced the student's ability to appraise the epistemological grounds of a claim to facticity, and illustrated that what "reality" is, is to varying degrees mediated by representations, which entail both scientific and aesthetic considerations.

To close, a discussion of the course's pedagogical method is crucial to understanding how I see myself working practically at this juncture of different worlds, acutely aware of the traditional power dynamics of the classroom—a dynamic that mirrors the flows of power in rendering present the objects of scientific and artistic activities. Because the course employs a seminar format, it is largely discussion-oriented, and students play an active role in ensuring the success of the course. Students are required to come in having read the assigned texts for the day, in order to present and defend their interpretations of the texts, as well as critique those of others and pose clarificatory questions. I post extended discussions via e-mail during the periods between sessions, to help set up and continue generating class momentum. This is because even three-hour periods are often insufficient for the amount of critical engagement the material often spurs. Students are required to log in at least once a week, during an assigned day, to carry on these electronically mediated conversations. Students are also required to visit their teaching apprentices or me during their office hours once every two weeks for small-group discussions, which afford further opportunities for the contextualization and application of apparently abstract concepts, and also helps establish an atmosphere of greater rapport, intimacy, and collegiality because it is often less daunting for students to speak up in informal, small-group discussions rather than formal, large-group settings. The pedagogical thrusts of the course, precisely because they rely heavily upon student engagement, require that various discussion settings be utilized, through formal presentations in class as well as informal discussions via e-mail and small groups outside of official class hours. Students are challenged to explore what it means to be engaged as a leader of a discussion, a critical interlocutor, and a sensitive listener.

The course begins with a number of sessions that I lead with the help of the apprentices, who have been supervised ahead of time. These teaching apprentices are advanced undergraduate students who have either taken an earlier class with me or worked on a collaborative project with me; in both cases, I actively recruit promising students who show an interest in learning what teaching is like from the perspective of a liaison between professor and student. The active incorporation of teaching apprentices is a crucial pedagogical dimension, because it not only provides them with practical behind-the-scenes training of what preparing a lecture/discussion session requires and provides them with extensive and sustained guidance and feedback in developing their own teaching styles, but also serves as an important exemplar for the other students in class, who often find the difference in pedagogical styles instructive.

After a few preliminary lectures in which I sketch the general outlines of the class and explain how each subarea fits into the larger blueprint, the duty of giving a brief summary and critique of some of the assigned texts for the day, and of generating discussion, is rotated, first, among the teaching apprentices, and then among the students. Prior to the dates they are scheduled to briefly take over one segment of the seminar, I meet with the teaching apprentices and students to give them feedback on their proposed lesson plans. In addition to these discussions, each student is required to give a five-minute oral report and hand in a short book report (two to three pages) on a book of his or her choice from the list of supplementary texts (refer to the syllabus outlined later) or a related text I approve. This simple exercise not only enables students to pursue a topic of their choice in greater depth, but also gives them an exercise in writing book reviews—an essential skill for parsing and critiquing the essentials of a chosen text.

At the end of the course, students are required to hand in papers (nine to ten pages) on topics of their choice related to the course. Movement toward the completion of the paper is achieved through a step-wise procedure that exposes students to the fundamental steps involved in producing an academic research paper. These steps move from heading a discussion on a particular topic, to writing up a preliminary topic statement, then a slightly more extended project description, a review of related literature or context review, a first draft, and finally to incorporating revisions based on student/peer/teaching apprentice reviews and comments from the professor. The last three meetings of the course are devoted to fifteen-minute presentations of students' papers, followed by ten-minute periods of questioning by the class. Such a setting gives students exposure to a conference format in which papers are professionally delivered, and the final paper is seen as raw material that may be refined in preparation for possible publication with a journal or further presentation at a conference.

In conclusion, perhaps the best testimony to the success of the colloquium was the quality and variety of the final papers produced, a significant number of which were accepted for future publication with *Prism*. The final papers ranged across, to name only a few examples, an examination of the problematization of "identity" and "body" on the Internet; to underlining gendered stereotypes of action and portrayal in fairytale illustrations; to using the concepts of *machismo* and *mestizaje* to trace the gender dynamics of Laura Esquivel's 1994 *Como Agua Para Chocolate*; to unveiling the mirror-imaging sufferings Jewish and German women underwent in Nazi Germany as a result of the mythopolitical configuration of their races and genders; to a comparative analysis of Alice Walker's and Toni Morrison's literature as illustrative of African-American women authors' portrayal of their own gender and race. By the time the colloquium closed with oral presentations of these final papers, the class had developed enough of a common vocabulary that scientists and artists/humanists alike could talk to, rather than through each other, and intelligently respond to each others' papers within the tightly constrained time frame of a miniconference. The joy of that experience, above all, sustains me when the frustrations and contingencies of working at the limen seem to loom large.

Course Topics and Readings

Authority, Science, and Art: Frankenstein as a Protofeminist Critique of Male Romanticism

Mary Shelley, *Frankenstein*, esp. 1–16, 42–48, 80–134, 150–153, 172–206.
Slides of Henri Fuseli's *Nightmare* and stills from several *Frankenstein* films.
Slides illustrating Dionysus's birth from the thigh of Zeus; sections from *Mythology*, a CD-ROM.
Video excerpts from James Whale's *Frankenstein*; Kenneth Branagh's *Mary Shelley's Frankenstein*, and *The Handmaid's Tale*.
Janice Hocker Rushing and Thomas S. Frentz, *Projecting the Shadow: The Cyborg Hero in American Film*, esp. 1–8, 165–221.
Caroline J. S. Picart, "Re-Birthing the Monstrous: Whale's (Mis)Reading of Mary Shelley's *Frankenstein*."
Clips from the videos of *Blade Runner* and *Terminator I* and *II*.

Sociology versus Philosophy of Science: Politics and Aesthetics in Science

Caroline J. S. Picart, *The Darwinian Shift: Kuhn vs. Laudan*.
Video excerpts from *Kuhn's Paradigm Paradigm*, *The Way of Science*, *A Glorious Accident: Stephen Jay Gould*, and *It's a Wonderful Life*.

Decentering the Sovereign Subject

Sandra Harding, "Why 'Physics' Is a Bad Model for Physics," in *Whose Science? Whose Knowledge?*
Trinh T. Minh-ha, "Questions of Images and Politics," in *When the Moon Waxes Red: Representation, Gender, and Cultural Politics*.
Video excerpts from Trinh Minh-ha's *Naked Spaces—Living Is Round*.

The Politics of Gender and Race in Science and the Eroticization of the Machine

Donna Haraway, "Apes in Eden, Apes in Space: Mothering as a Scientist for *National Geographic*" and "Metaphors into Hardware: Harry Harlow and the Technology of Love," in *Primate Visions*.
Video excerpts from *Gorillas in the Mist*.

The Epistemology and Ethics of Biological Essentialism in Science and Art

Moira Gatens, *Imaginary Bodies: Ethics, Power, and Corporeality*, 3–18, 125–150.
Londa Schiebinger, *Nature's Body: Gender in the Making of Modern Science*, 1–114.
Video excerpts from *The Sex Files*.

Nature, Science, and Art

Londa L. Schiebinger, *Nature's Body: Gender in the Making of Modern Science*, 115–212.
Mary Garrard, "Leonardo da Vinci and Creative Female Nature."
Slides of some of Da Vinci's works.

The Multicultural Gaze: Standpoint Theories and the Relevance of Social Location

Sandra Harding, " '. . . and Race?' Toward the Science Question in Global Feminism" and "Common Histories, Common Destinies: Science in the First and Third Worlds," in *Whose Science? Whose Knowledge?*

Responsibility—Epistemic, Moral, and Political

Donna Haraway, "A Cyborg Manifesto: Science, Technology, and Socialist-Feminism in the Late Twentieth Century," in *Simians, Cyborgs, and Women: The Reinvention of Nature*.

Feminist Activism as Related to Science

Donna Haraway, "The Biopolitics of Postmodern Bodies: Constitutions of Self in Immune System Discourse" and "The Contest for Primate Nature: Daughters of Man-the-Hunter in the Field, 1960–1980," in *Simians, Cyborgs, and Women: The Reinvention of Nature*.

Feminist Activism as Related to the Arts

Trinh T. Minh-ha, "Cotton and Iron" and "The Story Began Long Ago," in *When the Moon Waxes Red: Representation, Gender, and Cultural Politics*.
Trinh T. Minh-ha, "Commitment from the Mirror-Writing Box," in *Woman, Native, Other: Writing Postcoloniality and Feminism*.
Video excerpts from Trinh T. Minh-ha's *Naked Spaces*.

Some Feminist Critiques of Bioethical Issues

Tom Beauchamp and James Childress, *Principles of Biomedical Ethics*, excerpts from chapters 1 and 2.

Helen Bequert Holmes and Laura M. Purdy, *Feminist Perspectives in Medical Ethics*, selected excerpts.

Video excerpts from *The Sex Files* and *A Clash of Minds*.

Note

1. Encouraged by a grant from the Network for Excellence in Teaching at the University of Wisconsin, Eau Claire, and the active recruitment of the honor's program head, Ron Mickel, I reworked a senior seminar into a 300-level honor's colloquium.

Works Cited

Adams, Alice. "Molding Women's Bodies: The Surgeon as Sculptor." In *Bodily Discursions: Genders, Representations, Technologies*, ed. Deborah Wilson and Christine Moneera Laennec. Albany: State University of New York Press, 1997.

Beauchamp, Tom, and James Childress. *Principles of Biomedical Ethics*. New York: Oxford University Press, 1989.

Garrard, Mary. "Leonardo da Vinci and Creative Female Nature." In *Feminism and Tradition in Aesthetics*, ed. Peggy Zeglin Brand and Carolyn Korsmeyer. University Park: Pennsylvania State University Press, 1995.

Gatens, Moira. *Imaginary Bodies: Ethics, Power, and Corporeality*. New York: Routledge, 1996.

Harding, Sandra. *Whose Science? Whose Knowledge?* Ithaca, NY: Cornell University Press, 1988.

Haraway, Donna. *Simians, Cyborgs, and Women: The Reinvention of Nature*. New York: Routledge, 1991.

———. *Primate Visions*. New York: Routledge, 1989.

Holmes, Helen Bequert, and Laura Purdy. *Feminist Perspectives in Medical Ethics*. Bloomington: Indiana University Press, 1992.

Kuhn, Thomas. *The Structure of Scientific Revolutions*, 3rd ed. Chicago: University of Chicago Press, 1996.

———. *The Essential Tension*. Chicago: University of Chicago Press, 1977.

Laennec, Christine Moneera. "The 'Assembly-Line Love-Goddess': Women and the Machine Aesthetic in Fashion Photography, 1918–1940." In *Bodily Discursions: Genders, Representations, Technologies*, ed. Deborah Wilson and Christine Moneera Laennec. Albany: State University of New York Press, 1997.

Mellor, Anne. "Possessing Nature: The Female in *Frankenstein.*" *Romanticism and Feminism.* Bloomington: Indiana University Press, 1988.

Minh-ha, Trinh T. *When the Moon Waxes Red: Representation, Gender, and Cultural Politics.* New York: Routledge, 1991.

————. *Woman, Native, Other: Writing Postcoloniality and Feminism.* Bloomington: Indiana University Press, 1989.

Picart, Caroline Joan S. "Re-Birthing the Monstrous: James Whale's (Mis)Reading of Mary Shelley's *Frankenstein.*" *Critical Studies in Mass Communication* 15 (1998): 382–404.

————. *The Darwinian Shift: Kuhn vs. Laudan.* Acton, MA: Copley, 1997.

Rushing, Janice Hocker, and Thomas S. Frentz. *Projecting the Shadow: The Cyborg Hero in American Film.* Chicago: University of Chicago Press, 1995.

Schiebinger, Londa. *Nature's Body: Gender in the Making of Modern Science.* Boston: Beacon Press, 1993.

Shelley, Mary. *Frankenstein.* New York: Bantam Books, 1818.

From Teaching to Learning

A Course on Women, Gender, and Science

→ Haydee Salmun

Over the past ten years the increased concern about the status of women in the sciences and engineering has led to the initiation of programs at many institutions with the goal of increasing the recruitment and retention of women in these divisions at the undergraduate and graduate levels.[1] Typically these efforts concentrate on the mechanics of recruitment and the establishment of specific programs geared to make women feel more comfortable in scientific and engineering environments. I believe that it is essential to link the approaches that have been tried so far (more and better mentoring through seminars, panel discussions and advising, role models, and a strong emphasis on the development of a supportive intellectual community for women and other minorities) with an informed reflection on the nature of the scientific project itself. An open and effective dialogue must be created between feminist scholars of science and technology and women actively engaged at all levels in science and engineering programs in order to increase the participation of women in science and engineering and provide them with better tools to critique and reshape the state and nature of scientific inquiry in new and innovative ways.

I am a woman trained in the physical sciences and working in an engineering discipline. I am committed to talking to and with female scientists because I am a female scientist myself; I am committed to talking to and with members of minority groups because I belong to one. For the past three years, while actively engaged in research and teaching in my own scientific discipline, I have taught the only course at my institution that explores the complex interrelationship between scientific knowledge/practice and social dynamics arising from the intersections of gender, culture, and science. The course, which mutated from "Women in Science/Women on Science" to "Women, Gender, and Diversity in Science and Engineering,"[2] is a reading seminar (initially taught with Erica Schoenberger, a professor of geography) that explores the role, contributions, and experience of women in the science and engineering disciplines and examines the linkages (and possible disjunctions) between feminist theory *on* science and the lived life of women *in* science. The course is now part of the normal curriculum of the engineering school, as it is a course offered by the Department of Geography and Environmental Engineering. It has attracted students (both men and women) from various disciplines, most of whom have not been inclined to seek courses in the women's studies program.[3] The course is carefully organized to avoid the common schism between the insights of practicing scientists and the critiques of cultural/social theorists who do not work as so-called hard scientists. It is structured around two main themes: (1) women in the world of science, engineering, and technology, and (2) the contribution of feminist critiques to our understanding of science and the role of science in the production of knowledge. I have encountered some resistance and in some cases hostility to the course, but I have also encountered enthusiasm in the students, many of them starting out with little or no background in feminist theory.

The Institutional Context and Student Perspectives

It is important to understand the institutional context in which students' reactions to the course take place. Unlike a liberal arts institution or a major state university, Johns Hopkins is firmly attached to a scientific endeavor dictated by corporate competitive values and establishment research requirements. The nature of this institution is such that many students leave it without ever having attended a class that takes science itself as an object of study. They are hardly ever encouraged to do so. It is safe to say that most science, pre-med, and engineering undergraduates, which constitute the majority of the undergraduate population, leave Johns Hopkins without having had an occasion to reflect upon the construction of the knowledge that they work many years to acquire. They never reflect upon the apparently straight line that leads to science. There are, to be sure, cross-listed courses with the women's studies program (presently restructured as Women, Gender, and Sexuality Studies) that are social science- or humanities-based and examine the process of knowledge formation. It is almost a matter of chance, however, whether or not an engineering or science student will stray into one of them, since women's studies is seen as belonging firmly within the humanities and arts programs of the School of Arts and Sciences. Institutional, and disciplinary, division is very strong at Johns Hopkins, and this dissuades easy collaborations and fluent intellectual exchanges among schools and disciplines. In light of these considerations, it is essential, if perhaps much more difficult at research institutions like mine, that such a course be taught within the orbits of the engineering and sciences departments.

Many women scientists and engineers, particularly those who have successful careers at an institution like Johns Hopkins, think that obstacles related to gender discrimination are all but things of the past, even if not so distant a past. If things have not changed as much as one would wish, the way to press for more change is simply and firmly to show that "we can do it" and the rest will follow. Most would assert, "I am not a feminist, I am a scientist" and firmly believe, whether they state it or not, that "those feminists know nothing about science anyway so what can they teach me?" These women will more likely than not reject the idea that science is gendered. They are unlikely to be familiar with the fact that many of "those feminists," such as Evelyn Fox Keller, Donna Haraway, Ruth Bleier, Karen Barad, Barbara Witten, Margaret Wertheim, and Bonnie Spanier, to name a few, do know more than a word or two about science! They typically go about their daily chores implicitly sharing a view best summarized in Steven Weinberg's (1974) words: "The laws of nature are as impersonal and free of human values as the rules of arithmetic. We didn't want it to come out that way, but it did" (43). From this perspective, feminist theory does not seem to speak, at least in any significant and meaningful way, to the experience of women scientists.

Teaching Science/Feminism Connections

The alternative perspective that I claim is centrally relevant to women's lives in science and engineering comes from feminist science studies, which have helped us understand how the construction of scientific knowledge is, among other things, highly gendered.[4] It is within this framework that questions about how scientific epistemology, language, values, and cultures might hamper the ability of women to successfully pursue scientific careers are usually discussed. The recent interest in the field of gender and science from scholars trained primarily in the sciences and engineering attests to the tremendous impact of feminist critiques of science on how we view, conduct, and project our research (an example of which is this anthology).

However, given institutional and disciplinary contexts, making the connections between a mode of scientific inquiry that participates in the construction of gendered knowledge and the unsatisfactory situation of women in science is not easy. On the one hand, there are women scholars working on feminist theory (mostly based in the humanities) who can articulate important critiques of science but who seem to have a little or no experience of the day-to-day life of women in science and engineering and often little inside understanding of how work in those fields is typically organized. On the other hand, there are women scientists who cannot transfer feminist insights to their own terrain or even translate their distinctive experiences as women into terms understandable to mainstream feminist scholarship.

The original title of the course, "Women in Science/Women on Science," summarized my sense of frustration with this apparent lack of communication between these two groups. I believed then, as I do now, that my course could talk to students in the sciences about feminist approaches to science and expose students in the social sciences and humanities to the world, beliefs, and practices of scientists. To some extent, I had bridged the gap that seemingly existed between these two "cultures" and now wanted to help others do the same.

The goal of the first part of the course, now titled "Women, Gender, and Diversity in Science and Engineering," is to expose students to real people and real lives. We explore in some detail the experience of women in engineering fields and different scientific disciplines, such as biology, long considered "woman-friendly," and physics, seen by many as the ultimate male preserve. Of all the very enlightening recent autobiographical material that is available for this part of the readings, I selected sections from *Journey of Women in Science and Engineering: No Universal Constant* (Ambrose et al. 1997), *Women in Mathematics: The Addition of Difference* (Henrion 1997), an autobiographical essay by Evelyn Fox Keller (1977), and the account of the almost hard to believe failure of the Royal Swedish Academy of Sciences to recognize the work and contribution to the discovery of fission of Lise Meitner (Crawford et al. 1997). These readings have a tremendous impact on the students. They make them aware of past and present realities of talented women and force them to question their own preconceptions. To give some perspective to these accounts, I guide the students in class discussions to ask: Can the history of the struggles of women and people of color for equality within society at large help us to understand these struggles within the scientific professions? Can these struggles teach us anything about the nature of science as a social enterprise?

In order to foster an appreciation for the subtleties of the evolution of the status of women in science and engineering, we read a summary review of the results of Harvard University's Project Access. This is a detailed study of a large sample of high-achieving female and male scientists aimed at determining the degree and causes of gender disparity in their career outcomes. This work, which is an example of "hard facts and evidence," is complemented with a discussion of issues of "critical mass" in the different fields of science today, for which we read "The Paradox of 'Critical Mass' for Women and Science" (Etzkowitz et al. 1994). We begin to understand that increasing the number of women and other minorities in science without a change in the structure of the scientific workplace does not decrease gender disparity significantly. We then explore the social structure and internal values that determine the culture of science and engineering and the possible connections to the situation of women in these professions by reading *Women in Engineering: Gender, Power, and Workplace Culture* (Meilwee and Robinson 1992) and *Beamtimes and Lifetimes: The World of High Energy Physicists* (Traweek 1992).

The second theme of the course begins with an introduction to the very diverse gender and science literature by reading "The History and Philosophy of

Women in Science: A Review Essay" (Schiebinger 1987a). The class generally is re-
ceptive to beginning an examination of the power of metaphors in scientific research and scientific texts, and in particular their subtle and in some instances not
so subtle gendering. Our discussions are guided by more recent readings from *Nature's Body: Gender in the Making of Modern Science* (Schiebinger 1993), *Reflections
on Gender and Science* (Keller 1985), and *Refiguring Life: Metaphors of Twentieth-
Century Biology* (Keller 1995). We trace the persistence of such metaphors on gender relations within the sciences by discussing "Skeletons in the Closet: The First
Illustrations of Female Skeletons in Eighteenth-Century Anatomy" (Schiebinger
1987b), "His and Hers: Male and Female Anatomy in Anatomy Texts for U.S.
Medical Students, 1890–1989" (Lawrence and Bendixen 1992), and *The Woman in
the Body: A Cultural Analysis of Reproduction* (Martin 1987).

Next, we explore the social construction of systems of authority, legitimacy,
and credibility and the role gendered power relations play in that construction.
For this and other aspects of the course, *Pythagoras' Trousers: God, Physics, and the
Gender Wars* (Wertheim 1995) is invaluable. In particular, students enjoy the historical analysis, and it is not uncommon to hear them praise this book as "the
best history of science book I studied here." We complement this work with
readings from the social critique of science presented in *A Social History of Truth:
Civility and Science in Seventeenth-Century England* (Shapin 1994) to explore the
connections between the identities of individuals making claims and the credibility of what they claim. We look at the enduring importance of these connections in examples of today's definitions of what is and who does "good science."
The class uses this context to explore the overt and covert ways in which scientific knowledge gets used to perpetuate biases, in particular gender bias, and to
begin to think about whether science is fundamentally defined by gender-spe-
cific values and methods.

The final session is centered on feminist pedagogy and the implications of
feminist critiques of science on the teaching of science, as exemplified in "Feminist Pedagogy, Interdisciplinary Praxis, and Science Education" (Mayberry and
Rees 1997), "An Exploratory Attempt toward a Feminist Pedagogy for Science
Education" (Roychoudhury et al. 1993/94) and "Implications of Feminist Critiques of Science for the Teaching of Mathematics and Science" (Shulman 1994).
This discussion leads to an assignment all students undertake enthusiastically, to
write a short essay detailing how they would teach the subject of their choice.

Throughout the term we stress the importance of including more women and
other minorities in the sciences in order to contribute new ideas to the research
priorities for the United States over the next decade. The course's main emphasis,
however, is on connecting the question of "women in science" with the question
of "scientific knowledge production." That is, we question the relationship between who is and is not included in the process of creating knowledge and how

the social construction of science affects the kind of science that gets done, and how it is done. In sum, we stress that the question of equality is intimately related to the knowledge that science produces, not just to a question of the "numbers" of women in the sciences. By the end of the term, students are equipped to tackle questions on whether women have affected or can and do affect the culture and professionalization of science by changing social values.

Teaching to Learn

I consider the evolution of "Women, Gender, and Diversity in Science and Engineering" to be the result of the exchange that takes place between teacher/mentor and the students and an expression of a synthesis between students' responses and my responsiveness to them. For instance, one frustrating aspect associated with teaching this course relates in part to students making generalized or sloppy statements with little or no supporting evidence beyond "we know it" or "personal experience tells us so"—responses that I know they would not so quickly have in a traditional science course. The idea that the rigorous thinking exercised in science courses is not necessary here, and that casual relativism is perfectly fine, is frustrating and hard to combat. In as many cases as possible and in as gentle a manner as possible, I call such statements into question, and I do so by appealing to "our common scientific training and approach" to knowledge. I make use of my training in and my knowledge of science as well as my experience in teaching science to bring into the classroom the myriad of examples in which science moves along the path of "we know it *because* personal experience tells us so." In this rather constructive way, I attempt to validate personal experiences as legitimate knowledge (incidentally, I do this when teaching traditional science material as well), not so different from the knowledge we obtain in textbooks, while simultaneously stressing the need to develop a critical approach to the anecdotal, as we do in the laboratory.

The airing of grievances and dilemmas that we have encountered—as teachers and students—strengthened our engagement with the course and its materials, even among those students in their senior year who enrolled to satisfy nonmajor requirements with what they originally perceived to be an easy course. Consequently, a group of students from one class continued to meet regularly the following semester to discuss and read about the relationship of science, gender, and technology to their own work. This group consisted of students in engineering, geoscience, history of science, geography, and philosophy. Students have continued to seek my advice and subsequently some have enrolled in related courses, others decided to take courses in the women's studies program, and several engineering students arranged to continue studying feminism, gender, and science for another semester by enrolling in an independent reading course. Stories like these continue to inspire my desire to both teach and learn from my students and sustain my belief in the necessity of developing more courses aimed at examining the intersections of gender, culture and science as part of the core education in all science and engineering programs. Changes can, in this way, shape long-term transformations.

Guide to Course Readings[5]

Week 1

Mary Beth Ruskai, "How Stereotypes about Science Affect the Participation of Women."

H. Etzkowitz et al., "The Paradox of 'Critical Mass' for Women in Science."

G. Sonnert and G. Holton, "Career Patterns of Women and Men in the Sciences."

S. Ambrose et al., *Journeys of Women in Science and Engineering: No Universal Constants* (preface—"No Universal Constants?" and introduction—"Women, Science, Engineering, and Technology through the Ages").

Week 2

Londa Schiebinger, "The History and Philosophy of Women in Science: A Review Essay."

Elisabeth Crawford et al., "A Nobel Tale of Postwar Injustice."

Evelyn Fox Keller, "The Anomaly of a Woman in Physics."

Evelyn Fox Keller, *Reflections on Gender and Science* (Part III—"Theory, Practice and Ideology in the Making of Science").

Week 3

J. Meilwee and J. Robinson, *Women in Engineering: Gender, Power, and Workplace Culture.*

Week 4

Emily Martin, *The Woman in the Body: A Cultural Analysis of Reproduction* (Part Two—"Science as a Cultural System").

Londa Schiebinger, "Skeletons in the Closet: The First Illustrations of Female Skeletons in Eighteenth-Century Anatomy."

Evelyn Fox Keller, *Reflections on Gender and Science.*

S. Lawrence and K. Bendixen, "His and Hers: Male and Female Anatomy in Anatomy Texts for U.S. Medical Students, 1890–1989."

Week 5

N. Katherine Hayles, "Gender Encoding in Fluid Mechanics: Masculine Channels and Feminine Flows."

Barbara Whitten, "What Physics Is Fundamental Physics? Feminist Implications of Physicists' Debate over the Superconducting Supercollider."

Week 6

Steven Shapin, *A Social History of Truth: Civility and Science in Seventeenth-Century England* (chapter 4—" Who Was Robert Boyle? The Creation and Presentation of an Experimental Identity" and chapter 6—"Knowing about People and Knowing about Things: A Moral History of Scientific Credibility").

Week 7

Claudia Henrion, *Women in Mathematics: The Addition of Difference.*

Weeks 8 and 9

Margaret Wertheim, *Pythagoras' Trousers: God, Physics, and the Gender Wars.*

Week 10

Sharon Traweek, *Beamtimes and Lifetimes: The World of High Energy Physicists.*

Week 11

Londa Schiebinger, *Nature's Body: Gender in the Making of Modern Science.*

Week 12

Maralee Mayberry and Margaret N. Rees, "Feminist Pedagogy, Interdisciplinary Praxis, and Science Education."

Anita Roychoudhury et al., "An Exploratory Attempt toward a Feminist Pedagogy for Science Education."

Bonnie Shulman, "Implications of Feminist Critiques of Science for the Teaching of Mathematics and Science."

Notes

1. The Women in Engineering Initiative at the University of Washington, which began in 1988, the Women in Science and Engineering Institute at Penn State, formally institutionalized in 1994, and the Women in Science Program at the University of Wisconsin System, formalized in 1996, are some of the well-established and best-known examples of institutions that responded to studies of a decade ago outlining the barriers facing women in engineering and science careers.

2. As the course evolved, I became aware that the expectation of attracting students from underrepresented groups in science and engineering (other than white women) was not being fulfilled. This factor led to my reconsidering the name, course description,

structure, and content of the course. As a result of these changes, the student population became much more diverse, with a significant percentage of African-American women enrolled in the course.

3. Only 15 percent of the students who attended this course had previously taken a course in the women's studies program.

4. See, for example, Evelyn Fox Keller's *Reflections on Gender and Science* (1985); Donna Haraway's *Primate Visions: Gender, Race, and Nature in the World of Modern Science* (1989); and Sandra Harding's *Whose Science? Whose Knowledge? Thinking from Women's Lives* (1991).

5. This guide is intended to provide information about materials that, while used in the course most of the time, are not always used as detailed here. Rather, they provide me with a basic framework that I sometimes improvise upon by altering the order in which the material is presented or inserting new and different readings. While these materials guide this course, I urge other educators to be creative and improvise as they see fit.

Works Cited

Ambrose, S., K. Dunkle, B. Lazarus, I. Nair, and D. Harkus. *Journey of Women in Science and Engineering: No Universal Constant.* Philadelphia: Temple University Press, 1997.

Crawford, E., R. Sime, and M. Walker. "A Nobel Tale of Postwar Injustice." *Physics Today* (September 1997): 26–32.

Etzkowitz, H., C. Kemelgor, M. Neuschatz, B. Uzzi, and J. Alonzo. "The Paradox of 'Critical Mass' for Women in Science." *Science* 266 (1994): 51–54.

Haraway, Donna. *Primate Visions: Gender, Race, and Nature in the World of Modern Science.* New York: Routledge, 1989.

Harding, Sandra. *Whose Science? Whose Knowledge? Thinking from Women's Lives.* Ithaca, NY: Cornell University Press, 1991.

Hayles, N. Katherine. "Gender Encoding in Fluid Mechanics: Masculine Channels and Feminine Flows." *Differences: A Journal of Feminist Cultural Studies* 4 (1992).

Henrion, Claudia. *Women in Mathematics: The Addition of Difference.* Bloomington: Indiana University Press, 1997.

Keller, Evelyn Fox. *Refiguring Life: Metaphors of Twentieth-Century Biology.* New York: Columbia University Press, 1995.

——— . *Reflections on Gender and Science.* New Haven, CT: Yale University Press, 1985.

——— . "The Anomaly of a Woman in Physics." In *Working It Out: 23 Women Writers, Artists, Scientists, and Scholars Talk about Their Lives and Work*, ed. S. Ruddick and P. Daniels. New York: Pantheon Books, 1977.

Lawrence, S., and K. Bendixen. "His and Hers: Male and Female Anatomy in Anatomy Texts for U.S. Medical Students, 1890–1989." *Social Science Medicine* 35 (1992): 925–934.

Martin, Emily. *The Woman in the Body: A Cultural Analysis of Reproduction.* Boston: Beacon Press, 1987.

Mayberry, M., and M. N. Rees. "Feminist Pedagogy, Interdisciplinary Praxis, and Science Education." *NWSA Journal* 9 (1997): 57–73.

Meilwee, J., and J. Robinson. *Women in Engineering: Gender, Power, and Workplace Culture.* New York: SUNY Press, 1992.

Roychounhury, A., D. Tippins, and S. Nichols. "An Exploratory Attempt toward a Feminist Pedagogy for Science Education." *Action in Teacher Education* 15 (Winter 1993/94): 36–46.

Ruskai, Mary Beth. "How Sterotypes about Science Affect the Participation of Women." Lecture presented at the American Association for Women in Science annual meeting, 1989.

Schiebinger, Londa. *Nature's Body: Gender in the Making of Modern Science.* Boston: Beacon Press, 1993.

———. "The History and Philosophy of Women in Science: A Review Essay." *Signs: Journal of Women, Culture, and Society* 12 (1987a): 305–332.

———. "Skeletons in the Closet: The First Illustrations of Female Skeletons in Eighteenth-Century Anatomy." In *The Making of the Modern Body*, ed. T. Laqueur and C. Gallagher. Berkeley: University of California Press, 1987b.

Shapin, Steven. *A Social History of Truth: Civility and Science in Seventeenth-Century England.* Chicago: University of Chicago Press, 1994.

Shulman, Bonnie. "Implications of Feminist Critiques of Science for the Teaching of Mathematics and Science." *Journal of Women and Minorities in Science and Engineering* 1 (1994): 1–15.

Sonnert, G., and G. Holton. "Career Patterns of Women and Men in the Sciences." *American Scientist* 84 (1996): 63–71.

Traweek, Sharon. *Beamtimes and Lifetimes: The World of High Energy Physicists.* Cambridge, MA: Harvard University Press, 1992.

Weinberg, Steven. "Reflections of a Working Scientist." *Daedalus* (Summer 1974): 33–46.

Wertheim, Margaret. *Pythagoras' Trousers: God, Physics, and the Gender Wars.* New York: Random House, 1995.

Whitten, Barbara. "What Physics Is Fundamental Physics? Feminist Implications of Physicists' Debate over the Superconducting Supercollider." *NWSA Journal* 8 (1996).

Scientific Literacy → Agential Literacy = (Learning + Doing) Science Responsibly[1]

Karen Barad

Joe Smith is a truck driver who knows nothing about inertia. "So he throws the hammer onto the shelf right behind his head and loads his truck behind the cab with some heavy iron ingots, stacked up high. Then and there, a knowledge of inertia and the principles of motion may mean the difference between life and death to Joe Smith. On a sudden, short stop that hammer may hit him in the head and kill him.

His load of ingots may crash through the cab and crush him. This lesson should be driven home to our pupils. *Physics is a life and death subject.*"
—*Hyman Ruchlis, 1953*

One physics teacher reported on his offering of "Kitchen Physics" as a response to dealing with "the wail from the feminine members of . . . physics classes, 'Gee! I'll never get this. And what good would it be to me, anyway? It's a boy's subject; boys are more mechanically inclined than girls.'" Examples included tips on keeping the coffee warm and distinguishing eggs that had been hard-boiled from uncooked ones. He explains, "All this merely points out that one may live more graciously and understandingly with a small amount of knowledge acquired in a high school physics course, even if one happens to be of the feminine sex.
—*James B. Davis, 1951*

Relevance and context. These are the ingredients that are supposed to make science more palatable to students—the cultural coatings specially formulated to ease the digestion of physics, which, like castor oil, is as good for you as it is notoriously difficult to swallow. The "relevancy coated" approaches to teaching science promoted today are no less well intentioned—and no more successful—than they were nearly half a century ago. The limited success of such approaches should not be surprising: there's something paradoxical about the notion that something can be "made" relevant—as if relevancy could be imposed or added

226

onto an existing structure. The starting point is all wrong: taking an existing course and contemplating superficial alterations to it in an effort to make it relevant is a poor substitute for designing a relevant course or curriculum. Another important limitation is that relevancy is undertheorized. Relevant for/to whom? is a crucial question that needs to be addressed; but it is insufficient if posed in isolation from the issue of how the "whom" is to be understood. Questions of relevancy are intertwined with questions of subjectivity and epistemic responsibility. For example, although the physics teacher who creatively suggests a "kitchen physics" approach for the "ladies" has clearly thought about the fact that relevancy has different meanings for different audiences, his approach is essentializing: it fixes what is considered "feminine" in particular ways (historically, culturally, and so on) and erases an array of socially relevant differences. Implicit in the example are numerous cultural assumptions, including the following presumptions: that girls and women can identify with and are responsible for cooking and other aspects of gracious living; that keeping coffee at an appropriate equilibrium temperature and distinguishing the different states of matter of eggs (as opposed to learning the preparation of chapati or strategies for feeding children on poverty-level wages) are useful skills; that "ladies" don't want to be mechanics or, heaven forbid, pursue careers in physics.[2]

Alternatively, some approaches attempt to place science in its historical, philosophical, sociological, or cultural context by adding snippets from other disciplines, such as the history and philosophy of science, which seem appropriate to the topic at hand. But these approaches often reenact the very problem they are trying to address by pulling only single strands of history or philosophy out of a complex cloth in order to patch together a background against which to view science. Or, to switch back to the coated caplet metaphor, the approach is to first fabricate an idiosyncratic cultural shell around the curricular content and then explain the molding of the malleable interior—the self-same scientific content—in terms of the shell's form. The science-in-context perspective, in its single-minded focus on providing historically situated explanations for particular accounts of "nature," presents a rigidified and oversimplified view of "culture," and the relationship between them. It also gives students a distorted view of the history and philosophy of science and their respective disciplinary trajectories and intricate and interlocking structures. Presuming science to be embedded in a given cultural context—fixed in a specific surrounding—places a particular limitation on our understanding of science, of culture, and of their heterogeneous and multiple interactions.[3]

Whether the focus is on the influence of culture on science, or vice versa, these "context coated" approaches play off an assumed nature/culture dualism, reifying one pole or the other in an attempt to identify linear causal lines of influence between science and culture. Courses that explain the development of science on the basis of cultural factors alone (culture unilaterally influences science) are just as problematic as those that paint a picture of the modern world as the direct descendant of the triumphant victory of the scientific worldview (science unilaterally influences culture). Treating either nature or culture as a determining factor or holding one or the other as fixed and self-evident fudges on presenting a realistic view of both science and culture. Clearly, this deficiency cannot be addressed by adding the results of separate unidirectional examinations.

Often even more problematic is the genre of courses carrying the designation "Physics for Poets." These courses are often random and idiosyncratic pastiches of the "relevancy coated" and "context coated" approaches in which a host of different topics are presented with a uniform disregard for rigor. Entertainment is often accorded high value in such courses; however, entertainment often becomes a substitute for, rather than a way of promoting, learning. The glassy-eyed—"gee isn't that neat"—look on students' faces may be less a sign of enthusiasm for the subject matter and more an indication of their disempowerment. What is it that students really learn to appreciate in these so-called science appreciation courses?

And in all of this where is the science student? No doubt some readers will have assumed that I was referring all along to the teaching of science to non-science majors. Although some courses for majors enjoy a "splash" of relevancy and/or context here and there, generally speaking, no serious efforts are made in this direction. The standard response is that attention to these "peripheral issues" would rob the course of precious time needed for the "important stuff," which there simply isn't enough time as it is to adequately cover. As a physicist, I appreciate the responsibility we have to our majors, and I think that matters of content are real and important. But I also think that this goes hand in hand with another responsibility: to teach science in a way that promotes an understanding of the nature of scientific practices. This will make for better, more creative, more responsible participation in the various technoscientific enterprises in which we are all implicated at this historical moment. If science students do not learn that doing responsible science entails thinking about the connection of scientific practices to other social practices, then what is the justification for our current confidence as a society in the ability of scientists to make socially responsible decisions?

What other approaches are possible? How do we design pedagogies that go beyond these "coated caplet" methods of acknowledging relevancy and context? What approaches might be employed in the interest of capturing something of the complex nature of the relationship between science and culture, rather than seeking causal explanations for one strictly in terms of the other? Approaches that take account of discursive *and* material constraints on knowledge production? Approaches that contest the conception of the nature/culture dichotomy as transhistorical, transcultural, and self-evident? Approaches that teach students to think reflexively about the nature of science and about what it means to do responsible science while teaching them the science as well? Approaches that enable students to see the beauty, power, and delight in doing science, without placing science at a distance from other human practices? Approaches that inspire students to a mature love of science growing out of a respect for its strengths and its limitations, rather than a form of puppy love in which the infatuation is held hostage to one of two modes of expression: complete awe and blindness to its vulnerabilities, or disillusionment and wholesale rejection? Approaches by which all students, majors and nonmajors alike, can come to understand how important it is to participate in making decisions about the technoscientific world within which we live and the responsibility and accountability that must accompany technoscientific endeavors?

In this essay, I will outline one pedagogical approach, in the early stages of development, that seeks to speak to each of these issues. This approach is based upon a reconceptualization of scientific literacy as "agential literacy." It also pushes the boundaries of current discussions concerning the nature of (inter)disciplinarity.

A need for joint conceptual shifts in our understanding of scientific literacy and the nature of disciplinary knowledge may not be obvious from the academically segregated discussions of these issues. Generally speaking, these issues have been the separate province of noncommunicating sectors of the academy. Questions of disciplinarity are not common preoccupations of scientists and neither is scientific literacy a pressing issue for nonscientists. Why is this so? Why isn't it common for scientists to concern themselves with questions of disciplinarity (for example, What are the means by which particular knowledge relations among otherwise disparate elements develop? What is the nature of the epistemic constraints and enabling conditions constituting particular disciplines?)? Similarly, why is scientific literacy generally taken to be a curricular responsibility of science departments, and not other academic disciplines? What assumptions go into supporting these particular divisions of intellectual labor?

In recent efforts to examine and intervene in how knowledge is disciplined a variety of closely related approaches have been suggested. *Multi-, inter-, trans-, cross-, extra-, counter-, post-,* and *anti-* are among the prefixes that have been appended to *disciplinarity* in these attempts at border-crossing. Which of these versions, if any, speak to the imbrication of epistemology, ontology, and ethics? Reflections on the nature of knowledge and knowledge production alone just won't do; rather, as I will argue here, what is required is the study of something we might call "epistem-onto-logy" or "ethico-epistem-onto-logy" in rethinking a concept that is expected to do as much work as "scientific literacy."[4]

To attempt to talk across disciplinary divides as wide and as deep as the gulf separating the humanities from the sciences comes with certain risks. Nonetheless, I want to offer a joint reconsideration of scientific literacy and disciplinarity here, based upon the framework of agential realism (Barad 1996, 1998a). From the perspective of agential realism, technoscientific practices are particularly potent sites in which epistemological, ontological, ethical, and other issues are richly interwoven. This assertion has implications for science pedagogy as well as science policy. It also pushes the boundaries of current discussions concerning the nature of disciplinarity that have focused solely on the disciplining of knowledge, to the exclusion of other important dimensions. In particular, the reconceptualization of scientific literacy and disciplinarity that I will offer here takes account of the ontological as well as epistemological dimensions of boundary-drawing practices, and material as well as discursive constraints. The notion of responsible science that is offered turns on questions of agency, accountability, and objectivity.

The viewpoint of responsible science espoused here is based on the framework of agential realism. Agential realism is an epistem-onto-logical framework that takes as its central concerns: the nature of scientific and other social practices; the nature of reality; the role of natural, social, and cultural factors in scientific knowledge production; the contingency and efficacy of scientific knowledge; the nature of matter; the relationship between the material and the discursive in epistemic practices; the coconstitution of "objects" and "subjects" within such practices; the material conditions for intelligibility and for objectivity; the nature of causality; and the nature of agency. Agential realism takes its inspiration from the general epistemological framework of physicist Niels Bohr. Bohr's search for a coherent interpretation of quantum physics led him to more general epistemological considerations that challenge some of our most basic assumptions. His careful analysis of the relationship between the conceptual and physical apparatuses involved in scientific practices has relevance for contemporary efforts to understand the nature of science. Building on Bohr's insights, agential realism theorizes the relationship between the material and discursive, and human and nonhuman dimensions of these practices, moving us beyond the dichotomized realism and social constructivism positions and the accompanying well-worn debates between these positions.[5]

In the next section, I outline Bohr's general epistemological framework.[6] I then present some of the key features of agential realism and explore its implications for thinking about scientific literacy. Finally, I offer a specific example of a course specifically designed to increase the level of agential literacy.

Bohr's Epistemological Framework[7]

Bohr's careful analysis of the process of observation led him to conclude that two implicit assumptions needed to support the Newtonian framework and its notion of the transparency of observations were flawed: (1) the assumption that observation-independent objects have well-defined intrinsic properties that are representable as abstract universal concepts, and (2) the assumption that the measurement interactions between the objects and the agencies of observation are continuous and determinable, ensuring that the values of the properties obtained reflect those of the observation-independent objects, as separate from the agencies of observation. In contrast to these Newtonian assumptions, Bohr argued that theoretical concepts are defined by the circumstances required for their measurement. It follows from this fact, and from the fact that there is an empirically verifiable discontinuity in measurement interactions, that there is no unambiguous way to differentiate between the "object" and the "agencies of observation." As no inherent cut exists between "object" and "agencies of observation," measured values cannot be attributed to observation-independent objects. In fact, Bohr concluded that observation-independent objects do not possess well-defined inherent properties.[8]

Bohr constructs his post-Newtonian framework on the basis of quantum wholeness—that is, the lack of an inherent distinction between the "object" and the "agencies of observation." He uses the term *phenomenon*, in a very specific sense, to designate particular instances of wholeness: "While, within the scope of classical physics, the interaction between object and apparatus can be neglected or, if necessary, compensated for, in quantum physics *this interaction thus forms an inseparable part of the phenomenon*. Accordingly, the unambiguous account of proper quantum phenomena must, in principle, include a description of all relevant features of the experimental arrangement" (Bohr 1963c, 4, emphasis mine).

Bohr's insight concerning the intertwining of the conceptual and physical dimensions of measurement processes is central to his epistemological framework. The physical apparatus marks the conceptual subject-object distinction: the physical and conceptual apparatuses form a nondualistic whole. That is, descriptive concepts obtain their meaning by reference to a particular physical apparatus, which in turn marks the placement of a constructed cut between the "object" and the "agencies of observation." For example, instruments with fixed parts are required to understand what we might mean by the concept "position." However, any such apparatus necessarily excludes other concepts, such as "momentum," from having meaning during this set of measurements, since these other variables require an instrument with movable parts for their definition. Physical and conceptual constraints and exclusions are coconstitutive.

Since there is no inherent cut delineating the "object" from the "agencies of observation," the following question emerges: What sense, if any, should we attribute to the notion of observation? Bohr suggests that "by an experiment we simply understand an event about which we are able in an unambiguous way to state the conditions necessary for the reproduction of the phenomena" (Bohr quoted in Folse (1985, 124). This is possible on the condition that the experimenter introduces a constructed cut between an "object" and the "agencies of observation."[9] That is, in contrast to the Newtonian worldview, Bohr argues that no inherent distinction preexists the measurement process, that every measurement involves a particular choice of apparatus, providing the conditions necessary to give definition to a particular set of classical variables, at the exclusion of other equally essential variables, and thereby embodying a particular constructed cut delineating the "object" from the "agencies of observation." This particular constructed cut resolves the ambiguities only for a given context; it marks off and is part of a particular instance of wholeness.

Especially in his later writings, Bohr insists that quantum mechanical measurements are "objective." Since he also emphasizes the essential wholeness of phenomena, he cannot possibly mean by "objective" that measurements reveal inherent properties of independent objects. But Bohr does not reject objectivity out of hand; he reformulates it. For Bohr, "objectivity" is a matter of "permanent marks—such as a spot on a photographic plate, caused by the impact of an electron—left on the bodies which define the experimental conditions" (Bohr 1963c, 3). Objectivity is defined in reference to bodies and, as we have seen, reference must be made to bodies in order for concepts to have meaning. Clearly, Bohr's notion of objectivity, which is not predicated on an inherent distinction between "objects" and "agencies of observation," stands in stark contrast to a Newtonian sense of objectivity as denoting observer independence.

The question remains: What is the referent of any particular objective property? Since there is no inherent distinction between object and apparatus, the property in question cannot be meaningfully attributed to either an abstracted object or an abstracted measuring instrument. That is, the measured quantities in a given experiment are not values of properties that belong to an observation-independent object, nor are they purely artifactual values created by the act of measurement (which would belie any sensible meaning of the word *measurement*). My reading is that the measured properties refer to phenomena, remembering that phenomena are physical-conceptual "intra-actions" whose unambiguous account requires "a description of all relevant features of the experimental arrangement." I introduce the neologism *intra-action* to signify *the inseparability of "objects" and "agencies of observation"* (in contrast to "interaction," which reinscribes the contested dichotomy).

While Newtonian physics is well known for its strict determinism—its widely acclaimed ability to predict and retrodict the full set of physical states of a system for all times, based upon the simultaneous specification of two particular variables at any one instant—Bohr's general epistemological framework proposes a radical revision of such an understanding of causality.[10] He explains that the inseparability of the object from the apparatus "entails . . . the necessity of a final renunciation of the classical ideal of causality and a radical revision of our attitude towards the problem of physical reality" (Bohr 1963b, 59–60). While claiming that his analysis forces him to issue a final renunciation of the classical ideal of causality—that is, of strict determinism—Bohr does not presume that this entails overarching disorder, lawlessness, or an outright rejection of the cause-and-effect relationship. Rather, he suggests that our understanding of the terms of that relationship must be reworked: "the feeling of volition and the demand for causality are equally indispensable elements in the relation between subject and object which forms the core of the problem of knowledge" (Bohr 1963a, 117). In short, he rejects both poles of the usual dualist thinking about causality—freedom and determinism—and proposes a third possibility.[11]

Bohr's epistemological framework deviates in an important fashion from classical correspondence or mirroring theories of scientific knowledge. For example, consider the wave-particle duality paradox originating from early-twentieth-century observations conducted by experimenters who reported seemingly contradictory evidence about the nature of light: under certain experimental circumstances light manifests particlelike properties, and under an experimentally incompatible set of circumstances light manifests wavelike properties. This situation is paradoxical to the classical realist mind-set because the true ontological nature of light is in question: either light is a wave or it is particle; it can't be both. Bohr resolves the wave-particle duality paradox as follows: "wave" and "particle" are classical descriptive concepts that refer to different mutually exclusive phenomena and not to independent physical objects. He emphasizes that this saves quantum theory from inconsistencies since it is impossible to observe particle and wave behaviors simultaneously because mutually exclusive experimental arrangements are required. To put the point in a more modern context, according to Bohr's general epistemological framework, referentiality is reconceptualized: the referent is not an observation-independent reality, but phenomena. This shift in referentiality is a condition for the possibility of objective knowledge. That is, a condition for objective knowledge is that the referent is a phenomenon (and not an observation-independent object).

Agential Realism

Bohr's notion of science is limited by an underdeveloped account of the social dimensions of scientific practices. The framework of agential realism elaborates upon Bohr's epistemology, taking particular inspiration from his insights concerning the nature of the relationship between subject and object, nature and culture, and the physical and conceptual, and articulates a notion of practices as processes involving the intra-action of multiple material-discursive apparatuses. According to agential realism, apparatuses of observation are not simple instruments but are themselves complex material-discursive phenomena, involved in, formed out of, and formative of particular practices. This elaboration is accomplished in part through the theorization of an ontology and the specification of its relationship to the epistemological issues. I will not give a complete account here.[12] Rather, my focus in this section will be on the nature of apparatuses and questions of ontology, agency, and accountability.

Apparatuses, in Bohr's sense, are not passive observing instruments. On the contrary, they are productive of (and part of) phenomena. However, Bohr leaves the meaning of "apparatus" somewhat ambiguous. He does insist that what constitutes an apparatus only emerges in the context of specific observational practices. But while focusing on the lack of an inherent distinction between the apparatus and the object, Bohr does not directly address the question of where the apparatus "ends." In a sense, he establishes only the "inside" boundary and not the "outside" one. For example, is the "outside" boundary of the apparatus coincident with the visual terminus of the instrumentation? What if there is an infrared interface (that is, a wireless connection) between the measuring instrument and a computer that collects data? Does the apparatus include the computer? the scientist performing the experiment? the scientific community that judges the value of the research and decides upon its funding? What precisely constitutes the limits of the apparatus that gives meaning to certain concepts at the exclusion of others?[13]

A central focus in Bohr's discussion of objectivity is the possibility of "unambiguous communication," which can take place only in reference to "bodies which define the experimental conditions" and which embody particular concepts, to the exclusion of others. This seems to indicate Bohr's recognition of the social nature of scientific practices: making meanings involves the interrelationship of complex discursive and material practices. What is needed is an articulation of the notion of apparatuses that acknowledges this complexity.

Theorizing the social and political aspects of practices is a challenge that is taken up by Michel Foucault. Like Bohr, Foucault is interested in the conditions for intelligibility and the productive and constraining dimensions of practices embodied in "apparatuses."[14] Significantly, for both Bohr and Foucault, apparatuses are productive, constraining but nondetermining, specific material and discursive arrangements. Reading Foucault's and Bohr's analyses of apparatuses through one another provides a richer overall account of apparatuses: it extends the domain of Bohr's analysis from the physical-conceptual to the material-discursive more generally; provides a further articulation of Foucault's account, extending its domain to include the natural sciences and an account of the materialization of nonhuman bodies; and offers an explicit analysis of the inseparability of the apparatus from the objects and subjects of knowledge practices, and of the coconstitution of material and discursive constraints and exclusions.

As I will indicate below, an agential realist account entails the following important points: apparatuses of observation are not simple instruments but are themselves complex material-discursive phenomena, involved in, formed out of, and formative of particular social processes, including technoscientific ones. Power, knowledge, and being are conjoined in material-discursive practices. I briefly summarize a few of the main points of the analysis in what follows.[15]

How does this recognition of the material-discursive character of apparatuses matter to the ontological issues at stake in debates between realism and social constructivism? Petersen notes an important aspect of Bohr's response to such questions:

> Traditional philosophy has accustomed us to regard language as something secondary, and reality as something primary. Bohr considered this attitude toward the relation between language and reality inappropriate. When one said to him that it cannot be language which is fundamental, but that it must be reality which, so to speak, lies beneath language, and of which language is a picture, he would reply "We are suspended in language in such a way that we cannot say what is up and that is down. The word 'reality' is also a word, a word which we must learn to use correctly" (Petersen 1985, 302).

Unfortunately, Bohr is not explicit about how he thinks we should use the word *reality*. I have argued elsewhere (Barad 1996) that a consistent Bohrian ontology takes phenomena to be constitutive of reality. Reality is not composed of things-in-themselves or things-behind-phenomena, but things-in-phenomena. Because phenomena constitute a nondualistic whole, it makes no sense to talk about independently existing things as somehow behind or as the causes of phenomena.

The ontology I propose does not posit some fixed notion of being that is prior to signification (as the classical realist assumes), but neither is being completely inaccessible to language (as in Kantian transcendentalism), nor completely of language (as in linguistic monism). That reality within which we intra-act—what I term agential reality—is made up of material-discursive phenomena. Agential reality is not a fixed ontology that is independent of human practices, but is continually reconstituted through our material-discursive intra-actions.

Shifting our understanding of the ontologically real from that which stands outside the sphere of cultural influence and historical change to agential reality allows a new formulation of realism (and truth) that is not premised on the representational nature of knowledge. If our descriptive characterizations do not refer to properties of abstract objects or observation-independent beings, but rather describe agential reality, then what is being described by our theories is not nature itself, but our participation within nature. That is, realism is reformulated in terms of the goal of providing accurate descriptions of agential reality—that reality within which we intra-act and have our being—rather than some imagined and ide-alized human-independent reality. I use the label agential realism for both the new form of realism and the larger epistem-onto-logical framework that I propose.[16]

According to agential realism, reality is sedimented out of the process of mak-ing the world intelligible through certain practices and not others. Therefore, we are not only responsible for the knowledge that we seek, but, in part, for what ex-ists. Scientific practices involve complex intra-actions of multiple material-dis-cursive apparatuses. Material-discursive apparatuses are themselves phenomena made up of specific intra-actions of humans and nonhumans, where the differ-ential constitution of "nonhuman" (or "human") itself designates a particular phenomenon, and what gets defined as an "object" (or "subject") and what gets defined as an "apparatus" is intra-actively constituted within specific practices. Intra-actions are constraining but not determining.[17] The notion of intra-actions reformulates the traditional notion of causality and opens up a space for mater-ial-discursive forms of agency, including human, nonhuman, and cyborgian vari-eties. According to agential realism, agency is a matter of intra-acting; it is an enactment, not something someone or something has. Agency cannot be desig-nated as an attribute of "subjects" or "objects" (as they do not preexist as such). Agency is about the possibilities and accountability entailed in refiguring mater-ial-discursive apparatuses of production, including the boundary articulations and exclusions that are marked by those practices.[18]

Reconceiving Scientific Literacy as Agential Literacy

What are the implications of agential realism for thinking about scientific liter-acy? Agential realism provides an understanding of the nature of scientific prac-tices that recognizes that objectivity and agency are bound up with issues of responsibility and accountability. We are responsible in part for what exists not because it is an arbitrary construction of our choosing, but because agential real-ity is sedimented out of particular practices that we have a role in shaping. Which material-discursive practices are enacted matters for ontological as well as epistemological reasons: a different material-discursive apparatus materializes a different agential reality, as opposed to simply producing a different description of a fixed observation-independent world. Agential realism is not about repre-sentations of an independent reality, but about the real consequences, interven-tions, creative possibilities, and responsibilities of intra-acting within the world. Hence, according to agential realism, scientific literacy becomes a matter of agential literacy—of learning how to intra-act responsibly within the world.

What kind of education is needed to work toward the goal of agential liter-acy? Agential literacy requires understanding the nature of our intra-actions within the world. Therefore, it will be necessary to have the ability to analyze the intra-actions of multiple material-discursive apparatuses. A partial list of skills that will be required includes:

- the ability to identify the relevant apparatuses entailed in particular practices;
- the ability to analyze the material-discursive nature of each apparatus (including each apparatus' specific sedimented history);
- the ability to analyze the mutually constitutive relationship among intra-acting apparatuses (in their local specificity as well as their global intra-connectivity);
- the ability to analyze the intra-active constitution of "objects" and "subjects" (including, for example, the differential constitution of "human");
- the ability to recognize the boundaries drawn in the enactment of particular practices;
- the ability to imagine and understand the possibilities for reconfiguring apparatuses and reconstituting boundaries; and
- the ability to analyze, as best as possible, the consequences of new practices.

In turn, these analyses will require:

- understanding and taking account of the multiple forms of agency;
- attention to the requirements of objectivity (including attentiveness to marks on bodies);
- ongoing development of new methods for exposing background assumptions, including attention to the active inclusion of communities affected by different technoscientific practices;
- attention to issues of responsibility and accountability; and
- ongoing reflection on the nature of scientific knowledges and practices as part of the practice of doing science.

Although it may seem that agential literacy raises the standards so high as to make the goal unreachable, introducing a notion of literacy with more complexity does not mean that it is less achievable. On the contrary, an oversimplified model may be an important cause of the lack of progress that we have seen in achieving the goal of scientific literacy, not only because such a model misses the mark when it comes to understanding our complex intra-actions within the world—undermining much of what it is hoped that scientific literacy will achieve—but also because the goal of scientific literacy may not be compelling to many of the "scientifically illiterate" who have already grasped its irrelevance. One common complaint made by students taking science courses is that what they are learning does not seem relevant to their lives. According to the conception of agential literacy presented here, one does not make the subject matter relevant by starting with an unchanged traditional curriculum and coating scientific facts with "relevant examples" to make them go down easier. In teaching for agential literacy, science is understood (not "in context") but in complex intra-action with other practices.

If, unlike multidisciplinary or interdisciplinary approaches, a transdisciplinary approach "does not merely draw from an array of disciplines but rather inquires into the histories of the organization of knowledges and their function in the formation of subjectivities . . . mak[ing] visible and put[ting] into crisis the structural links between the disciplining of knowledge and larger social arrangements" (Hennessy 1993, 12), then the latter approach contains some of the elements of the methodology that is needed in teaching for agential literacy. Additionally, agential realism suggests that these considerations be supplemented by insights that follow from an appreciation of the nature of the disciplining of knowledge as particular material-discursive practices. This approach inquires into:

- the material-discursive nature of boundary-drawing practices as both the enabling and exclusionary workings of power;
- the coconstitution of different domains of knowledge through the intra-action of multiple apparatuses;
- the intra-active constitution of "objects" and "subjects" within practices;
- the epistem-onto-logical consequences of particular boundary cuts; and
- questions of agency and accountability in terms of the possibilities of refiguring apparatuses and the constitutive boundary cuts through which knowledge is disciplined.

I will use the term *trans/disciplinary* to signify this enlarged set of considerations, where the slash is inserted as a physical marker, a visual symbol, of the material nature of boundary-drawing practices (a crucial dimension of disciplinary practices too often omitted in discussions of disciplinarity), and to emphasize the fact that the intra-action of different disciplinary apparatuses does not negate the epistem-onto-logical import of the different histories and institutional structures of various disciplinary practices that it draws upon, nor does it constitute an undoing of the disciplinary nature of knowledge—boundaries are always necessary for making meanings.[19]

Teaching Agential Literacy

The mass of our children should be given something which may not be terribly strenuous but should be interesting, stimulating and amusing. They should be given science appreciation courses just as they are sometimes given music appreciation courses.

—*Edward Teller, testifying at a hearing
of the Senate Armed Services Committee,
November 1957* [20]

The epitome of the general education course for non–science students, the so-called "Physics for Poets" course, puts the philosophy expressed by Teller into practice. This genre of courses misses the mark completely when it comes to teaching students about responsible science. In fact, these courses can actually result in the further mystification of science and the disempowerment of students. [21] What kind of pedagogy would help students to learn about practicing responsible science?

In this section, I describe a course that I specifically designed to advance the agential literacy of my students, called "Situated Knowledges: Cultural Studies of Twentieth Century Physics." I chose twentieth-century physics as the subject matter on the basis of my own interests and expertise and because it brings to the fore crucial epistemological issues—though the basic pedagogy can be adapted to other subject matters. Since twentieth-century physics is a popular choice of topic for non–science major physics courses, this also allows an easier comparison between pedagogies that teach with the traditional notion of scientific literacy in mind and a pedagogy that has agential literacy as a goal. For starters, these pedagogies differ in motivation, audience, and methodology. What often motivates the choice of this subject matter in "Physics for Poets" courses is its "sexiness" (Stephen Hawking's best-seller litters coffee tables across the country— *quantum leap, chaos theory, black holes,* and *quark* are terms that circulate in the popular culture), its "shock" value (the counterintuitive findings about the universe), and the fact that it is fairly easy to draw (weak, surface) parallels to the humanities (that is, the work of the "poets"). Furthermore, "Physics for Poets" courses are directed at non–science majors and generally offer only a handwavy presentation of the main ideas. In contrast, the course that I will briefly describe is motivated by the desire to challenge both non–science *and* science majors to a greater understanding of the nature of scientific practices and of what it means to do responsible science. Every attempt is made to be as rigorous as possible in the presentation of the physics and the other related issues.

This course carries three different course identifications (designating it as a physics course, as an interdisciplinary women's studies course, and as a science, technology, and society course) at the Claremont Colleges, where it was originally taught. It has a laboratory component and satisfies a science distribution requirement for the liberal arts colleges and a humanities distribution requirement for the science and engineering college. It is also cross-listed with the Five-College Women's Studies and the Science, Technology, and Society (STS) programs. The course is open to all undergraduates.

The approach used is trans/disciplinary, and the readings are drawn from a range of literatures including anthropology, philosophy, history, sociology, feminist theory, cultural studies, and physics. This approach is different from ones that merely attempt to place physics in its historical, philosophical, sociological, or cultural "context" by adding tidbits from other disciplines (such as the history and philosophy of science) that seem appropriate to the topic at hand.[22] To begin with, unlike the "science in context" approaches, the agential literacy approach does not play off an assumed dualism between culture and science—trying to then draw out definitive causal lines of influence between one and the other—a fact that may be as disconcerting to social constructivists as it is to realists. Rather, the approach used is to examine the intra-action of different apparatuses constituting different knowledge practices. Emphasis is placed on an examination of different boundary cuts enacted in the formation of particular categories of analysis and how they relate to one another. For example, contrary to some "science, technology, and society" approaches, it is not presumed that the question of how physicists make sense of the world can be answered by simply identifying appropriate cultural influences, treating nature as mediated by culture, and treating culture as itself an implicitly transparent and separate surrounding or context. Rather than presuming some inherent demarcation between nature and culture as the starting point for the analysis, an agential realist analysis includes an examination of the way different disciplinary cultures define what counts as "nature" and what counts as "culture." Furthermore, it privileges neither the material nor discursive dimensions of scientific practices, but seeks to understand the relationship between material and discursive constraints and conditions. In this way, the role of (human and nonhuman) agency in the production of objective knowledge can be appreciated, and students can begin to see the importance of their own participation in doing responsible science, of learning how to intra-act responsibly within the world.

This course was designed to enable students to learn science while thinking about science, and to learn that thinking about science is part of doing science. Students did calculations and laboratory exercises, experienced the power and efficacy of science, and learned to appreciate the value of doing responsible science, while thinking about the nature of scientific practices and its relationship to other social practices. In a sense the course itself was a meditation on scientific literacy, disciplinarity, and the consequences of particular boundary practices. I believe that the success of the course is in part due to the fact that agential literacy is the kind of literacy that is achievable because it is more realistic—it has more to do with the world within which we intra-act, and students know it. (For a more detailed account of this course see Barad 2000b).[23]

Conclusion

The teaching of scientific literacy has been considered to be the sole responsibility of scientists. If by scientific literacy we mean simply knowledge of scientific facts and methods, then this seems reasonable. But if our goal is agential literacy—knowing how to intra-act responsibly within the world—then we must all share the responsibility for preparing future generations to meet the challenges that lie ahead. Agential literacy cannot be taught in one course or even within one curriculum. It is a responsibility that cuts across disciplinary boundaries in the academy and beyond.

The making of science is not separate from the making of society. Scientific practices are not just any kinds of doings, they are material-discursive intra-actions with intertwined epistemological and ontological significance. The making of what we call "science" and what we call "society" are mutually constitutive, not because they impact one another, but because the constitutive intra-actions do not honor the arbitrary boundaries we construct between one and the other. The multiple material-discursive apparatuses that are consciously or unconsciously mobilized and implicated in particular practices are not isolatable pieces of instrumentation contained within the walls of a laboratory. The apparatuses that are constitutive of practices (be they "scientific" or "social") are themselves material-discursive phenomena with particular sedimenting histories.

The fact that Luis Alvarez, a physicist who worked on the Manhattan Project at Los Alamos during the war, mined the postwar thermonuclear bomb project for equipment to be used in the construction of his bubble chamber at Berkeley to do high-energy physics experiments is not sufficient reason, in and of itself, to condemn or to desist from engaging in experimental particle physics. After all, appropriation can prove to be an effective intervention in the structures of power. But knowing this history is important for understanding the nature of the material cultural that brings pieces of Los Alamos to Eniwetok and back to northern California (Galison 1997, 4). And understanding the flow of materials, information, concepts, styles of engagement,[24] and more across the leaky boundary between pure and applied science is important for getting at the "genealogy of instruments [that] helps to explain how they became certified as legitimate keys to the domain of the subvisible" (5)—and how, I might add, the scientific authority of such projects lends legitimization to other cultural endeavors that share pieces of these sedimenting histories. What we need more generally is to understand the construction, circulation, and enfolding of elements of material-discursive culture: a genealogy of apparatuses (experimental, theoretical, pedagogical, economic, and so on), not simply of instruments. For apparatuses are

242

Feminist Science Studies

themselves phenomena—the result of particular material-discursive practices—
and the enfolding of phenomena into subsequent iterations of particular situated
practices (which may be traded across space, time, and subcultures) constitutes
important shifts in the nature of the intra-actions, that result in the production of
new phenomena, and so on. Which shifts occur matters for epistemological as
well as ontological reasons. We are responsible for the world within which we live
not because it is an arbitrary construction of our choosing, but because agential
reality is sedimented out of particular practices that we have a role in shaping. To
understand what it means to do responsible science, to engage in responsible actions more generally, requires that we learn how our practices come to matter.

Acknowledgment: I gratefully acknowledge support from the Irvine Foundation and
from the Mellon Foundation for funding related to the development of the course.

Notes

1. This paper is an abridged version of my "Reconceiving Scientific Literacy as Agential Literacy, or Learning How to Intra-Act Responsibly within the World," In *Doing
Culture + Science*, ed. Roddey Reid and Sharon Traweek. New York: Routledge, 2000b).
2. This is not an isolated example. And while certain specific features mark it as a cultural product of the 1950s, it would be wrong to think that the approach (or even the
theme: I can see it now— a Martha Stewart segment on the physics of gracious living!) is a
relic of that era. Similar examples—that rely upon fixed and homogeneous notions of
gender, race, nationality, sexuality, class, and other social variables—continue to be offered
today, with the best of intentions, by both women and men, feminists and nonfeminists.
3. Their heterogeneous and multiple "intra-actions," rather than "interactions," are
more to the point here, as explained below.
4. See Barad (2000b), the unabridged version of this paper, for a brief historical account of the discourses on scientific literacy and how its conceptualization has influenced
the development of different pedagogies for science.
5. For more details on agential realism see Barad (1996, 1998a, 1998b, forthcoming [b]).
6. Before I present my reading of Bohr's general epistemological framework, I want to
be clear about the precise focus of the discussion concerning Bohr. As Bohr scholar and
philosopher Henry Folse (1985) points out:

> While Bohr himself understood from the beginning that he was concerned with philo-
> sophical issues extending far beyond his proposed solution to the specific quantum
> paradoxes that have held the center of attention since 1927, unfortunately, history has
> not been altogether kind to his philosophical endeavors. Instead of being understood as
> a general framework within which the new physics was to be justified as an objective

description of nature, complementarity came to be identified with the so-called "Copenhagen Interpretation" of quantum theory (6).
It is Bohr's general epistemological framework, and not the interpretation of quantum mechanics, that is of interest here.

Although Bohr has been called a positivist, an idealist, an instrumentalist, a (macro)phenomenalist, an operationalist, a pragmatist, a (neo)Kantian, and a realist by various scholars, I would argue that Bohr's philosophy does not fit neatly into any of these categories because it questions many of the dualisms upon which these philosophical schools of thought are founded. For example, while Bohr's understanding of quantum physics leads him to reject the possibility that scientists can gain access to the "things-in-themselves," that is, to the objects of investigation as they exist outside of human conceptual frameworks, he does not subscribe to a Kantian noumena/phenomena distinction. And while his practice of physics shows him to hold a realist attitude toward his subject matter, he is not a realist in any conventional sense since he believes that the nature of the interaction between the objects of investigation and what he calls "the agencies of observation" is not determinable, and therefore cannot be "subtracted out," leaving us with a representation of the world as it exists independently of human beings.

A separate issue of importance should be noted at this juncture as well. Bohr did not see the epistemological issues with which he was concerned as being circumscribed by Planck's constant. That is, he did not see them as being applicable solely to the microscopic realm. In fact, if Planck's constant had been larger, Bohr insists that the epistemological issues that concern him would have been more evident (and we wouldn't have been as inclined to being fooled into representationalism).

Finally, I want to be clear that I am not interested in mere analogies but rather widely applicable philosophical issues such as the conditions for objectivity, the appropriate referent for empirical attributes, the role of natural as well as cultural factors in scientific knowledge production, and the efficacy of science (especially in the face of increasingly numerous and sophisticated demonstrations of its contingent nature).

7. This section and the next are excerpted from Barad (1998a).

8. For more details see Barad 1995. *Agencies of observation* is Bohr's term, which he seems to use interchangeably with *apparatus*. Because of the usual association of agency with subjectivity, "agencies of observation" hints at an ambiguity in what precisely constitutes an apparatus for Bohr. For further discussion see the section "Agential Realism."

9. Bohr called this cut "arbitrary" to distinguish it from an "inherent" cut. But the cut isn't completely arbitrary and so I use "constructed" as a contrast to "inherent."

10. According to Newtonian physics, the two variables that need to be specified simultaneously are position and momentum. According to Bohr, our understanding of causality as Newtonian determinism must be revised because mutually exclusive apparatuses are required to define *position* and *momentum.*

11. For more details see Barad (1998b and forthcoming [b]).

12. For more details see Barad (1998b and forthcoming [b]).

13. For quantum mechanics aficionados this issue may seem to have resonances with the "collapse problem." However, there are significant differences. The concern here is

with Bohr's general epistemological framework and not with his interpretation of quantum mechanics. (The notion of the collapse of the wave function was von Neumann's contribution, which Bohr never embraced. Some scholars have argued that Bohr's interpretation does not require a collapse-type mechanism; others see this as a failure of Bohr's interpretation.) Once again, the concern here is not with Bohr's interpretation of quantum mechanics, but with his general epistemological framework.

14. See especially Foucault (1977), particularly the discussion of "observing apparatuses" such as the panopticon.

15. For more details see Barad (1998b and forthcoming [b]). See Rouse (1987, 1996) for a detailed philosophical analysis of the extension of Foucault's notion of power/knowledge to the domain of the natural sciences.

16. I use the term *epistem-onto-logy* here instead of *ethico-epistem-onto-logy* only because this latter neologism is too unwieldy, not because the ethical issues are not central.

17. See Barad (1998b, forthcoming [b]), for details on how to understand the notion of intra-action as a reworking of the traditional notion of causality.

18. Questions of agency, responsibility, and accountability are central to the framework of agential realism (see Barad 1996). For further elaborations see Barad (1998b, 2001, forthcoming [b], and Rouse 1999).

19. The inclusion of the slash is inspired by Leela Fernandes's construction "trans/national." Fernandes inserts the slash to emphasize the fact that the production of boundaries has different political and material effects in different national contexts, that the boundaries that are drawn in one national context have simultaneous material effects in other national contexts, and that the "crossing" of national boundaries symbolized by "trans" does not negate the historical importance of what is constituted as "nation" (that is, the material effects of national boundaries). Fernandes's notion of the "trans/national" was discussed during the presentation of her work at the "Women in the Public Sphere: Power, Practice, Agency" seminar at Rutgers University on March 12, 1998. Fernandes's (1997) *Producing Workers* is a brilliant exposition on the material and structural dimensions of boundary-making practices; see Barad (2001, forthcoming [b]) for a discussion of this work in relation to agential realism.

20. Quoted in Shamos (1995, 197). The hearing, from which this quote is taken took place shortly after the launching of Sputnik. Perhaps more important, it took place a few years after Teller's hydrogen bomb was built and tested, and a few years after Teller, a militant anti-Communist, testified against Oppenheimer at the McCarthy hearings (some believe as retaliation for Oppenheimer's opposition to building the hydrogen bomb). The Stars Wars program was another brainchild of Teller's.

21. What, after all, were the goals that Teller was interested in promoting? Conformity of nonscience students to the social order? The transformation of students into pliant consumers of science-related goods? Continuing unquestioning public support of future science projects? No doubt Teller was sensitive to the fact that even in good economic times proactive public relations efforts are required to ensure the continued support of "Big Science."

22. I taught such a course in the mid-1980s at Barnard College. The course was called "Physics in Historical Perspective"; its originator was experimental physicist Samuel Devons (a student of Ernst Rutherford). One of the first of its kind, the "History of

Physics" laboratory at Barnard was the realization of this Columbia University professor's vision and labor. As Sam explained to me, the lab was built at Barnard because such a project lacked legitimacy on the "east side of Broadway" and because he wanted to inspire young women to major in physics. When I first inherited the course and the laboratory, as a newly minted recipient of a doctorate in theoretical physics, I knew hardly anything about the history of physics and its value to understanding physics (not just pedagogically, but epistemologically speaking). Though I naturally tailored the course and the laboratory to my own interests, I am indebted to Sam Devons for making this historic and pedagogically visionary project a reality at Barnard, and for teaching me some very far reaching lessons about the disciplining of knowledge and pedagogy. (Sadly, the lab and the course are now defunct.)

23. I have begun work on a "textbook" for the course (Barad forthcoming [a]).

24. "A bubble chamber of the 1950s came with an industrial and military notion of how to partition teamwork in the laboratory" (Galison 1997, xviii).

Works Cited

Barad, Karen. *Cultural Studies of Twentieth Century Physics*. Unpublished manuscript, forthcoming (a).

———— . *Meeting the Universe Halfway*. Unpublished manuscript, forthcoming (b).

———— . "Re(con)figuring Space, Time, and Matter." In *Feminist Locations: Global/Local/Theory/Practice*, ed. by Marianne DeKoven. New Brunswick, NJ: Rutgers University Press, 2001.

———— . "Reconceiving Scientific Literacy as Agential Literacy, or Learning How to Intra-Act Responsibly within the World." In *Doing Culture + Science*, ed. Roddey Reid and Sharon Traweek. New York: Routledge, 2000.

———— . "Agential Realism: Feminist Interventions in Understanding Scientific Practices." In *The Science Studies Reader*, ed. Mario Biagioli. New York: Routledge, 1998a.

———— . "Getting Real: Technoscientific Practices and the Materialization of Reality." *Differences: A Journal of Feminist Cultural Studies* 10 (Summer 1998b).

———— . "Meeting the Universe Halfway: Realism and Social Constructivism without Contradiction." In *Feminism, Science, and the Philosophy of Science*, ed. Lynn Hankinson Nelson and Jack Nelson. Dordrecht: Kluwer, 1996.

———— . "A Feminist Approach to Teaching Quantum Physics." In *Teaching the Majority: Breaking the Gender Barrier in Science, Mathematics, and Engineering*, ed. Sue V. Rosser. New York: Teachers College Press, 1995.

Bohr, Niels. *The Philosophical Writings of Niels Bohr, Vol. I: Atomic Theory and the Description of Nature*. Woodbridge, CT: Ox Bow Press, 1963a.

———— . *The Philosophical Writings of Niels Bohr, Vol. II: Essays 1932–1957 on Atomic Physics and Human Knowledge*. Woodbridge, CT: Ox Bow Press, 1963b.

———— . *The Philosophical Writings of Niels Bohr, Vol. III: Essays 1958–1962 on Atomic Physics and Human Knowledge*. Woodbridge, CT: Ox Bow Press, 1963c.

Davis, James B. "For the Ladies, Kitchen Physics." *Science Teacher* 18 (October 1951).

Fernandes, Leela. *Producing Workers: The Politics of Gender, Class, and Culture in the Calcutta Jute Mills*. Philadelphia: University of Pennsylvania Press, 1997.

Folse, Henry. *The Philosophy of Niels Bohr: The Framework of Complementarity*. New York: North Holland Physics Publishing, 1985.

Foucault, Michel. *Discipline and Punish: The Birth of the Prison*. Trans. Alan Sheridan. New York: Vintage Books, 1977.

Galison, Peter. *Image and Logic: A Material Culture of Microphysics*. Chicago: Chicago University Press, 1997.

Heldke, Lisa. "Responsible Agents: Objectivity as Responsibility and Agential Realism." Paper presented at the 20th World Congress of Philosophy, Boston, August 13, 1998.

Hennessy, Rosemary. *Materialist Feminism and the Politics of Discourse*. New York: Routledge, 1993.

Petersen, Aage. "The Philosophy of Niels Bohr." In *Niels Bohr: A Centenary Volume*, ed. A. P. French and P. J. Kennedy. Cambridge, MA: Harvard University Press, 1985.

Rouse, Joseph. "Feminism and the Two Poles of Naturalism." Paper presented at the Feminism and Naturalism Conference, St. Louis, 1999.

——— . *Engaging Science: How to Understand Its Practices Philosophically*. Ithaca, NY: Cornell University Press, 1996.

——— . *Knowledge and Power: Toward a Political Philosophy of Science*. Ithaca, NY: Cornell University Press, 1987.

Ruchlis, Hyman. "New Approaches Needed in Physics." *Science Teacher* 20 (February 1953).

Shamos, Morris H. *The Myth of Scientific Literacy*. New Brunswick, NJ: Rutgers University Press, 1995.

DESTINATION

Reintegrating Science, Community, and Activism

Section IV

Fertile Futures
Grounding Feminist Science Studies Across Communities

→ Swatija Manorama and J. Elaine Walters

We have chosen to work together as feminist women from our respective homes in India and the United States as much out of curiosity and friendship as from any intention to change the world. Over the course of our relationship, through e-mail and in person, we have discovered similarities and differences that shape our worlds and thinking. We are both activist-workers.[1] Swatija has a background in the sciences, and Elaine in sociology. In this essay we will share our work on reproductive technology as an example of how feminist science studies intersects with our activist work in our communities. We have been inspired by the work of Evelyn Fox Keller (1985, 1995, 1996), Donna Haraway (1989, 1991), and Vandana Shiva (1993) to ground and complement the analysis and vision of our activist work within a feminist science framework.

Here we argue that feminist progressive politics must first and foremost resist the placement of women's bodies and good health as raw material for technological manipulation. In different ways, several of the authors in this section discuss the observation that now dominant sciences—what Sandra Harding will refer to in her essay as "international" sciences—have evolved to serve the very limited interests of a powerful few to the detriment and exclusion of many, especially women. This service and exclusion occurs at every point along the continuum from prioritizing (or ignoring) particular research questions to limiting the definition of what counts as legitimate science, to the distribution of the information and technology generated as a result. For example, Bonnie Spanier describes the healthcare/scientific community's response—and early lack of response—to breast cancer. She highlights the exclusion of survivor input into research and practices, and the skewing of research data in favor of pharmacological remedies (and company profits) that may in fact do as much (or more) harm than good in preventing breast cancer. Valerie Kuletz discusses the denial of credibility and exclusion of data and information—what Sandra Harding will call "everyday science"—compiled by the survivors, advocates, and the families and communities of people who have been harmed by the nuclear industry. In addition to her detailed

248

description of the uranium development process and its cost to (mostly) indigenous people, Kuletz also provides a historical framework for understanding the way science has been used as "a mechanism of exclusion" in the service of "progress" and unbridled development.

In her depiction of the expansion and integration of "scientific motherhood," Jacquelyn Litt gives us the stories and voices of Jewish and African-American women parenting in the 1930s and 1940s in Philadelphia. While she makes it clear that these women embraced and in fact fought to integrate and gain access to these "modern" practices and beliefs, she shows the ethnoracial and class delineations that defined and reinforced the terms and patterns of access and adoption in the process. What is also clear in some of the stories Litt shares with us is how the drive to assimilate and access these new ways required these mothers to reject their own expertise, remedies, and wisdom of the past and fostered their dependence on information and expertise that came from outside of their own experiences and communities. These mutually constituted realities—a rejection of self with no access to its replacement—have the same familiar sting experienced by women in relation to dominant modern sciences.

If you enter the sciences you are expected to leave your identity as a woman outside, yet you aren't ever really allowed all the way in. Evelyn Fox Keller (1992, 43) calls this move to assimilate and our dismissal in the process the "two-one step." Assimilation for the sake of professional development has meant the silencing and even complete annihilation of certain voices and the ultimate disappearance of their collective knowledge. But some of us keep struggling. In "Laboratories without Walls," Lisa Weasel begins with a disclosure of her own disappointment at not being "lucky enough to practice a consciously feminist science" within her chosen field. She describes her own pursuit of liberatory practice within the seemingly divergent worlds of feminism (women's studies) and science. Though she notes the lack of "socially engaged action" in both worlds, she is working to bring science back into the community. In the process she has found a model she believes can be "adopted, modified, and put into practice as a means of implementing feminist science activism." The model of the science shop provides an opportunity for community members and scientists to work together, and fosters the pursuit of research that pays attention and gives voice to the people most often neglected in current configurations of scientific practice. In her view, if this model were to be infused with feminist principles and awareness of oppression, it could be an even more inclusive and liberatory forum for social activism.

The dominant modern sciences and the knowledge generated from them has been commodified for sale or is otherwise inaccessible. At the same time, historical common knowledge bases—from languages to indigenous plant and animal life to agriculture and healing—are dissipating from our memories at an alarming rate. This dispossession has been cultivated, first in the West and now globally, by the advance of capitalism as the dominant economic and political paradigm. In line with Valerie Kuletz, we see this path as initially most disastrous for those whose labor and land and very bodies are either dismissed or exploited at the service of capital accumulation. Yet even pure logic predicts (and we are beginning to see the signs of) the spread of destruction without regard to status, wealth, or isolation, with serious implications for *all* life on this planet. Simply put, we now understand that destroying any part of a living system will harm all the life it supports.

In her essay, Sandra Harding provides a starting point for reclaiming those sciences, which have been excluded or denied legitimacy by the "absolute neutrality ideal," which she very quickly and eloquently debunks. She focuses on five "knowledge-seeking practices" she thinks become good candidates for counting as "real sciences"—science that "work in everyday life as well as in institutional projects, that do reveal nature's order, whether or not recognized as 'modern' sciences." If the push to legitimize these sciences is successful, "more accurate accounts of our bodies, environmental hazards to us, nature's pharmacological resources, sustainable agriculture, energy and water supplies, and other aspects of nature where the prevailing sciences have not yet fully responded to women's scientific and technological concerns" will be more accessible to us and will wield more influence in our activism.

In this section, we and several of the contributors use examples from our own lives and from the everyday lives of other real and marginalized people to illustrate the disconnections we see deepening between our needs, our experiences, our bodies, and nature. We examine how certain sciences and technologies are legitimated while being used on and against us for the sake of domination and profiteering. In turn, we each look at the harm done as a result and the difficulties encountered in various attempts at redress. Each of us highlights efforts and successes and the lessons that we suggest can be drawn from them. As this essay and the others in this section illustrate, hope comes as we acknowledge and grieve our losses, become conscious of and sustain our collective efforts, and work thoughtfully to heal divisions between human (and other) beings and to meet our common needs. Our own work addresses the current situations of women in our two countries with respect to fertility control and assistance.

Controlling Fertility and Compulsory Reproduction

Looking at the impact of science and technology on the reproduction of women of the United States and India, two main themes emerge: the idea that fertility must be curbed in the name of "overpopulation" (applied largely to poor women), and the converse notion that fertility must be technologically assisted and enhanced to cure an "infertility epidemic" (applied mostly to rich and privileged women). For almost a century, eugenicists, population planners, and researchers have worked toward the development of long-acting, provider-controlled contraceptives for women with the marketed perception that there is "unrestrained female fertility" in the third world and among the poor and people of color in the first world (Soloway 1995). These temporary sterilization methods are meant to complement permanent sterilization methods, and to enable providers to "override" women's cycles. Adopted for mass-scale use in India and for focused application in the West, the outright goal of these technologies has always been to reduce the numbers of dark-skinned and poor bodies (Roberts 1997). Unless we are teenagers, poor, or a person of color in the United States, we can never fully know the emotional, social, or physical impact of these policies. If we are Indian, we cannot help but know them.

In both India and the United States, for example, poor women are encouraged or coerced into using Norplant rather than other safer, user-controlled methods, with the government picking up the tab. When they suffer from side effects or decide to have a child, they have extreme difficulty getting anyone to remove it and the government has sometimes refused to pay the cost (Roberts 1997). In the United States, welfare and early-intervention programs working with low-income or teen women use acceptance of long-acting contraceptives or sterilization as a measure of success.[2] Sterilization and forced acceptance of temporary sterilization methods have been used as conditions of release or probation for women convicted of drug offenses or child abuse (Roberts 1997). In India, "family planning" programs include sterilization camps (targeted primarily at women) and the pressure to accept a long-acting contraceptive method or sterilization as a precondition for any kind of government assistance (Kerkel 1998).

Despite their alleged advantages for achieving the goals of population control, these technologies have not been the panacea promised by their promoters. In fact, the focus on population control, and on developing methods and technology to implement it, diverts attention and critical resources away from the real and root causes of these complex social problems. In the process, women and children's human rights, general health concerns, and needs for economic and environmental securities are neglected, undermined, and even assaulted. From inadequate, unethical, and harmful research practices to the coercive and covert use of invasive and dangerous reproductive technology (Forum for Women's Health 1995), women serve as the guinea pigs and the scapegoats for their development and application. At the same time, powerful arguments by feminists advocating reproductive freedom as a means to liberation for women have been reduced, decontextualized, and easily coopted (as an argument over "choice") by population planners to enhance legitimacy for their eugenic efforts (Raymond 1993; Soloway 1995). Couched as a debate over choice, some feminists argue blindly that more options are good for women and increase reproductive freedom. In reality, however, this definition of *choice* is both reductionist and privileged. Those of us who actually have a choice (accurate information, access to better options, and the power to decide for ourselves) would never knowingly choose to use harmful or pain-producing technology in our bodies.

In contrast to these eugenic efforts to curb the reproduction of certain groups of people is the development of technology for the privileged to expand the procreative options open to individuals and therefore enhance human "freedom" (Roberts 1997). Marketing infertility as a modern "crisis" and targeting women's bodies as the problem to be solved (while denying or ignoring men's infertility and the physiological and environmental causes of infertility) justifies the use of "invasive medical intervention, drugs, and surgery on women" (Raymond 1993). These methods put enormous pressure on women to conceive while at the same time reducing their direct involvement and power in the process. From in-vitro fertilization (IVF) to cloning, physicians and researchers, rather than women patients themselves, take charge of the process and in fact see themselves as integral to procreation and reproduction (Roberts 1997).

These so-called fertility assistance methods do not, in fact, assist fertility; instead they facilitate and allow conception for those who can afford it without addressing problems of infertility at all. Environmental factors and health problems that disparately impact poor people and people of color and that are known to impair fertility get little or no attention while literally billions of dollars are currently spent on expensive, highly ineffective, high-tech interventions that are known to be dangerous (Raymond 1993). Providers "mix and match" drugs and methods in combinations and doses that have not been tested, with no guidelines for, or regulation of, their decisions. They go against their own industry standards by using heroic, experimental interventions, taking a level of risk usually reserved for cases of life-threatening illness (Raymond 1993).

Women, in this case privileged women, are used as guinea pigs for research geared toward giving modern science more power over female reproduction and procreation. Though some feminists argue that the use of these methods offers more options to some people, and have some capacity to expand options for nontraditional families, "they more often reinforce the status quo than challenge it" (Roberts 1997, 247) and are generally inaccessible to the majority of people faced with infertility. As Dorothy Roberts (1997) argues, "the profile of people most likely to use IVF is precisely the opposite of those most likely to be infertile. The people in the United States most likely to be infertile are poor, black, and poorly educated. Most couples who use IVF and other high-tech procedures are white, highly educated, and affluent" (252–253). In addition, "most IVF clinics accept only heterosexual married couples as clients, and most physicians have been unwilling to assist in the insemination of women who depart from this norm. They routinely deny their services to single women, lesbians, welfare recipients, and other women who are not considered good mothers" (248).

As an activist on this issue, Swatija has worked with Forum against the Oppression of Women (FAOW[3]) and the Forum for Women's Health (FFWH), taking stands against the use, misuse, and misrepresentation of harmful reproductive technologies. She has been involved in tracking and documenting the ways Indian women are targeted and impacted by the application of these technologies. These groups, for example, are now calling for a ban on antifertility vaccine (AFV) research and development. Yet feminists are far from agreement on these and other issues relating to reproductive technologies.

In a situation like this, in which women around the world are the subjects of stories of harm, exploitation, and disappointment, it is a painful reflection to see ourselves as feminists so divided over the issue of reproductive freedom. But the fact is, "choice"—defined rigidly as access to limitless options—no matter what the safety or effectiveness of the option, so dominates the discussion of reproductive technologies in the West that it is almost impossible to recognize the injuries that are done to women. This blindness continues to have a detrimental effect on the efforts of women's groups worldwide who are working to ensure the development and advancement of safe reproductive options. Only a unified effort rooted in sound ethical and feminist principles will allow us to demand and expect not only more and better reproductive technologies, but also appropriate technologies (Raymond 1993) that meet our needs and our high standards.

New Possibilities

Bringing together our diverse perspectives and sharing our experiences as feminists has been understandably difficult and contentious. The voices and perspectives of Donna Haraway, Vandana Shiva, and Evelyn Fox Keller have been constantly with us—in our heads, in our dreams at night, and in regular conversations in our own homes and across the planet—for a full year.

From their very different backgrounds and perspectives, these three women have each challenged and enriched our understanding of the sociopolitical dimensions that define and promote some forms of science as legitimate and dismiss others as nonscience. Individually they unearth and tease at boundaries and relationships, examine the inherent and inherited patterns of oppression present in multiple contexts and practices, confront and challenge reductionism, and participate in liberation efforts based on feminism and egalitarian values. In her own way, each suggests that despite (and perhaps because of) their exclusion from the dominant contemporary discourse, liberatory science movements continue to emerge, gaining influence and offering resistance, new perspectives, and hope for the way forward. The following is our effort to draw out—from these and other "partial perspectives" (Haraway 1991)—a credible, inclusive articulation of some guiding principles we believe to be inherent in liberatory, feminist ways of understanding, reorienting, and doing science in general, and science related to human reproduction in particular.

Our scientific theories and practices must be grounded in the awareness that life is interdependent and that we are inextricably part of that life. As a priority for research, investigating and valuing interdependence reorients the focus of scientific inquiry and at the same time alters what gets defined as science. This principle requires our sciences to attend to the intricacies and complexities of interactions at all levels. Instead of objectifying and reducing our focus of study to the smallest possible "mechanized" components, we are forced to expand it to include not only the interrelationships of organisms (including humans) but also to include the contexts in which the organisms exist. With regard to human reproduction this means we must investigate the whole-body reproductive systems of men as well as women along with the emotional, social, and physical aspects of our interactions with one another. It also means that we must attend to differences and discrepancies in the ways our complex bodies work rather than attempting to reduce every aspect to only those that are common, predictable, or exploitable.

As women, we must be restored to our rightful place as active subjects. Feminist, liberatory sciences that seek to provide safe technology for contraception and fertility assistance must be grounded in the real experiences and knowledges of diverse local women (and men). Diversity within local communities must not only be accounted for, it must be accessed and integrated into the research and development process. Any pretense of "absolute neutrality" must be abandoned in acknowledgment of the appropriate subjective interest on the part of women involved in or impacted by such efforts. When women are the initiators of research for their own benefit and use they are empowered to pursue and generate knowledge based on their own experiences and to foster the development of technology and resources that meet their needs and standards. Both Elaine and Swatija have been involved in working with preadolescent and adolescent girls in this way, hoping to engage them in constructive curiosity and the lifelong practice of "everyday"—and perhaps other—sciences. Working in support-group settings, we have focused on giving girls accurate information about their bodies as well as facilitating their own discovery process through supported self-observation and sharing. We have seen over time that their direct involvement in defining the terms of the group, of generating their own questions, and of producing their own materials has helped to build their confidence in questioning and has enhanced their abilities to present what they've learned or discovered to others. We have noticed across the board, and in many contexts, that as we are activated as subjects, we embark on the path to becoming activists. Knowledge *is* power, but it is also responsibility. Once we are aware of this, for most of us, there is no going back.

Research, development, and use of science and technology must be ethical and not cause harm. This is the principle of zero tolerance for harm. We see, for example, that there are already methods and technologies for contraception that are very effective and not harmful, yet they are abandoned in favor of provider-controlled methods with no consideration for the short- or long-term harm they cause. As a member of FAOW and FFWH Swatija has seen first-hand the unethical and dangerous practices that have been used to test some of the most powerful chemicals on vulnerable or uninformed women. Elaine has been to conferences at which health care providers were given biased information about Norplant, which dismissed the side effects—such as heavy bleeding—as mere "inconveniences." She has also worked with young women in a juvenile detention facility who described being coerced into accepting either Norplant or Depo Provera. These practices flourish because the women and girls who are the targets are blamed by society for social problems far beyond their control, because they are poor or otherwise vulnerable, because their children are unwanted or not provided for, because they are not allowed by custom or house rule or by their partners to make their own decisions, or because they do not have other options. At the other end, we both know women who have gone through heroic efforts to conceive children using dangerous chemicals because the pressure was so strong on the part of their male partners to produce genetically related offspring.

Liberatory, feminist sciences must work to identify, respect, and protect boundaries. This principle follows directly from the last and is at the heart of feminist movements all over the world working to stop violence against women and against nature. One way to think of boundaries is to view them as frames that support what Evelyn Fox Keller refers to as "structural integrity" (1986, 43). In living systems these frames are protective; without them the system is vulnerable to damage or extermination. Boundaries are also the interfaces between systems, filtering and preventing harmful interactions and facilitating necessary ones. Vandana Shiva insists that ecological boundaries are necessary protections that have been steadily violated at every level, from the molecular to the species, for the sake of unrestrained human development and exploitation (Shiva 1993). In human beings boundaries are emotional as well as physical, and violations come from both fronts. In the case of the most harmful reproductive technologies the violations may be both physical and emotional. Physical boundaries, such as those protecting delicately balanced endocrine systems, are crossed without regard to their harmful impact. Emotional boundaries, such as resistance, discomfort, or fear, are seen as disruptive, irrational, or inconsequential if they are seen at all and are overrun without question.

We must acknowledge men's role in reproduction and facilitate their responsibility and involvement in child-rearing. This principle is based on the belief that men are responsible for contraception as well as for conception and that they are capable of and should be responsible for nurturing and caring for children. We believe that their doing so is good for women, good for children, and good for them. In fact, it may be the case that our liberation as women will be possible only when men participate in and value caretaking work. As women we see that our work as caretakers is devalued and considered inferior in many cultures.

Feminist activists, scientists, and academics must work cooperatively for liberatory social change. They must also stay connected to the communities and take their lead from people likely to benefit from, or be impacted by, the outcomes of their work. As activists, we must pay attention to the work of feminist scientists and academics and begin to see its importance in our worlds. We must also make our needs for scientific and academic research and information known. This means that we will sometimes step into confusing territory, where it feels as if the people around us are speaking a foreign language—which they are. We must also carry ourselves in the knowledge that *our* work is vital, and that the work of feminist scientists and academics is given life through us. In addition, it is critical that we represent and support the presence of those whose voices are often neglected or denied in the worlds of science and academia.

As scientists and academics, we must make sure that our work is useful to activists in the field. We must allow their expertise and interests to guide our priorities. We must present information in common language and make it accessible in multiple formats. Importantly, we must build relationships with social change organizations and become comfortable in working-class settings and in the field. As often as possible, we must make clear invitations to activists and make our conversations and planning sessions accessible to their full participation. Ultimately, by consciously and honestly attending to our relationships in practical terms we can heal the divisions, close rank, and advance and sustain one another as work partners in these multiple movements toward social change and liberation.

Notes

1. We use the term *activist-worker* to connote the fact that we spend time in the trenches of our respective movements more or less as part of our daily lives. We are volunteers, staff, and general laborers as opposed to politicians, public relations professionals, or academics.

2. Coercion by omission, neglecting to explain side effects or provide information on alternative contraceptives, is standard practice among U.S. providers determined to keep young women from becoming pregnant.

3. Formerly known as the Forum against Sex Determination and Pre-Selection. The name was changed in 1992 as the focus of the group expanded after the limited success of the group in 1989 in initiating a selective ban on sex determination tests.

Works Cited

Forum for Women's Health. "Contraceptives: Our Chioices, Their Choices." In *Our Lives, Our Health*, ed. Malini Karkal. Bejing: World Conference on Women, 1995.

Haraway, Donna. *Simians, Cyborgs, and Women: The Reinvention of Nature*. New York: Routledge, 1991.

————. *Primate Visions: Gender, Race, and Nature in the World of Modern Science*. New York: Routledge, 1989.

Keller, Evelyn Fox. "Feminism and Science." In *Feminism and Science*, ed. Evelyn Fox Keller and Helen E. Longino. Oxford: Oxford University Press, 1996.

————. *Refiguring Life: Metaphors of Twentieth-Century Biology*. New York: Columbia University Press, 1995.

————. "Gender and Science: Why Is It So Hard for Us to Count Past Two?" In *Inventing Women: Science, Technology, and Gender*, ed. Gill Kirkup and Laurie Smith Keller. Cambridge, MA: Blackwell/Open University Press, 1992.

————. "How Gender Matters: Or, Why It's So Hard for Us to Count Past Two?" In *Perspectives on Gender and Science*, ed. Jan Harding. New York: Falmer Press, 1986.

————. *Reflections on Gender and Science*. New Haven, CT: Yale University Press, 1985.

Kerkel, Malini. "Population Control: State Sponsored Violence against Women." Presented at the International Conference on Preventing Violence and Caring for Survivors. *YMCA, Mumbai* (November 1998).

Raymond, Janice. "The Production of Fertility and Infertility: East and West, South and North." In *Women as Wombs*, ed. Janice Raymond. San Francisco: HarperCollins, 1993.

Roberts, Dorothy. *Killing the Black Body: Race, Reproduction, and the Meaning of Liberty*. New York: Pantheon, 1997.

Shiva, Vandana. "Reductionism and Regeneration." In *Ecofeminism*. New York: Zed, 1993.

Soloway, Richard. "The 'Perfect Contraceptive': Eugenics and Birth Control Research in Britain and America in the Interwar Years." *Journal of Contemporary History* 30 (1995): 636–664.

"Your Silence Will Not Protect You"

Feminist Science Studies, Breast Cancer, and Activism

Audre Lorde's trenchant assertion about silence from *The Cancer Journals* (1980) that titles this chapter speaks to a fundamental feminist principle, voiced over and over throughout many forms of activism around breast cancer.

> I was going to die, if not sooner then later, whether or not I had ever spoken myself. My silences had not protected me. Your silence will not protect you. But for every real word spoken, for every attempt I had ever made to speak those truths for which I am still seeking, I had made contact with other women while we examined the words to fit a world in which we all believed, bridging our differences. And it was the concern and caring of all those women which gave me strength and enabled me to scrutinize the essentials of my living (Lorde 1980, 20).

From her keen scrutiny and her commitment to widespread, collectively organized challenges to the normality of sexism, heterosexism, racism, and class bias, Lorde exposed the repressive qualities of the well-meaning "Look Good . . . Feel Better"[1] approach following treatment for breast cancer: hiding the breast amputation with a prosthesis, covering the visible results of radiation and chemotherapy by wearing a wig, denying the anger arising from getting the disease, and being treated as a woman patient—especially a black woman, especially a black lesbian, woman-centered woman—in our medical system.[2] Well documented in the first edition and then in subsequent editions of *Our Bodies, Ourselves: A Book by and for Women* (Boston Women's Health Book Collective 1970, 1973, 1998), many women have broken the silences that have suppressed society's accountability for—along with our own consciousness of—the harm from various forms of violence against women by those who love us and those who are supposed to serve us.

I believe that Lorde's insights and arguments speak powerfully to women in science as well, privileged women sometimes afraid to speak for themselves and the collective good. I propose that women (and feminist men) in the sciences

258

have a responsibility to "first, do no harm" and, through feminist science studies and related perspectives,[3] to become a force for constructive and necessary change in science and technology. To do less is to pervert our commitment to good science, to misuse our privilege as educators, researchers, and practitioners, and to abrogate our responsibility to society.

In this essay, I discuss my analysis that connects feminist science studies in academe to an engagement with national and local activism about breast cancer. What does it mean to take a feminist perspective on molecular biology, my original field, and what difference does it make for women's lives? The situation of breast cancer research and the efforts of breast cancer survivors and friends to create research and a medical system based on our experiences and concerns provides insight into the importance of a feminist approach to science. At the same time, the analytical approach taken by some feminist activist groups to biomedicine can provide a model for feminist science.[4]

Breast Cancer Advocacy in the 1990s

> New science, a new advocacy movement, a new political commitment, and new money—great promise.
>
> —*Karen Stabiner, 1997*

A constellation of forces surfaced in the 1990s as breast cancer became a pivotal focus in the movement to recognize the dire neglect of women's health in this country (see Clarke and Olesen 1999 14–24; Stabiner 1997). Activism from many quarters (such as Dr. Susan Love, breast cancer surgeon and author of the breast cancer "bible," and Dr. Bernadine Healy, first woman to head the National Institutes of Health, in 1991) forced some promising changes. Congress dramatically increased funding for breast cancer research, both lab experimentation and clinical trials, and new grant categories were created to promote innovative, high-risk research.[5] For the first time in history, breast cancer survivors who were not scientists were allowed to participate in some of the groups that decide which research proposals would be funded.

One of a number of key organizations that shaped those accomplishments is the National Breast Cancer Coalition (NBCC), whose founders were responsible for sending millions of signatures to Congress. Each year since 1993, NBCC has created a legislative agenda, and it has been clear from those agendas that NBCC is trying to work for all women, not just privileged ones; for example, NBCC lobbies for all women—especially uninsured and underinsured women—to have access to diagnosis and full treatment for breast cancer as well as participation in clinical trials. NBCC hosts an annual Advocacy Training Conference (mainly presentations on the newest developments in breast cancer treatment and prevention) and lobbying day in Washington plus intensive institutes (Project LEAD) for citizens concerned about breast cancer research,[6] education about breast cancer for the media and for politicians, and other efforts.

A key women's health organization that predates NBCC and has made critically important contributions to feminist analysis of women's health and related scientific claims is the National Women's Health Network. Founded in 1976, this organization questioned standard breast cancer treatments (such as radical mastectomies for benign or localized tumors) early on and pioneered critiques of hormone replacement therapy.[7] More recently, the National Women's Health Network published a scrupulously careful analysis of the P-1 American study of tamoxifen (Fisher et al. 1998) that played a key role in NBCC's controversial position on tamoxifen.

Breast cancer is not the number one killer of American women (as a group)[8]—heart disease is. It's not even the number one cancer killer statistically—lung cancer deaths beat out breast cancer (but not among African-American women), thanks to cigarettes and consumerism-driven changes in mores (for example, the Virginia Slims ad, "You've come a long way, baby"). So why did women become so concerned and upset about breast cancer around 1990?

Several reasons have been highlighted by activists. Because in the United States breast cancer *is* the number one killer of women aged thirty-five to forty-four—relatively young women in their prime. Because the United States has a relatively high incidence of breast cancer, and that incidence has been increasing by about 1 percent per year since 1940 (Feuer et al. 1993). Because it took too long for the medical establishment to change the standard treatment—radical mastectomy—to less invasive surgeries, even after evidence was published that long-term survival after radical mastectomy or lumpectomy plus radiation is the same. Most of all, perhaps, because of the static nature of the statistic that about one-third of women who get breast cancer will die from it; that has not changed significantly in more than fifty years. And because, in spite of this statistic, so little research money had been targeted to breast cancer research prior to 1993. In this light, perhaps a different question is in order: Why did it take women so long to get upset (see Leopold 1999)?

Feminist activism around the issue of breast cancer provides an opportunity to understand the complex relationship of science, politics, and feminism, while also promoting the practice and values of feminist science studies. In this essay, I will assess the consequences of these recent changes for women, for science, and for medicine.

From Science to Activism, a Quest for Wholeness

Hundreds of local grassroots groups offer support, education, and advocacy about breast cancer and make a difference in women's (and their families') lives.[9]

In 1997 I became involved in forming such an organization in the Albany, New York, area, where I live. After experiencing breast cancer about six years ago, my friend, Patricia Stocking Brown, who is also a scientist with a radical feminist analysis, shared with me what she had learned about the state of knowledge and practice surrounding this disease. What she had found stunned her. As a scientist committed to evidence, she found an appalling gap between the scientific literature on breast cancer and the accepted practices of physicians. As a feminist and endocrinologist, she was amazed at how little was actually known about women's healthy breasts, much less those with cancer cells and tumors. As a feminist scientist, she recognized that the assumptions guiding the treatment and understanding of breast cancer were rife with sexism, and that all of the assumptions had to be reexamined: for example, the assumption that women's hormones rule (the effect of estrogen on cancer cells is a central explanation of the problem and the solution); and the assumption that what's good for the physician is good for the patient (removing many or all lymph nodes gives some information about whether the cancer has spread, but it does not increase long-term survival; it does, however, increase the risk of underplayed problems such as lymphedema).

At Catholic Siena College, where she was the first woman hired as a regular faculty member, Pat Brown offered a one-credit course on the biology of breast cancer ("Breast Cancer: Are We Asking the Right Questions?") that was so successful that she has continued to teach regular biology courses to both biology majors (many of whom go on to medical school) and nonmajors. Committed to evidence-based medicine combined with a strong feminist analysis, she is known for empowering both scientists and nonscientists with the ability to read primary research papers and analyze the data themselves, rather than accepting the conclusions and interpretations of the authors.[10]

I joined her quest to bring informed decision-making to as many women as possible in our area and to learn more about effective political advocacy as part of a group of interested women, many already at the forefront of some aspect of breast cancer or environmental issues locally. We agreed on an agenda for action that focused on access to information for all women and access to analytical tools for making informed decisions. Calling ourselves CRAAB![11] (Capital Region Action against Breast Cancer!), we developed a number of educational projects aimed at fostering skills for analyzing biomedical and personal literature about breast cancer.[12] The skill of reading the original scientific literature was the one that Pat Brown and some of the rest of us felt was key to empowering women as advocates for themselves and for possible participation on funding panels and in policy development. Upon reflection on what characterizes feminist science studies, or feminist approaches to the sciences, I have realized that Pat's commitment to evidence-based medicine together with an analysis of the forces affecting what counts as evidence—and thus a goal of our monthly discussions—are examples of Sandra Harding's (1991) "strong objectivity," a form of objectivity that is dependent on context and takes into account the forces that affect meaning.

CRAAB! started a monthly discussion group, which alternated reading a book, usually an illness narrative, with reading scientific papers.[13] In our discussions, the group does not formally advocate one "correct" choice on any controversial topic such as treatment or preventive drug therapy, although individuals may have strong positions based on our reading and experiences. We are very sensitive to the idea that each individual must find those answers that are "right" for her in contexts in which evidence suggests there *is* no best treatment. For example, a woman might choose not to take tamoxifen after surgery because the daily reminder of potential recurrence, or the increase in risk for blood clots, outweighs the possible decrease in recurrence risk. This could be understood as a feminist stance and another aspect of strong objectivity, because it takes into account both the limitations of statistics in predicting what one individual will experience (without denying the validity of the statistics based on the population studied) and the importance of psychological, economic, and social factors in each individual woman's health. As a group, we have chosen to take the role of providing skills and analyses to help women (and men) be heard in their doctor's offices, often against the rising tide of pressure from pharmaceutical companies to use the newest drug.

Our close scrutiny of the data in scientific articles, as compared to the researchers' conclusions, reveals some serious shortcomings in the scientific claims, and this ability to analyze the data arms each individual with knowledge and perhaps more confidence to negotiate the biomedical world. We are exposing and analyzing a world of uncomfortable but very real uncertainty, a world of insufficient knowledge about how our bodies work within the places we live, insufficient scientific knowledge about the many diseases that constitute cancer and breast cancer in particular, and evidence-based uncertainty about a best choice in treating breast cancer and in claims about preventing it.

Feminist Scientific Analysis and Strong Objectivity

What characterizes a feminist analysis of science, and what principles do we find in theory and in practice? A key argument for the necessity of feminist science studies and its contributions to "good" science and a "good" society is located in the principles found in feminist theory and practice, including activism. I believe that feminist science studies and women's health activism hold the promise for significant change because of two key aspects of what I make of Sandra Harding's (1991) strong objectivity in science : (1) a close analysis of the data itself and a meta-analysis of the collective data in a field compared to the conclusions offered by scientists and the media, combined with (2) a feminist analysis of power, of the ways that particular economic and social forces ("interests" and their values) shape both the framework and practice of science, and how the science is used. Both of these analytical practices are at the heart of feminist science studies, and they are also found in parts of women's health activism. I believe that strong objectivity is a necessary component of all areas of women's health activism that enables the current movement (like the American women's health movement of the 1970s) to refuse to accept the authority of the medical system and the blame for our ailments (Steingraber 1998, 262) implicit in the common view that we can prevent and cure breast cancer if we do breast self-exams, have regular mammograms, do what our physicians recommend, take "preventive" drugs like tamoxifen or raloxifene, and so on.

One way (among several) of describing what it means to bring feminist critiques to the sciences is to consider how social, political, and economic interests can affect scientific knowledge at different points in its production: which priorities scientists set for research, which questions they ask about a topic, what theory or explanatory framework they use in a given scientific study, what methods are used, what data are considered valid as compared to spurious, how the data are interpreted, what conclusions scientists draw from their analysis of the data, and what directions they choose for future research.[14]

When I investigated how gender ideology has affected my original field of molecular biology (and microbiology), I found the imprints of a sexist belief system—of one sex naturally dominant over another, of hierarchy and centralized control as natural arrangements—that in general biology have been more obviously superimposed onto organisms we can see (Spanier 1995). For biology at the macro and micro levels, cultural beliefs about natural difference and about "sex" reinforced reductionist tendencies and a cult of simplicity in science to produce the distorted idea that genotype dictates phenotype, that biology is destiny. For molecular biology, the distortions were both more subtle and more sweeping.

The predominant ideology of molecular genetics as the lens through which we are to understand biology distorts and limits our approaches to cancer research. While the authors of a major textbook in their summary of the chapter on cancer (1) state that susceptibility to human cancers is rarely inherited; (2) point to the "multicausal, multistep nature of carcinogenesis"; and (3) admit that their model of how cancer develops is "certainly simplistic—for one thing, it does not include nongenetic influences"; the textbook's chapter on cancer nonetheless focuses solely on genetic mechanisms as the best promise for cancer prevention and therapy and provides little guidance for developing a more comprehensive research approach (see Spanier 1995). We must contend with the political and social consequences of this worldview in molecular biology.

Breast Cancer Research: Overemphasizing Genetics while Underplaying Environmental Toxics

Has the predominant ideology affected the quest to eliminate breast cancer? Examples abound in the current overemphasis on an individual's genetics in research on breast cancer and the inadequate attention to the carcinogens in our environment and where they originate.

As a result of the power of recombinant DNA technologies and the focus of research funding on understanding how genes work in cells, much attention has been given to finding genes that influence breast cancer (among many diseases). Because breast cancer appears to be inherited in 5 to 10 percent of all cases, we are able to use our well-developed genetic techniques to learn about normal and abnormal activity at the molecular and genetic levels. By studying families in which breast cancer is very prevalent, genes called BRCA1 and BRCA2 have been identified and implicated in increased susceptibility to breast, ovarian, and prostate cancers. However, the usefulness of this approach as a tool tends to become overshadowed by our belief system that understanding genetics will lead to the best solutions to our disease problems. One company rapidly developed an expensive genetic test for mutated BRCA1 genes and marketed it for use. Several problems arose with this approach. The original hype around BRCA1 suggested that everyone who carried the mutant form of the gene would get breast cancer. From that logic came the proposal of prophylactic double mastectomies—remove the breasts in those with a mutant gene, it was assumed, and the threat of breast cancer is removed. However, every piece of breast tissue cannot be removed with a mastectomy, so the possibility exists of cancer arising in the remaining tissue. Further, mastectomy carries the risk of subsequent lymphedema, a painful, chronic problem that can be life-threatening. Also, if a woman has the mutation, that does not mean she will get breast cancer; that is, genotype does not dictate phenotype, since the penetrance of a gene (the likelihood it will be expressed phenotypically and be clinically apparent) is not necessarily 100 percent. For example, early studies suggested that the penetrance of BRCA1 was 85 percent in women and less than 1 percent in men; but subsequent studies show the risk in women to be significantly lower (Weber 1996; Struewing et al. 1997).

Thus, a first well-meaning response to the availability of a test for mutations that increase risk might be that all women should have access to it, particularly those from populations, such as Ashkenazi Jews, with a higher frequency of the mutation. But knowing that you have a mutant gene does not tell you that you will get breast cancer. In addition to the question of whether and to what degree genotype determines phenotype (the gene's penetrance), screening tests have false-positives as well as false-negatives.

The force of current hospital structures and medical professions must also be factored in as part of a feminist analysis of power. Genetic counselors are usually linked to hospitals, and their job is to encourage the use of genetic information in health decisions. While that may sound neutral, the ideological context that makes genetics the center of disease analysis and solutions predisposes genetic counseling toward using genetic tools. Activist groups have played a key role in presenting information and arguments that counter some of that force. The Massachusetts Breast Cancer Coalition[15] explains in a handout, "What You Need to Know before Considering Genetic Testing for Heritable Breast Cancer," that "the test for BRCA1 . . . can only indicate a susceptibility to get breast cancer, which means that you *might* have a higher risk of getting breast cancer." It explains that no therapy can be offered to prevent breast cancer in someone with a positive test, and that a negative test does not mean a person will not get the disease. An understanding of all of this information is necessary for making a truly informed decision about this genetic test and its consequences for the individual and her family.

Moreover, the coalition puts its premises up front: "The technology of genetic testing has moved forward much faster than the scientific, ethical, and social understanding of its implications." This is followed by proposals for education and legislation that would protect confidentiality and protect against discrimination by insurers and employers.

In biomedicine, the current overemphasis on genetics and a noncontextual way of thinking about genetics, obscures the question: What caused the genetic changes in those 90 percent of cases that were not inherited? And what caused the original BRCA1 and BRCA2 mutations found in the approximately 10 percent of inherited cases?[16] Furthermore, the steady increase (estimated at 1 percent per year since 1940) in breast cancer incidence in the United States cannot be explained by evolutionary changes in our gene pool. Evidence has mounted that World War II and related economic forces switched our society over to industries (pesticides, plastics, and so on) that practically bathe us in cancer-promoting and endocrine-disrupting toxics (Procter 1995; Chlorfene-Casten 1996; Steingraber 1998). Yet the National Cancer Institute's report on breast cancer research priorities limits concern about environmental toxics to studies of how they interact with the body to produce disease (Breast Cancer Progress Review Group 1998). It has been only relatively recently that mainstream cancer organizations such as the American Cancer Society have paid any attention to environmental cancer risks at all, and now its prevention focus is mainly on "tobacco control" and reducing the risk of skin cancer, focusing on prevention of these "lifestyle" risks while playing down the accumulating evidence of cancer's relationship to chemicals such as PCBs, vinyl chloride, and pesticides.

Because our incidence of breast cancer is so high and the hundreds of chemicals in question so ubiquitous, it may be difficult to get a definitive scientific answer.

Given that situation, some scientists are reexamining our assumptions about requiring definitive scientific answers before taking action. Known as "the Precautionary Principle," this view says, "Where there are significant risks of damage to the public health, we should be prepared to take action to diminish those risks even when the scientific knowledge is not conclusive, if the balance of likely costs and benefits justifies it" (Davis et al. 1998, 1). For example, Devra Lee Davis and her colleagues (1998) analyzed what is known about breast cancer from epidemiologic and toxicologic studies and proposed a focus on those probable risk factors that can be changed, such as exposure to mutagens and chemicals that mimic hormone action. Physicians for Social Responsibility, particularly concerned about the increase in cancer in children, have mounted an international program to decrease exposure to persistent organic pollutants (POPs). The Precautionary Principle shifts the weight toward possible and probable risks and away from the requirement for absolute scientific proof in those cases in which definitive scientific answers may not be achievable.

A feminist cancer research agenda would include finding ways to remove the known and suspected carcinogens and endocrine-disruptors from our environment. It would understand "prevention" to mean changing the risk factors we can change, instead of claiming that a drug such as tamoxifen, with both mild and serious side effects, will do the trick.

Tamoxifen, Feminist Activism, and Strong Objectivity

Tamoxifen (marketed as Nolvadex by AstraZeneca) has been used in the treatment of breast cancer since the 1970s and is known to act mainly as a selective estrogen receptor modulator (SERM). As the first drug to specifically target tumors that show sensitivity to estrogen, it appeared to have fewer side effects than chemotherapy drugs that target all dividing cells in the body. However, serious side effects were detected in studies after a longer time—uterine cancer, vision problems, strokes, and blood clots—so groups like the National Women's Health Network were concerned about studies using tamoxifen on healthy women to "prevent" breast cancer.

The major American study (Fisher et al. 1998) showed a significant (45 percent) *relative* decrease in risk for breast cancer. In contrast, two European studies showed no effect of tamoxifen on breast cancer risk (Powles et al. 1998; Veronesi et al. 1998), and British medical journals were more cautious in reporting their findings than their American counterparts because of the contradictory results. However, the National Cancer Institute publicized the results of this P-1 study on the Internet even before they were published, and announced that the study would be "unblinded" because the results at that point showed a strong effect of tamoxifen. That meant that the women in the placebo group were free to take tamoxifen;

it also meant that no long-term information would be obtained from this expensive study. That is, we will get no information about the long-term effects of healthy women taking tamoxifen compared to a control group.

By doing a close reading of the American article, the National Women's Health Network pointed out that the large-sounding relative reduction in risk was actually a decrease from an absolute incidence of only 2.7 percent to 1.4 percent. In effect, one woman out of one hundred did not get breast cancer compared to the untreated control group. However, taking tamoxifen increased the risk of endometrial cancer by 250 percent overall, with the risk for women over fifty increasing by 400 percent (a four-fold increase compared to the placebo group). Furthermore, the increased risks of two types of life-threatening vascular events (pulmonary embolism and deep vein thrombosis) were three-fold and 1.6-fold respectively, regardless of age. Thus, the network highlighted the equivalent increase of life-threatening endometrial cancer, blood clots, and other vascular problems in the group getting the drug. The network argued that taking tamoxifen simply exchanged one problem (breast cancer) for others (uterine cancer and blood clots). Further, reducing the risk of breast cancer, particularly in a study that ended after only four years, is not the same thing as preventing it.

The National Breast Cancer Coalition also advised caution about the claims. But the group of distinguished scientists in the Breast Cancer Progress Review Group for the National Cancer Institute (1998) concluded: "Anti-estrogen therapy has been shown to be beneficial not only for treatment but also for prevention." And the American Society of Clinical Oncology recommended that physicians offer tamoxifen as an option to healthy women to "prevent" breast cancer, saying that "a woman's personal fear of breast cancer is perhaps the most important consideration in deciding whether to take the drug" (*Albany, New York, Times-Union*, May 10, 1999).

Zeneca (which became AstraZeneca) embarked on a major advertising campaign, telling women, "There is something you can do." The National Women's Health Network prompted the Food and Drug Administration to make the company change its ad to include the drug's side effects and more information about the study participants, who were women defined by certain criteria as being at high risk for breast cancer. Yet the advertising blitz grabbed the attention of many women, and the company's "education" of physicians has been felt. One physician pressured his client to take tamoxifen, calling it "a miracle drug." Another physician recommended the drug to his client, and when she hesitated, he shook his finger at her and said she was not being responsible. Other reports include a mother asking if her twelve-year-old daughter should be on tamoxifen. The next step is the STAR (Study of Tamoxifen and Raloxifene) trial currently under way, another large clinical trial to see whether another SERM, raloxifene (sold by Eli Lilly as Evista), is as effective as tamoxifen in decreasing the risk of getting breast cancer. There is no control group in this study, a shocking decision for those who question the safety and efficacy of this approach.

What difference has feminist activism made for women concerned about breast cancer? The National Breast Cancer Coalition has adopted the same position as the National Women's Health Network and Dr. Sidney Wolf's Public Citizen Health Research Group of "serious concerns" with the STAR trial, pointing out that it differs from other clinical trials because

> it is a prevention trial and involves giving toxic drugs with serious side effects to healthy women. NBCC believes that this difference is crucial and requires an extremely cautious approach to trial design and implementation. NBCC believes that since the tamoxifen prevention trial was stopped early, it is not known if the drug saves lives, or whether it is possible to determine the long-term risks or benefits of the drug or the optimal length of time a woman should remain on it. Tamoxifen, a toxic drug with life-threatening side effects, is being tested on healthy women. The potential adverse effects associated with the trial are very serious and there is no tool to assess a woman's risk of those events. . . . NBCC believes the STAR trial design, which does not include a placebo arm, is flawed (NBCC 1999, 8).

Researchers have quickly recognized how useful, even essential, activist networks might be in recruiting women, particularly breast cancer survivors, into clinical trials in the numbers needed for statistically valid data. Indeed, as more money for such trials comes from the government, pharmaceutical companies, and philanthropic groups such as the Susan G. Komen Foundation, competition is stepping up for trial participants (no longer explicitly referred to as "subjects"). Journalists have reported a drug company practice of offering physicians monetary bonuses for each woman the doctor recruits into a clinical trial (Eichenwald and Kolata 1999, 1), exposing to more public view the longstanding relationship between allopathic physicians and drug companies in the United States (Starr 1982), and raising questions about the impartiality of our physicians. The tension is palpable between advocates who deeply desire a magic bullet to cure breast cancer and those who are deeply suspicious of research done or supported by drug companies.[17]

Bringing strong objectivity to a feminist analysis of current research and clinical trials, then, requires understanding the interests and power of pharmaceutical companies and their relationship to biomedical research and researchers. Analyzing the published studies of treatments or preventives also requires knowing the questionable record of some powerful corporations, particularly pharmaceutical companies, in sharing all of their data, including information about those (human) participants who dropped out of studies. Indeed, much of the information on the efficacy and safety of marketed drugs is not easily available because it has not been published (Fried 1999). Uncertainty about whether we are able to assess all relevant data may require leaving some question marks above certain claims.

To judge how to weigh information from different sources also involves understanding the relationship of drug and medical device companies to organizations for women's health. The National Women's Health Network, a part of the radical women's health movement since the 1970s, has raised this issue and provides information essential to strong objectivity (Zones and Fugh-Berman 1999). While some women's health organizations have adopted policies of not accepting corporate funding (National Women's Health Network, National Latina Health Organization, and Breast Cancer Action [BCA] in San Francisco), the National Alliance of Breast Cancer Organizations (NABCO) lists more than fifty companies that sponsor it, including Bristol-Myers Squibb (a manufacturer of chemotherapy drugs), GlaxoWellcome, and Zeneca (maker of tamoxifen).[18] As Zones and Fugh-Berman (1999) point out, "While accepting corporate donors does not necessarily compromise an organization, it gives the appearance of doing so, and in many cases corporate influences on an organization's views and actions are very subtle" (7).

NBCC is an important organization to study in this regard, as its projects, including the valuable Project LEAD, are supported by Avon, Bristol-Myers Squibb (maker of Taxol, an anti-tumor drug), and GlaxoWellcome. NBCC explicitly fosters a working relationship between activists and drug companies to promote research and clinical trials.[19] At the same time, at its meetings, NBCC features the full spectrum of views on controversial topics and has taken a strong position against tamoxifen as preventive medicine. Time will tell how influential NBCC can and will be in keeping women away from questionable clinical trials such as STAR. Here is where activist groups have potentially great power. Should women participate in clinical trials? Which ones? And if NBCC is heard, how long will the drug companies continue to sponsor a powerful critic?

Conclusion

Feminist perspectives reveal recurring themes of conceptual errors or questionable value judgments in biology that distort our understanding of life and our vision of solutions to problems. These include: (1) a reductionist approach to understanding life in terms of constituents, often neglecting properties that emerge from structural organization of interacting parts; (2) assuming hierarchy to be natural, with one component, in this case DNA, as most important in controlling the other components; (3) isolating each component and thus stripping away its context at many levels of structural organization; (4) a belief in parsimony, seeing simplicity as elegant and therefore better (looking in physics for the grand theory of everything may or may not be useful; in biomedicine looking for

the single cause or theory that explains breast cancer is unwarranted and misleading in light of the complexities of cancer within our bodies); and (5) a belief that
science is separate from society and that the paths taken in research are not influenced by political, social, or economic interests.

A feminist analysis of the current state of breast cancer research must also address forces (both ideological and economic) within the American system of
medicine, such as: the tendency toward aggressive overtreatment compared with
other industrialized countries (Lerner 1998, especially chapter 3); partnerships
with pharmaceutical companies (Starr 1982); acceptance of the view that corporate (and individual) profits from the medical system are ethical and create a
market-driven system that is the best in the world; the lack of evidence for standard treatments together with the assumption that those treatments are evidence-based, while complementary and alternative ones are not based on
evidence; and a belief that health care is a privilege, not a right. Just as feminist
science studies claims to promote a more accurate, less partial science, the recent
activism around breast cancer is becoming a vocal force in the call for evidence-
based medicine, struggling against a medical establishment with a history characterized by slow change and a close relationship to pharmaceutical companies.[20]

Breast cancer is also at the center of social change issues such as the power of
for-profit HMOs, the need for equitable health care and health insurance for
everyone, the relationship of "basic" research to applied or targeted research,
health care without harm, and environmental justice.[21] If, together, breast cancer
and feminist activism provide us with a model of feminist science, then scientists, physicians, and educators who apply the principles of strong objectivity
and feminist responsibility will acknowledge and support the full range of concerns about women's health and science in context.

Acknowledgments: I want to acknowledge the State of New York/United University Professions Professional Development and Quality of Working Life Committee and the Faculty Research Awards Program of the University of Albany for their support of my
research on breast cancer activism. I also want to thank the University of Albany, SUNY,
for my sabbatical leave, a great privilege.

Notes

1. The American Cancer Society (ACS) offers "Look Good . . . Feel Better" as a "free
public service . . . designed to teach women cancer patients beauty techniques to help restore their appearance and self-image during chemotherapy and radiation treatments."
The Cosmetic, Toiletry, and Fragrance Association Foundation and the National Cosme-

tology Association cosponsor the program (see American Cancer Society 1999). The ACS acknowledges "a generous grant" from GlaxoWellcome, one of the largest pharmaceutical companies.

2. Published in 1980, *The Cancer Journals* remains one of the most powerful and constructively angry readings, provoking strongly positive as well as negative responses from breast cancer survivors and fellow travelers.

3. The Center for Consumer Medicine and Public Health and the Center for Science in the Public Interest suggest the same principles and approaches to medical research and practice.

4. In her wonderful collection of essays, *The Politics of Women's Biology* (1990), Ruth Hubbard proposes that *Our Bodies, Ourselves* is a model for what feminist science might be: women-centered, created from women's values and concerns, based on women's experiences analyzed through feminist lenses that address inequities of power and resources. *Our Bodies, Ourselves*, however, does not include sufficient information about how biomedical claims are analyzed for accuracy; nor does it usually include sufficient references to that end.

5. This started nationally in the Department of Defense Breast Cancer Research Program (although not every funding panel includes a nonscientist consumer advocate), and at the state level in, for example, the California Breast Cancer Research Program.

6. Project LEAD (Leadership, Education, and Advocacy Development) consists of five-day intensive courses, offered periodically around the country, on how to read and analyze scientific papers on the biology of cancer and on epidemiology so that more advocates can make informed decisions not only about their personal concerns, but also about what funding panels should support and what the research agenda of the future should look like. I attended a Project LEAD course and found it very educational.

7. I want to thank Smith College for a travel grant to use the Sophia Smith Collection and the archives of the National Women's Health Network.

8. According to Susan Shinagawa (1999), founder of the National Asian American and Pacific-Islander Cancer Survivors and Advocacy Network, in collaboration with the Asian American and Pacific Islander American Health Forum, native Hawaiian and African-American women have the lowest breast cancer survival rates in the United States. The incidence of and mortality rates from breast cancer for Marshalese Islander women is five times greater, and their cervical cancer rate is seventy times greater than for U.S. women. For more information about the network, call 415-954-9964.

9. These are some useful resources for women concerned about breast cancer:
National Support/Health Groups
National Women's Health Network 202-347-1140
National Y-ME (referrals to local chapters) 800-221-2141
National Asian Women's Health Organization 415-989-9747
National Latina Health Organization 510-534-1362
National Lymphedema Network 800-541-3259
U.S. Government
Information on NCI-sponsored BC/clinical trials 800-4-CANCER.
Information on many cancers, delivered via fax, CANCERFAX, 301-402-5874.
Information on adverse reactions to drug therapy 800-FDA-1088.

Additional

National Breast Cancer Coalition 202-296-7477

Breast Cancer Action, 55 New Montgomery Street, #323, San Francisco, CA
   94105. Toll free: 877-2STOPBC. Barbara Brenner, Executive Director.
   Excellent critiques in newsletter.

Tell Washington White House Hotline, 202-456-1111, House/Senate
   switchboard 202-224-3121

10. Patricia Stocking Brown has her doctorate in comparative endocrinology and is a professor of biology at Siena College. Her research in developmental endocrinology has focused on the function of prolactin in vertebrate evolution, which has given her a broader perspective on the biology of breast cancer. She has been recognized by the community in a variety of ways, for example, through awards from the Susan G. Komen Foundation and Siena College.

11. Named for the sign of cancer, the crab, and for our need to be appropriately crabby and angry about the current state of affairs with regard to breast cancer.

12. CRAAB! has many members and people who receive our mailings (more than one hundred). But the core group consists of about a dozen women who attend our monthly business meetings, set up our monthly public programming, write grants, work on our projects (publishing a "Guide to Resources on Breast Cancer" for the region, choosing an "Essential Breast Cancer Bookshelf" for libraries and printing the list on bookmarks), and help host the New York State Breast Cancer Network meetings and advocacy days in 1999 and 2000 at the state legislature. About two-thirds of the group are breast cancer survivors, while the rest of us are concerned women whose mothers, sisters, or friends have experienced the disease. So far we have received grants for more than $60,000 from the local Susan G. Komen Foundation, administered by the Junior League of Albany, Long Island's 1 in 9, the New York State Legislature, and the Candle Foundation. In addition, Siena College (and, to a lesser degree, the University at Albany) has provided space, refreshments, xeroxing, interns, and other support.

13. Some topics we have investigated are the effects of weight and weight gain on breast cancer risk, the effects of tamoxifen and raloxifene, the effects of psychosocial support on survival and quality of life, and diagnosing and treating lymphedema. Some authors of illness narratives include Terry Tempest Williams, Audre Lorde, Reynolds Price, and Rachel Naomi Reman.

14. The word *choose* is not an accurate representation of how scientists set priorities and what they do, but it does reflect most scientists' belief system.

15. The Massachusetts Breast Cancer Coalition can be contacted at: 85 Merrimac Street, Boston, MA 02114, 617-624-0180, 800-649-6222.

16. The 1998 National Cancer Institute's agenda stated: "It is recommended that a genetics definition of each type of normal mammary epithelial and stromal cell be created [along with] a biological and biochemical elucidation of the functions of mammary gland gene products that appear to have regulatory functions" (Breast Cancer Progress Review Group 1998, p. 1 of conclusion). If the agenda were balanced with concern about the sources of environmental toxics and their elimination, genetic priorities would be less problematic.

17. Personal observation at Project LEAD, Philadelphia, May 1998, and elsewhere.

18. Breast Cancer Action's (2000) statement of "Core Principles and Values" includes: "We cannot be bought" (3). In contrast, "the American Medical Women's Association has taken money in exchange for endorsing commercial products including particular vitamins, Gyne-Lotrimin (cream for vaginal yeast infections), and Citrus Hill calcium-fortified orange juice" (Zones and Fugh-Berman 1999, 6).

19. NBCC honored Genentech, the corporation that markets Herceptin (an antibody that works against breast cancer from a specific defect, multiple copies of a gene called HER-2/neu that contributes to normal cell growth control), as a model for the industry on "how much can be accomplished when the advocacy and pharmaceutical/biotechnology/research communities work together" (NBCC 1999).

20. I have proposed significant changes for molecular biology: "What must be changed is not only the paradigmatic polarization that occurs at all levels, constructing dichotomies such as genetic/nongenetic and nature/nurture, but also the sociopolitical values and assumptions that structure and define molecular biology. . . . We can present the parts of the cell as equally important in 'life' and in 'regulation' and avoid fallacies inherent in a reductionist worldview by understanding qualitative differences among the levels of organization we consider 'life.' And we can teach the history and sociopolitical significance of genetics, molecular biology, molecular genetics, and related subfields as an integral part of the construction of knowledge. . . . Other issues, such as that raised about . . . the definition of 'life' based on the gene, require more radical reconceptualizing of whole areas of biology" (Spanier 1995, 110).

21. HealthCare without Harm is an organization committed to transforming the health care industry so it is no longer a source of environmental harm. This includes phasing out the use of polyvinyl chloride and persistent toxic chemicals. For information, call 703-237-2249, or visit the website (www.noharm.org).

Works Cited

American Cancer Society. "Cancer Facts and Figures 1999." Atlanta, GA: American Cancer Society, 1999.

Boston Women's Health Book Collective. *Our Bodies, Ourselves for the New Century*. New York: Simon and Schuster, 1998.

————. *Our Bodies, Ourselves: A Book by and for Women*. New York: Simon and Schuster, 1973.

————. *Women and Their Bodies*. Boston: New England Free Press, 1970.

Breast Cancer Action. "BCA Newsletter." Newsletter 57 (January/February 2000).

Breast Cancer Progress Review Group. "Charting the Course: Priorities for Breast Cancer Research." National Cancer Institute, 1998.

Chlorfene-Casten, Liane. *Breast Cancer: Poisons, Profits, and Prevention*. Monroe, ME: Common Courage Press, 1996.

Clarke, Adele E., and Virginia L. Olesen. *Revisioning Women, Health, and Healing: Feminist, Cultural, and Technoscience Perspectives*. New York: Routledge, 1999.

Davis, Devra Lee, Deborah Axelrod, Lisa Bailey, Mitchell Gaynor, and Annie J. Sasco. "Rethinking Breast Cancer Risk and the Environment: The Case for the Precautionary Principle." *Environmental Health Perspectives* 106 (1998): 523–529.

Eichenwald, Kurt, and Gina Kolata. "Drug Trials Hide Conflicts for Doctors." *New York Times,* May 16, 1999, sec. 1, p. 1.

Feuer, E., et al. "The Lifetime Risk of Developing Breast Cancer." *Journal of the National Cancer Institute* 85 (1993): 892.

Fisher, Bernard, et al. 1998. "Tamoxifen for Prevention of Breast Cancer: Report of the National Surgical Adjuvant Breast and Bowel Project P-1 Study." *Journal of the National Cancer Institute* 90 (September 16, 1998): 1371–1388.

Fried, Stephen. *Bitter Pills: Inside the Hazardous World of Legal Drugs.* New York: Bantam, 1999.

Harding, Sandra. *Whose Science? Whose Knowledge?* Ithaca, NY: Cornell University Press, 1991.

Hubbard, Ruth. *The Politics of Women's Biology.* New Brunswick, NJ: Rutgers University Press, 1990.

Leopold, Ellen. *A Darker Ribbon: Breast Cancer, Women, and Their Doctors in the Twentieth Century.* Boston: Beacon Press, 1999.

Lerner, Michael. *Choices in Healing: Integrating the Best of Conventional and Complementary Approaches to Cancer.* Cambridge, MA: MIT Press, 1998.

Lorde, Audre. *The Cancer Journals.* San Francisco: Aunt Lute Books, 1980.

National Breast Cancer Coalition (NBBC). *Call to Action* 5 (Summer 1999).

Powles, T., et al. "Interim Analysis of the Incidence of Breast Cancer in the Royal Marsden Hospital Tamoxifen Randomised Chemoprevention Trial." *Lancet* 352 (September 22, 1998): 98–101.

Proctor, Robert N. *Cancer Wars: How Politics Shapes What We Know and Don't Know about Cancer.* New York: Basic Books, 1995.

Shinagawa, Susan M. "Breast Cancer in Asian American and Pacific Islander Women: Myths and Realities." *The Breast Cancer Fund Report* (Winter 1999): 3, 6.

Spanier, Bonnie. *Im/partial Science: Gender Ideology in Molecular Biology.* Bloomington: Indiana University Press, 1995.

Stabiner, Karen. *To Dance with the Devil: The New War on Breast Cancer.* New York: Dell Publishing, 1997.

Starr, Paul. *The Social Transformation of American Medicine.* New York: Basic Books, 1982.

Steingraber, Sandra. *Living Downstream: An Ecologist Looks at Cancer and the Environment.* New York: Random House/Vintage, 1998.

Struewing, Jeffrey P., et al. "The Risk of Cancer Associated with Specific Mutations of BRCA1 and BRCA2 among Ashkenazi Jews." *New England Journal of Medicine* 336 (May 15, 1997): 1401–1408.

Veronesi, U., et al. "Prevention of Breast Cancer with Tamoxifen: Preliminary Findings from the Italian Randomised Trial among Hysterectomized Women." *Lancet* 352 (September 22, 1998): 93–97.

Weber, Barbara L. "Genetic Testing for Breast Cancer." *Scientific American* (January/February 1996): 12–21.

Zones, Jane Sprague, and Adriane Fugh-Berman. "Corporate Conflict of Interest among U.S. Non-Profit Women's Health Organizations." *The National Women's Health Network News* (May/June 1999): 1, 6, 7.

Taking Science to the Household

Scientific Motherhood in Women's Lives

───➤ Jacquelyn S. Litt

The phrase *scientific motherhood*, which dates to Catherine Beecher's *Treatise on Domestic Economy* (1842), refers to the idea that motherhood should be guided by scientific supervision and principles (Apple 1995). Prior to the 1920s much of the scientific education women received about motherhood in the United States took place in settlement houses, public health clinics, milk dispensaries, and public schools. But by the 1920s pediatricians and general practitioners defined themselves as the exclusive purveyors of expert advice on child health, and successfully nudged aside much of the public health and maternalist reform work that defined the Progressive era's scientific motherhood movement (Halpern 1988; Ladd-Taylor 1994). From the late 1920s on, one-third to one-half of all visits to physicians concerned child care issues for managing healthy children, as mothers consulted physicians in record numbers. Between 1920 and 1950 more and more mothers reported that their children's feeding was under a physician's care (Apple 1987). During this time, childbirth practices were also medicalized, as hospitalized births supplanted home births in increasing numbers (Leavitt 1986). With new professional authority and public deference, the medicalized[1] approach to motherhood fueled a new normative model for mothers: mothers' lack of compliance with medical rationales came to be seen as a sign of maternal neglect (Abel 1995).

Medical historian Rima Apple shows that the formal rhetoric of scientific motherhood limited women's control over child-rearing, making women "both responsible for their families and incapable of that responsibility" (1995, 162). This chapter examines scientific motherhood from the perspectives of women's everyday lives, focusing on the negotiated meanings and uses of this discourse, which came to constitute women's relations to scientific authority. By reclaiming women's voices and agency for the history of scientific motherhood, this essay shows the new expert discourse as heterogeneous: despite medicine's efforts to limit women's autonomy, and despite its promise to link women in a common, virtuous motherhood, mothers created scientific motherhood to meet their daily

275

needs, and did so in ways that drew upon and activated ethnoracial and class divisions among women.

I approach feminist science studies by exploring women's relations to expertise in arenas beyond formal scientific settings, such as in communities and at kitchen tables. Using feminist standpoint theory, I argue for a feminist study of science that considers expertise and science as contextual—produced by women as they respond to daily contingencies in these quotidian settings. From this perspective, we see medical science and practice as highly contested cultural objects and as deeply entwined with the production of gender in everyday life.

The data and analysis are drawn from my book (Litt 2000), which offers a fuller discussion of the topics raised in this chapter. The data on women's lives come from oral-history interviews I conducted with twenty African-American and eighteen Jewish women who raised their children in the 1930s and 1940s in Philadelphia. I interviewed the women in their homes in Philadelphia, soliciting volunteers through both informal snowball sampling and through connections I made with social service agencies. I used semistructured interviews (Reinharz 1992), which had a thematic focus on medical and child care issues in mothering. The interviews lasted from one and a half hours to four hours each. Each interview was tape-recorded and transcribed. When possible, I mailed the transcribed copy to the respondent. I provide all women with fictitious names.[2]

The New Medicalized Mother

Medicalization is the process through which biomedical interpretations of conditions have acquired cultural legitimacy, eclipsing (or at least pushing aside) other perspectives, such as custom, religion, and traditional knowledge, on human problems and conditions. Throughout the twentieth century, the domain of medicine expanded to include mothering practices, as well as childbirth, old age, death, child development, sexuality, appearance, alcohol use, and eating problems as requiring the intervention of medical experts and frames of reference. Through cultural and institutional practices (such as legal and economic supports), medical understandings have become the dominant frame for understanding and regulating a large range of personal and social activities and have come to undergird modern systems of social control and beliefs (Clarke and Olesen 1999; Martin 1987, 1994a; Rapp 1999).

By the 1930s scientific motherhood had been institutionalized as the province of professional medicine, particularly pediatrics and obstetrics. Advice manuals targeted maternalist reformers as dangerous for child health, warning women that only physicians were qualified to distinguish between the superstitious and the scientific (Apple 1987; Litt 1993). In turn, the emphasis of pediatricians shifted to managing the activities of healthy infants and children in private medical practice. Infectious disease rates had dropped, and many of the earlier life-threatening infectious diseases were controlled with the new antimicrobial sulfa drugs by the late 1930s and penicillin therapy by the mid-1940s. Defining themselves as the "new counselors of health," pediatricians now built their practices by attracting and recruiting the mothers of essentially healthy children. Sydney Halpern (1988) describes the new medical approach as revolutionary: "Never before had practicing professionals concerned themselves in a systematic manner with normal growth and development of individual children" (96).

Moving toward these more middle-class concerns involved physicians' administrations of meticulous feeding recommendations (see Apple 1987), vaccinations, growth and development tests, and "well-baby care," which included weighing and measuring the child. Check-ups offered more than good health. The medical visit, according to practitioners, promised a reformed motherhood. Just as scientific and technological advances were thought to improve industrial work and transportation, the advances of medical practice were said to bring mothers an orderly, progressive—and monolithic—practice of child care. The ethic of scientific motherhood was rooted in the conviction that science held the potential for straightening out the putative irrationality, backwardness, and diversity of mothers' child care health practices. In an *Archives of Pediatrics* article (1921) entitled "Hysteria in the Nursery and in Warfare: A Comparison and Contrast," Dr. Hector Charles Cameron warns, "To examine a child without an opportunity of making acquaintance with the mother is to be deprived of evidence which may prove essential for correct [medical] judgment" (199). "Medical therapy" was directed toward teaching mothers "about their own shortcomings," warned Dr. R. S. Miles (1921, 667). The medical ethos of well-baby care brought mothers' routine activities under medical surveillance, fastening the tie begun in the Progressive period between mothers' work in households, children's health needs, and expert authority.

The reform of motherhood that was promised in the ethos of medicalized motherhood took on particular strength as an ideology of ethnic and racial regulation. White professionals found scientific motherhood an appealing response to gender, racial, ethnic, and class conflicts of the late nineteenth and early twentieth centuries, particularly the animosities wrought by immigration, industrialization, and urbanization. Scientific motherhood was held out as offering a new scientific basis for promoting social stability in the midst of these radical social upheavals, for reinscribing, above all, the traditional gender order, cultural homogeneity, and white dominance (Fraser 1998; Kraut 1994; Meckel 1990; McBride 1989). As racial and ethnic minorities, African-American and Jewish women were targeted by professionals as inferior mothers. It was from their position as "outsiders-within" (Collins 1998) that the women I interviewed negotiated the new cultural authority of medicalized child care.

I will argue in this essay that it was not through a universal experience or location of motherhood that women approached scientific authority on motherhood. As Rayna Rapp found in her study of women's understandings and uses of amniocentesis in the United States in the late twentieth century, social inequality challenges the hegemonic discourse espousing science's universality: "The powerful universal explanatory claims and attendant technological interventions of science are continually constructed, crosscut, and sometimes undercut by the social hierarchies, identities, and economies through which 'science as culture' is shaped, and its resources distributed and contested" (1999, 16). By focusing on multiplicity and inequality, Rapp finds women negotiating with the dominant meanings, uses, and resources surrounding this new reproductive technology, actively creating their relations to scientific findings and recommendations as one of many cultural systems upon which they draw. Emily Martin's (1987, 1994a, 1994b) work also shows how individuals create meanings of science through their daily experiences, overturning dominant assumptions of women's (and men's) passivity in relation to the meaning and techniques of scientific knowledge: "Seeing science as an active agent in a culture that passively acquiesces does not provide an adequately complex view of how scientific knowledge operates in a social world" (1994a, 64). While formal texts and practices provide a backdrop around which women take up scientific discourse, much of its force is generated in spaces well beyond scientific/medical texts or doctors' offices, in places such as women's informal network relations and in their negotiations of social inequality and discrimination. This approach to the social studies of science features women as agents, producing and using expert discourse "on the street" (Martin 1994a, 64) while at the same time negotiating their relation to dominant codes of difference and gender.

Feminist standpoint methodology is useful for studying the question of difference and inequality in women's relations to expert authority. As Patricia Hill Collins describes it, "Standpoint theory posits a distinctive relationship among a group's position in hierarchical power relations, the experiences attached to differential group positionality, and the standpoint that a group constructs in interpreting these experiences" (1998, 194; see also Harding 1986). Dorothy Smith uses such a standpoint approach for analyzing textual discourse. She refers to textual discourse as occupying a "ubiquitous point of reference" (1990, 175) for dominant forms of femininity (including mothering), holding all women accountable despite their different positions, resources, and identities. Standpoint analysis of this "point of reference" involves searching for the contested and multiple meanings women create of it, for "spaces where discourses meet agentic actors" (Clarke and Olesen 1999, 18).

"He Was Just Like One of Us": Jewish Women and Scientific Motherhood

Sixteen of the eighteen Jewish women I interviewed were daughters of Russian immigrants and defined in very strong terms their acceptability as American mothers through scientific motherhood. As children they were subject to the ubiquitous acculturation pressures, which included the idea that modern medicine was essential for family health. White women, and established Jewish immigrants of earlier generations, directed their efforts toward "protecting immigrant children" and "modernizing immigrant families" and used the tenets of scientific motherhood to do so (Glenn 1990; Ladd-Taylor 1994, 5; Rose 1994). Young immigrant mothers were targeted and were taught the "American way" (Meckel 1990). The Jewish women I interviewed embraced this new way:

> No. I never took my mother-in-law's remedies. She came from the other side. I mean, after all, we're American. We're not from the little *shtetla*. I [had] the biggest man [doctor] in the city when Phyllis [my daughter] was born. So this is who I felt had more knowledge than old-fashioned remedies. I didn't use old-fashioned remedies. It wasn't my way of living. I wanted to know what we do today. Not what we did thirty, forty years ago. What good was thirty, forty years ago? You have to know today.

Using medical discourse to guide them through their own mothering constituted an engagement with the modern style of motherhood these women wanted to adopt. Sarah Rosenfeld vividly portrays the lengths to which she went to create herself as the new modern mother in relation to her immigrant mother's practices: "I had moved to the second-floor bedroom apartment in my parents' house, and the baby'd be crying. Well, the baby was due to get her next feeding at 2 o'clock, and if it was five of 2, she cried." I asked Sarah why she let the baby cry?

> I was a perfect mother, no reason why. The hospital sent you home with a list, and they told you exactly what to do. . . . [My mother] used to come up and knock on the apartment door. I locked her out. And she called me a murderer. I remember her saying it in Jewish: "It doesn't cost anything. I'll pay you. Give her some milk." This was the way it had to be. If the doctor said every four hours, every four hours. It was the right thing to do. I had a little bolt on my door, and she couldn't come in.

While scientific motherhood forced a divide between women such as Sarah and previous generations of Jewish women, the authority on child-raising previously garnered from these women was replaced by that of men. Unlike other immigrant groups, Jews had many physicians in their personal networks (see Watkins and Danzi 1995). Indeed, it was a physician's immersion in a common Jewish social network that provided the foundation for a Jewish woman's faith in him. Jewish mothers consulted almost exclusively Jewish physicians, with whom they felt a common identity. Rose Kleiner explains that she "used the best pediatrician for [my daughter] Phyllis." I asked her how she knew that he was the best:

"Well, in the first place, he happened to be my mother's cousin." And Estelle Sein explains that she preferred going to Jewish doctors: "Because I could talk [to them]. I don't know. I felt that they would understand me better or whatever. I think you could talk more openly with a person of your own religion. . . . That doesn't mean that Christian doctors aren't good doctors." It was through a gendered framework that they explained their relations to Jewish physicians. As men—neighbors, brothers, friends—pursued medical degrees or other business and professional opportunities to achieve their own social advance, mothers promoted their social position by supporting these men, and by reshaping their households and mothering orientation to meet "American" ideals.

If scientific authority gained its attractiveness in the Jewish community because it was transmitted by known community physicians in the context of familiar ethnic traditions, it gained much of its power because it connected mothers to a socially advanced status group of Jewish women who were similarly oriented to modernization and advancement. Women described their motherhood as indebted to friendships and information sharing with other Jewish women, and they spoke of their relations to physicians as mediated by this network:

> [My friends and I] used to confer . . . if one had a cold or something. Being we used the same doctors and things, a lot of times I'd go with her when she'd take Arlene for a check-up and she'd go with me, you know. We were that close. And we did use the same doctor, Dr. Weidman. I was using him first. And then she automatically, just cause I was using him, she liked him too.

These same network relations also involved mothers in drawing distinctions between insiders and outsiders to their social group—distinctions, in other words, about whose child care knowledge they would solicit and take. Shirley Rivers's descriptions of her fears about living in an ethnically mixed neighborhood, where she and her family had their pharmacy business, illustrate the sense of distance from non-Jewish families that she felt:

> The worst thing [with the new baby] was that I [had previously] moved away from my family. . . . All my married sisters lived in a radius of one block, and don't forget we lived with my mother. And [when I moved] I am going into this wilderness with no Jews because . . . where we had our business was Italian, Irish, and some black. Not knowing anything, but somehow or other the Lord looks and then I never had it so good, let me just tell you. We worked our butts off. Then we moved after that . . . I decided that it was time to bring them . . . to meet some Jewish friends.

Defining the absence of Jews as a "wilderness," Shirley sets herself off from the "Italians, Irish, and blacks" with whom she shared her neighborhood and on whom her family's livelihood depended. Feeling alone in this uncharted terrain of an ethnically mixed neighborhood, feeling no comfort from the insights of her neighbors, she appears to have lost her capacity to "know anything." It was only when she was securely situated with Jewish friends that she felt able to depend on her community for child health and mothering support.

The inclusions and exclusions Jewish mothers believed in and worked to create provided the basis for their relations to scientific authority. Only on the rarest of occasions did they consider going outside this ethnic group for medical help. On a routine basis, it was Jewish physicians and other Jewish mothers who provided the legitimation of scientific motherhood. Here we see how deeply women's understandings of scientific motherhood were tied to their collective investments in securing social standing and in their constant negotiations of insider and outsider boundaries. What mattered less to them was the technical right and wrong of the practices. What they could evaluate was the symbolic meaning of their practices, and it was on this basis that they forged their relations to scientific motherhood.

"We Tried to Work with Our People": African-American Upper-Middle-Class Networks and Scientific Motherhood [3]

I interviewed two women who were part of an upper-middle-class African-American network in Philadelphia. Sue Thomson's parents migrated to Philadelphia from South Carolina in the 1920s, and established a prominent mortuary business. Sue explains her mother's social advance as framing the medicalized culture her mother developed:

> My mother at that point . . . would have been considered a career woman. I mean, she was a career woman with, you know, the housekeeper and whatever. And she didn't do that . . . medical stuff to us you know. She just would send us to the doctor. . . . And she was just that much ahead of [her time].

Marion Marks—herself a migrant to Philadelphia when she was an infant—also directed her mothering in the 1930s toward securing her family's social acceptability. She did not use her mother's remedies, as she explains:

> Well, it's just like the change of that time. . . . And it's just an adjustment that you yourself had to make. Not only were you supposed to, that's what you had to do. You need a doctor. You needed a doctor.

Scientific motherhood held a strong attraction for these women, one that was as much a moral pull as a technical one. Adopting medical standards constituted the sign and practice of their advanced social position. Sue and Marion do more than distinguish between different knowledge systems. They construct this distinction to mark a boundary around themselves and their social networks—a boundary they see as evidence of their active participation in "the change of the time."

In these interviews, the women emphasized how the legacy of racism harmed African Americans' health. It was in this context of exclusion that they defined their relations to dominant medicine, emphasizing that their networks served as a lever for breaking down racial barriers. In their descriptions we find another segregated culture of scientific motherhood, one directed less toward medicalizing daily neighborhood life than toward citywide activism and institution building for African Americans. African-American women used their network ties to secure access to the advances of dominant medicine and to create themselves as acceptable mothers.

Philadelphia's medical system was almost entirely segregated, and as late as World War II it was still the case that twelve of Philadelphia's hospitals would admit black patients only in "colored wards." Other discriminatory practices included separate attendance hours with long waiting periods, verbal abuse by white hospital staff, lack of maternal and child health facilities, and a shortage of chronic care and convalescence facilities (McBride 1989). In this isolation from access to medical and scientific resources, we see a pattern that Collins (1998) argues symbolized African Americans' exclusion from the status of citizen; they symbolized the essence of the primitive and superstitious against which science defined its modernity and superiority. African-American women faced a white scientific and reform establishment that viewed them as primitives, objects of study and control, rather than potential citizens, objects of uplift and assimilation (Fraser 1998). These factors, combined with poverty and poor housing, produced higher morbidity and mortality rates among African Americans than among whites. Gertrude Fraser describes how African-American mothers were positioned as permanent outsiders to the promises of scientific motherhood:

> Even with the best maternal and infant care, whites assumed that African Americans would retain what they had defined as inferior traits. For them, it would be impossible for a "Negro" really to participate in American society, except in the narrow boundaries that had been reserved for him or her. In the case of maternal and infant health care, African Americans received few of the idealized rewards of scientific progress and permanently lost much of that which had helped to sustain them (1998, 127).

Therefore, it was up to the African-American community itself to marshal efforts toward medicalization, to eliminate racism in medicine, and to forge access to medical advance. Gaining access to medical care was a battle fought along the same lines as the Civil Rights movement. Philadelphia had its own health movement that developed along a track parallel to the national movement for health by African Americans (McBride 1989). And it was left to African-American professionals and mothers—in their everyday practices as caretakers—to secure the health and well-being of the black population (Fraser 1998).

Sue explained that it was to African-American physicians in their network that her family turned: "We didn't have much choice. I mean, we weren't as welcome [by white physicians]." And to illustrate how white racism could be interrupted by these network ties, she describes a childhood incident of racism by white opticians to whom she had been referred by Dr. Fay, an African-American ophthalmologist:

> [I went to see] opticians. The guy at the front door . . . told me that "We're not hiring today and we don't need any help." And I was a teenager and I said, "What did you say?" And he said, "We're not hiring anybody today. . . ." I said, "Dr. Fay sent me here to get my glasses."

In describing the barrier she encountered to medical services and how her network relation to Dr. Fay helped her to overcome it, Sue emphasizes the security provided by network ties, security that was contingent on the social-class connection forged among her upper-middle-class parents and the network of professionals with whom they identified. Dr. Virginia Alexander, who was part of this network, was featured in "Can a Colored Woman Be a Physician?" in *The Crisis* (1933, 33) for her work to combat discrimination against African Americans.

> [Alexander] spends an endless amount of time following her patients to hospitals, checking on [the] diagnosis both medical and surgical, standing by her patients when operated upon and visiting them afterwards. . . . This service probably more than anything else has had the effect of staving off or definitely dulling the edge of increased practices of segregation and discrimination in most if not all of the hospitals of Philadelphia.

As members of this upwardly mobile network, which included Dr. Alexander and her partner, Dr. Helen Dickens, Sue's mother and Marion were protected from many of the worst practices of a racist medical system. They, in turn, felt obligated to support the African-American professionals (women and men) who were building their own practices. Marion describes this responsibility:

> Dr. Gary was Negro, Dr. Andrews, Dr. Alexander, Negro. So we tried to work with our people as much as we could, you know. After all, you wanted to give them work too, see. The others didn't have any trouble getting their work because as a rule it was more of them than it was of us. . . . So that's why I'm saying that we tried to favor and help them because they're trying to get through life, the same way all other nationalities are, too.

When Marion was a child, her family supported and helped to establish this network. They attended the fund-raising fairs sponsored by Mercy Hospital, for example, one of the city's two black hospitals:

> As a little girl I was in ballet and dance school and what-not. We used to go, they'd have fairs at the Mercy Hospital out on the grounds. People would come from everywhere to these fairs. And as a dancing group, we would go out, do little dancing and acting like fools, see. [Laughs.]

By participating in these networks Marion saw herself as having secured her ties to an advancing social group and supported collective mobility, while at the same time gaining access to a network of protective caretakers.

Sue Thompson's parents also were active members of this tightly knit network. She represents the network as self-consciously oriented toward buffering the effects of racism against African-American professionals: "One of the things, and this is the way that I think we got close to Dr. Dickens, [was] in those days, we would have teas. We had teas from house to house." One of the houses, she remarks, "actually had a music room":

> [The house] had a floor-to-ceiling library on one wall. And then the concert grand [piano] and so people used [this] house for the teas. On Sunday afternoons, so what they would do, new professionals coming to town, new professionals would be introduced at a tea. Someone would come in and they would say, "This is the new doctor."

Like the Jewish women, these African-American mothers cultivated ties with others in a similar class and racial position as they constructed their relations to scientific authority. Both upper-middle-class African-American women and Jewish women pursued social-class mobility and protection from racism and anti-Semitism through their ethnic enclaves, and constructed their domestic lives in relation to these network obligations and resources. Through these ties and interdependencies, medicalization developed its meaning as a gendered and racialized enterprise. Seen from the perspective of science's promise of a unified motherhood, we find an important contradiction. Medicalization and the appeal (and presumed safety) of being a respectable mother characterized the women equally. Yet their lives, mothering practices, and personal networks were entirely separate. Scientific motherhood was taken up by these women not as a basis for their commonality with other women, but as a site where social divisions along class and racial ethnic lines were reproduced. As they responded to their various "outsider-within" locations in U.S. society, they had little choice but to remake medical discourse as yet another social practice that re-created ethnoracial and class differentiation.

*"I Don't Know Any Doctors": Working-Class African-American Women
and Scientific Motherhood*

The working-class African-American women I interviewed also organized their
mothering in terms of network responsibilities and resources, although these
were not oriented toward the tenets of scientific motherhood. Rose Lyons, a
poor, single African-American mother, offers an example of network ties that
produced her distance from the norms, demands, and privileges of scientific
motherhood. She relied on informal networks of other women for help with
child care for her son as well as emotional and financial support. Her household
was part of a larger web of households, all contributing to the everyday survival
of each other. She called these networks a "family." Like the other women in similar circumstances, Rose gave priority to patching together a household routine
that enabled her to maintain paid employment. She explains that relying on a
doctor for monthly check-ups was simply out of the question:

> See, we couldn't go the doctor's every time anything happened when I was rais-
> ing him. You went to the doctor, but not every time, every little thing. You had
> to know things yourself. My mother did. [And my grandmother] pulled us
> through when the flu was raging.

These working-class women were not oriented toward medicalized contexts, in
part because they had little or no access to private medical care facilities where scientific motherhood was widely practiced. Without known and trusted community figures, medical institutions and practices seemed distant, removed from
their daily lives. Their closest associations were with women in similar social circumstances, who went to public health care facilities, not private medical offices,
for medical attention. When they turned to formal medicine it meant forging ties
to medical institutions and scientific advance in sites outside of their close networks, such as in hospital parenting lessons, in the homes of their white domestic
employers, and in the white doctors' offices where they worked as housekeepers—
in places, in other words, where their class and racial status were marginal.

In her memoir of being "a white mother of Black sons," Jane Lazarre explores
the daily negotiations of race and racism embedded in her cross-racial mothering, one aspect of which is recognizing her own privilege and power in relation
to her sons, husband, and in-laws. At one point in her narrative she speaks to her
own racial power as something her black mother-in-law, Lois, uses to get medical
attention in an emergency room:

> In . . . matters of race consciousness and Black pride, of wariness and readiness
> of battle, Lois' ability to win out over fate and survive dire social conditions,

are famous. Once, waiting for admission to an emergency room when Simeon [Lois's son] was sick, she told me bluntly: "Go tell them we've been here for hours. They'll believe you cause you're white." She is a resistance fighter at heart and by necessity. I obey her, resent her, tease her, am angry or grateful or frustrated and always full of admiration (1996, 106).

After many years of witnessing, participating in, and learning from this community of resistance, the "life stories" of her black kin come to affect Lazarre as well, and shape a new identity for her. Yet when the African-American women in my study borrowed the status and power of white privilege just as Lois did, these were not occasions when established connections (amid division) could find a place. Rather, there were stories of temporary alliance conspicuous more by differences than by coming together across ethnoracial or class divides.

Many women, for example, turned to friends' employers, coworkers, bosses, or landlords who offered a link to the important but out-of-reach resource of modern medicine. For childbirth, for example, Gloria Jones used the obstetrician for whom her mother did domestic work. Blanche Pierce decided that vaccinations and other medical technologies were important after learning that her sister's employer, "the first [person] to receive insulin," benefited from new medical knowledge. These provided important links to medicine, not links of familiarity and commonality but essentially of difference. Instead of a celebration of social progress, inclusion, and safety, we find in these narratives a struggle with unsatisfactory care and lack of power in relation to medical establishments and personnel.

Cheryl O'Neil's narrative of seeking better medical care shows this dynamic of difference in women's relations to expert authority. Cheryl learned of the dominance of medicine for child care when she worked as a domestic for white employers who used pediatricians. Because her employers were "schooled" people, Cheryl decided that she too would pursue the use of a private doctor rather than the clinic, as she explains:

> I was doing housework and child care, taking care of people's children. And a lot of the people I would work for used 'em. They were schooled, maybe doctor, lawyer, something like that. And that's what I did. So I found me one. I looked in the *Yellow Pages* and found one closest to me, and [if] the name sounded good, [I went].

Cheryl never spoke directly with her employers about this decision; she simply followed the example they set. Nor did she consult a physician who was known to—and proven by—her own network. It was on her own terms—with her own scant resources—that Cheryl switched from free to paid services. She became so convinced of the superiority of private, paid care that she worked longer hours and sacrificed other purchases:

I had a medical card. I didn't use it. I took my money out of work for it and paid [for] the [doctor]. I figured that they wouldn't . . . give you the right stuff [with the medical card] because they were giving you something. I would work extra hours to make extra money, make sure that I paid for it. So my [children], they got top-notch everything. When I stopped going to the hospital, to the regular clinic, I had a private pediatrician for them to go to. I will always get baby doctors. I will always find me one somewhere.

Like others who came to identify the advantages of private medical care through the model of those outside of their immediate and closest ties, Cheryl copied the practice of her more privileged employers but did so without the resources or advantages they enjoyed. Working twelve hours a day, commuting from the central city to the suburbs, taking care of her employer's children while her own were looked after by others, all point to the limits of structuring her relation to medical discourse in the terms her employers could adopt. In seeking private medical care Cheryl identified with these more privileged women; in this commonality she pictured herself as carrying out the kind of mothering she respected in her employers. Yet without the social networks and artifacts of status mobility, this was an approach to medical discourse that approximated but could not reproduce the scientific mothering of the middle class. Cheryl's approach was not mixed with a broader status advance nor her integration into a new, socially mobile network of other mothers.

Medical discourse's unifying model, or its "ubiquitous point of reference" (Smith 1990, 175) for mothering, holds all women accountable despite the variety of settings and circumstances in which women actually live. In the narratives of these African-American mothers we find a mirroring of the exclusivity that middle- and upper-middle-class women developed in and through their segregated medicalized cultures. In this case, scientific discourse does not function simply as a set of textual directives that these women find harder to meet than others. Instead, these women confront scientific motherhood as a normative force and in spaces far removed from physicians' offices. They negotiate this power largely through relations with other women for whom medicalization represented and enacted personal and collective advancement. Their relations with other women, as Smith puts it, were "mediated by the standardization of . . . norms organized by [medical] discourse" (1990, 175).

Conclusion

My goal in this essay has been to direct attention away from a perspective toward science that assumes, however implicitly, either women's victimization by medical discourse or the idea that women commonly accepted medicine's premise on its own scientific terms. This chapter approaches women's relations to scientific authority through a feminist standpoint approach, searching out how actual women engaged and produced the new tenets of medicalized motherhood. Analytically, this means focusing on women's group position and social inequality in elaborating what science means for women. What is distinctive about the power of scientific discourse here is not only that it locates some women inside the dominant model of motherhood and others outside on the basis of race and social-class differences, but that it affects how and with what meanings mothers enter into social relations with other women.

In women's narratives of scientific motherhood we can identify struggles between old and new practices, conflicts over the most health-producing techniques for raising healthy children. Yet what structures this conflict is another, larger contest between social groups over boundaries, status, and acceptability. In these women's daily negotiations we find scientific motherhood serving as a prime meaning of expert authority: women brought medical discourse into being as a project of creating motherhood within ethnoracial and class boundaries. The processes through which women brought scientific motherhood into being were not a progressive, acultural, and unified "march of science." Instead, I have shown scientific motherhood as a divided and contradictory discourse, refracted through relations of inequality and difference among women. Instead of establishing links across race, ethnicity, and class, scientific motherhood cemented existing social divisions and gave them new, scientifically justified resilience.

Notes

1. I use the terms *medicalized motherhood* and *scientific motherhood* interchangeably in this chapter.

2. For an extended discussion of the method and the consequences of status differences and commonalities between me and my respondents, see the introduction to my book, *Medicalized Motherhood: Views from the Lives of African-American and Jewish Women.*

3. The data on which the Thompsons' family story is based was collected during an interview I had with their daughter, who reflected on her mother's child care practices. This was the only occasion in the study when I went outside of my sample of mothers of the 1930s and 1940s. I did so because of the importance of this social group's relation to medicine, and to the movement for civil rights, including health rights, in Philadelphia. I also interviewed a key physician in this network, Dr. Helen Dickens, and did archival work at the Medical College of Pennsylvania to investigate her senior partner, Dr. Virginia Alexander (see Litt 2000).

Works Cited

Abel, Emily K. "A 'Terrible and Exhausting' Struggle: Family Caregiving during the Transformation of Medicine." *Journal of the History of Medicine and Allied Sciences* 50 (1995): 478–506.

Apple, Rima D. "Constructing Mothers: Scientific Motherhood in the Nineteenth and Twentieth Centuries." *The Society for the Social History of Medicine* 8 (1995): 161–178.

———. *Mothers and Medicine: A Social History of Infant Feeding, 1890-1950*. Madison: University of Wisconsin Press, 1987.

Beecher, Catharine. *A Treatise on Domestic Economy, for the Use of Young Ladies at Home, and at School*. Boston: T. H. Webb and Co., 1842.

Cameron, Hector Charles. "Hysteria in the Nursery and in Warfare: A Comparison and Contrast." *Archives of Pediatrics* 38 (1921): 193–200.

"Can a Colored Woman Be a Physician?" *The Crisis 40* (1933): 33–34.

Clarke, Adele, and Virginia Olesen. "Revising, Diffracting, Acting." In *Revisioning Women, Health, and Healing: Feminist, Cultural, and Technoscience Perspectives*, ed. Adele E. Clarke and Virginia L. Olesen. Routledge: New York, 1999.

Collins, Patricia Hill. *Fighting Words: Black Women and the Search for Justice*. Minneapolis: University of Minnesota Press, 1998.

Fraser, Gertrude. *African American Midwifery in the South: Dialogues of Birth, Race, and Memory*. Cambridge, MA: Harvard University Press, 1998.

Glenn, Susan Anita. *Daughters of the Shtetl: Life and Labor in the Immigrant Generation*. Ithaca, NY: Cornell University Press, 1990.

Halpern, Sydney. *American Pediatrics: The Social Dynamics of Professionalism, 1880–1980*. Berkeley: University of California Press, 1988.

Harding, Sandra. *The Science Question in Feminism*. Ithaca, NY: Cornell University Press, 1986.

Kraut, Alan M. *Silent Travelers: Germs, Genes, and the "Immigrant Menace."* New York: Basic Books, 1994.

Ladd-Taylor, Molly. *Mother-Work: Women, Child Welfare, and the State, 1890–1930*. Chicago: University of Illinois Press, 1994.

Lazarre, Jane. *Beyond the Whiteness of Whiteness: Memoir of a White Mother of Black Sons*. Durham, NC: Duke University Press, 1996.

Leavitt, Judith. *Brought to Bed: Child-Bearing in America, 1750–1950*. New York: Oxford University Press, 1986.

Litt, Jacquelyn. *Medicalized Motherhood: Views from the Lives of African-American and Jewish Women*. New Brunswick, NJ: Rutgers University Press, 2000.

———. "Pediatrics and the Development of Middle-Class Motherhood." *Research in the Sociology of Health Care* 10 (1993): 161-173.

Martin, Emily. *Flexible Bodies: Tracking Immunity in the Age of AIDS*. Boston: Beacon Press, 1994a.

———. "Anthropology and the Cultural Study of Science: Citadels, Rhizomes, and String Figures." Keynote address to the Society for Social Studies of Science, 1994b.

———. *The Woman in the Body: A Cultural Analysis of Reproduction*. Boston: Beacon Press, 1987.

McBride, David. *Integrating the City of Medicine: Blacks in Philadelphia Health Care, 1910–1965*. Philadelphia: Temple University Press, 1989.

Meckel, Richard A. *Save the Babies: American Public Health Reform and the Prevention of Infant Mortality, 1850–1929*. Baltimore: Johns Hopkins University Press, 1990.

Miles, R. S. "Common Nervous Conditions of Children." *Archives of Pediatrics* 38 (1921): 664–671.

Rapp, Rayna. *Testing Women, Testing the Fetus: The Social Impact of Amniocentesis in America*. New York: Routledge, 1999.

Reinharz, Shulamit. *Feminist Methods in Social Research*. New York: Oxford University Press, 1992.

Rose, Elizabeth. "From Sponge Cake to *Hamentashen*: Jewish Identity in a Jewish Settlement House, 1885–1952." *Journal of Ethnic History* 13 (1994): 3–23.

Smith, Dorothy. *Texts, Facts, and Femininity: Exploring the Relations of Ruling*. New York: Routledge, 1990.

Watkins, Susan Cotts, and Angela Danzi. "Women's Gossip and Social Change: Childbirth and Fertility Control among Italian and Jewish Women in the United States, 1920–1940." *Gender and Society* 9 (1995): 469–490.

After Absolute Neutrality

Expanding "Science"

$\longrightarrow$ Sandra Harding

In 1962, Thomas Kuhn's influential account of scientific change showed how the new social histories of modern science revealed "the historical integrity of that science in its own time" (Kuhn 1962). More than three decades of subsequent studies have produced accounts of modern sciences that are far more accurate to the recorded history of science and to current scientific practices (for example, Bloor 1977; Galison and Stump 1996; Latour 1988; Latour and Woolgar 1979; Quine 1953; Schuster and Yeo 1986; Shapin 1994; Shapin and Shaffer 1985). Moreover, gender analyses have extended such "postpositivist" accounts to show the significant respects in which modern sciences have displayed a historical integrity with the gender relations of their era (for example, Braidotti et al. 1994; Haraway 1989; Harding 1986, 1991; Keller 1984; Merchant 1980; Plumwood 1993; Rooney 1994; Schiebinger 1993; Shiva 1989; Wajcman 1991). Finally, multicultural and postcolonial science and technology studies have revealed how modern sciences have been permeated by distinctively European projects that have often been Eurocentric, racist, imperial, and colonial ones. Sciences have been part of the imperial and colonial projects of their cultures (Goonatilake 1984; Harding 1998; Joseph 1991; Lach 1977; Needham 1954ff; Watson-Verran and Turnbull 1995).[1] These three fields of post–World War II science studies eliminate the possibility of justifying modern science as culturally neutral, and thus as the kind of unique historical phenomenon that is the preoccupation of the older histories and philosophies of science. If it is not unique in such ways, do we then need to revisit and reevaluate the value and viability of other cultures' science traditions?

Such issues are not the topic only of scholarly projects. Over the last half century the base of the global economy has shifted from heavy industry to the production and management of information. Scientific and technological productions are now the foundation of the global political economy. This economy continues to expand into new areas around the globe, and to structure more deeply and completely daily life in societies in which it has already been present. Furthermore, as this capitalist economy spreads around the globe, so too does the shared conceptual framework common to European and American democracies, modern sciences, and capitalist economies. Emerging in the same historic eras, all three value the "disenchanted" material world, cultural neutrality, rational processes, objective decisions, the interchangeability ("equality") of their central actors, and other features. Which conceptual components of this scientific, political, and economic framework should be preserved and which revised or abandoned? In addressing this issue, feminist science studies continues to provide an important voice in renegotiating the terms of global democracy as it critically examines such notions as objectivity, rationality, good method, and—the topic of this essay—what should be considered to constitute "real science."

A central challenge for anyone reflecting on the sciences these days is to figure out how to think about knowledge claims that are permeated by cultural values and interests, and yet are also "true": empirically reliable, and by other conventional measures, the result of "good science." As long as cultural partisanship was automatically considered a sign of impure science, the production of false claims, or "bad" or "not really" science, this difficult issue never arose. We could all safely stay preoccupied with excluding politics and cultural values from scientific inquiry and the results of its projects. However, if even the very best of international sciences are considered to be fully part of their historical eras, bearing the cultural fingerprints of those eras and the subsequent ones that practice and maintain them in their cognitive core—their methods, formal results of research, and basic metaphysics (for example, distinguishing between primary and secondary properties)—then this difficult issue looms before us. It is not just that the questions sciences ask reflect culturally specific concerns, although this is a major source of the "localness" of international as well as of other kinds of sciences. Equally significant, the resources materially and culturally available to seek answers to such questions, including methods of inquiry and standards for justifying knowledge claims, also bear such cultural fingerprints. Consequently, modern international sciences, no less than the knowledge systems of other cultures, reveal culturally distinctive patterns of systematic knowledge and of systematic ignorance and error.

To say this is by no means to deny that nature's order must play a central role in the knowledge system of any culture that manages to survive for even a day. And even if international sciences cannot achieve absolute cultural neutrality, clearly many of their elements regularly do achieve a kind of relative neutrality and autonomy. International sciences obviously have developed effective strategies for downplaying the influence of many of the kinds of values and interests of their eras on the results of research. But so too, it turns out, do elements of knowledge systems of other cultures achieve such degrees of cultural neutrality, as evidenced, for example, by their adoption into modern sciences—a point I will address below.

Moreover the culture-permeated versus culture-free contrast has turned out to obscure other important issues, such as which kinds of cultural elements do and should we want to permeate our sciences for scientific and/or political reasons? And who should make such decisions if they are not trusted solely to scientific experts who, it was presumed, know how to eliminate all social values and interests from their projects? Should we seek answers to such questions in the abstractly democratic rhetorics that modern sciences have favored since their origins—for example, in their concerns for the social equality of observers, for research processes that avoid "might makes right" in the production of knowledge, for public access to the results of research? What concrete social relations in and around the sciences could make such democratic sentiments more effective, in gender and global contexts, too? Such questions are not ones that scientists are prepared through their training to think about, nor have most nonscientists gained the skills and knowledge necessary to answer them.

Feminist science studies have made important contributions to raising and advancing thought about such issues. Around the world women have called for more accurate accounts of our bodies, environmental hazards to us, nature's pharmacological resources, sustainable agriculture, energy, and water supplies, and other aspects of nature where the prevailing sciences have not yet fully responded to women's scientific and technological concerns. In addition, we have wanted such projects linked to pro-democratic agendas that benefit and empower women, and that do so for women around the world (Braidotti et al. 1994).

My project here is to try to identify kinds of knowledge-seeking practices that have become good candidates for counting as real sciences once the absolute neutrality ideal is left behind. By "real sciences" I mean to refer to ones that work in everyday life as well as in institutional projects, and that reveal nature's order, whether or not modern, international sciences have recognized them as such. Once the contrast between culture-free and culturally embedded sciences is abandoned, the importance of many more of women's interests and practices, in Europe and America and around the globe, can be appreciated.

In the next section, I look at new ways of thinking about the necessity (and desirability) for all sciences to be permeated by aspects of their historical era. I then outline how five kinds of inquiry not regarded as fully scientific in the older philosophies and histories of modern, international sciences gain that status in the analyses developing today that are guided by the new science studies. Along with what we can now see as culturally embedded international, modern sciences should be included overtly mission-directed research, much of engineering and technology development, hybrid sciences composed of natural and social elements (such as medicine or environmental sciences), the everyday science of farmers, mechanics, and infant caretakers in modern Western societies, and—last but not least—non-Western cultures' scientific and technological traditions.

Local Knowledge Systems

The three science studies movements referred to above reveal the current widespread understanding that all knowledge systems have been in significant respects "local"—that is, they have an integrity with their historical era, in Kuhn's words. Equally important, they reveal the necessity of this historic integrity, and the cognitive resources available to sciences when they make use of such local resources. Most surprising, it turns out that in some cases it is precisely a science's permeation by a set of cultural values that is responsible for its cognitive advances (Harding 1998). Therefore, to eliminate all of the cultural features of a scientific system would be to deprive it of its most energizing and fruitful elements.

Consider how, first, different societies inhabit different parts of heterogeneous nature. Some live on the shores of the Atlantic, others in the Sahara Desert, some in arctic and others in tropical climates, some in terrains afflicted with tornados and others in monsoon territories. Some travel from Polynesia to Australia, others from Spain to the Americas, or from Cape Canaveral to the moon. Obviously, each culture will have distinctive interests in the environment with which it must interact. However, even in the same environment, different cultures will ask different questions. On the borders of the Atlantic Ocean, some will want to fish in the ocean, others to use it as a coastal trading route. Still others will want to use it as a vista and playground for expensive homes built along its shores, to mine the oil and minerals beneath its floors, as a dump for toxic wastes, or to restore it to sustainable environmental health. Each such culture will develop distinctive patterns of knowledge and of ignorance that are created by their interests in the waters before them—by the questions that they ask, and those they don't ask.

If the familiar jigsaw puzzle model of nature's order were a reasonable one, all of the patterns of knowledge could be fit together into the one true account of nature's singular order, each culture's pattern of knowledge filling in spaces occupied by another culture's patterns of ignorance. For example, the environmentalists would neatly replace the patterns of ignorance found in the "spaces" between the patterns of knowledge of the miners and toxic dumpers, not disturbing the patterns of knowledge but merely expanding them to include the information produced by other social interests. To take another example, the Asian acupuncture pattern of knowledge would be thought of in this model as substituting for international biomedicine's historic ignorance of how to manage chronic pain. Even if we retained this jigsaw puzzle model of the growth of scientific knowledge, we can see the importance of appreciating the culturally distinctive values and interests that would lead different cultures to ask different kinds of questions about nature's order. Whenever any of these knowledge systems are lost, other cultures are deprived of valuable resources, now and in the future.[2]

Yet the jigsaw puzzle model is problematic. Cultural interests sometimes conflict, producing conflicting patterns of "knowledge." For example, interests in maximizing industrial expansion and in agribusiness can conflict with interests in keeping environments sustainable. The former interests assume that nature will always renew itself regardless of how humans interact with it; environmental analyses deny this assumption. Since scientific theories are always underdetermined by their evidence—they always, and usefully, generalize to cases not yet observed—a conceptual framework valuable for success in one project, such as industrial expansion, can be disastrous for success at another, such as sustaining environments. My point here is that the cultural permeation of scientific questions by historical interests can by no means be conceptualized as an innocent fact that can be accommodated by the standard jigsaw puzzle model of scientific advance.

However, two other culturally local features of every knowledge system make the jigsaw puzzle model even less reasonable. Complete cultural neutrality is not only impossible in principle, it is also undesirable for scientific and epistemological (as well as political) reasons. The mention of theoretical frameworks above points to how cultures develop distinctive discursive resources to think about nature's order. They draw on or develop culturally relevant metaphors, models, and narratives to conceptualize and direct their research projects. For example, in the history of European sciences, nature has been conceptualized as a benevolent mother ("Mother Nature"), as a cornucopia of endless resources, as a product of a Christian God's mind, as a mechanism like a clock, and—to skip five centuries—as a complex and different kind of mechanism such as a self-correcting computer, or as a spaceship or lifeboat in the recent environmental models. These metaphors, models, and narratives are not just useful pedagogical or heuristic devices. Instead, they are an integral part of scientific inquiry, directing scientists to examine certain kinds of phenomena instead of others, and guiding how science will expand or correct its hypotheses in the course of research. To eliminate this kind of cultural specificity would be to lose for science the endless supply of such resources that enable human cultures to imagine effectively the constantly changing phenomena with which they must interact.

Moreover, different cultures have different ways of organizing the production of knowledge. As modern science has always argued, how one interacts with nature shapes what one can know about it. Modern physicians and indigenous healers can both learn things that laboratory medical research cannot. Farmers, herders, and sylviculture workers come to understand aspects of nature's order that scientific agriculture accidently or intentionally ignores (Braidotti et al. 1994; Shiva 1989). Pasteur had to reorganize where, how, and by whom scientific knowledge was produced in order to achieve the results of his research (Latour 1988). Physicists, engineers, and mathematicians with different disciplinary-based notions of randomness had to invent new such notions that would be suitable for the virtual reality project in which they were jointly involved (Pickering 1992). Hundreds of other studies also reveal the importance to cultures' scientific projects of local discursive resources and ways of organizing the production of knowledge.

These studies bring us a long way from the older ideals of absolute cultural neutrality for real sciences. Let us turn to analyze the kinds of knowledge-seeking practices that these studies in effect situate as "real sciences." What relevance do these have to those interested in women, gender, and science?

More Real Sciences and Their Gender Aspects

Mission-Directed Research

The fall of the neutrality ideal reveals the difficulty of locating the border between what used to be thought of as "pure science" and mission-directed research. In thinking about the former, conventional accounts have tended to focus on the epistemic goals and motivations (for example, the search for the facts or truth about a phenomenon) that overtly guided the research of individual scientists, or of whole laboratories and fields of science. They have been little concerned with the professional ambitions of individuals, scientific fields, or institutions, or with the larger social projects that explicitly or implicitly made a research topic "interesting." Furthermore, if scientists were unaware of any mission toward which their research was directed, then the research could be counted as "pure science." This view of science as a product of individual scientists' conscious motivations is problematic in a number of respects.

In the first place, there are certain kinds of research that clearly are directed by social missions, and yet these social and even political goals have not been thought to impugn the objectivity of the research in any distinctive way. One such example was, until at least as late as World War II, military research. As Margaret Jacob says in her influential account of the scientific revolution,

> Western science at its foundations, as promoted by its most brilliant as well as its most ordinary exponents, never questioned the usefulness of scientific knowledge for warmaking. I know of no text from the early modern period which suggests that the scientist should withhold his knowledge from any government, at any time, but especially in the process of preparing for warmaking. Indeed most texts that recommend science also propose its usefulness in improving the state's capacity to wage war more effectively, to destroy more efficiently (1988, 251).

During World War II, nationalism and just wars were considered acceptable missions for science that would not impugn the cultural neutrality of their research. Moreover, the entrance of the United States into international science was made possible by the shift of research agendas in physics to national security in the period from 1940 to 1960 (Forman 1987). The Manhattan Project in particular gained the United States membership—indeed, leadership—in postwar scientific research. Mission-directed research, even when the mission permeates the cognitive content of the results of research, can produce the highest-quality science. Thus empirically true scientific claims can be cognitively permeated (in the ways indicated in the preceding section) by cultural projects.

Another such area is medical and health sciences. No one thinks that the desire of entire research communities to find a cure for cancer or AIDS in itself threatens the validity of the research that such communities certify as objective. Yet such desires are by no means culturally neutral as we can recognize if we think of such groups as Christian Scientists, who refuse biomedical intervention in health matters, or of other groups who believe that what international science conceptualizes as a curable physical illness is often a consequence of bad social relations or of God's will, and is more effectively dealt with in social or religious relations. (Such arguments are common about both AIDS and cancer.)

There are two additional problems with conventional thinking about mission-directed research. It is clear that funders can have goals of which scientists are unaware. For example, military funding of "basic research" is selective about which kinds of research it funds. It expects to reap military benefits from knowledge of some aspects of nature's order but not from knowledge of other aspects. Cultures' patterns of knowledge and ignorance represent the combined interests of all the various social forces shaping scientific research. Finally, this belief puts a premium on supporting and maintaining the ignorance of scientists about the possible or even obviously inevitable social assumptions and consequences of their research. Scientists, individually or collectively, can feel most confident that they are conducting objective research if they remain conscientiously ignorant of what goes on outside the laboratory door. Yet, if scientists are to be partners with others concerned with improving scientific practice and theories about science, such "scientific illiteracy" on the part of scientists is insupportable.

What implications do these facts about mission-directed research have for feminist concerns? For one thing, just because a research project is guided by feminist "missions" should not be sufficient reason to deny it the status of real science, or even of maximally objective science. Feminist concerns for promoting research on women's health issues, sustainable environments for women, or on technical developments to serve women's needs do not in themselves create the kinds of "biases" that damage the reliability of the results of research. To argue otherwise would be to admit that any scientific research directed to the interests of a particular group of people—children, the sick, the hungry, victims of environmental destruction, ocean travelers—is thereby damagingly biased. The language of "bias" that associates any cultural interests with a damaging lack of objectivity obscures issues about how partisan research, engaged to promote culturally distinctive interests and values, is inevitable, but not necessarily detrimental to the growth of scientific knowledge. Of course, such interests and values can indeed lead to empirically unreliable results of research, but this is not automatically the case. The fact that a project is guided by feminist concerns is not in itself reason to suspect the objectivity of the results of that research. Thus judgmental relativism is not inevitable if we give up the language of "bias."

On the other hand, just because a scientist is a "good feminist" in every conscious area of life doesn't ensure that the research such a scientist produces is gender-neutral and unbiased. It is not always obvious to the recipient of research funds what the funders' missions are. Sometimes even the latter can intend to support only gender-neutral work or even feminist work and yet make assumptions that support larger social missions of which they would disapprove were they were aware of them. For example, the understandable interests in discovering how men and women differ psychologically, biologically, or in some other way support the androcentric mission to sustain the belief that men are fundamentally different from women. Similar arguments have been made about the only apparently innocent search for racial differences. Thus mission-directed sciences can be just as "real" as those that do not carry their missions on their sleeves, so to speak.

Engineering and Technology Development

Engineering and technology development constitute another such real science. Three important shifts have changed the way these are conceptualized in the new science studies. In the first place, modern sciences cannot be separated from technology development, since their projects frequently seek to provide information to resolve what are defined as technological problems, as much military-directed or agricultural research does.[3] Moreover, scientific advances make possible new technologies and, in some contexts, make them virtually inevitable. What forces could have controlled the development of car-centered cultures in the cultural and political environment of the United States once the basic information for constructing internal combustion engines became available? Most important, sciences' own methods of inquiry are themselves technologies. A research design can usefully be understood as a production device or machine, made up of instructions, various skills and techniques, sometimes hardware, and the individuals who use and maintain these components, for interacting with natural and social worlds in order to generate distinctive types of information. And we can reflect that while sciences do make technologies available, it is equally true that new technologies make new sciences available. Photography and computers provide just two such examples of technologies that have led scientific inquiries in new directions.

Second, such research technologies are not themselves culturally neutral. Artifacts have politics, including gender politics, though they do not *determine* social consequences, as the older technological determinists supposed (Lie 1995; Wajcman

1991; Winner 1977). Gadgets, tools, machines, and built environments, among other kinds of technological achievements, make possible some kinds of social projects and limit others. They require various kinds of expertise that are rarely made available to everyone, and they organize human labor and leisure in culturally specific ways. Consider, for example, the diverse politics of birth-control devices, some of which can make it possible in a particular social environment for women to express their sexuality while controlling their own fertility or, in other environments, can ensure that poor or racially marginalized women will be prohibited from birthing the children they desire.

For these reasons, it is a mistake to think of engineering and technology development as only applied science. Instead, technology development is itself an integral part of scientific growth, and it can produce distinctive knowledge about nature's order. Gender analyses have made important contributions to such understandings. Moreover, responding to women's technological needs can advance the growth of scientific knowledge in diverse fields. However, attention to the gendering of technologies is especially important for women in the so-called developing societies, where the bad effects of development sciences and technologies on women have been a major feminist concern (Braidotti et al. 1994; *Gender, Technology, and Development* 1997ff; Harcourt 1994; Harding and McGregor 1996; Mies 1986; Shiva 1989; Sparr 1994). The de-development and mal-development of the already most economically and politically disadvantaged groups around the world, in which women and their dependents are disproportionately represented, turns out to have been a precondition for the economic growth of elites, through which benefits of development flow to those already economically and politically advantaged, in the so-called developed as well as developing world.

Natural-Social Hybrid Sciences

The fall of the absolute neutrality ideal has also improved the scientific status of such fields as medical and health sciences, environmental sciences, and others in which it has been recognized that one needs knowledge of both nature and social relations in order to understand the phenomena of interest. Bodies and their environments are influenced by social factors as well as natural causes. Social processes bring certain natural causes into play, and natural processes can stimulate social responses. One cannot even specify which features of a human or his or her local environment are due to nature and which to culture, since cultural processes shape how genes are expressed and species develop. Moreover, as we have seen above, the objects of study of the natural sciences are always socially constituted as such objects—for example, as races versus populations, as a biologically weak sex versus a physically restricted one, or as weeds versus not profitable for export, or as contributors to biodiversity. Furthermore, as historians and sociologists point out, social knowledge has always been crucial for the development of scientific processes in the history of international science, though this feature was obscured by the ideology of the neutrality ideal (Latour 1988; Schuster and Yeo 1986; Shapin 1994; Shapin and Shaffer 1985).

Feminism has long insisted that the binary of nature versus culture obscures ways that the purportedly purely natural is also a historically shifting cultural category. Such analyses have stressed the importance of exploring the joint and even coconstituting operations of nature and culture in such areas as health and environmental sciences rather than restricting funding primarily to research projects that ignore the social influences on health and sustainable environments. It is also important to consider whether gender analyses should give greater attention to ways in which the purportedly only cultural also has roots in the natural. Their failure to do so has tended to reify the cultural in just the kinds of ways that they have criticized mainstream philosophies of science for reifying the natural.

Other Cultures' Sciences

I have focused primarily on international sciences in the catalogue above of new kinds of "real sciences." However, the scientific status of many other cultures' knowledge systems also is enhanced by the demise of the absolute neutrality idea. It was precisely the contrast between purportedly value-neutral international sciences and what was considered to be "only" ethnosciences or folk sciences in other cultures, permeated by religious and other culturally local assumptions, that gave so much status to the absolute neutrality ideal of international sciences. Most obviously, other cultures have in the past also developed many kinds of effective systematic knowledge-seeking about their bodies and environments (Goonatilake 1984; Lach 1977; Watson-Verran and Turnbull 1995). Many of these continue to develop today in other cultures' medical and health systems, agricultural practices, and environmental management, to pick three of the most obvious such areas. The sciences that became international sciences have long borrowed elements of other cultures' knowledge systems, and continue to learn from them today. As I indicated earlier, acupuncture has recently been adopted into modern biomedicine for the management of chronic pain, and pharmaceutical companies are prospecting in indigenous knowledge of communities in Amazon forests and in the knowledge of Asian and other health therapies. International development agencies are learning how to support some of the existing practices of farmers in developing countries rather than replacing these with what often turned out to be inferior, scientific, modern practices (Bass 1990; Braidotti et al. 1994; Hess 1995; Shiva 1989).

There is no justification for believing that international sciences could in principle tell us everything we want to know about our bodies and their environments, now or in the future. Nature continually produces new phenomena, and cultures continuously generate new interests, discursive resources, and ways of organizing the production of scientific and technological knowledge. The world contains multiple scientific traditions, and it is crucial to the continuing creativity of each that the others flourish. Human cognitive diversity is as much a fragile and threatened resource as is nature's biodiversity. Moreover, to the extent that international sciences are embedded in the expansionist projects of the already economically and politically advantaged societies, and thus directed toward narrow, economistic, and antidemocratic conceptions of "human welfare," rather than also social, political, cultural, aesthetic, or even spiritual aspects of human development, the knowledge projects of other cultures provide especially valuable resources for guidance in understanding noneconomistic aspects of natural and social relations.

Women have made and continue to make important contributions to the knowledge traditions of other cultures. Moreover, to the extent that the gender-integrationist ideal characteristic of public agenda feminism in the United States and Europe has been less powerful in other cultures, women's and men's knowledge systems are more distinctive. Women farmers, herders, sylviculturalists, traders, healers, physicians, pharmacologists, and artisans are some of such groups that have developed distinctive knowledge traditions. Women's scientific and technological creativity is more easily visible in societies traditionally more sex-segregated than U.S. society today, yet in any context in which human activities tend to be gender segregated, women, like men, will develop and maintain distinctive systematic bodies of knowledge about the world with which they interact. This leads to a consideration of one more kind of systematic knowledge.

Everyday Science

What about the challenges to gain knowledge in everyday life? Sciences of other cultures and the natural-social hybrids mentioned earlier have often been developed through institutions and processes very different from those characteristic of the ideal of pure sciences. The availability of abstract principles to guide research and its application is more important in some kinds of sciences than in others. Farmers, fishermen, artisans, mothers, and indigenous healers also develop systematic knowledge about the constantly changing bodies and environments with which they interact, and they constantly seek to improve the knowledge they have. Indeed, some observers have argued that their work is often more original and creative than the work of highly trained scientists for whom the factorylike structure of much contemporary research blocks the possibility of their conceptualizing and designing their own research projects (Goonatilake 1984).

This kind of inquiry has been one of the major influences on feminist science studies and its philosophies of science. In everyday life, women tend to develop distinctive knowledge about their own bodies and the bodies of children, family, the sick, and the elderly that they tend. The women's health movement is one group that has "started from women's lives," as the feminist standpoint theorists put the point (Harding 1986, 1991), to ask the kinds of questions that have been ignored or devalued in the purportedly culturally neutral mainstream sciences. Feminist approaches to environmental sciences grew out of the everyday knowledge and questions of women. It is mothers who are often the first to chart patterns of neighborhood childhood sicknesses and of household water quality. Women farmers map environmental changes. And such kinds of everyday science have led to central feminist science studies concerns about whose interests are served by the projects of mainstream sciences. By starting from everyday life in order to "study up"—to critically examine the dominant institutions and their conceptual frameworks—feminist science studies has asked how to improve the very standards for what should count as objectivity, rationality, good method, and, indeed, science itself.

An Epistemological and Political Question

I have been arguing that the demise of the absolute neutrality ideal has made possible the expansion of science's horizons to include a number of other kinds of systematic knowledge-seeking with which international science conventionally contrasted its own purportedly culturally neutral results of research. Women's scientific and technological interests and desires gain status once these kinds of inquiry are also understood to be making important contributions to the growth of knowledge. Concerns to protect purportedly culture-free sciences from contamination by social values and interests can now be replaced with questions of which social values, interests, discourses, and ways of organizing the production of knowledge can and should flourish, and which should be eliminated or carefully controlled. The democratic elements of traditional "modern" scientific thinking offer great resources here, though feminist and other pro-democratic political philosophies must help us all to critically evaluate how to revise and transform such elements into ones that benefit women around the world. What should count as science will remain both an epistemological and a political question. Feminist science studies has come to have a central voice in the contemporary global project of redefining the terms of democracy. At its best, it has insisted that the democratic development of science and society requires that those who bear the consequences of science and technology policy decisions have a proportionate share in making them—in short, that women's interests and values count.

Notes

1. Indeed, it should be regarded as Eurocentric to imply, as I did above, that only the dominant science traditions today in the West are "modern sciences." All scientific tradi-

tions existing today are modern, since they have developed in response to the new ideas to which they have been exposed as well as to changing environmental conditions. I shall frequently refer to the European "modern science" tradition by another of its familiar names: "international science." This term captures the extent of its adoption today without implying that its claims are transcultural or universally valid in the conventional sense.

2. And, of course, when the cultures themselves are intentionally destroyed or happen to die out from plagues, starvation, or environmental destruction, the disappearance of their knowledge systems is only one of the losses to humanity.

3. I use the phrase "defined as technological problems," since military actions are not the only way to solve political problems, nor is the "green revolution" the only way to solve local food shortages.

Works Cited

Bass, Thomas. *Camping with the Prince and Other Tales of Science in Africa.* Boston: Houghton Mifflin, 1990.

Bloor, David. *Knowledge and Social Imagery.* London: Routledge and Kegan Paul, 1977.

Braidotti, Rosi, et al. *Women, the Environment, and Sustainable Development.* Atlantic Highlands, NJ: Zed, 1994.

Forman, Paul. "Behind Quantum Electronics: National Security as Bases for Physical Research in the U.S., 1940–1960." *Historical Studies in Physical and Biological Sciences* 18 (1987).

Galison, Peter, and David J. Stump (Eds.). *The Disunity of Science.* Stanford, CA: Stanford University Press, 1996.

Gender, Technology, and Development. New Delhi/Thousand Oaks/London: Sage Publications, 1997ff.

Goonatilake, Susantha. *Aborted Discovery: Science and Creativity in the Third World.* London: Zed, 1984.

Haraway, Donna. *Primate Visions: Gender, Race, and Nature in the World of Modern Science.* New York: Routledge, 1989.

Harcourt, Wendy (Ed.). *Feminist Perspectives on Sustainable Development.* London: Zed, 1994.

Harding, Sandra. *Is Science Multicultural? Postcolonialisms, Feminisms, and Epistemologies.* Bloomington: Indiana University Press, 1998.

——— . *Whose Science? Whose Knowledge? Thinking from Women's Lives.* Ithaca, NY: Cornell University Press, 1991.

——— . *The Science Question in Feminism.* Ithaca, NY: Cornell University Press, 1986.

Harding, Sandra, and Elizabeth McGregor. "The Gender Dimension of Science and Technology." In *UNESCO World Science Report 1996,* ed. Howard J. Moore. Paris: UNESCO, 1996.

Hess, David J. *Science and Technology in a Multicultural World: The Cultural Politics of Facts and Artifacts.* New York: Columbia University Press, 1995.

Jacob, Margaret. *The Cultural Meanings of the Scientific Revolution.* New York: Knopf, 1988.

Joseph, George Gheverghese. *The Crest of the Peacock: Non-European Roots of Mathematics.* New York: I. B. Tauris, 1991.

Keller, Evelyn Fox. *Reflections on Gender and Science*. New Haven, CT: Yale University Press, 1984.

Kuhn, Thomas S. *The Structure of Scientific Revolutions*. Chicago: University of Chicago Press, 1962.

Lach, Donald F. *Asia in the Making of Europe, Vol. 2*. Chicago: University of Chicago Press, 1977.

Latour, Bruno. *The Pasteurization of France*. Cambridge, MA: Harvard University Press, 1988.

Latour, Bruno, and Steve Woolgar. *Laboratory Life: The Social Construction of Scientific Facts*. Beverly Hills, CA: Sage, 1979.

Lie, Merete, and Anne-Jorunn Berg. "Feminism and Constructivism: Do Artifacts Have Gender?" *Science, Technology, and Human Values* 20 (1995): 332–351.

Merchant, Carolyn. *The Death of Nature: Women, Ecology, and the Scientific Revolution*. New York: Harper and Row, 1980.

Mies, Maria. *Patriarchy and Accumulation on a World Scale: Women in the International Division of Labor*. Atlantic Highlands, NJ: Zed, 1986.

Needham, Joseph. "The Laws of Nature and the Laws of Man." *The Grand Titration: Science and Society in East and West*, ed. Joseph Needham. Toronto: University of Toronto Press, 1969.

———. *Science and Civilization in China*. Cambridge: Cambridge University Press, 1954ff.

Pickering, Andrew. "Objectivity and the Mangle of Practice." *Annals of Scholarship* 8 (1992).

Plumwood, Val. "The Politics of Reason: Towards a Feminist Logic." *Australasian Journal of Philosophy* 72 (1993): 436–462.

Quine, W. V. O. "Two Dogmas of Empiricism." In *From a Logical Point of View*, ed. W. V. O. Quine. Cambridge, MA: Harvard University Press, 1953.

Rooney, Phyllis. "Recent Work in Feminist Discussions of Reason." *American Philosophical Quarterly* 31 (1994): 1–21.

Schiebinger, Londa. *Nature's Body: Gender in the Making of Modern Science*. Boston: Beacon, 1993.

Schuster, John A., and Richard R. Yeo (Eds.). *The Politics and Rhetoric of Scientific Method: Historical Studies*. Dordrecht: Reidel, 1986.

Shapin, Steven. *A Social History of Truth*. Chicago: University of Chicago Press, 1994.

Shapin, Steven, and Simon Shaffer. *Leviathan and the Air Pump*. Princeton, NJ: Princeton University Press, 1985.

Shiva, Vandana. *Staying Alive: Women, Ecology, and Development*. London: Zed, 1989.

Sparr, Pamela (Ed.). *Mortgaging Women's Lives: Feminist Critiques of Structural Adjustment*. London: Zed, 1994.

Wajcman, Judy. *Feminism Confronts Technology*. University Park: Pennsylvania State University Press, 1991.

Watson-Verran, Helen, and David Turnbull. "Science and Other Indigenous Knowledge Systems." In *Handbook of Science and Technology Studies*, ed. S. Jasanoff, G. Markle, T. Pinch, and J. Petersen. Thousand Oaks, CA: Sage, 1995.

Winner, Langdon. "Do Artefacts Have Politics?" In *Autonomous Technology*, ed. L. Winner. Cambridge, MA: MIT Press, 1977.

Laboratories Without Walls

*The Science Shop as a Model for Feminist
Community Science in Action*

→ Lisa H. Weasel

A Personal Path to Feminist Science Action

I belong to a generation of feminist scientists lucky enough to have had their feminism and their scientific training side by side, yet still not lucky enough to be able to practice a consciously feminist science within our chosen fields. By this I mean that I became a feminist as I became a scientist, that like many feminist scientists of my generation I was drawn to feminism through my politics, and to science through my passion for understanding and untangling the mysteries of nature. Behind my commitment to both science and feminism was the belief that both paths provided a means for promoting positive change in the world. Through feminist theories and community activism, I believed that I could help to understand and alleviate social inequities based on the intersecting power imbalances constructed around categories such as gender, race, class, ethnicity, age, and sexual orientation. Through my scientific work in the laboratory, I believed that I could make an active impact on people's lives by understanding and alleviating physical maladies affecting the body, such as breast cancer, autoimmune disease, and malnutrition.

Yet while these twin paths of feminism and science may have paralleled each other in the early stages of my education, I found that these two paths never fully intertwined. On the contrary, they seemed to diverge ever more and in fact threatened to pull one another off course as I made my way through graduate school, postdoctoral training, and as I entered the faculty ranks. Now, having held faculty positions in both women's studies and biology, I have at times been seen as an outsider in comparison to fellow women's studies colleagues from the humanities and social sciences, while at other times been chided and even exiled by fellow scientists for using the "F" word (*feminism*) in my courses and research. To many, I am no longer considered a "proper" scientist since I do not run a laboratory, yet my training in science has often precluded me from full membership within the supposed interdiscipline of women's studies. Looming behind this split has been my growing frustration with the lack of models for putting my feminism into action through my scientific practice, for applying the specialized knowledge and skills that I have gained through my scientific training to the kinds of issues and community activism that feminism has taught me to recognize and address.

In this sense, it seems that both feminism and science have failed to embody their supposed commitment to action in the world. The kind of research and teaching on science that has until this point been cultivated within women's studies in the academy has tended to focus on critique and philosophical issues more than practical or applied aspects of actually carrying out science from a feminist perspective, and how such a practical approach might relate to issues of alleviating oppressive power relations constructed by society. While feminist critique and philosophies of science are important, engaging, and inherently useful, one of the tenets that drew me to feminism was its commitment to integrating theory and action, an integration that I have struggled to find and construct within the bounds of science as it is contained within women's studies.

Likewise, as I have looked down on the world through the hydraulically sealed windows of my third- or fifth- or twenty-fifth-floor laboratories, or through the lenses of 10 or 20 or 20,000 multi-magnification microscopes, I have come to the equally disappointing realization that through my isolation in the laboratory and my consumption of the vast volumes of hazardous and toxic materials required for this work I am no more contributing to the alleviation of societal disease than I may be promoting its causation. Science has proven no better a route to socially engaged action than the feminist theories of science have.

As a feminist scientist, I can either view this as a bitter failure, a choice that I am once again forced to make between my love of science and my passion for the world of women's studies, between the intellectually titillating world of the academy and the embodied, grassroots approach of community activism; or, I can view this state of affairs as a necessary challenge, an invitation to seek out new models of feminist science praxis that can combine research and activism and in doing so can help to redefine the place of science within women's studies, simultaneously constructing a new relationship between the academy and the community. Obviously, I have opted in favor of this latter choice. In my academic work, I have made difficult choices that have allowed me to pursue research projects with direct community relevance, such as those integrating feminist principles into science education and outreach. As a teacher, I have taught my students in both biological science and women's studies to develop strategies and projects that bring their scientific training to bear on the community. The many projects that have stemmed from intervention assignments as well as direct student initiatives in my undergraduate classes include outreach and mentoring programs in local schools, an HIV education and prevention program for migrant farm workers, and a community water-quality monitoring program. While individually and through my students I have been able to make a commitment to an integration of science and community, I have continued to search for models for adequately institutionalizing such an integration within the academy. In doing so, I have discovered a particularly promising model that I believe could be adopted, modified, and put into practice as a means of implementing feminist science activism. The remainder of this essay is devoted to describing this model, known as the "science shop," and articulating how it might build upon and be informed by the important and already well-developed feminist theoretical studies of science to serve as a new model for implementing cross-disciplinary feminist activism partnerships between academic women's studies initiatives and local communities, while at the same time helping to center science within women's studies.

The Science Shop: Origins and Organization

The community partnership model of scientific research known as the "science shop" originated in the 1970s in the Netherlands, during an era of political reform concerning public influence and access to government-sponsored scientific research. During this time, university-based projects known as "science shops" were independently implemented at several Dutch universities, with the shared goals of encouraging "socially relevant research in the universities, to relate this work to the needs of society, and to provide client groups with technical information" (Nelkin and Rip 1979, 21).

Science shops are typically staffed by students under faculty supervision, as well as a small number of paid support staff in some cases. Most science shop–related research is carried out by students who receive university academic credit for their work under faculty supervision, usually as part of master's or doctoral theses. This is a structure that takes advantage of and fits within the standard procedures of the university: "because students are doing research and writing papers, and faculty are supervising and evaluating their work, both groups are doing what they would be doing as part of their regular workloads; thus the extra cost and time are minimal" (Sclove, Scammell, and Holland 1998, 63). Because of their independent origins, structures vary among different science shops, but all share the common goals of providing community groups who otherwise could not afford such services with access to scientific and technological expertise and problem-solving, while at the same time reorienting the research priorities of academic scientists to focus on issues with direct social impacts. Science shops typically solicit research questions from community groups or organizations, rather than from individuals. This ensures that the questions have broader merit and that solutions and resources provided will be disseminated beyond an individual level. Community groups and organizations must demonstrate that they are unable to commission such research on their own, although in some cases science shops will accept questions and research agendas from organizations and/or local governments that are willing to contribute to the cost of the research, as long as such research is socially relevant and not commercially motivated. Beneficiaries must also have a plan for implementing or applying the results of the research. Publicity campaigns involving newspaper advertisements, publicly disseminated bulletins, and other media outlets serve to inform the public about the existence of science shops and availability of their services.

The range of research questions accepted by science shops is quite broad and is in many cases interdisciplinary, particularly traversing the divide between social and natural science issues and approaches. Examples of research questions that have been pursued by science shops in the Netherlands include health effects of industrial and toxic chemicals; local environmental and ecological questions; traffic safety issues; design of household appliances for handicapped residents; recycling studies; and research documenting the competence of lesbian and gay couples as parents in comparison to heterosexual partners (Zaal and Leydesdorff 1987; Sclove, Scammel, and Holland 1998; Nelkin and Rip 1979). Many of the questions that are brought to the science shops require no further original research; for those questions that require original research, the science shop serves as both a resource and a clearinghouse, with some science shops providing links to researchers and others performing the research either on their own or together with the community groups.

Although the goal of the science shops is to redirect academic science research and as such many of the questions are likely to appear inappropriate or unacceptable within conventional academic frameworks, follow-up research on projects pursued at the Amsterdam science shop illustrates that this is not always the case. A significant number of projects resulted in scientific publications and congress papers, approximately 20 percent resulted in follow-up studies, and in one-third of the cases, the resulting output from the research was incorporated into educational materials (Zaal and Leydesdorff 1987). Other science shop projects have led to the development of new research methods and interdisciplinary collaborations (Lydesdorff and Van den Besselaar 1987). These impacts are in addition to those applications and dissemination efforts outside of the academy, and illustrate that there can be a significant overlap between research problems identified and articulated by community groups, and those deemed interesting, worthwhile, and productive within academia. Because science shop projects usually conclude with a printed research report and a press release that is widely disseminated, they also serve to bring media attention to the university and help to create a positive image of scientific research in the eyes of the public.

Historically in the United States, the role of integrating science and public concerns has been assigned to land grant universities, established over a century ago through an act of Congress. However, land grant institutions' missions differ from the science shop model in that their primary goal is to conduct and disseminate research to the public, rather than to restructure science so that community members are directly involved in defining and conducting the research. While many land grant universities continue to serve as an interface between science and the public through extension services, more recently Richard Sclove, a nuclear engineer and political scientist, has spearheaded a "community research network" movement in the United States, based on the Dutch science shop model.[1] While the model appears to be catching on, the American science shop movement has fewer direct ties to academia than do the Dutch science shops, with many of the community research institutes in the United States existing as nonprofit organizations or community centers rather than bona fide university units. This has some positive effects, in the sense that the research model used in most U.S.-based community research is more closely linked to the methods of participatory research (PR) or participatory action research (PAR) (Sclove, Scammel, and Holland 1998; for an overview on PAR see Park et al. 1993), in which community groups not only pose and articulate the questions that will be asked, but also take a lead in carrying out the research, side by side and in collaboration with so-called experts. The participatory research framework upon which many U.S.-based science shops are modeled has its origins in third world resistance movements opposing colonial and neocolonial research agendas; such participatory research efforts have been documented in Africa, Latin America, and Asia (Fals Borda and Rahman 1991; Hall et al. 1982).

The Science Shop as a Model for Feminist Science in Action

The science shop provides a model that might usefully be adapted as a means for bridging the current divide that seems to exist between feminist theory on the one hand and the goal of an activist feminist scientific practice on the other hand. As I mentioned earlier, a great deal of important theoretical work has been carried out concerning feminist critiques and epistemologies of science, but a means of putting these theoretical perspectives into scientific practice, particularly for translating them into activist scientific projects, in most cases has not been articulated. In this sense, the science shop model can provide a practical framework within which feminist critical and epistemological perspectives can be enacted and extended.

One well-developed feminist epistemological lens through which the science shop model can be viewed is that of feminist standpoint theory. While some strands of feminist standpoint theory originated from the idea that women's gendered social activities and experiences of oppression provide them with a privileged vantage point from which to construct knowledge (Rose 1983; Hartsock 1983), other more recent articulations of feminist standpoint theory have traced its deeper history as one of "criticisms of prevailing institutions, their cultures, and practices that appear when formerly silenced peoples begin to gain public voice" (Harding 1998, 149) and have expanded its implications to include an emphasis on the value of the perspective of the "outsider within" (Collins 1991). Underlying all feminist standpoint approaches is an emphasis on beginning the process of knowledge formation from marginalized perspectives, a process that problematizes conventional methods and approaches that dominant standpoints take for granted. Feminist standpoint theory is both politically and epistemologically compelling for those who wish to expand the realm of questions that are considered in science and to shift the power dynamics within and out of which scientific knowledge is created. Consistent with the goals of science shops, making science "public" requires incorporating the voices and experiences of those outside of science, those beyond the walls of the academies and industries where science tends to be conjured. Many socially relevant scientific questions that never make their way into research laboratories lie waiting to be discovered on the margins of science and society.

The science shop model provides a structure through which voices outside of the dominant discourse of science can bring their own questions into the laboratory, and through which dominant scientific practices can be critically scrutinized and reformulated by outsiders in the interest of pursuing marginalized and socially relevant knowledges. The requirement that questions brought to the science shop come from organizations or groups rather than individuals and that these groups must lack the economic base to pay for such research is designed to ensure that research questions not only are of relatively broad relevance to the community, but also that they are questions that might not normally be asked and answered within the confines of conventional scientific research. The emphasis on participatory action research methods in the U.S. science shops also promotes a further level of accessing and incorporating marginalized perspectives and of questioning conventional methods. As alluded to above, in this approach community members work side by side with scientific "experts" in creating and carrying out the research methodology and in articulating and disseminating research questions and findings. Including "outsiders" in the scientific research process can help to bring to light assumptions, biases, and inconsistencies that members of the dominant scientific community take for granted or are unable to recognize. By including marginalized and "outsider" participation in all stages of the scientific process, this approach allows for a more thorough reorientation and reconstruction of science, not only by redefining the types and kinds of questions that are asked but also by critically evaluating and reformulating research methodologies from a marginalized perspective. Collaboration between such marginalized "outsiders" and scientists with more privilege and authority is a key aspect of the participatory action research approach. As Robin McTaggart emphasizes, "Both the politics and epistemology of participatory action research require broad participation; it must not be confused with 'political activism' or 'oppositional politics' among the less powerful, the poor, or the disenfranchised. Participatory action research is an obligation undertaken by people at all levels and in all kinds of institutions who seek to develop the quality of their work and the symmetry and reciprocity of their relationships with others" (McTaggart 1997, 6).

The participatory action research process that is promoted in U.S. science shops also serves to shorten the distance between observer and observed; "it adopts a view of social science that is distinct from a view based on the natural sciences (in which the objects of research may legitimately be treated as 'things')" (McTaggart 1997, 40). Such an approach has been identified within several feminist critiques as a way of dismantling the false sense of separation between objectivity and subjectivity and of the image of the scientist as a distant, detached authority (Keller 1985; Bleier 1984). When scientific research is carried out by those whose life experiences have generated the questions, and by those who have a direct and invested interest in applications of the outcome, new kinds of questions can arise and innovative methodologies can be developed, and the false dichotomy separating observer and object of study becomes blurred. Furthermore, including the subjects of research as active participants in their own self-study can serve to challenge and redirect power relationships that are imbedded within the research-at-a-distance approach, and can help to disseminate scientific literacy within an applied context; "because participatory action researchers sought to redefine the often privileged relation of the researcher to the researched, the vindication of participatory action research methodology required more than the validity of arguments to achieve acceptance by the research establishments it confronted and by the people it claimed to support" (McTaggart 1997, 1).

Not only the approach to research but also the nature of questions generated in science shops is likely to be relevant to feminist theory. Because questions brought to science shops originate in everyday life, they tend to reach across disciplinary boundaries that are often artificially kept in check within the academy. As such, the interdisciplinary and applied nature of these research agendas is ideally suited to the kinds of collaborations that feminist theory seeks to cultivate, and can open up new kinds of research that might not be adequately addressed within a single discipline. On a practical level, women's studies programs and departments have long been characterized by commitments to common feminist social and political goals and analyses rather than a uniform subject matter or methodology. Scholars and students within women's studies programs therefore have developed skills and frameworks for carrying out interdisciplinary dialogues and research, which can be directly applied to the types of research questions generated within the science shop model.

On a practical level, the science shop model can provide an interdisciplinary, community-oriented action approach to practicing science that is consistent with feminist theories and philosophies. One example of a community-based research project that embodies such an approach is the Chicago-based Policy Research Action Group (PRAG) assessment and intervention study of refugee women's health needs (Sclove, Scammel, and Holland 1998). Based on collaborative research between a community-based organization and a student intern from Northeastern Illinois University, the project assembled a literature review and administered questionnaires to assess refugee women's access to health care. In response to their findings, the group instituted a women's health program intervention aimed at improving access and applicability of health services for refugee women (Sclove, Scammel, and Holland 1998).

Another example involves the nongovernmental organization (NGO) Center-Perzent, based in Karakalpakstan, an independent republic of Uzbekistan in Central Asia, which collaborates with several local and international universities to research and address issues relevant to women's health and the environment: "these projects incorporate women's perspective into the research and analysis of the crisis as well as directly involve them in programs such as health education and organic food farming" (Ataniyazova 1998). The numerous research and advocacy projects that Center-Perzent has undertaken include an epidemiological study of women's reproductive pathology and toxicity in a region where 90 percent of women have complications during pregnancy, 99 percent of women suffer from anemia, and the frequency of birth defects is five times higher than in Europe; a study of pesticide levels and types in food, water, and women's breast milk in an environment that has been devastated by ecological damage from intensive cotton farming and irrigation; and an investigation establishing general women's reproductive health indicators in several countries including Uzbekistan, Brazil, and Mexico (Ataniyazova 1998). New scientific research questions and findings are emerging from the community-based model embraced by Center-Prezent; for example, studies of trace element disorders and placental analysis have been used to assess maternal health and fetal exposure to environmental agents (Oral Ataniyazova, interview, August 1996). As an intervention, Center-Perzent has trained local women in the community to conduct workshops on health and environmental issues and to staff "health desks" to provide advice and information (Ataniyazova 1998).

By reorienting the kinds of questions that are asked and the ways in which scientific research is carried out, the science shop offers an avenue through which the very nature of science, its premises, practices, and applications, can be redefined within a feminist context. By soliciting its research questions from the community and developing its research methods and strategies in collaboration with "nonexperts," the science shop model allows contextualization and accountability to be built into the research approach, elements important to a feminist articulation of a scientific agenda. Structurally, the science shop can provide a site for linking scholars and community in outreach and activist efforts, further reinforcing the interaction between theory and practice that feminism embraces.

Two-Way Streets: What Feminism Can Offer the Science Shops

While offering a potential model for feminist science in action, the science shop can best be understood as a structure that can allow feminist principles to be enacted through scientific practice, rather than as a methodology guaranteed to produce a preformed, inherently feminist science. Furthermore, although liberatory in its aims, the science shop model as it has been developed to date has not been deliberately feminist in its design. Therefore, if this model is to be adapted as a way of carrying out and applying feminist science in action, it can benefit from a conscious incorporation of feminist aims and resources. In the same way that the science shop can serve as a structural model for a feminist science, the theories and practices of feminism can provide resources to support the successful functioning of science shops.

Although the theoretical underpinnings of participatory action research upon which many science shops are based has a strong connection to historical materialism and critical theory, scant attention has been paid to feminist theories or issues in the development of participatory action research approaches (Maguire 1993, 163). Despite this neglect, feminism has an important role to play in highlighting issues of gender, race, class, and other intersecting social categories within science shop practices. By drawing attention to these categories, feminism can help to reshape the aims, articulation, execution, and application of research in science shops to further redistribute scientific power and knowledge along equitable lines (Maguire 1987). For example, feminist theory would direct attention to the roles of gender, race, and class in the projects carried out by science shops. In some instances, these connections will be explicit, such as in cases relating to health issues that have direct gender, race, or class implications. For example, a group of individuals with breast cancer may seek assistance from a science shop in order to gain access to scientific information that could help them to decide which course of treatment will be most effective (see Spanier, this volume). In this case, issues of race, class, gender, and sexuality are at the fore, since the causes, effects, and potential options for treatment may be influenced by these factors (in addition to others). Different groups of individuals may need different types of information in order to make adequate decisions, and the kinds of questions posed by those who are experiencing the disease may be different from those who have primarily an intellectual or academic interest in cancer biology.

In other cases, although direct influences of these factors may not be apparent on the surface, they will still be present in the relationship between the scientific "experts" and the members of community groups in the articulation and investigation of research questions. As research is carried out and results are applied, feminism would draw attention to the composition of the research team and the power dynamics within it, to gendered language use in interpersonal interactions and in written reports, and to the composition and power relations of those who will benefit from the research. In overall evaluation of the project, feminism would lead to the inclusion of questions such as "How has power, based on gender, been redistributed or maintained by the project?" (Maguire 1987). Not only the results of the research but also the experiences and outcomes relating to participants' lives and relationships with each other must be considered. Because PAR-based science shops operate on a collaborative model in which academic researchers work side by side with the individuals posing the questions, issues of difference will naturally be present in the course of the work. By attending to these differences up front, they can be addressed and accounted for, and incorporated into the research model or format. While the traditional model of science tends to cast scientific knowledge as value-free, feminist science studies reminds us that the selectivity of the kinds of questions that are asked, articulated, and answered in science means that it is necessarily value-laden. Furthermore, when practiced without a critical lens or widespread participation, the power wielded by science can reinforce existing social inequities. By bringing different types and kinds of questions and approaches into the research process, knowledge can be restructured and power redistributed. For example, individuals living with a problem in their community, such as ecological degradation or pollution in their neighborhood, may be able to pose different types of questions and provide data and models that researchers within the academy may not be trained or able to see. On the other hand, academic researchers may have access to particular techniques or bodies of information, in this case specific data on chemical properties, health effects, or weather patterns, or expensive measuring and detection equipment, that would be otherwise unavailable to the general population. By integrating these perspectives and acknowledging their differing origins and motivations, applications can be developed that help to structure social change. Furthermore, by providing a lens through which power inequities based on gender, race, class, and other intersecting categories can be identified and dismantled, feminist theory can help to further the goals of the science shop movement in promoting community-based research.

Theoretical resources are not the only ones that feminism can offer to support and enhance the enactment of science shops. By now, feminism has amassed a certain degree of power and privilege within the academy as it has been institutionalized within women's studies programs and departments. While still marginalized within the academic hierarchy, women's studies units often have power over faculty hiring and tenure decisions, as well as control of student supervision and curriculum design. These are resources that can be drawn upon to promote and facilitate the development of science shops within academia. Because the science shop model relies upon varying levels of collaboration (between researchers within the academy; between academics and community members; between students, faculty, and community), it is a model that may be accessible and appealing to many women's studies programs. By hiring, promoting, supporting, and awarding tenure to scientists who engage in feminist community research, women's studies programs can help to reshape and reinstitutionalize scientific research agendas along feminist lines. Having scientists in women's studies departments and programs is also essential for forging connections and eliciting collaboration with university science departments, which can serve as sites for recruiting student participation, as well as provide necessary expertise and laboratory and field study resources. In an era when more attention is being given to community effects of science and improving science education at the secondary level, the emphasis on outreach that the science shop model provides can be an asset for science departments. While science shops aim to make links between the academy and the community, in this way they can also facilitate connection and collaboration within academia. By attracting and supporting students' involvement in community-based research through the science shop model, women's studies programs can reinforce and train the next generation of community-oriented scientific scholars, as well as strengthen links between feminist activism and academia.

From Theory to Practice: Promoting Feminist Science through the Science Shop Model

While the science shop model may theoretically provide an attractive structure for promoting feminist science in action, to date the science shop model has not been implemented within women's studies programs in academia or through many science-oriented feminist community organizations. In order to constructively facilitate the implementation of the science shop model within a consciously feminist context, practical steps need to be taken. Here, I will offer suggestions primarily directed at ways in which science shop models of feminist science in action can be developed through collaborative interactions between academic women's studies programs, science departments, and community groups or organizations. These suggestions focus on faculty development, community outreach and collaborations, and teaching and curriculum development.

   Although science shops need not be centered within academia, and indeed in the United States most are not, universities can provide certain resources, some

of which have been articulated above, that can support the development of community-based research. Likewise, science shops may offer attractive alternatives to
conventional scientific research aims and agendas within the academy. This is particularly true in the case of women's studies programs, which although committed
to interdisciplinarity and community outreach have not yet found sufficient models for incorporating an activist feminist scientific practice within their purview.

Faculty Development Efforts

Women's studies programs can promote an awareness of the science shop model
for practicing science and stimulate a constructive dialogue around ways in
which feminist theories can augment the practice of socially relevant and responsible science. By sponsoring seminars and invited speakers on the science shop
model and explicitly inviting scientists to attend, women's studies programs can
facilitate an awareness of this model within the academy and of its relevance to
feminism, particularly in places such as the United States, where few science
shops operate within university settings. In addition to inviting faculty, students,
and administrators to such events, active community attendance and involvement should be sought both to forge constructive collaborations and to promote
widespread awareness of the availability of community-based research opportunities. Faculty hiring decisions within women's studies programs can also take
into account this new vision of what scientists can bring to the field of women's
studies. Although hiring science faculty can seem prohibitively expensive to
women's studies programs (start-up costs for laboratories, research support, and
so on), due to the collaborative nature of the science shop model and its ability
to take advantage of conventional academic set-ups, new faculty hiring may not
be a prerequisite for beginning a science shop practice associated with a women's
studies program. By making practicing scientists in other academic departments
aware of this model, women's studies programs can actively seek out scholars
who are willing and able to support such efforts, and promote their association
and assimilation into women's studies programs. Women's studies programs can
also sponsor grant writing workshops and seminars aimed at fostering interdisciplinary, community-based science projects that incorporate feminist principles
and that involve individuals from women's studies, the sciences, and the community. The Loka Institute has compiled a listing of U.S. agencies that fund community-based research,[2] which can be used as a resource for such efforts.

Integration of Community Groups and Members

While an academic women's studies program can provide an institutional base
and resource for promoting a feminist science shop model, at the heart of the science shop is the community and its concerns. Thus, while women's studies programs can work within the academy to develop awareness and resources for

feminist science in action, it is essential that community members and groups be an integral part of all planning and promotion stages. Many women's studies programs' advisory boards include community members; this is particularly important in the case of science shops, which aim to reorient the focus of science to the needs and participation of the community. In cases where formal women's studies units do not exist or have few ties to the community, campus women's centers may provide a more accessible link between community groups and feminists in the academy. At the same time that women's studies programs sponsor seminars and workshops to promote awareness of the science shop model among faculty and students, community groups can also be invited to give presentations publicizing their concerns and needs. Women's studies units can compile databases of local community group contacts and requests, and seek to recruit interested and qualified students and faculty to interface with them. An international database listing community-based research organizations, individuals, and science shops has been compiled by the Loka Institute,[3] and can be consulted as a resource—and can be expanded by such local initiatives.

Curriculum Development and Teaching Efforts

Finally, in order to fully promote community-based, feminist science in action, we must train coming generations in methods and theories that will support an ongoing effort to make scientific practice more equitable, inclusive, and socially relevant. This requires curriculum development and teaching efforts that extend a feminist vision of science into the community, and trains students to be responsible scientists and community members. Depending on the context, these courses can be offered through women's studies, through science departments, or as part of general education, internships, or outreach activities (ideally a combination of these). Incorporating community outreach and activism into feminist science courses that already exist or specifically creating such courses is a necessary first step in teaching students how to work across theory-practice divides. Such curricular interventions are particularly important in these courses, since much of the feminist science literature does not address community or activist issues, and most areas of science fail to instruct students in the relevance of their subject to society. Incorporating descriptions of science shop efforts and community-based research projects relevant to women's issues, such as those described in this essay, can provide models and promote awareness of the progress that is being made in these areas. A "Community Report Card"[4] developed by the Women's Environment and Development Organization (WEDO) can be a useful tool for initiating and structuring student evaluations and involvement in health and environment issues in the local community. Similarly, student internships with health and environmental organizations, already a part of many women's studies programs, can serve as a link between academia and activism, and can build a foundation for future research alliances and activities. These internship experiences can be extended by requiring students to develop follow-up activities and articulate questions for future research upon completion of the internship, which can then be pursued by future interns or taken up by a faculty member. Providing credit for follow-up activities can serve to bring students' community experiences back into the academy, and provide time and space for deeper exploration of potential collaborative research topics. Literature on the science shop model and feminist perspectives on participatory action research can be incorporated into course syllabi on feminism and science, and team teaching between academics (feminists and/or scientists) and activists can be pursued as a further means of instructing students and cultivating research networks. Because science shops tend to depend heavily upon student involvement, providing structures and opportunities that allow for substantial student-community networking and collaboration is important for the development of community research networks.

Conclusion

The science shop model represents only one possible interpretation of and path toward a potential feminist science practice in action. I have chosen to focus on this model because I believe that it provides a structure that lends itself particularly well to the types of issues that feminists have critiqued and theorized within feminist science studies. Likewise, I believe that feminist theories and practices can also enhance the work of science shops, particularly by helping to center issues of power and social inequalities based on gender, race, and other identities within their research frameworks. Because it has been implemented successfully within the Dutch university system over several decades and is receiving growing interest in the United States as a model for equitable and socially relevant scientific practice, the science shop model provides a relatively well developed and effective structure for implementing community-based science within the academy. Given that many science shops within the United States are not formally connected to universities, women's studies programs can serve as a useful site for integrating community science into academia, and for helping to reorient the focus and direction of science along feminist lines. Given the need for a feminist practice of science to accompany the growing body of feminist science studies literature, the science shop offers a promising structure that can help to further feminist goals of integrating theory and practice and facilitating interdisciplinary links within and between the academy and the community.

Notes

1. Sclove is currently the executive director of the Loka Institute, a nonprofit organization dedicated to making research, science, and technology more responsive to democratically decided social and environmental concerns. The Loka Institute can be reached at P.O. Box 355, Amherst, MA 01004, or on the Internet at www.loka.org
2. A listing of organizations and agencies that fund community-based research in the United States can be found on the Loka Institute website, www.loka.org
3. Loka's Community Resource Network (CRN), an international listing of individuals and organizations interested or engaging in community-based research, is available on the Loka Institute website, www.loka.org
4. A "Community Report Card" (1992) developed by the Women's Environment and Development Organization (WEDO), available in several languages, can be obtained free of charge by writing to WEDO, 355 Lexington Avenue, 3rd Floor, New York, NY 10017. Materials can also be ordered from WEDO's website, www.wedo.org

Works Cited

Ataniyazova, Oral. "Women Respond to a Shrinking Aral Sea." Report prepared by Center-Perzent in association with Women in Europe for a Common Future, in *Women Transform the Mainstream: Eight Case Studies of Women Activists Challenging Industry, Demanding Clean Water, and Calling for Gender Equity in Sustainable Development.* New York: Women's Environment and Development Organization, 1998.

Bleier, Ruth. *Science and Gender: A Critique of Biology and Its Theories on Women.* Elmsford, NY: Pergamon Press, 1984.

Collins, Patricia Hill. *Black Feminist Thought: Knowledge, Consciousness, and the Politics of Empowerment.* New York: Routledge, 1991.

Fals Borda, Orlando, and Muhammad Anisur Rahman. *Action and Knowledge: Breaking the Monopoly with Participatory Action Research.* New York: Apex Press, 1991.

Hall, Budd, A. Gillette, and R. Tandon. *Creating Knowledge: A Monopoly: Participatory Research in Development.* Toronto: International Council for Adult Education, 1982.

Harding, Sandra. *Is Science Multicultural? Postcolonialisms, Feminisms, and Epistemologies.* Bloomington: Indiana University Press, 1998.

Hartsock, Nancy. "The Feminist Standpoint: Developing the Ground for a Specifically Feminist Historical Materialism." In *Discovering Reality: Feminist Perspectives on Epistemology, Metaphysics, Methodology, and Philosophy of Science,* ed. S. Harding and M. Hintikka. Dordrecht: Reidel, 1983.

Keller, Evelyn Fox. *Reflections on Gender and Science.* New Haven, CT: Yale University Press, 1985.

Leydesdorff, Loet, and Peter Van den Besslaar. "What We Have Learned from the Amsterdam Science Shop." In *The Social Direction of the Public Sciences: Causes and Consequences of Cooperation between Scientists and Non-Scientific Groups,* ed. Stuart Blume et al. Dordrecht: Reidel, 1987.

Maguire, Patricia. "Challenges, Contradictions, and Celebrations: Attempting Participa-
tory Research as a Doctoral Student." In *Voices of Change: Participatory Research in the
United States and Canada*, ed. Peter Park et al. Westport, CT: Bergin and Garvey, 1993.
——— . *Doing Participatory Research: A Feminist Approach*. Amherst, MA: Center for In-
ternational Education, 1987.
McTaggart, Robin. "Reading the Collection." In *Participatory Action Research: International
Contexts and Consequences*, ed. Robin McTaggart. Albany, NY: SUNY Press, 1997.
Nelkin, Dorothy, and Arie Rip. "Distributing Expertise: A Dutch Experiment in Public
Interest Science." *Bulletin of the Atomic Scientists* 35 (1979): 20–23, 54.
Park, Peter, Mary Brydon-Miller, Budd Hall, and Ted Jackson. *Voices of Change: Participa-
tory Research in the United States and Canada*. Westport, CT: Bergin and Garvey, 1993.
Rose, Hilary. "Hand, Brain, and Heart: A Feminist Epistemology for the Natural Sci-
ences." *Signs* 9 (1983): 73–90.
Sclove, Richard, Madeleine Scammell, and Breena Holland. *Community Based Research in
the United States: An Introductory Reconnaissance*. Amherst, MA: Loka Institute, 1998.
Zaal, Rolf, and Loet Leydesdorff. "Amsterdam Science Shop and Its Influence on University Research: The Effects of Ten Years of Dealing with Non-Academic Questions."
Science and Public Policy 14 (1987): 310–316.

Feminist Science Studies, Objectivity, and the Politics of Vision

Valerie Kuletz

Nature and the Nuclear Landscape

Feminist science studies concerns "nature" in all its trope-laden complexity. It's about how we interpret nature, construct it, interact with it. It's about who gets to name it, who gets to own it, and who holds legitimate control over its representation. In most fields—but particularly in the study of nuclear landscapes—all of these interactions over "nature" are highly contentious. Nature here is not a thing-in-itself, a gene, for instance, or an ecosystem, from which we can separate ourselves, our cultures, or our politics. Rather, it is, as Donna Haraway (1997) describes it, something more akin to "heterogeneous relationality"; or, as I describe it in *The Tainted Desert* (1998), an intersubjective process of relation. As Haraway (1997), Harding (1991), Longino (1990), and many others have taught us, this complex relationality of nature—which includes us—is what feminist science studies is about. It's about a process and practice of knowing that is ongoing. If we understand nature in this way we cannot pretend to isolate it from the cultural and political fields through which we constitute it. "Objectivity," then, in a feminist science study of nature, requires inclusion of its interconstitutive social and political fields, of which we, as practitioners, are part.

Whether it takes form as a subatomic particle, a human body, or an ecosystem, at every level of scale, for human beings, "nature" is culturally and historically constructed. For example, before nature was an ecosystem constructed within a language of cybernetic inputs and outputs based on a systems electromechanical model derived largely from engineering, nature was a holistically balanced and ordered community based on a functionalist organismic model. "Nature's" move from organism to ecosystem is accompanied by economistic analogies and metaphors, in which bioeconomic ecology mirrors post–World War II capitalist political-economy. While well known among science studies scholars, this particular representational history about "nature" bears repeating.

321

It's a history that reminds us to stay vigilant in the midst of the powerful and convincing unexamined tropes for nature within which we are enmeshed.

In my work on the nuclear landscape, "nature" exists on multiple levels, from the human-created transuranic elements such as plutonium, to the human bodies whose genetic structures and cellular behavior are modified by such elements. "Nature" also pertains to landscapes, such as desert valleys, that are used to test nuclear weapons devices, as well as pertaining to the mountains and salt caverns in which humans bury transuranic elements in the form of high-level radioactive waste. In the nuclear landscape "nature" is also a highly contested field of social struggle, fetishization, imagination, political power plays, celebrations, fears, and constructions of self and society. This being the case, both scientific and nonscientific representations of nature, and practices with nature, require vigilance, constant reinterpretation, reassessment, and self-critique. It's a practice of ongoing negotiation with nature—human and nonhuman.

Understanding "nature" in the nuclear landscape requires active awareness of three distinct but interrelated issues. The first concerns the extraordinarily political nature of vision; the second concerns the ongoing multiethnic struggles over the meaning and use of "nature"; and the third concerns how science, or scientific knowledge, is used as a mechanism of exclusion. Together, these issues call attention to the question of objectivity, which—in the study of militarized science—is problematic in the extreme. While not attainable in a universal or absolute sense, objectivity is enhanced by a commitment to the politics of vision, recognition of multiethnic contestation, and recognition of the exclusionary principle in a great deal of scientific practice. Unfortunately, too many scientists working in this highly contested domain get positioned (by government and industry forces) outside the social unrest swirling about them, as though their work cannot or should not be concerned with the political and cultural nature of the world in which they practice their craft, or, indeed, of which their craft is constituted.

But political and cultural their work is, as is the nuclear landscape itself. The nuclear landscape is the material manifestation of the merging of Cold War politics with certain scientific beliefs and practices common to the second half of the twentieth century. Nature here became the experimental field upon which a new and well-funded militarized science emerged and proceeded to overdevelop itself with strong steroidlike injections of Cold War money. Nature has responded to the coupling of science and war. The offspring of such a coupling is revealed in the constellation of pollution sites across the western United States, and in the bodies of the victims of radioactive fallout or radioactive waste pollution, which register as intimate battles fought over cancer, miscarriages, childhood deformities, and death. Part of the politics of vision concerning my work in this landscape was to reveal the far-reaching extent of this legacy of experimentation, in which vast geographies of desert and sky became the laboratories of war. In the process I discovered many groups engaged in battles over compensation for illness (such as uranium miners and fallout victims), over the siting of deep-geologic, shallow, or temporary nuclear waste dumps at places like New Mexico's Waste Isolation Pilot Project (WIPP) or Nevada's Yucca Mountain,[1] and over the question of possible contamination from the U.S. nuclear weapons complex. Inhabitants of the nuclear landscape are struggling with what has happened to them in the past, as well as what they fear will happen in the future as the Department of Energy plans the disposal of tens of thousands of tons of nuclear waste and begins the construction of a new nuclear weapons complex for the twenty-first century.

In these struggles I have sometimes found scientists fighting scientists (demonstrating the malleability of scientific "facts"), but mostly it was nonscientists who were struggling—local people, indigenous people, and environmentalists—as they confronted scientific "experts," often employed by large corporations (such as Anaconda or Westinghouse) or employed by powerful government agencies (such as the Department of Energy or the Department of Defense). Most compelling to me was the struggle of indigenous peoples against those who ran the uranium mining concerns, the U.S. nuclear testing program, and the toxic waste consortiums. Here the power differentials were enormous, matching the nearly insurmountable differences in perception of the environment held by each of these groups. Such differences—concerning both political power and epistemology—make communication between the different parties very difficult. While not present in large numbers, American Indian people were (and still are) everywhere in the nuclear landscape—at all concentrated sites of nuclear activity within the larger nuclear landscape, in the uranium mining fields, around the nuclear testing ranges, living next to the deep-geologic repositories, and targeted (by both industry and the U.S. government) for temporary high-level nuclear waste storage sites. Although ubiquitous, Indian people are often invisible, especially to the forces of power surrounding them. There are many examples of this invisibility: their presence was not taken into consideration when nuclear weapons were tested in Nevada (resulting in radioactive fallout); they were not taken into consideration when the DOE released radioactive materials from experiments in New Mexico (resulting in radioactive fallout over Pueblo communities); they were not included in epidemiological studies of radioactive fallout in government-sponsored studies; and the list goes on.

The field of difference that I encountered—between local and indigenous groups who understand nature one way, and government and scientific groups who understand nature very differently—was the framework in which the three trajectories of concern mentioned above began to take shape. Fundamentally, the most important difference between these two groups concerns objectivity: whether one holds an intersubjective view of nature, or whether one "objectifies" nature, making an epistemological separation between subject and object, self and other, nature and culture.

Vision

The Tainted Desert (1998), from which the following section is extracted, is the product of over seven years of study and fieldwork in the American Southwest, where I investigated the impact of nuclearism and militarization on the land and on the various communities living there, primarily (although not exclusively) American Indian. Perhaps the most interesting aspect of this work from my perspective concerned vision and invisibility. For most people, and even for a semi-outsider like myself, it is easiest to begin with an investigation of that which is most easily seen—the "legitimate" accounts of nature supporting a view of the region as an experimental laboratory for waste disposal or weapons testing. Thus, I talked with scientists (many of whom were employed by the Department of Energy and the Department of Defense or by large corporations contracting with the government) and studied the narratives of geologists, physicists, volcanologists, hydrologists, ecologists, environmental scientists, and archaeologists. Often, although not always, related to this group were the ever-present government bureaucrats and corporate representatives—those who choose not to see the cancers in Indian communities if they cannot be "scientifically" correlated with uranium mining, nuclear testing, or toxic waste dumping (which was unregulated until the 1970s). Often there exist multiple and sometimes conflicting scientific narratives about the effects of radiation on downwinders, uranium mining villagers, or communities close to nuclear waste dumps. When governments and corporations choose not to see the harmful effects of toxic contaminants it becomes most expedient for them to embrace the scientific reports that are financially most beneficial to them and their shareholders—that is, those that find no correlation.

Seeing the unseeable in this domain was more difficult. It became an epistemological practice and a passion. What at first seemed to be sparse and uninhabited, empty, vast desert space soon became a collection of interrelated, multilayered, highly textured, and hotly contested socio-natural environments. Seeing the obscured, the secret, and the hidden required time in the field at sites of public protest with "oppositional" groups, or making contact with Indian people in private homes and tribal council halls. Such people live on the margins, or on the edge of military reservations, uranium mining fields, and nuclear waste sites. Indeed, Indian people have lived along the edge of militarized science since its inception with the transformation of the West after World War II, but, outside of tourism, they remain largely invisible to most Euramericans. Seeing the obscured or invisible also required research into recently declassified documents, such as the President's Advisory Committee's report on human radiation experiments, as well as investigating countless activist and military watchdog organizations' documents and maps. Another avenue into the unseen was provided by Indian newspapers and other "subaltern" artefacts, which document what's going on in Indian country, and which rarely receive exposure in traditional news venues.

Although visible and invisible narratives about nature are often very much at odds with one another, if put together, they produce a more comprehensive field of study about nature and society in this part of the world—one that's inclusive, not exclusive. By enlarging the field of study, the politics of vision can simultaneously facilitate objectivity as well as support the goals of environmental justice.

Contestation

Because accounts of nature vary so dramatically in the nuclear landscape, sites of multiethnic struggle are everywhere. The hearings on uranium mining reclamation at the Laguna Pueblo—the subject of the extract below—constitute only one site of multiethnic struggle among many. In addition, demonstrations outside the Nevada Test Site are ongoing sites of struggle over land-use, nature, militarized science, and Western Shoshone sovereignty rights (the Nevada Test Site is on Western Shoshone land by right of the Treaty of Ruby Valley). In the same geographic region as the Nevada Test Site there exist important multiethnic demonstrations against the use of Yucca Mountain (a holy mountain to the traditional tribes of the area) as a high-level nuclear waste repository. One of the most striking examples of contestation here was the time Indian ceremonial demonstrations were held on the northwest flank of the mountain while (in one of the largest earth science projects in history) scientists and engineers drilled into the southeast side of the mountain in preparation for creating one hundred miles of tunnels meant to contain nuclear waste forever. The cresting ridge of Yucca Mountain was the dividing line between vastly different activities, forms of knowledge, and understandings of power. These two groups were aware of each others' presence as, together, they engaged in the dance of conflict on Yucca Mountain.

Sites of struggle, especially between groups with vastly different worldviews, are richly textured places that reveal the social constructedness of nature by means of contrast—including how science constructs nature. Sites of struggle are also composed of actors who are galvanized to tease out, or unmask, the political and cultural situatedness of their opponents' "facts." Everyone here becomes a deconstructionist, at least temporarily, as they attempt to delegitimate their opponents' claims of truth. Indians, locals, and environmentalists accuse scientists working for the government of "bias," while some scientists at the Yucca Mountain Project accuse environmentalists of distortion of the "facts," and Indians of strategic myth making. What is most important is that these sites of struggle propel all the players into engagement, so that everyone is "marked" in the process of marking others. Here, a feminist science study is synonymous with active engagement, and the practitioner of such studies becomes himself or herself one of the marked or situated players. Thus, a field of inquiry that includes oppositional voices and bodies is necessarily large and extended, approaching Helen Longino's concept of the broad inclusive field upon which social knowledge can practice "objectivity."

What the activists are saying in the nuclear landscape is that they be included in decisions about what is studied and how it is studied. All of this translates to a demand to open the field of investigation. Science, if separated from its cultural and political context, is not enough to inform decisions pertaining to the siting of nuclear waste. The nuclear waste experiment at Yucca Mountain or the experimental bombing laboratory at the Nevada Test Site includes the local activists— their bodies, their families, their communities. They are part of the experiment that is called a nuclear waste dump out in the desert and they want to be recognized as such. Indeed, it is no more than the right of the experimental subject to know the nature and possible effects of the test he or she undergoes and to give or withhold consent. To not grant that right is to perpetuate the radiation experiments of the 1950s.

It would be nice to be able to create such an open field without antagonistic struggle, but power relations and inequities will always disrupt the social ideal of a "level playing field." For now, multiethnic struggle continues along the razor-sharp line between "us" and "them." And here lies a challenge. How does a feminist science study negotiate such agonistic confrontations? Where do we stand in this bifurcated field of contestation? The struggles become so heated and divisive between government or industry-sponsored scientists and activist-supported scientists and nonscientists that communication—which is necessary for objectivity— becomes nearly impossible. Because of this, it becomes imperative that we find a way to negotiate these deeply troubled waters, while not silencing anyone. This is exactly the challenge that faces the practitioners of feminist science studies as we move out of the academy and into the field of contestation—a field at once contentiously messy and very promising. However powerful, the traditional scientific model for producing knowledge—even the ecological model—is not sufficient to adequately address social, political, and cultural problems (including environmental problems). This is not to say it isn't extremely useful; it is. But since science is ultimately *practiced* out in the messy world, in society, it needs to be seen as capable of producing only what it does, and that is partial knowledge. If we, as feminist science studies scholars, keep this in mind, we will have come a long way on the path toward communication between opposing parties in the field.

Exclusion

Exclusionary science does not help us achieve that comprehensive field of social knowledge so crucial to the pursuit of objectivity. In my work on nuclearism in the Southwest, where I attended Department of Energy–sponsored community meetings called scoping sessions and open hearings (where the DOE, by law, is required to meet with the community about new nuclear weapons complex facilities planned for their region), it was clear to me that so-called objective scientific facts were repeatedly marshaled against those who would question government and industry—this, in a forum purporting to be an open arena of community debate and discussion. Anyone who has attended these meetings is familiar with these tactics. Having witnessed such meetings numerous times it is my view that Department of Energy bureaucrats use the exclusionary tactic purposefully and strategically, while scientists (whom the DOE brings in as experts) do so sometimes unconsciously, and sometimes quite consciously. However, while sometimes seemingly unconsciously, scientists do make a choice to testify on behalf of the government, and so cannot ever be completely unaware of the political aspect of their alliances. Those who opposed the DOE are characterized often as emotional, ignorant, irrational, or as trouble-makers. Although this is an old story—at least as old as the anti-nuclear movement itself—the problem still remains with us. Scientific expertise (and the use of specialized scientific language) continues to be used to silence questions about health and the possible harmful effects of certain scientific-industrial or scientific-military activities, as the following extract from *The Tainted Desert* (chapter 2, 19–37) on uranium mining demonstrates. If science excludes social context, it can much more easily be used as an exclusionary tool. The message is that if scientific "facts" constitute unchanging, incontestable truths (unaffected by or, more appropriately, not constituted by various interests— commercial, military, national, or otherwise), then we need only listen to "reason" for oppositional struggle to end. However, radioactive mining, nuclear testing, and waste burial experiments (and I do mean experiments) are seriously dangerous practices, all of which include nearby human and nonhuman communities. Thus, it is not incorrect to say that, in these cases, the scientists' laboratories are the people's lives themselves. One way to demonstrate the fallibility of what seem to be incontestable scientific "facts" is to counter them with other scientific "facts." In the nuclear landscape this occurs at all sites of contestation. So-called reputable studies directly contradict the findings of other so-called reputable studies. The rift at Yucca Mountain between the scientists employed by the State of Nevada (which is opposed to nuclear waste in Nevada) and those employed by the Department of Energy (which supports nuclear waste in Nevada) is a case in point. Radioactive contamination at particular sites is said to be harmless by some scientists while it is said to be dangerous by others. In either case, the community is too often left outside such assessments. In my own work as a feminist science studies scholar I was committed to the inclusion of the concerns and knowledge of the surrounding communities, as well as both sets of contradictory scientific pronouncements, if they existed.

How science is conducted also contributes to its propensity to be used as an exclusionary tool, and is linked to the issue of vision and invisibility. In the case of the impact of radioactive fallout from above-ground nuclear testing at the Nevada Test Site on surrounding communities in the 1950s, 1960s, and 1970s, the few epidemiological studies that were done did not take into consideration different living habits of rural Indian groups compared to non-Indians living in urbanized places like Las Vegas. By not seeing or listening to Native peoples in the region, and thus not recognizing different eating and living habits among them (many of whom drank unprocessed water and ate wildlife and wild plants), epidemiologists studying harmful effects of radiation contamination had no way of *seeing* that Indians were ingesting greater amounts of contaminated food and water. Neither can we absolve ourselves from such "biased" studies by arguing that they were done by scientists in the past, when they didn't know any better. Recent studies conducted in the 1980s and 1990s on the effects of fallout were as bereft of Indian living conditions and practices as older studies had been.

Conclusion

Multiethnic struggle and science used as a mechanism of exclusion both concern invisibility, the invisibility of particular peoples in the nuclear landscape. These "virtual uninhabitants," also called by the U.S. government the "low-use segment of the population," are part of the scientific field in these scientific-militarized landscapes. To bring them into the field of scientific consideration is to include environmental and social justice into the construction of nature in this part of the world. These are the people who insist that Yucca Mountain, or the Nevada Test Site, or New Mexico's Grants Uranium Belt be seen as nature whose meaning goes beyond that of being only an object of experimentation, a nuclear testing laboratory, or an extraction landscape. That trope-laden interrelational, intersubjective process called "nature," which everyone is fighting over, has many, many meanings, and it is a site of different and conflicting engagements. It is a wasteland, an outdoor laboratory, a toxic container, a holy mountain, traditional homeland, a spiritual landscape, a complex ecosystem, and so much more. It is an environment defined by its aridity by some, and by others by its underground water and healing resources. Objectivity in this field of nature, then, requires that we consider it all. In order to consider it, we first have to be able to see it, which is why, for me, feminist science studies begins with the politics of vision.

The section, Environmental Justice in Uranium Country, that follows is taken from the second chapter of *The Tainted Desert*. Within this extract the reader is presented with an example of the three issues detailed above: the politics of vision, multiethnic struggle, and scientific exclusion. As indicated above, these three issues emerged in many parts of the nuclear landscape and as such were documented in the course of my book. They are found from the Yucca Mountain Project in Nevada to the rad-waste dumps surrounding Los Alamos National Nuclear Laboratory in New Mexico. The Grants Uranium Belt is but one more example of an environment that cries out for a feminist science study dedicated to social and environmental justice.

Environmental Justice in Uranium Country

The Uranium Story

On a crisp autumn afternoon in 1995 my husband and I drove west from Albuquerque to the Laguna Pueblo and then to the small village of Paguate to interview Mrs. Dorothy Purley, a Laguna Pueblo woman who had worked in New Mexico's Grants uranium district when its mines were viable. Paguate is an old village, the requisite Catholic church at its center, with dirt roads winding around clusters of small, earth-colored adobe dwellings. To get to Paguate we had to drive through the recently capped-off Jackpile-Paguate uranium mine. The disrupted landscape appeared endless; one could not see where the mine began and where it ended — it was everywhere. From Mrs. Purley's kitchen, its walls painted a brilliant turquoise blue, I could see the massive mine stretching out in all directions. I could also see the enlarged thyroid on Dorothy's neck. She later confirmed she was suffering from cancer, which is not uncommon in this section of the nuclear landscape. As she told me:

> My mother died of it . . . my brother died of it! My aunt! How many aunts and how many uncles have died? And you know it's just a shame that the DOE doesn't believe what's going on. . . .
>
> I'm in that same situation right now. This cancer has really ruined my health. . . . You know it really hurts, and I'm standing here living on borrowed life right now. I don't know when my time is going to expire, but all I do is keep praying that God will continue to give me my strength. . . . I'm too young to die. I'm not ready to die. That's why I'm up and about, going here and there [speaking on behalf of radiation victims]. When they call me, I go![2]

At first Dorothy stayed home because she felt ashamed of her sickness, but her sister convinced her to make her story public, even within her own community, to break the unspoken code of silence. As her sister said: "People have to know what's wrong, people have to see what's wrong, maybe that way our people will understand what is going on on the Laguna Reservation, mainly in Paguate."[3] Dorothy said that a nineteen-year-old had recently passed away because of prostate cancer, as had a fifteen-year-old with leukemia; that her brother-in-law had skin cancer; and that the number of miscarriages on the reservation had increased radically since the uranium mining began, as well as birth defects and serious respiratory and allergy ailments. The list of radiation-related incidents was not unlike that enumerated by the Moapa Paiute women living near the Nevada Test Site. Only the Laguna landscape was pitted with uranium mines instead of bomb craters.

Those who have attempted to inform the public about uranium mining and milling in the Four Corners area refer to the postwar period as a "hidden holocaust," a tragic legacy of the Cold War. Still, today, few Americans are aware of this particular story of national sacrifice. Most tourists speak about the Four Corners area with admiration for its beauty and share the colonist's fascination with its "picturesque" Indian cultures. Uranium fields aren't on the AAA road map of Indian country.

The Four Corners area, where New Mexico, Arizona, Utah, and Colorado meet, contains two-thirds of U.S. uranium deposits, most within reservation boundaries. Located within much of the Navajoan Desert, or Painted Desert (also regarded as an extension of the Great Basin), this uranium-rich area of the Colorado Plateau is known as the Grants Uranium Belt. It is the first node on the network of pollution sites stretching out across the map of the nuclear landscape.

Arid-ecosystems geologists who promote hazardous waste disposal in desert regions describe the region this way:

> [The Navajoan Desert] is located in northeastern Arizona, southeastern Utah, and the northwestern corner of New Mexico and is best correlated with the exposure of the Chinle Formation, which contains variously colored clay shales. Most of the area is composed of valley slopes, plains, and badlands, located between sandstone hogbacks. *The Chinle Formation is of interest to the energy industry because of the naturally occurring deposits of uranium in the interbedded sandstone and conglomerate strata and the clays of the deep shale beds, as well as oil and gas deposits in deeper formations* [emphasis added]. The clays were formed in swamplands and frequently have high concentrations of smectite (a swelling clay) that may reduce the hydraulic conductivity of the soil, an important consideration in waste disposal facility siting (Reith and Thomson 1992, 38–39).

This geologic discourse is typical of those that, while noting the importance of these formations for "the energy industry," leave out the existence of its human inhabitants, many of whom are Indian. What first appears as a purely objective scientific account upon closer inspection is little of the sort; it is an account for use by the energy industry. However, living on the "Chinle Formation" is one of the largest concentrations of Indians in North America, as well as a significant number of Spanish-speaking people.

At the height of the second uranium boom in the late 1970s, the Bureau of Indian Affairs "approved 303 uranium leases covering 250,000 Indian acres in the region, and the federal government estimated a total of 3.5 million acres, including federal uranium, were going to be developed" (Ambler 1990, 150). Near the Navajo Reservation, at the Laguna Pueblo, more uranium mining and milling occurred, most notably the Jackpile-Paguate mine—until 1980 the largest uranium mine in the world (and the largest ever in the United States), covering approximately 2,800 acres. During its thirty-year operation, the mine produced 22 million tons of ore and removed 44 million tons of materials from three open pits and several underground mines (U.S. Department of Interior 1986). This was the mine I gazed out upon from the window of Dorothy Purley's kitchen. Uranium development's legacy has been one of a severely polluted environment, human and nonhuman radiation contamination, cancers, birth defects, sickness, and death. Health risks associated with uranium mining and milling have been identified and examined by different investigators and reported in a variety of sources including the Southwest Research and Information Center publications and the *New England Journal of Medicine* as well as others (see Taylor 1983; Samet et al. 1984; Navajo Health Authority 1981; Robinson 1990).[4]

In seeking federal assistance to study the effect of low-level radiation on the health of their children, Navajo health officials called attention to at least two preliminary studies—one conducted by the March of Dimes (principal investigator Dr. L. Shields) and the other by the Navajo Health Authority (principal investigator Dr. D. Calloway). Calloway's (1983) study suggested that Navajo children may have a five times' greater rate of bone cancer and a fifteen times' greater rate of ovarian and testicular cancer than the U.S. average. However, despite these preliminary findings, no funding was granted for extended epidemiological studies of the impact on Navajos living near uranium tailings and mines (Southwest Research and Information Center 1983).

Further extending the nuclear landscape and causing harm to those who live there, millions of gallons of water in the Four Corners area were subjected to radiation pollution by the extractive processes of uranium mining.

Science as a Mechanism of Exclusion

Today—because they are "invisible"—the uranium mines and tailings are, for the most part, left unreclaimed. Although a 1983 Environmental Protection Study confirmed that the Navajo Reservation alone had approximately one thousand significant nuclear waste sites, the Environmental Protection Agency (EPA) deemed them all "too remote" to be of "significant national concern" (Churchill 1993, 271). A 1978 study by Los Alamos National Laboratory concerning rehabilitation of land and water contaminated by uranium mining and milling offered one solution: to zone such areas as forbidden to human habitation (Dreeson 1978). A report in 1972 by the National Academy of Science suggested that the Four Corners area be designated a "national sacrifice area" (Churchill 1993, 275).

Other scientific accounts, as noted below, were completely contrary to these findings and denied that any significant pollution problems existed or that adverse health effects could be associated with living in the region. Though seemingly different in content, all these reports belie the same prejudice: the land and by implication the people living on the land were better left ignored. That is, neither was worth saving.

To understand how an entire society could ignore an environmental disaster on the scale of the open-pit uranium mines, it is necessary to examine some of the ways scientific discourse can be used as a mechanism of exclusion, particularly when it is marshaled against anecdotal evidence presented by nonscientists (evidence like that offered by Dorothy Purley). In the case of the Grants uranium district, anecdotal statements from Native speakers may be in themselves incontestable—but they carry no weight in establishing a causal link between the reported illnesses and the existence of radioactive mine tailings or unreclaimed pits. Although anecdotal testimony has sometimes been accepted in court cases regarding other issues, the history of anecdotal statements in this region is one marked by what social scientists call *delegitimation*. Anecdotal statements about the health risks associated with unreclaimed uranium mines and tailings are gathered in preliminary studies or as testimony in open hearings and may be incorporated into draft environmental-impact statements but do not constitute scientific evidence. They are simply reported; any claim they may have on the truth can be—and in some cases has been—diminished by the overwhelming weight of contrary "scientific" evidence. The statements are, in effect, excluded from consideration, and the people who speak them are, by extension, excluded from any decision-making process bearing on their welfare.

Many "preliminary studies" suggested serious health risks to children in communities near abandoned uranium districts. One preliminary study showed "a twofold excess of miscarriages, infant deaths, congenital or genetic abnormalities, and learning disabilities among uranium-area families" (Shields 1992, 500) compared with Navajo families in nonuranium areas. Even after being informed of these and other findings, no federal or state agencies provided funding for further study. In fact, in 1983, one agency, the Indian Health Service (a division of the U.S. Department of Health and Social Services) had sent a report to Congress ("Health Hazards Related to Nuclear Resources Development on Indian Land," 1983) stating that there was "no evidence of adverse health effects in Indians in uranium development areas and that there is no need for additional studies or funding for such studies" (Taylor 1983). The one "official" scientific investigation of birth defects that was funded, primarily by the March of Dimes Birth Defects Foundation, was too "small" to render "significant" results. Its conclusion states: "It was unlikely that our small study population would have demonstrated a real effect in terms of statistical significance" (Shields 1992, 550).

Since statistical significance in epidemiological studies generally requires large study populations, Indian communities are disadvantaged because they are usually quite small.

Thus, inadequate funding and the shortcomings of statistical analyses for small populations can result not only in a lack of "official" documentation to support the "preliminary" and "anecdotal" knowledge of health risks, but in the production of official documentation that is contrary to the preliminary studies. For the communities living in uranium districts, a little (underfunded) science is *not* better than no science at all. What gets circulated, and what has credibility, is the "official" report—even if that report is based on inadequate foundations.

Scientific knowledge in this contested terrain is deeply influenced by state and federal agencies, funding, and many other nonscientific factors. Epidemiological studies are costly, as are the "experts" who administer them. Poor communities do what they can, but their findings have little purchase when it comes to lawsuits against state agencies or private companies. In the end, we must look seriously at the discrepancies between community-sponsored "preliminary" studies and federally funded "expert" accounts of health risks.

In the 1986 open hearings concerning the environmental and human impact of the unreclaimed Jackpile-Paguate mine, a radiation scientist representing Anaconda argued that the individual lifetime risk of cancer in the most exposed individuals at Paguate (the village overlooking the 2,800-acre mine) under the no-action alternative (the proposal that Anaconda need not engage any reclamation of the massive mine) is far less than the lifetime risk of dying due to excess cosmic rays received by living in Denver, Colorado (U.S. Department of Interior 1986, A-10). In his testimony, this specialist does not tell the audience how he arrives at this analogy, nor what the standards are for such a statement. He does not tell the audience that standards on the hazards of radiation exposure have changed drastically over time, such that smaller and smaller doses are recognized as sufficient to cause cancer. Since he is an "expert" in this field, his analysis overrides the anecdotal statements of the residents claiming to be adversely affected.

Public hearings for the environmental-impact draft statement for the Jackpile-Paguate mine's reclamation project began with no fewer than ten Ph.D.'s and other "technical" experts in a variety of scientific disciplines, including a mining engineer, a plant ecologist, a radiation ecologist, an expert in biomedicine, and others. All testified in obfuscating technical language that America's largest uranium mine could be safely left unreclaimed. All were under contract with Anaconda.

Even if we ignore the fact that these testimonies are paid for by the uranium mining company, the discrepancy between these statements and earlier studies of the general area made by Los Alamos scientists and those made by the National Academy of Science (mentioned above), in which the uranium mining districts were called "national sacrifice areas" and zones in which human habitation should be forbidden, cannot be ignored. Since the Jackpile-Paguate mine was the largest in the area (and one of the largest in the world), it would be safe to assume that it was included in these assessments. In addition, scientists agree universally that uranium mining at this mine has caused cancer and death in miners (if not in nearby residents). Uranium ore and tailings, as well as the water used in the mining process, are known to be radioactive.

The role of the scientist providing "expert knowledge" and scientific validation for corporations and the government in determining environmental and health standards for the production, processing, and disposal of radioactive materials and for mine reclamation demonstrates a persistent collaboration between some scientific knowledge producers and what can only be described as highly biased interests (in our example, the subsidiary of the Atlantic Richfield Corporation, Anaconda).[5] Of course, such collaborative relations do not include all scientists. Scientific "expert" knowledge is also marshaled *against* government and industry interests by anti-nuclear activists so that "objective" testimony ends up comprising multiple voices, demonstrating the malleability of scientific data and its interpretation. Even among partners, such as certain scientific communities and energy industries, disagreement exists. "Science" does not come as a hegemonic package of truth when its subject matter concerns politically charged and contested areas such as land and the environment. Though the report from the Anaconda-hired scientists (claiming the uranium mine harmless) seems to contradict the Los Alamos National Laboratory report (claiming the uranium district uninhabitable), the underlying message and the political ends appear to be the same: that the Indians, if not expendable, can be displaced. From the Indian perspective displacement may mean the same as expendability.[6]

Because scientific analysis is costly and requires specialized skills, open hearings more often than not consist of contestations between "expert" scientific knowledge and local "commonsense" anecdotal knowledge. Confronting the "experts" in formal public hearings, such as those held for the reclamation of the Jackpile-Paguate mine, often feels like an exercise in futility—especially when technoscientific discourse is marshaled in opposition to "simple" fears and commonsense knowledge—to those most affected, the local populace.

The discourses of science (and of the law) are formidable tools for legitimating dubious claims and delegitimating counterclaims. As became apparent in the hearings on reclamation mandates, Anaconda attempted to shield itself with scientific discourse that claimed that one of the world's largest uranium mines did not need to be reclaimed, that it could be left open with its tailings blowing in the wind, that it posed no risk to human or animal health. In response to the "experts," the Pueblo Indians of Laguna cited case after case of deaths caused by cancer. As Herman Garcia of the village of Paguate commented:

and now I think the reason why the people in the Pueblo of Laguna are kind of concerned about this cancer illness is because like—and please don't compare it with the City of Albuquerque or New York. I come from a very small village, and I don't know how you'd figure that out; but, last year, in the Village of Paguate alone, we lost five people from cancer . . . these people that I'm talking about were nondrinkers and nonsmokers. . . .

That's why we're having such a hard time, and I think we've been as reasonable as we possibly could be, but how much longer do we have to wait to cover the land, the one we consider dangerous. I have to work because I can't really go by these studies, I'm no expert, and I think it would really make me feel good—like the ponds we consider hazardous, I'd like for some of these experts to go out there and swim in those ponds. Then when I see them swim, then maybe I feel more secure, and we might be able to swallow some of these studies that have been introduced here today (U.S. Department of the Interior 1986, statement by Mr. Herman Garcia of Paguate Village).

Besides presenting the oral accounts in open hearings, Anaconda substantiated its claims with voluminous scientific texts in the form of technical documentation produced by expert witnesses. In addition to the obscurity of the language, the sheer volume of documentation functions as a barrier to the uninitiated.

The dominance of text-based scientific and legal arguments and validation of the "facts" concerning Indian cultures by Euramerican scientific experts is particularly problematic, because Indian peoples' heritage of knowledge is often based on oral traditions and organized around a very different set of legitimating strategies. Of course, increasing numbers of Indians wield the sword of legal and scientific discourse today with great skill and some notable success, but many Indians still do not use (and disdain to use) the master's tools to bring down the master's house.

Confronting scientific "truth" for many Indians, as well as non-Indians, in the nuclear landscape can be an extremely disempowering experience. Those not trained in the specialized discourse of radiation science confront an apparent discrepancy between what they experience in their bodies, such as cancer and its connection to the open uranium mine down the road, and what they are told is the "truth" about the risks from radiation exposure.

Objectivity and a Multicultural Voice

Increasingly, scientific and legal discourse is also being marshaled in support of the disenfranchised, the communities of color, and the poorer segments of society. In the uranium mining districts, important alternative studies have been initiated by the Southwest Research and Information Center, particularly the work of Chris Shuey and Paul Robinson. Investigating pollution surrounding Los Alamos, the Concerned Citizens of Nuclear Safety have produced scientific data of their own to support their claims of deliberate violations of environmental safety standards in disposing of radioactive waste. The same is true for other Indian and community groups throughout the country. The alternative technical data presented by these groups constitute one of the strongest weapons available to affected communities to force the state and private industry to act responsibly. However, lack of funding leaves many important studies undone. And although they are important, scientific studies are useless in contending with the historical and political patterns of abuse that underlie much of the nuclear landscape. Nor can they contend with harm done culturally to communities. Not only do social and historical knowledge need to be part of environmental discourse, but so do non-Euramerican forms of knowledge. True "objectivity" is rendered only within an inclusive field of knowledge, which is especially crucial in multicultural situations.

Open hearings in this contested domain far too often limit the field of objectivity, serving only as a staging ground upon which mechanisms of exclusion—achieved by the use of expert witnesses—are deployed. But some Indian voices from the margin, while humbled by these opposing technical discourses, assert themselves and a different kind of knowledge and experience, as exemplified by the testimony of Harold Lockwood of the Laguna Tribe:

Good afternoon. My name is Mr. Lockwood. I'm a tribal member of the Laguna Tribe and I'm sorry I don't have any scientific credentials or anything. The only thing that I have that I can lay claim to, I'm an ex-Marine and Vietnam Veteran. Social responsibility. It seems some—while some us were going to school, there was some of us still fighting in Vietnam for the rights of big companies to make profit. . . .

Religious meaning. The land is laying there open like a sore wound. My people believe in the land. We believe in our Indian ways. We believe in the heavens and stars (U.S. Department of Interior, October 1986).

Scientific discourse may serve as a mechanism of exclusion in public hearings and in government documents at every stage of the nuclear cycle, but it hasn't entirely silenced the traditional Indian voice with its appeal to the heavens, the stars, and the earth. Although such public voices don't wield as much power as they should in the institutionalized process, they are still important. They exist in the public record as a vision of what the centers of power look like to those on its margins. Sometimes, the voice of the people is the only record we have of what is going on within the dark zones of the nuclear landscape.

But though these two opposing voices (scientific and traditional Indian) are clearly present, increasingly a mixed, multicultural voice that aligns scientific analysis with traditional indigenous knowledge is also heard. Communication between scientists who support and respect traditional knowledge and Indians that make use of scientific knowledge from the Euramerican tradition comprise a discourse that emerges out of the multiracial and multicultural collaborations made necessary by far-reaching environmental problems such as nuclear landscapes.

Notes

1. There are two deep-geologic repositories now under construction as permanent burial grounds for the country's nuclear waste. WIPP (Waste Isolation Pilot Plant) is for transuranic waste produced by the military. The Yucca Mountain Project is for industry-produced high-level nuclear waste from nuclear power plants (only approximately 10 percent is said to be from military sources).

2. Dorothy A. Purley, interview by author, Paguate Village, Laguna Pueblo reservation, New Mexico, September 16, 1995.

3. Dorothy Purley's statement should be read as a personal discussion with the author only, not as an official statement from the Laguna Pueblo. Dorothy's outspoken stand and her criticism of the uranium mines are not necessarily shared by all Pueblo or Navajo people.

4. See also Makhijani, Hu, and Yih (1995), chapter 5. Their book, *Nuclear Wastelands*, identifies the major health studies conducted on uranium miners. It also documents the historical disregard of the studies' results (that certain aspects of uranium mining were dangerous to miners and should be altered) by the uranium companies and the Atomic Energy Commission.

5. This kind of collaboration between scientists and private or government interests also occurred in lawsuits between the Department of Energy and downwind victims of nuclear testing at the Nevada Test Site.

6. Even though the final settlement with the Anaconda Company gave the Laguna Pueblo Indians enough money to unsatisfactorily reclaim the mine, they are still left working with uranium tailings as one of their primary means of making a living. Again, they appear to be at risk, excluded, and expendable.

Works Cited

Ambler, Marjane. *Breaking the Iron Bonds.* Lawrence: University Press of Kansas, 1990.

Calloway, Donald. "Neoplasms among Navajo Children." *The Workbook* 8, no. 6. Albuquerque: Southwest Research and Information Center, 1983.

Churchill, Ward. *The Struggle for Land: Indigenous Resistance to Genocide, Ecocide, and Expropriation in Contemporary North America.* Monroe, ME: Common Courage Press, 1993.

Dreeson, D. R. "Uranium Mill Tailings: Environmental Implications." *Los Alamos Scientific Laboratory Mini-Report*, February 1978.

Haraway, Donna J. *Modest_Witness@Second_Millennium.FemaleMan©_Meets_OncoMouse™*. New York: Routledge, 1997.

Harding, Sandra. *Whose Science? Whose Knowledge?* Ithaca, NY: Cornell University Press, 1991.

Kuletz, Valerie. *The Tainted Desert: Environmental and Social Ruin in the American West.* New York: Routledge, 1998.

Longino, Helen. *Science as Social Knowledge: Values and Objectivity in Scientific Inquiry.* Princeton, NJ: Princeton University Press, 1990.

Makhijani, Arjun, Howard Hu, and Katherine Yih. *Nuclear Wastelands: A Global Guide to Nuclear Weapons Production and Its Health and Environmental Effects.* Cambridge, MA: MIT Press, 1995.

Navajo Health Authority. "Neoplasms among Navajo Children." Grant proposal. Window Rock, AZ, February 1981.

Reith, Charles C., and Bruce M. Thomson (Eds.). *Deserts as Dumps? The Disposal of Hazardous Materials in Arid Ecosystems.* Albuquerque: University of New Mexico Press, 1992.

Robinson, Paul. "Uranium Production and Its Effects on Navajo Communities along the Rio Puerco in Western New Mexico." In *The Proceedings of the Michigan Conference on Race and the Incidence of Environmental Hazards*, ed. Bunyan Bryant and Paul Nohai. Ann Arbor: University of Michigan School of Natural Resources, 1990.

Samet, Jonathan M., et al. "Uranium Mining and Lung Cancer in Navajo Men." *The New England Journal of Medicine* 310 (June 7, 1984).

Shields, L. M., et al. "Navajo Birth Outcomes in the Shiprock Uranium Mining Area." *Health Physics* 63 (1992).

Southwest Research and Information Center. *The Workbook* 8, no. 6. Albuquerque: Southwest Research and Information Center, 1983.

Taylor, Linda. "Uranium Legacy." *The Workbook* 8, no. 6. Albuquerque, N.Mex.: Southwest Research and Information Center, 1983.

U.S. Department of Interior. Final Environmental Impact Statement for the Jackpile-Paguate Uranium Mine Reclamation Project. Albuquerque: Bureau of Land Management, October 1986.

Notes on Contributors

CAITILYN ALLEN is an associate professor of plant pathology and women's studies at the University of Wisconsin-Madison.

PAMELA BAKER is an associate professor in the Department of Biology at Bates College.

KAREN BARAD is currently the Chair of the Women's Studies Program at Mount Holyoke College, where she is also a professor of women's studies and philosophy. Her Ph.D. is in theoretical partical physics.

INGRID BARTSCH is an assistant professor of women's studies at the University of South Florida. She also has a significant affiliation with the Environmental Studies Program, where she teaches interdisciplinary courses.

DEBBIE P. BAUTISTA is currently a medical student at the New York College of Podiatric Medicine.

MONTSERRAT CABRÉ is a research associate at the Department d'Història de la Ciència, Consejo Superior de Investigaciones Científicas, Institució Milà i Fontanals, Barcelona, and at Duoda, Centre de Recerca de Dones, Universitat de Barcelona, Spain.

JAN CLARKE received her Ph.D. in sociology from York University in Ontario. She currently teaches sociology at Red Deer College in Alberta, and taught sociology and women's studies at Augustana University College in Alberta.

MICHELLE ELEKONICH is a research associate in the Department of Entomology at the University of Illinois at Urbana-Champaign.

MICHAEL J. FLOWER is an associate professor at Portland State University, where he holds a joint appointment in the University Honors Program and the Center for Science Education.

ANGELA B. GINORIO is the director of the Northwest Center for Research on Women, an associate professor in women's studies, and an adjunct associate professor in the departments of psychology and American ethnic studies—all at the University of Washington.

DONNA HARAWAY is a professor in the History of Consciousness Department at the University of California, Santa Cruz.

SANDRA HARDING is a professor in the Graduate School of Education and Information Studies and in the Women's Studies Program at the University of California, Los Angeles, where she also co-edits *Signs: Journal of Women in Culture and Society.*

KATE HAUSBECK is an associate professor of sociology and women's studies at the University of Nevada, Las Vegas.

ELIZABETH HENRY is a lecturer in the School of Communications at the University of Denver.

REBECCA M. HERZIG is an assistant professor of gender, race, and science in the Program in Women's Studies at Bates College.

MELISSA HONRADO received undergraduate degrees in women's studies and biology from the University of California at Irvine, where she helped to initiate the Biology Outreach for Science Scholars Program.

J. KASI JACKSON is finishing her dissertation at the T.H. Morgan School of Biological Sciences and Behavior, University of Kentucky. She has also completed a graduate certificate in the Women's Studies Program.

LESLIE S. JONES is an assistant professor of biology and science education in the Department of Biology at the University of Northern Iowa.

SHARON KINSMAN is an associate professor in the Department of Biology at Bates College, where she also teaches interdisciplinary biology and women's studies courses.

VALERIE KULETZ is currently a lecturer in American studies at the University of Canterbury in New Zealand.

JACQUELYN S. LITT is an assistant professor in the departments of Sociology and Women's Studies at Iowa State University, where she also teaches in the women's studies program.

C. PHOEBE LOSTROH is a Ph.D. candidate in the Department of Microbiology and Molecular Genetics at the Harvard Medical School.

SWATIJA MANORAMA is a feminist health activist and a freelance researcher. She is a voluntary member of the Forum Against Oppression of Women (FAOW) and the Forum for Women's Health (FFWH) in Bombay, India.

MARALEE MAYBERRY is an associate professor of sociology and women's studies at the University of Nevada, Las Vegas.

JAIME PHILLIPS is a Ph.D. candidate in the Department of Sociology at the University of Nevada, Las Vegas, where she currently teaches courses in the women's studies program.

CAROLINE JOAN ("KAY") S. PICART is an assistant professor of humanities and English at Florida State University, where she also teaches women's studies courses.

HAYDEE SALMUN was an associate professor in the Department of Geography and Environmental Engineering at Johns Hopkins University, and is currently an assistant professor at Hunter College of CUNY.

KATHRYN SCANTLEBURY is an associate professor in the Department of Chemistry and Biochemistry and Secondary Science Education Coordinator for the College of Arts and Science at the University of Delaware.

BONNIE SHULMAN is an associate professor in the Departments of Mathematics and director of the Women's Studies Program at Bates College.

BONNIE SPANIER received her doctorate in microbiology and molecular genetics. She is currently an associate professor in the women's studies department at the State University of New York, Albany.

BANU SUBRAMANIAM is an assistant research professor at the Southwest Institute for Research on Women and in the departments of women's studies and ecology and evolutionary biology at the University of Arizona.

ELIZABETH H. TOBIN teaches history at Bates College, specializing in labor and women's history in Europe. She is also associate dean of the faculty.

J. ELAINE WALTERS coordinates the Domestic Violence Intervention Project at the McKenzie-Willamette Hospital in Eugene, Oregon.

LISA H. WEASEL is an assistant professor in the department of biology at Portland State University.

MARTHA P. L. WHITAKER received her Ph.D. in hydrology and water resources from the University of Arizona, Tucson, where she is now completing her master's degree in women's studies.

MICHAEL WITMORE is an assistant professor of English at Carnegie Mellon University.

MARY WYER is an assistant professor in the Women and Gender Studies and Multidisciplinary Studies at North Carolina State University, where she directs a curriculum initiative on "women and gender in science and engineering."

Acknowledgments

Index